TERRITORIES OF LIFE

EDITED BY
MARIO BLASER
SYLVIE POIRIER
PENELOPE ANTHIAS

TERRITORIES OF LIFE

EQUIVOCATIONS, ENTANGLEMENTS, AND ENDURANCES

Published by
University of Alberta Press
1-16 Rutherford Library South
11204 89 Avenue NW
Edmonton, Alberta, Canada T6G 2J4
amiskwaciwâskahikan | Treaty 6 |
Métis Territory
ualbertapress.ca | uapress@ualberta.ca

Library and Archives Canada Cataloguing in Publication

Title: Territories of life : equivocations, entanglements, and endurances / edited by Mario Blaser, Sylvie Poirier, and Penelope Anthias.
Names: Blaser, Mario, 1966– editor | Poirier, Sylvie, 1953– editor | Anthias, Penelope, 1980– editor
Description: Includes bibliographical references and index.
Identifiers: Canadiana (print) 20250160544 | Canadiana (ebook) 20250160633 | ISBN 9781772128253 (softcover) | ISBN 9781772128475 (EPUB) | ISBN 9781772128482 (PDF)
Subjects: LCSH: Indigenous peoples—Land tenure—Case studies. | LCSH: Indigenous peoples—Ethnic identity—Case studies. | LCSH: Indigenous peoples—Social conditions—Case studies. | LCGFT: Case studies.
Classification: LCC GN380 .T47 2025 | DDC 305.8—dc23

First edition, first printing, 2025.
First printed and bound in Canada by Rapido Books, Montreal, Quebec.
Copyediting by Clorinde Peters.
Proofreading by Aalap Trivedi.
Indexing by Tanvi Mohile.

GPSR: Easy Access System Europe | Mustamäe tee 50, 10621 Tallinn, Estonia | gpsr.requests@easproject.com

This book has been published with the help of a grant from the Federation for the Humanities and Social Sciences, through the Awards to Scholarly Publications Program, using funds provided by the Social Sciences and Humanities Research Council of Canada.

University of Alberta Press gratefully acknowledges the support received for its publishing program from the Government of Canada, the Canada Council for the Arts, and the Government of Alberta through the Alberta Media Fund.

CONTENTS

ACKNOWLEDGEMENTS

The editors would like to thank the Centre for Indigenous Conservation and Development Alternatives (CICADA), especially its director, Dr. Colin Scott, and its project manager, Lucia Justo. We also want to thank Dr. Cristina Rojas, principal investigator of the Social Sciences and Humanities Research Council (SSHRC) funded project "Territory Making as World Making," who responded with enthusiasm to our proposal of channeling the results of that project through this volume. All the chapters about South America come from that project. In addition, Mario Blaser wants to recognize the support of SSHRC and Memorial University. Penelope Anthias's participation in this collective project was made possible by postdoctoral funding from the European Research Council and the Independent Research Council of Denmark. A British Academy Mid-Career Fellowship supported her contributions to the edited volume.

Mario Blaser, Sylvie Poirier,
and Penelope Anthias

INTRODUCTION

TERRITORIES OF LIFE AND THE STRUGGLES FOR HETEROGENOUS WORLDS

We start with a proposition: the vast and profound diversity of modes of existence and their complex inter- and intrarelationships enlivens what many call Planet Earth.[1] This proposition, expressed in as many ways and languages as there are modes of existence, has fostered traditions that evidence the crucial importance of nurturing such heterogeneity. While the modern science of ecology has only recently, belatedly, and rather unsophisticatedly caught up with this idea, its manifold practical expressions have, for a long time, given shape to myriad collectives and continue to do so. These collectives are agentive assemblages—veritable sympoietic worlds—that weave themselves into being through emplaced relations of exchanges and reciprocity between entities that transcend the modern distinction between humans and non-humans, even if (following such distinctions) many would call them peoples, animals, plants, geophysical entities, or supernatural beings.[2] "Territories of life" is the label we use in this volume to speak about the shapes that these collectives or worlds adopt in the present as they endure under the shadow of modernization and its coloniality.[3] Our choice to use this label requires some explanation, which also provides the rationale of the volume.

As diverse collectives encountered the colonizing "modernization front" and its categorizations (see Latour 1993), they were generally redefined (and split) as—to use the latest accepted term—"Indigenous Peoples" (humans) and "the land" (non-human nature) upon which they lived. From this colonial redescription of their being, collectives have had to adopt the language and concepts of colonial institutions, especially those associated with the nation-state, such as "territory," "sovereignty," "property," "citizenship," and "rights," among others. In effect, while those concepts presume the modern distinction between "the human" (as subject) and "the land" (or non-human nature—as object) and purport to describe or regulate their mutual relations, they have become central to the struggles of collectives to sustain the practices and relationships that make them just that: assemblages that exceed the human/non-human divide. In this context, we use the label "territories of life" to foreground that the struggles of collectives to sustain themselves nowadays proceed within fields of equivocations. Succinctly, an equivocation is a situation in which interlocutors are not referring to the same thing but are unaware of their divergence (see Viveiros de Castro 2004).[4] Colonial relations are full of equivocations, albeit unevenly so: when the colonized has to adopt the colonizer's words and categorizations, these words mean something else, and while the colonized usually know it, the colonizers usually do not.

An exemplary equivocation happens when, as we suggested, collectives struggle to sustain themselves using terms such as "Indigenous Peoples" and "territory." From the perspective of territories of life, both terms mean something that exceeds what contemporary states (and modern publics in general) can see and recognize; that is, on the one hand, humans (Indigenous Peoples) and, on the other hand, demarcated spaces of non-human nature (land or territory) over which the former claim rights.[5] The equivocation is compounded by the fact that the label "Indigenous" (or cognate terms such as "Natives," "Aboriginals," and so on) have been unevenly used across diverse colonial geographies. In some cases, peoples emerging from the colonial partition of collectives were never called "Indigenous"; in others, as Yamila Gutierrez-Callisaya shows in this volume, communities entangled with the land were renamed as "peasants," "traditional peoples," "caboclos" or "gauchos." While some communities have reclaimed the colonial label "Indigenous," many others do not find that necessary. In some places (like Asia, Africa, Oceania, and some parts of Latin America), many communities have taken up the term "Indigenous" more recently as a way of contrasting themselves from national majorities, because the term foregrounds their unique entanglements with the land (see Simon, this volume).[6] For other groups (mostly in North America), rather than implying a necessary relation to a particular land, the label "Indigenous" has become a matter of human genealogies and identity (Ingold 2000); a situation that sparks bitter controversies about who can and cannot legitimately claim the label for themself (see Bouchard et al. 2022; Leroux 2019; Simpson 2014). In other cases, like that of the Black communities in Colombia, territories of life have never claimed nor sought to claim the label "Indigenous" to describe themselves (see Rojas, this volume).

Thus, while the struggles of territories of life might often appear in association with the category "Indigenous Peoples," the former do not map exactly onto the latter; in fact, they exceed it. It is this excess that interests us the most, as we will explain later. The label "territories of life" also highlights that the agents that animate these struggles are never only human but are rather those of entire (more-than-human) collectives (Bawaka Country et al. 2014; Deloria and Wildcat 2001; Ruiz Serna 2023; Sundberg 2014; Watts 2013). This broad understanding of agency has expansive consequences, some of which we explore in this volume through an idea that is becoming increasingly, if unevenly, accepted. This idea is that what is referred to as "the X's struggles for their territory" is often much more than simply a struggle for control of lands and resources; rather, it usually also involves the struggles of a certain collective or world to sustain itself *in its radical heterogeneity*.[7] At stake in these struggles is the heterogeneity of modes of existences writ large, that is, the very conditions for the possibility of life on this planet (Latour 2012). We (the editors) insist that the ways in which the struggles for territories of life are unfolding today and what they reveal about the challenges of the present matter to us all. Showing how and why this is the case is one of the purposes of this volume.

In order to explore what transpires in the struggles for territories of life, we have sought contributions from within an extensive network of scholars, activists, and practitioners that, through direct or indirect linkages, found a meeting point in the project "Territory Making as World Making"—funded by the Social Sciences and Humanities Research Council of Canada and led by contributor Cristina Rojas—and in the Centre for Indigenous Conservation and Development Alternatives (CICADA), which supported the preparation of this volume. Authors come from diverse backgrounds, both Indigenous and non-Indigenous, as well as from various walks of life. While some of them are more directly situated within the academy than others, they are all involved with the ongoing struggles and sustainability of various territories of life. This is the case for the editors as well. For over thirty years, Mario Blaser has researched and been involved with the Yshir Nation's struggle to defend and sustain the yrmo, their territory of life.[8] Since 1990, Sylvie Poirier has conducted collaborative research with the Atikamekw Nehirowisiw Nation in north-central Quebec related to sustaining relations of stewardship toward Nitaskinan, the collective they are part of, including through a Comprehensive Land Claim's negotiation with the federal and provincial government.[9] Since 2008, Penelope Anthias has conducted collaborative ethnographic research with Guaraní communities and organizations who are reclaiming territories in Bolivia's Chaco region.

The territories of life present in this volume are grounded in countries that have come to be called—over approximately the last two hundred years—Australia, Bolivia, Canada, Colombia, Paraguay, and Taiwan. The variety of settings provides us with different points of entry to take the pulse of the contemporary struggles of these territories. Paramount among these conditions is a general trend, since the 1970s, of nation-states to move toward recognizing Indigenous rights, in particular to land and/or territories. In the last two decades, an important corpus of literature from Indigenous and non-Indigenous scholars and activists has highlighted the manifold implications of this move, especially when the recognition of Indigenous rights to self-governance and territories is part of neoliberal (and bureaucratic) governance—what Elizabeth Povinelli has famously called the "cunning of recognition" (Povinelli 2002; see also Anthias 2018; Bryan 2012; Correia 2019; Coulthard 2014; Nadasdy 2017; Offen 2003; Samson 2016; Watson 2015).

Yet, the cunning of recognition has deeper roots than its minimization as a mere neoliberal ruse would allow us to see. This became patently evident in the mid-2000s with the arrival to power of administrations in Bolivia and Ecuador that, propelled by grassroots movements (including Indigenous ones), advanced an explicitly anti-neoliberal and decolonial agenda and were even headed (in Bolivia's case) by an Indigenous president. As the chapters focusing on Bolivia (Gutierrez-Callisaya and Ruiz Fournier) show, this did not prevent those administrations from unleashing repressive tactics against the mobilization of territories of life that struggled to defend their own integrity against the developmentalist plans of agrobusinesses and extractive industries. Governments would deny that anything but a struggle for natural resources was a stake in these mobilizations and would insist that those natural resources were necessary to bring national majorities—including the Indigenous majorities that some of them purported to represent—out of poverty (see Anthias 2018; Gustafson 2020; Postero 2017; Radcliffe and Radhuber 2020). What we are trying to foreground is that the fundamental trap of state recognition—operative regardless of the ideological persuasion of circumstantial governments—rests in the fact that the struggles of territories of life proceed through asymmetrical fields of equivocations within which they become unavoidably entangled with colonial concepts and their associated practices, with "territory" paramount among them. We do not deny that colonial capitalism's perpetual drive for accumulation by dispossession and the forms of violence that come with the imposition of the modern regime of univocity are part of what makes the unfolding of heterogeneous territories of life very difficult. However, we highlight how the politics of recognition obscures the deeper ontological stakes in these struggles by channelling the defence of territories of life into modern (colonial) conceptions of territory and property. In this volume, we use the equivocations and entanglements that transpire in the concept of territory as a lens through which to explore some of the challenges that territories of life must tackle to endure in their radical heterogeneity. Equivocations, entanglements, and endurances are thus the keywords that connect and organize the chapters.

EQUIVOCATIONS

Since first proposed by Eduardo Viveiros de Castro (2004), the concept of equivocation has shown its capaciousness to help us grasp both the radical heterogeneity of modes of existence and the limits of translation, all the while escaping the crippling effect of relativism. Viveiros de Castro suggests that, rather than a single world out there upon which we might have multiple cultural perspectives (multiculturalism), equivocation entails engaging with multiple realities (multinaturalism) or what others call a "pluriverse" (de la Cadena and Blaser 2018; Escobar 2014; Law 2015). We will not rehash the arguments that have already been made to advance this basic premise, which, like any ontological claim, is ultimately undecidable; instead, we will simply point out that one of its advantages is that it unsettles discussions that justify colonial practices as "realistic" (for example, when governments or corporations claim that treating non-humans as natural resources is a realistic stance to which everyone should submit). But what, exactly, are the implications of using the plural "realities"? Are we speaking of self-contained realities or worlds, and if so, would we not be falling into the old trap of relativism? If we were speaking of self-contained realities, we would indeed be falling into that trap, but we are not; we are speaking of something that looks more like the figure below.

The figure is multiple or, to use Marilyn Strathern's (2004) terms, "more than one"—both rabbit (looking to the right) and bird (looking to the left)—but less than two: one rabbit and one bird. This is what the concept of multiple realities (or reality multiple) tries to convey. Let the rabbit and the bird stand for different collectives and the practices that world them as well as the entire illustration for the pluriverse (although, for a better illustration of the latter we should imagine that it contains many more animal figures and that we are inside of it rather than looking at it). In part, these collectives are in the same spatio-temporal location, and they are articulated through common traces in the drawing, but those very same traces also articulate them as divergent; they make them equivocal. As we have noted, equivocation generally refers to situations in which interlocutors fail to understand that while using the same term, they are referring to different things (Henare et al. 2007). However, when related to the notion of multiple realities, equivocation describes the basic mode of articulation

FIGURE 0.1 | The bird/rabbit illusion evokes the concept of equivocation. (Source: Unknown artist, "Kaninchen und Ente," *Fliegende Blätter*, October 23, 1892. Public domain.)

that constitutes heterogenous modes of existence, collectives, and, by extension, the pluriverse. In effect, far from being errors that need to be fixed, equivocations are constitutive of the pluriverse; they allow for the very possibility of multiplicity, for the possibility that the rabbit *is also* the bird.

As might be apparent, in this setup, the trap of relativism cannot be laid down as we are missing its basic premise of two clearly distinct entities or domains in a relation. It is missing a set of subjects (with their cultural perspectives) on the one hand, and a set of objects (of which those subjects have a partial perspective, or unto which they project themselves) on the other. What we have, instead, are worldings or collectives bringing themselves into being *in and through their situated and manifold relations*. Avoiding relativism also frees us from its counterpart, universalism. Considering that knowledge is situated (Haraway 1988) and thus partial, no tradition of thought should claim the authority to enunciate so-called universals.[10] Given that there is no common or universal referent (a world out there), and no universal humanity or human nature, different collectives/interlocutors are never referring to exactly the same thing; here lies the limit of translation. Yet, this does not suggest (as supposed by many of those who reject the proposal of multiple realities) that communication is not possible; rather, it implies that, instead of being understood as the transfer of a stable and undistorted meaning, it has to be understood as a *working translation*, an articulation whose veracity is assessed not in terms of accuracy (i.e., a meaning that remains self-identical while moving) but of efficacy (i.e., it works for the articulated parties). We know that a translation or communication (as articulation) is good only insofar as it works. Viveiros de Castro calls these kinds of translations "translation as controlled equivocation": the articulation/translation is built on fully recognizing the equivocation at play, that is to say, the referents being articulated are not the same.[11]

A brief digression is in order here. Sometimes Viveiros de Castro's use of the qualifier "controlled" before "equivocation" is taken to simply mean aware, and consequently, that "uncontrolled equivocation" would simply mean unaware. However, this is only partially accurate. Viveiros de Castro uses the qualifier "controlled" to designate a method of translation that assumes that the interlocutors involved are all equally and fully aware of the equivocation and are working through and with it. Hence, the qualifiers "controlled" and "uncontrolled" were never meant to fully account for the asymmetrical and varying levels of awareness that interlocutors have of an equivocation. We find it important to stress that while controlled equivocations might be attempted in certain situations, most commonly only some—or none—of the interlocutors are aware of the equivocation. As we will see below, a situation in which only one party is aware is the most common in colonial settings. In such settings, thus, it is always important to highlight who is aware of an equivocation at play and who is not.

From a stance that embraces the proposition of multiple realities, different worldings relating or communicating with each other is never in question—obviously, they are always already related and communicated. What is in question is the quality of their relations, translations, and articulations, and what effects these have in their ways of being. Are equivocations controlled or uncontrolled? Do the articulations generated through them work? How? To what extent? With what results? These questions are addressed by the contributions to this volume.

Ultimately, for those who consider the radical heterogeneity of worlds as the primordial condition for a lively "Planet Earth," whether a certain translation/articulation works can only be assessed through the extent to which, returning to our illustration, the rabbit and the bird both remain even as their relations change and move. Let us explain.

Sometimes (most times), equivocations go unnoticed; the bird and the rabbit might persist, blissfully unaware of each other. Sometimes, the equivocation is productive; let's imagine the bird tells the rabbit, "We have to clean this" pointing to its beak, to which the rabbit agrees because it thinks that keeping ears clean is good. Although the bird is taking care of its beak and the rabbit its ears, the practices of one enhance the other's. It is when practices interrupt each other that attention to the equivocation becomes crucial, for how the interruption is addressed will either yield a pluriverse-enhancing response or one that denies it. For example, let's say that the rabbit is the modern collective and it decides it can make better use of its ears. Thus, it extracts parts of them without even realizing that it is simultaneously removing parts of the bird's beak, probably killing it. Now, let's say the ears are mountains, or animals, or natural resources in the rabbit's world, but they are also ancestors or powerful and respected non-human persons in the bird's world—that is, they are existents without which it might be difficult, if not impossible, to keep nurturing a livable life. The bird therefore tries to defend itself. The rabbit may hear the complaints of the bird but will dismiss them, for in the modern collective of one reality, of one single world, ears are ears. They cannot also be beaks; there cannot be bird where there is only rabbit. Translation here works (so to speak) through the imposition of univocity: "we are talking of the same thing, and I know it, unfortunately your understanding about the thing is not truly what the thing is, so you have to be silent."

While it is true that the modern collective for which the rabbit stands might gradually render the bird (as well as other collectives) invisible, inviable, and inexistent—implying that the pluriverse and its radical heterogeneity become attenuated—it can never fully exclude from its constitution that which exceeds it; it cannot evacuate the equivocal. In the face of the colonial imposition of univocity, collectives have consistently carved out spaces for their heterogenous modes of existence; in other words, they have actively mobilized the equivocations inherent to translations to advance and perform that which modernity refuses or denies.

But this is an uphill battle full of traps, as we hinted at above, because no matter how carefully and clearly the aim of a translation/articulation has been set up, its consequences change the parties in ways that are often unpredictable. This unpredictability is at the centre of what contributors to the volume explore through the equivocations inherent in translating (and articulating) the struggles of collectives to sustain their heterogenous modes of existence into struggles for territory. How is this translation working? What effects is it having?

By paying attention to how the concept of territory is mobilized in practice, research and critique in the past few decades have helped to reveal its complexity. From its common-sense meaning as areas of control that can be drawn (mainly by the state's hand) as polygons on topographic maps, "territory" has come to index the complex and entangled spatial projection of different political projects (Anthias 2018; Halvorsen 2019). This is aided by the fact that "territory" has accumulated equivocal conceptual baggage that makes it a prime vehicle for a variety of projects. Throughout colonial history and to this day, collectives—in their manifold relations with states, external corporations, and extractive industries—have mastered the art of negotiating with the powers in place to be able to exist more or less on their own terms. In their dialogues and negotiations with modern nation-states, and in a context of unequal relations of power, they adopt the language and terms of the state (and of the international system). Central to this terminology are the concepts of territory, rights, sovereignty, and (in some cases) Indigeneity. However, more recently, spokespersons for these collectives have put forward and defended their own concepts, political thought, forms of authority, and practices of stewardship, expressed in their native languages (see Atleo 2004; Huanacuni 2010; Simpson 2011, 2017). They have done so through various practices of affirmation and resurgence. Defiantly mobilizing their own relational ontological and epistemological principles, these spokespersons enact a work of translation that seeks to generate symmetry, in particular by making evident that the referent of the term "territory" is not the same; that is, by making the equivocation evident (or attempting what Viveiros de Castro would call a "translation as controlled equivocation").

Speaking of territories of life prolongs this translation as controlled equivocation to propose that, for many collectives, territory is the locus both of relations of reciprocity between active and sentient beings that transcend the human/non-human divide and of the interactions and frictions (Tsing 2004) between themselves and visions of a good life imposed by the state and corporations. While in the worlding practices of territories of life, it is assumed that those active and sentient beings have to be approached as cosmopolitical actors and partners or kin (Bird-David 2017; de la Cadena 2015; TallBear 2011; Watts 2013); in the worlding practices of modern states and settler capital, the operative assumption is that the territory is an abstract, an ahistorical space, a reservoir of natural resources passively awaiting to be extracted and exploited (more or less rationally) at the hands and machineries of "Man." With significant frictions and conflicts, these contrasting sets of assumptions are often co-present in the practices that make territories today. In other words, territory has become a diacritic, marking the sites where different visions and stories of the good life unfold, though not always harmoniously. Because visions and stories are enacted in practice, it can be said that territory is where and how diverse modes of existence *take place*, always complexly *entangled* with each other (Anthias 2017, 2019; Dussart and Poirier 2017; Moore 2005; Poirier and Westman 2020; Rivera Cusicanqui 2012), and where, by extension, the heterogeneity of modes of existence is sustained or curtailed.

ENTANGLEMENTS

As our contributors show, disputes, frictions, and tensions between distinct visions of a good life that have territory as their locus are not simply conflicts between modernity and its others. The lines of force and struggle are more complex than that, and the notion of entanglement foregrounds this complexity. It is helpful to revisit the question that orients our analysis: What are the results of ongoing translations/articulations between worlds? Is the bird still there? In what shape? The radical heterogeneity of modes of existence raises the question of encounters, co-presence, and coexistence, while the work of translations/articulations raises the question of practices and strategies of communication and negotiation between worlds and modes of existence. If the notion of equivocation brings forth the existence of multiple realities, the notion of entanglement intends to emphasize their co-presence, and how such co-presence is narrated, negotiated, and performed by the collectives concerned. In this volume, entanglement is addressed at different scales, within and between collectives.

The concept of entanglement has much empirical and analytical potential. "To be alive," writes Anishinaabe/Ojibway scholar John Borrows, "is to be entangled in relationships not entirely of our own making" (2017, xiii). Entanglements take shape and unfold at different scales within and between worlds and modes of existence. Entanglements are situated and emplaced, they engage human and non-human existents. Whatever is entangled in any spatio-temporal context cannot be easily disentangled, and any changes in one of the interconnected threads/entities/beings will affect the other (Dussart and Poirier 2017, 5). Within a forestland, for example, trees that grow side by side have their branches and roots entangled. That is to say that they grow together and thus separately; they are engaged in sharing—with a myriad of other beings—a common spatio-temporal world. In their entanglement, correlation, and co-evolution, these trees come to affect one another in complex, multifaceted, and unpredictable ways. Within a forestland, sounds and smells are also entangled and affect each other in their very expressions, in inextricable and unpredictable ways, as they move within a shared space-time.[12] They maintain their distinctiveness while sharing forms of attachment and interdependence with neighbouring others. Nowadays, these sounds and smells have become entangled with the noises and fumes of extractive machineries. Over time, the former have either ceased to exist, moved elsewhere, or made themselves hardly noticeable while becoming entangled with new and not-so-subtle presences.

Entanglements are multivalent. As Sophie Chao (2022, 208) points out, some are mutual and enable their respective constituents to thrive; others are imposed and may suffocate some constituents to support the propagation of others; and yet others may simultaneously generate collaborations and frictions, which in turn may act as factors of change, producing new entanglements (Quiroga, this volume). Furthermore, each existent or collective engaged in an entanglement maintains its own volition and some degree of "relative autonomy" (Morphy and Morphy 2013; see also Éthier and Flamand, this volume; Thomassin et al., this volume). As Françoise Dussart and Sylvie Poirier have underlined, "The concept of entanglement suggests also no coherence and ordering, no given direction and fixed categories, no boundaries, and leaves room for principles of uncertainty and unpredictability" (2017, 6). They add that the challenge is to figure out what does become entangled. Unpredictability, indeterminacy, co-presence, and relative autonomy mean that the bird continues to exist in its own way, though probably in a different shape. However, different collectives and modes of existence may conceive of and perform entanglement—and thus relationality—differently.

In non-modern collectives, relationality—and thus entanglements and attachments between human and non-human beings and entities—is an ontological and epistemological principle. In these modes of existence, entanglement is conceived and valued as a fact of life, whereas relationships constitute the very fabric of reality. These modes of existence have come to be called "relational ontologies" (Escobar 2014; Poirier 2008, 2013; Scott 2017) in contrast with the dominant naturalistic ontology and anthropocentric bias of modern modes of existence, as "the world of people without a world" (Danowski and Viveiros de Castro 2014, 242). In non-modern collectives, relations and thus entanglements with others (be they animals, plants, winds, rivers, ancestors, spirits, or places) are constitutive of beings and persons, human and non-human.[13] Being one is being multiple, as portrayed by the figure above. In these collectives, entanglement and relationality stress the "mutuality of beings" (Quiroga, this volume), human and non-human, as well as the meshwork of interactions and interrelations that shape their world and their common becoming. At the empirical level, such mutuality of beings translates into forms of affects and attachments that manifest as mutual obligations and responsibilities between kin.[14] Territories of life exist and are sustained through extended and emplaced kincentric meshwork, undoubtedly inclusive of non-humans. Such mutuality is sustained through ongoing communication, negotiation, exchanges, and alliances between humans and non-humans, and a sense of intergenerational indebtedness toward those who were and those yet to come. Therein lies their cosmopolitics, as portrayed in most of the contributions to the volume. However, when such mutuality of beings and entities can no longer be performed and sustained, forms of (di)stress occur within the collectives and are experienced by the modes of existence that constitute them.

With coloniality and the modernization front imposing a regime of univocity, territories of life have come to be constantly in the presence of and entangled with the bounded and de-subjectified "territories" of nation-states and settler capital, hence the equivocation. Local life projects have become increasingly entangled with those of global and national economies and territorialities. Modern systems of cartography and property impose arbitrary territorial delimitations and borders, enacting cuts in the processual networks through which territories of life are produced (Blomley 2011). The concept of entanglement "allows us to inquire into the dialectical and the dialogical dimension of the encounters and the coexistence" (Poirier 2017, 215) between divergent territorialities and modes of existence as each is aiming to sustain and reproduce itself. Global coloniality and unequal relations of power between divergent visions of a good life have intensified the entanglements and the work of translation between worlds. Over the last five hundred years of co-presence, the worlds have become entangled in complex, subtle, and unequal ways. As stressed by Lorna Quiroga (this volume), "navigating the equivocations entails partial connections between divergent worlds; and this type of encounter has the potential to generate unexpected and unpredictable new entanglements."

What are the effects of having to translate territories of life, with their principles of relationality and mutuality of beings, into the language of secular political modernity, settler states, and capitalism, with their conception of territory as a passive reservoir of natural resources to be controlled (and owned) by groups of (variously identified) humans?[15] What spaces are left to negotiate forms of co-presence that would allow sufficient scale, space, and autonomy for territories of life to sustain and reproduce themselves, albeit in a revisited form? What shape could such negotiations take, considering that the states and capitalist corporations have neither the conceptual tools nor the political will to engage in a fair dialogue with collectives that do not share their language and vision? Is the negotiation possible even when resting on a series of equivocations? All these questions are addressed in some way or another by the contributors to this volume, each in their particular setting.

To understand the work of translation and the indeterminacy inherent to it, many authors in our volume explore the effects of the ongoing co-presence of territories of life with modern territory; that is, the results of local practices and strategies of communication and negotiation with the state and corporations. They show that entanglement occurs at all levels and that local life projects (whether focused on economy, education, or political authority) are constantly in (more or less forced) conversation with the institutions of colonial states, and with national and global economies and the territorialities they delineate. In some cases, the struggles to sustain territories of life and their life projects amidst such entanglements bring forth emerging claims of Indigeneity (see Simon, this volume) and associated demands for autonomy and sovereignty (Éthier and Flamand, this volume). However, speaking of sovereignty again raises the question of equivocation. For the state and secular political modernity, "only human persons can be political subjects" and have rights (Nadasdy 2017, 181). Thus, the "institution of citizenship implicitly divides the human realm (where citizenship is possible) from the non-human (where it is not)" (180). We would add that through this division, another divide is enforced between those among the (now redefined) humans who have rights over specific non-humans (such as the land) and those who do not. In contrast, and as mentioned earlier, the cosmopolitics of territories of life are not only inclusive of non-human agencies as kin and thus as political subjects, but they also emphasize criteria beyond rights as relevant to determining whether someone/something belongs with the collective (for example, criteria such as responsibility, respect, and care toward all components of the collective).

In summary, rights and citizenship, as exclusive to humans, and kinship, as inclusive of non-humans, mobilize different forms of belonging. The latter involves a kind of sociality and (inter)subjectivity heavily imbued with feelings of obligation and responsibility that the terms "sovereignty" and "autonomy" (as conceived by the modern collective) cannot encompass. And yet, these terms currently seem almost unavoidable, and they have a kind of gravitational pull that transforms the practices that constitute territories of life. These transformations raise questions as to what emerges from these uneven entanglements: Is there still a bird? If so, in what shape? (see Simon, Ruiz Fournier, and Wattez, this volume).

ENDURANCES

Our contributors show that despite the gravitational pull of colonial conceptualizations and state laws, not to mention material processes of land depletion and destruction, territories of life continue to sustain relationships, obligations, and responsibilities toward the myriad of beings that constitute them. They also make new alliances. "Our sovereignty," writes Leanne Betasamosake Simpson, a Michi Saagiig Nishnaabeg scholar, "comes from an abundance of healthy, responsible and respectful relationships with all our relations" (2015, 22). But what to do "when your relations are destabilized, uprooted, or threatened with extinction?" (Thomassin et al., this volume) as is the case today with territories of life. To sustain their modes of existence, territories of life draw from an "ethic of connection" (Rose 2004), from their own local forms of solidarity, authority, and decisional processes that operate along family, clan, or community lines (as shown in the chapters by Éthier and Flamand, Gutierrez-Callisaya, Simon, Tytelman, and Wattez), but also by listening to the non-humans that constitute them (Moritz and Qwalqwalten; Thomassin et al., this volume). Of course, local forms of solidarity, authority, and decision-making processes endure and are constantly reimagined as they find themselves entangled with the centralized, secular, and anonymous power of the state and its institutions. In some cases, these forms of authority and accountability are not legible as sovereignty or relative autonomy in the eyes of the state and its representatives, but such invisibility allows some territories of life to sustain themselves as such away from the disciplining gaze of the modern state (see Rojas, this volume). The presence of equivocations lodged in terms such as "sovereignty" testifies to the endurance of the radical heterogeneity of modes of existence. Indeed, territories of life continue to find ways to reinvent and sustain themselves despite centuries of colonial and neocolonial violence in all its forms (structural, physical, symbolic, and ontological). Or, as Gutierrez-Callisaya (this volume) points out, borrowing from a concept that has become widely used by grassroots movements in Latin America (see Leff 2017; Porto-Goncalvez 2009), they (r)exist.

Playing with the similar sounds (in Spanish but also in English) of the words "resistance" (resistencia) and "existence" (existencia), the concept of (r)existence signals a way of being that somehow *endures* by changing and adapting against the grain. Merging public expressions of resistance with everyday practices that reproduce life (Sempértegui 2021), (r)existence denotes "practices of worldmaking that affirm and defend life in a context characterized but not exhaustively contained by modernity/coloniality" (Leinius 2024). For us, this literature aptly highlights two important aspects of territories of life and their modes of being in the present: first, that they change so that they can still be themselves, and second, that these changes take place not within a hospitable and inviting context but in one that constantly encroaches on them, threatening the heterogeneity of modes of existence.

For Elizabeth Povinelli (2011), endurance signals a refusal to disappear, an insistence on keeping going in spaces left abandoned (or completely drowned) by liberal and neoliberal forms of rule. This involves a constant struggle against social and material conditions of poverty, disease, and infrastructural ruin that are expected to exhaust Indigenous life projects. To endure, then, is to strive for existence, to swim against the tide, to persevere in the face of prevailing material obstacles. It also involves struggles over knowledge and representation. Anishinaabe scholar Gerald Vizenor's (1999) related concept of "survivance" describes the narrative strategies and forms—"trickster stories"—that enable Indigenous Peoples to resist the racializing tropes of "Indianness" imposed on them by settler colonial society. For Vizenor, survivance seeks an "active sense of presence" over absence, deracination, and oblivion. Endurance can also manifest in more overtly political acts, such as in the calculated acts of refusal (for example, of US and Canadian passports) that enable Indigenous sovereignty to endure "within and apart from" settler governance (Simpson 2014). As the above examples show, endurance is linked to entanglement in that it implies the preservation and reinvention of territories of life *in the midst* of colonial conditions of dispossession, erasure, and political disenfranchisement. Bolivian Aymara scholar Silvia Rivera Cusicanqui aptly captures this through her notion of ch'ixi (2012). An Aymara word that denotes "a color that is the product of juxtaposition, in small points or spots, of two opposed or contrasting colors," ch'ixi expresses "the parallel coexistence of multiple cultural differences that do not extinguish, but instead antagonize and complement each other" (2012, 105). Ch'ixi highlights how the "Indian world" continues to persist *amidst* the modern—not only in remote, "peripheral" territories of the Bolivian lowlands, but in mining centres , cities, and in Indigenous networks of commerce and contraband. It is in this endurance amidst entanglement—rather than in the politics of multicultural recognition—that Rivera Cusicanqui identifies the possibility of decolonization.

We see in various chapters of this volume how territories of life creatively refashion hegemonic practices to deflect, as far as possible, efforts at turning them into compliant relay points of modernizing logics. The strategies and practices of endurance as (r)existence are manifold and give way to a tremendous creativity of initiatives: agroecological projects; forms of "land as pedagogy" (Simpson 2014) oriented to intergenerational knowledge transmission; adapting school curricula; native language classes; bringing the "territory" into the classroom or the reverse; websites on local knowledge; storytelling; digital mapping (Hunt and Stevenson 2017; Éthier 2020; Povinelli 2011); and rangers' programs, to name but a few (in this volume see particularly Gutierrez-Callisaya, Moritz and Qwalqwalten, Thomassin et al., and Wattez). The endurance of territories of life rests also on non-linear conceptions of time and space, on patience, and on confidence in local knowledge, skills, and values. It also involves the co-presence, cooperation, actions, and power of other-than-humans, which are major agentive and communicative constituents of territories of life, and which also endure, entangled with the constituents of the modern collective (see Gutierrez-Callisaya and Quiroga, this volume; Dussart and Poirier 2021).

This endurance, which may be equated with transformative continuity and creative adaptability, is a testimony of a mature cosmopolitical thought. Through endurance over centuries and generations, territories of life have been able to reimagine/revisit/reinvent themselves with a view to reproducing and sustaining the core principles and values of relationality, reciprocity, and responsibility toward and between the myriad of existents that constitute them as collective. But endurance has manifested not only as (r)existence, but also as resurgence (see Éthier and Flamand; Gutierrez-Callisaya, and Thomassin et al., this volume). The capacity of territories of life to practise themselves into being has had its ebbs and flows, in part connected to changing regimes of visibility and invisibility in different places, under which—for varying reasons—the modernization front has allowed some practices to prosper while refusing to register others (see Rojas, this volume). Nowadays there seems to be an opening to the practices of territories of life, not so much because the modernization front allows them but rather because the promises that propelled it ring increasingly hollow and their catastrophic consequences are becoming evident. As a result, there has been a veritable resurgence of what we call territories of life. Alongside this resurgence, wider publics have become receptive to alternative stories about the good life. Many territories of life are eager to share their stories; not for others to copy them, but so that, as Annick Thomassin, Adam Nye, Jacinda Baragud, and Kim Spurway put it in their chapter, "the terms of our co-existence" can be collectively renegotiated. But what would such renegotiation imply? This question leads us to the second point that the concept of endurance helps to highlight: that the modes of existence of territories of life are present in an inhospitable context.

As argued above, chapters in this volume depict the ways in which territories of life endure against the grain of a relentless push to domesticate them. In effect, endurances (both as (r)existence and resurgence) within unequal relations of power, are "hard work"[16]—territories of life, often marginalized, must find the resources, time, and space to realize their innovative projects and to sustain their obligations and responsibilities toward the myriad of beings that constitute them. However, it should not be forgotten that the (human) communities that constitute the territories of life must remain accountable to states and their representatives, who may have quite divergent projects for them, more in tune with the modernization front. From this perspective, it seems that territories of life are constantly subjected to an all-encompassing plan of territorial ordering, whereby every unit must fulfill its assigned role within a system that is intended to benefit a selected set of humans to the detriment of everything else.[17] This is a compulsively voracious system that cannot leave anything to its own devices; its drive is to swallow everything, digest it, and, on that basis, continue to expand. Hence, from a bird's eye view, territories of life would appear as dispersed islands surrounded by a constantly rising ocean that threatens to swallow them. In this visual, the dynamics of equivocal translations and entanglements through which these islands endure could be equated to locating elements that make it possible to raise the island's ground just enough to remain above sea level. The problem is that while those elements raise the floor, they are also wet and heavy, so the more they pile up the less they work to raise the island. In other words, even if this effort has worked to some extent, it is becoming increasingly strenuous. This, we believe, should direct the attention of many of us to the task of finding elements not for raising the floor of the surviving islands but for building new islands, thus stopping the ocean from rising and even, perhaps, making it recede. To put it plainly, decolonial work should imply shrinking the sea so that rather than an archipelago of islands what emerges is a mosaic of different territories of life; we think that territories of life will only exist rather than (r)exist amidst other territories of life with which they can coexist.

The "us" we invoke above is intentionally vague as it refers more to a position in this discussion than a definite identity. The "us" mainly refers to those who are not fully or at all part of territories of life. We are thinking of the position of many authors and the potential main readership of this volume; that is, a position that could be described as allyship, actively contributing to the endurance work of territories of life, which are variously there. What we mean by "variously there" is that the quotidian lives of many of us are more thoroughly entangled with and dependent on the modern collective than the lives of many components of the territories of life we are involved with. In short, the everyday lives of many of us has more to do with the rising ocean than that with a territory of life. Being variously internal/external to territories of life does not take away from the importance of the work one may do to support their endurance but it does generate common conundrums. Most of us are aware that translations amidst uneven equivocations and entanglements work only to a degree; we are aware that our contributions equate to piling up wet elements to raise the floor of the island. And yet, we ask ourselves: "What else can be done under the circumstances? We must work with the elements/concepts that this overbearing ocean offers."

In the face of such a conundrum, we wonder whether our limited imagination for possible alternatives is not just an indication of the degree to which we are part of the ocean even as we reject it. If that is the case, then the invitation of many territories of life to work toward what St'át'imc elders call "visions of abundance for all" (see Moritz and Qwalqwalten, this volume) would imply a slightly different distribution of tasks for those variously involved with them. We return to our point that territories of life exceed the category of Indigenous Peoples. The potency of this excess is what we want to tap into when we tie the definition of the vague "'us"' we keep invoking to a position defined by varying degrees of entanglement with and dependence on both territories of life and the modern collective. With this move we want to emphasize that while everyone/everything is in one way or another entangled with the modern collective, that does not mean everyone/everything is in the same position. The point is important, not to assign blames or absolutions but for carefully assessing the kinds of entanglements that constitute "us" and what we might need to do about them. While the latter point will necessarily depend on the specificity of each one's situation, we want to propose as a rule of thumb that the primary (albeit not only) responsibility for those of "us" who are more thoroughly entangled with and dependent on the modern collective is not supporting the endurance of territories of life over "'there,"' but generating institutions, practices, and relations that might be constitutive of (our own) territories of life right "'here,"' where we are. Of course, doing so implies the parallel task of dismantling the institutions, practices, and relations that are rendering the endurance of territories of life so fragile. What this might entail in each circumstance is a question we want to invite our readers to consider. We think that the chapters in the volume provide a sense of the challenges that any project of generating or regenerating territories of life anew will need to face.

AN OVERVIEW OF THE BOOK: TOWARD HETEROGENOUS WORLDINGS

We begin with Aymara intellectual Yamila Gutierrez-Callisaya's chapter, focusing on the achievements of a project of reconstituting ayllus (the basic unit of Andean sociality) as territories of life. The reconstitution of ayllus began in the 1980s as a reaction to the imposition of peasant union structures and other civilizing agricultural policies that led to soil degradation, land parcellation, out-migration to cities, and a feminization of agricultural labour. Gutierrez-Callisaya asks how and to what extent the reconstitution of ayllus over the past two decades has brought solutions to the destructive effects of assimilationist policies, and what consequences such reconstitution has had for the roles of Aymara women. She argues that the erasure and marginalization of women's roles in territorial management—including their ritual roles in maintaining cosmobiotic relations—is a key feature of colonial state formation, but that women have always found ways to (r)exist based on their own ethic and cosmogenic vision as expressed through specific practices. Her chapter sheds light on how new socioproductive initiatives, imbued in this ethic and cosmogenic vision, constitute the practical expression of the reconstitution of Cantapa Marka, a collective of ayllus located in the highland plains of La Paz Department.

We have chosen this chapter to open the book because it sets the stage for some of the issues we want to foreground in this volume. Grounded in the processes that have since taken place in areas that formed part of the Twantinsuyu (Inca Empire) when the European invaders arrived, Gutierrez-Callisaya shows us how a territory of life was disarticulated by successive waves of colonial policies, and how since the early 1980s some sectors of the Indigenous movement have sought to reverse that process. Gutierrez-Callisaya underscores that this is not the goal of the "Indigenous movement" in general, but only of one sector. This distinction recalls a point we stressed above: there is no automatic equivalence between the category "Indigenous" and belonging to a territory of life. The point is important because it provides the basis for the question/challenge we pose about what might mean to enroll ourselves (regardless of our human-centred identity) in projects aimed at regenerating or generating territories of life, here where we are. We hope that by setting the stage in this way, this chapter will encourage our readers to navigate the subsequent ones with this question in mind.

The section "Equivocations" opens with Lorna Quiroga's chapter, in which she draws on collaborative research with the Yshir people in Paraguay to explore the productive potentialities of equivocation around the concept of "territory." Contrary to modern categorizations of territory as collective property, or as a bounded place of cultural attachment, Quiroga notes that Yshir demands for territory are associated with struggles for the right to exist as an assemblage, the Yrmo, which includes not only humans, but also animals, spirits, stories, plants, and sentient landscapes. However, rather than seeing this equivocation around territory as a limitation, she argues that it is precisely what enables Yshir people to "keep on walking towards the recovery of the Yrmo" without becoming "trapped by the modern category in the process." To this end, the chapter explores the legal framework that sets up territory as a site of equivocation and discusses how the Yshir organization UCINY (Unión de las Comunidades Indígenas de la Nación Yshir) grapples with and moves through this framework to advance its own agenda, associated with the defence of territories of life. A crucial point that Quiroga highlights is that the equivocation at play here is not only about the thing at stake, let's say between a polygon on a map (i.e., the state's notion of territory) and the human/non-human assemblage (i.e., the yrmo, the territory of life). Rather, she shows that the equivocation also involves the very process of "territorial claim." More than a legal process to escape the encroachment of state and agribusiness, under the rubric of territorial claim, UCINY supports concrete practices that enliven the heterogenous life projects of groups (like artisan women) that constitute the yrmo as a territory of life.

Carolina Tytelman's chapter shows a similar equivocation at play in forest co-management practices between the Innu people and the Canadian settler colonial state at a provincial level (Newfoundland) in Nitassinan/Labrador. She argues that Nitassinan and Labrador are different territorial entities that coexist uneasily, sometimes in open opposition. The chapter explores this unequal entanglement as it plays out in different facets of the co-management process. This includes competing constructions of the Labrador Forest as a resource with market value versus a more-than-human assemblage that is integral to Innu social relations and the imposition of colonial state cartography, English language, linear time, and human-centred notions of accountability over Indigenous knowledge practices that centre relationality, respect, and reciprocity. Despite this unequal encounter between territorial entities, Tytelman argues that Innu participation in co-management forms part of a wider strategy toward self-government and enables access to symbolic and material resources that contribute to reproducing Nitassinan.

In their chapter, Benoit Éthier and Sipi Flamand discuss the Atikamekw Nehirowisiwok (north-central Quebec, Canada) contemporary political structures and decision-making processes as an entanglement between their own forms of authority and responsibilities and those imposed by the settler state of Canada. They mobilize the equivocal concepts of "sovereignty" and "entangled sovereignties" to rethink the very terms of Atikamekw Nehirowisiwok self-determination outside of Western etymology and epistemologies and colonial politics. At the political and decisional levels, the authors present a complex and ongoing negotiated co-presence—an entanglement—between different forms and levels of autonomy and authority. These include the extended families (Wicican, as the primary institution, as a clan-like entity), the territorial leaders (ka nikaniwitcik), the elected members of the band councils (for each of the three communities) as an imposed colonial political structure, and the Council of the Atikamekw Nation, the political organization they have created to represent their interests to the settler state. Éthier and Flamand expose the various political agendas, initiatives, and forms of engagement that the Atikamekw Nehirowisiwok have developed over the last few decades to affirm their sovereignty (Otiperitamo[so]win) and to sustain their own life projects, relations, and responsibilities toward their unceded territory (Nitaskinan) as an assemblage of territories of life (notcimik). In opposition to the model of centralized and secular power favored by the state, the Atikamekw Nehirowisiwok promote a value of reciprocity and a politics of consensus (orocowewin) between themselves and the various local authorities, including the voices of Nitaskinan/notcimik.

In the section "Entanglements," we take a closer look at the limitations of translation in the uneven terrain of equivocation. We begin with a chapter by Scott Simon on territories of life in Formosa (commonly known as Taiwan), their political ontologies, and their entanglements with state rule over the last century—a period that has seen Japanese occupation, Taiwanese nationalism, and rule by the Republic of China. Highlighting how a focus on geopolitical tensions obscures the perspectives of peoples who are indigenous to the place, Simon insists that they have never renounced their sovereignty and continue to practise their own spatial ontologies. The chapter focuses particularly on the world that the Sediq and Truku peoples call dgiyaq, the mountain forests inhabited by animals and ancestors that are most intimately known by hunters and trappers. Ontological conflicts have emerged between this world and a nation-state ontology around land cadastres, classifications of ethnic groups, and state appropriation of mountain forests for extraction of natural resources. Simon shows how the state's recent embrace of Indigenous rights has not resolved these ontological conflicts; rather, this has imposed modern ideas of ethnicity and exclusive territories that conflict with Gaya (sacred law). Nevertheless, the chapter highlights how the Sediq and Truku peoples continue to practice sovereignty amidst these entanglements, including through storytelling, trapping, and hunting, and the mobilization of sacred law in negotiations with state and corporate actors.

The chapter by Hernán Ruiz Fournier—a longtime ally of the Guaraní People of Tarija Department in Southern Bolivia—grants insight into the complex politics of indigeneity in Bolivia, where the entanglement of the capitalist political economy and colonial land relations continue to place obstacles on Indigenous claims for territories of life even under a government led by—and a constitution avowedly made for and by—Indigenous Peoples. The chapter underlines the challenges of reconstituting territories of life in the context of a neo-extractivist development model profoundly rooted in colonial logics. As Ruíz Fournier notes, the demand for territory has been central to Indigenous struggles for citizenship in the Bolivian Chaco, following a long history of dispossession and debt peonage. For the Guaraní, territory is a "big house"; the source of life that permits the endurance of ñandereko (Guaraní ways of being). While state recognition of Tierras Comunitarias de Origen (Community Lands of Origin) has widely failed to accommodate this vision, Guaraní communities of Karaparí have faced an outright denial of their existence by state authorities. Ruíz Fournier explains how this politics of non-recognition plays out across multiple spheres—from a flawed land titling process to a lack of consultation over hydrocarbon development, to marginalization within local governance. Paradoxically, this has occurred despite a National Constitution in Bolivia that establishes the plurinational character of the state and the rights of Indigenous Peoples. Ruíz Fournier makes sense of this contradiction with reference to an extractivist development model that benefits local landowning elites at the expense of Indigenous Peoples and produces a rentier logic within public administration.

In his chapter, Paul Wattez turns our gaze from the immediate interface between state and territories of life toward the practices that are generated within territories of life as a consequence of those entanglements. Based on his ethnographic and collaborative work with the Iyiyiwch of Waswanipi (Northern Quebec, Canada), he addresses a major contemporary issue and challenge: how to reconcile the sedentary, professional, and scholastic lives of Iyiyiwch families with the sustenance of intimate relationships with their territories. In 1975, the Iyiyiwch signed the first modern treaty in Canada, the James Bay and Northern Quebec Agreement (JBNQA). In his analysis of Iyiyiw land tenure system in its contemporary coexistence with Quebec and Canadian land tenure systems, Wattez brings forth the equivocation between different conceptions of the "territory"—James Bay and iyiyiw istchee. His main objective is to better understand the Iyiyiw process of the "institutionalization of experiences of the land" over the last decades and its impacts on the social and cosmological intimacy with the land and its non-human inhabitants. He focuses on two initiatives of the Cree Nation Government, namely the "hunting breaks" ("moose break" and "goose break," created in the 1980s) and the "land excursions" (the "canoe brigades" and the "winter journeys," created in the 2000s), both dedicated to sustaining the Iyiyiw way of life, land-based activities, and knowledge transmission, to varying degrees. While the "hunting breaks" occur within the extended families and on the family hunting territories, thus favouring more intimacy with places and non-humans, the "land excursions," while beneficial to some youth, are perhaps more impersonal and their bureaucratic framework mismatches with Iyiyiw ways of acquiring knowledge. However, given ongoing challenges such as extractive projects and climate change, these might become the main forms of continuing that intimacy, which raises the question of how these will unfold in the future and with what effects.

In the first chapter of the section "Endurances," Annick Thomassin, Adam Nye, Jacinda Baragud, and Kim Spurway explore how Torres Strait Islanders (Queensland) and the Walbunja people (New South Wales South Coast) of Australia "work hard" to exercise their everyday sovereignty and sustain their intimate, reciprocal, and caring relations with the entities that compose the territories of life they are part of amidst the everyday impacts of climate change, including rising sea levels and extraordinary bush fires. The authors describe how, throughout colonial history and to this day, these two territories of life have become irremediably entangled with global processes and the Australian settler-state territoriality. However, by adopting a kincentric and relational perspective, they demonstrate how, despite colonial policies, dispossession, and ontological asymmetries, these territories of life have creatively adapted to the major changes of their lifeworld, maintaining their responsibilities and relative autonomy from settler state institutions. All along, the Torres

Strait and Walbunja people have carefully been listening to "the new narratives" conveyed by their territories of life and non-human kin. Thus, their knowledge, practices, and life projects, explain the authors, continue to be rooted in ethics of mutual care and responsibilities for non-humans, ancestors, and future generations. In view of the impacts of climate change and environmental disasters, the authors plead convincingly for the renegotiation of the very terms of coexistence and alliances between multiple ontologies and for considering the foundation for new ontological relations for Australian futures.

The chapter by Sarah Moritz and Qwalqwalten similarly sheds light on the unflinching and relentless love and responsibility for the territory of life that guides the St'át'imc (Salish) life projects in the Bridge River Valley (British Columbia, Canada). Following the territory's transformation from a "Land of Plenty" with abundant Chinook salmon stocks to a post-industrialist "food desert" as result of hydroelectric development over the past century, they discuss social and environmental continuities and changes in memory and praxis, including in the context of a St'át'imc knowledge–science collaborative environmental monitoring program that forms part of a 2011 Hydro Settlement Agreement. They argue that, despite having to translate their visions to communicate with non-Indigenous, settler, and industry partners, St'át'imc are nevertheless using this program to re-enact their knowledge of fishing, water use, and governance practices as part of their long-term goal to reclaim the Land of Plenty and finally return "home." This involves maintaining more-than-human social relationships, in which salmon, the Bridge River, and other beings emerge as sentient, active, and communicative social agents who have their own perspectives on socio-environmental change. By demanding recognition of these relationships, St'át'imc families prompt a fundamental rethinking of the bounds of community or society as interspecies, multispecies, and kin-based relationships and communication. The authors conclude that St'át'imc accept the equivocation of limited cross-cultural, social, and perspectival translatability, but also seek to enact relations with all beings (including both animals and non-St'át'imc humans) in order to work toward a vision of abundance for all. This, as we pointed out earlier, implies an open call for those of us who are not fully or at all part of territories of life to consider how can we become part of these visions of abundance for all. Perhaps by building our own?

Of course, this is not easy, especially if our modes of existence are profoundly imbricated with and conditioned by that which denies territories of life. And yet, we feel that this is not impossible. To provide some empirical grounding to our feelings, we conclude with Cristina Rojas's chapter on the territoriality of Black Communities in Colombia. She shows us how, since the eighteenth century, enslaved people and their descendants in Colombia have incrementally carved out spaces from where they could generate their own forms of relations with other non-human beings and places and how, from those spaces, veritable territories of life began to flourish. This process went through different regimes of visibilities and invisibilities, where the constitution of a divergent form of territoriality was at times invisible to the state, and hence was left to be, and sometimes it was visible and attacked. Even under relentless violence, a territory of life emerged out of the very entrails of modern territoriality, becoming a contemporary example and a horizon for an entire national project. We believe this chapter should encourage even the most sceptical to recognize the possibility of generating territories of life from the rising ocean of modernization itself—provided its elements are properly reworked, no matter how deeply constraining and conditioning they may be. After all, what could be more conditioned and constrained than the mode of existence of enslaved beings?

We hope the book offers a ground from which to discuss the challenges to and possibilities for the continuation of territories of life that have endured, for the renewal of those that have been severely damaged, and for the creation of those that must flourish to sustain the diversity of modes of existence that enlivens Planet Earth.

NOTES

1. The term "intrarelations" signals the precedence of relations over that which is related; that is, that entities are always already the result of relations.
2. Sympoiesis refers to a process of "making with," a form of self-making that can only happen collectively and collaboratively. See Donna Haraway (2007).
3. We borrow the concept from Arturo Escobar (2008) as well as from the ICCA consortium, a partner of this volume's sponsor, the Centre for Indigenous Conservation and Development Alternatives (CICADA). For ICCA consortium see https://www.iccaconsortium.org/; for CICADA see https://cicada.world/.

4. The equivocation differs from the "conflict of interpretation" of hermeneutics and semiotics (Ricoeur 1974) as it reveals not divergent interpretations of the same object, but different objects. The approach of material semiotics is most relevant here (see Blaser 2016; Law 2015).
5. It is worth noting, however, that Indigenous Peoples were until recently excluded from the category of human and included in the category of nature in earlier colonial moments (hence being exterminated, enslaved, or treated as objects to be managed by colonizers).
6. At the global level, since the adoption of the United Nations Declaration on the Rights of Indigenous Peoples in 2007, many marginalized communities of diverse traditions—either peasants, herders, or hunters and gatherers—have seen in that declaration and the status of "Indigenous" the opportunity to claim rights to their lands that are denied to them by the nation-states within which they are encompassed.
7. According to the Merriam-Webster dictionary, "radical" means; a) "relating to, proceeding from a root"; b) "relating to the origin," a "basic principle," and thus fundamental; c) "very different from the usual or traditional," and thus extreme. All these meanings are relevant to our understanding of "radical" heterogeneity. In view of the modernization front of the last two hundred years, and the forms of violence that it deploys to homogenize the modes of existence, the radical heterogeneity many collectives are struggling to sustain is fundamental to the continuing existence of territories of life on Planet Earth. Radical heterogeneity contrasts with the modern colonial understanding of one reality, one single world, and as such it presents itself as an extreme positioning.
8. Since 2009, he has been conducting collaborative research projects with Innu Nation of Labrador as well.
9. In the 1980s and onward, she has also conducted research in an Aboriginal community of the Australian Western Desert (Poirier 2005).
10. François Jullien writes: "There is no longer any doubt today that the universalism that Europe [and modern science] advocated was, in fact, only the universalization of its own culturalism" (2008, 144; our translation). Several authors have indeed characterized the Western and Modern quest for universals, or of a universal humanity, as an arrogant or cannibalistic universalism in the face of other modes of existence and the many ways of being human. Too often, such universalism has proven to be a very powerful theoretical and political tool to silence and neutralize Otherness and the heterogeneity of modes of existence. The Grand Modern Narrative of the Anthropocene is heir to that tradition (Hache 2014).
11. Viveiros de Castro has a beautiful analogy that explains this idea: translation through equivocation would be analogous as thinking of walking as controlled falling; we never have a final certitude that it works, only that it works so far (2004, 5)
12. See Steven Feld, Dennis Leonard, and Jeremiah Ra Richards's pathbreaking documentary *Voices of the Rainforest: A Day in the Life of Bosavi, Papua New Guinea* (2019).
13. Related to the principle of relationality, Escobar writes: "A fundamental principle is that all things in the world are *made of entities that do not pre-exist the relations that constitute them*" (2018, 75; original emphasis, our translation).
14. Donna Haraway would talk of "response-abilities" (2016).
15. In his seminal work, *Provincializing Europe* (2000), Dipesh Chakrabarty raises the following question about the politics of translation: "How do we conduct these translations in such a manner as to make visible all the problems of translating diverse and enchanted worlds into the universal and disenchanted language of sociology?" (89).
16. The expression "hard work" is borrowed from the Australian Aboriginal peoples when they refer to the hardships of maintaining their ritual practices and responsibilities to their "Country"—including the ancestral spirits that dwell there and as part of a continuing process of creation and re-creation—while having to be accountable to a secular modern state and settler capital that considers such practices unproductive and a waste of time.

17. This is a literal translation of the Spanish, "plan de ordenamiento territorial," a technical term that is usually translated to "land planning." The Spanish technical term is much more explicit about the reach and logic behind these practices.

REFERENCES

Anthias, Penelope. 2017. "Ch'ixi Landscapes: Indigeneity and Capitalism in the Bolivian Chaco." *Geoforum* 82: 268–275.

Anthias, Penelope. 2018. *Limits to Decolonization: Indigeneity, Territory, and Hydrocarbon Politics in the Bolivian Chaco.* Cornell University Press.

Anthias, Penelope. 2019. "Ambivalent Cartographies: Exploring the Legacies of Indigenous Land Titling through Participatory Mapping." *Critique of Anthropology* 39 (2): 222–242.

Atleo, Richard. 2004. *Tsawalk: A Nuu-chah-nulth Worldview.* UBC Press.

Bawaka Country, Sarah Wright, Sandie Suchet-Pearson, et al. 2014. "Working with and Learning from Country: Decentring Human Author-ity." *Cultural Geographies* 22 (2): 269–283.

Bird-David, Nurit. 2017. *Us, Relatives: Scaling and Plural Life in a Forager World.* University of California Press.

Blaser, Mario. 2016. "Is Another Cosmopolitics Possible?" *Cultural Anthropology* 31 (4): 545–570.

Blomley, Nicholas. 2011. "Cuts, Flows, and the Geographies of Property." *Law, Culture and the Humanities* 7 (2): 203–216.

Borrows, John. 2017. "Foreword." In *Entangled Territorialities. Negotiating Indigenous Lands in Australia and Canada*, edited by Françoise Dussart and Sylvie Poirier. University of Toronto Press.

Bouchard, Michel, Sébastien Malette, and Jo-Anne Muise Lawless. 2022. "Academia, Twitter Wars, and Suffocating Social Justice in Canada: The Case of Unrecognised Indigenous Peoples." *Dialectal Anthropology* 47: 97–107. https://doi.org/10.1007/s10624-022-09677-2.

Bryan, Joe. 2012. "Rethinking Territory: Social Justice and Neoliberalism in Latin America's Territorial Turn." *Geography Compass* 6 (4): 215–226.

Chakrabarty, Dipesh. 2000. *Provincializing Europe. Postcolonial Thought and Historical Difference.* Princeton University Press.

Chao, Sophie. 2022. *In the Shadow of the Palms: More-Than-Human Becomings in West Papua.* Duke University Press.

Correia, Joel E. 2019. "Unsettling Territory: Indigenous Mobilizations, the Territorial Turn, and the Limits of Land Rights in the Paraguay-Brazil Borderlands." *Journal of Latin American Geography* 18 (1): 11–37.

Coulthard, Glen. 2014. *Red Skin, White Masks: Rejecting the Colonial Politics of Recognition.* University of Minnesota Press.

Danowski, Déborah, and Eduardo Viveiros de Castro. 2014. "L'arrêt de monde." In *De l'univers clos au monde infini*, edited by Émilie Hache. Editions Dehors.

De la Cadena, Marisol. 2015. *Earth Beings: Ecologies of Practice Across Andean Worlds.* Duke University Press.

De la Cadena, Marisol, and Mario Blaser, eds. 2018. *A World of Many Worlds.* Duke University Press.

Deloria, Vine, and Daniel Wildcat. 2001. *Power and Place: Indian Education in America.* Fulcrum Resources.

Dussart, Françoise and Sylvie Poirier, eds. 2017. *Entangled Territorialities: Negotiating Indigenous Lands in Australia and Canada.* University of Toronto Press.

Dussart, Françoise and Sylvie Poirier, eds. 2021. *Contemporary Indigenous Cosmologies and Pragmatics*. University of Alberta Press.

Escobar, Arturo. 2008. *Territories of Difference: Place, Movements, Life, Redes*. Duke University Press.

Escobar, Arturo. 2014. *Sentipensar con la tierra: Nuevas lecturas sobre desarrollo, territorio y diferencia* (Primera edición). Ediciones Unaula.

Escobar, Arturo. 2018. *Otro posible es posible: Caminando hacia las transiciones desde Abya Yala/Afro/Latino-América*. Ediciones desde abajo.

Éthier, Benoit. 2020. "Analyzing Entangled Territories and Indigenous Use of Maps: Atikamekw Nehirowisiwok (Quebec, Canada) Dynamics of Territorial Negotiations, Frictions, and Creativity." *The Canadian Geographer* 64 (1): 32–48.

Gustafson, Bret. 2020. *Bolivia in the Age of Gas*. Duke University Press.

Hache, Émilie, ed. 2014. *De l'univers clos au monde infini*. Éditions Dehors.

Halvorsen, Sam. 2019. "Decolonising Territory: Dialogues with Latin American Knowledges and Grassroots Strategies." *Progress in Human Geography* 43 (5): 790–814.

Haraway, Donna. 1988. "The Science Question in Feminism." *Feminist Studies* 14 (3): 575–599.

Haraway, Donna. 2007. *When Species Meet*. University of Minnesota Press.

Haraway, Donna. 2016. *Staying with the Trouble: Making Kin in the Chthulucene*. Duke University Press.

Henare, Amiria, Martin Holbraad, and Sari Wastell. 2007. *Thinking through Things: Theorising Artefacts Ethnographically*. Routledge.

Huanacuni, Fernando. 2010. "Paradigma occidental y paradigma indígena originario." *América Latina en movimiento* 452: 17–22.

Hunt, Dallas and Shaun A. Stevenson. 2017. "Decolonizing Geographies of Power: Indigenous Digital Counter-mapping Practices on Turtle Island. *Settler Colonial Studies* 7 (3): 372–392.

Ingold, Tim. 2000. "Ancestry, Generation, Substance, Memory, Land." *The Perception of the Environment: Essays on Livelihood, Dwelling and Skill*. Routledge.

Jullien, François. 2008 *De l'universel, de l'uniforme, du commun et du dialogue entre les cultures*. Fayard.

Latour, Bruno. 1993. *We Have Never Been Modern*. Harvard University Press.

Latour, Bruno. 2012. *Enquêtes sur les modes d'existence: Une anthropologie des Modernes*. La Découverte.

Law, John. 2015. "What's Wrong with a One-World World?" *Distinktion: Scandinavian Journal of Social Theory* 16 (1): 126–139.

Leff, Enrique. 2017. "Las relaciones de poder del conocimiento en el campo de la ecología política1." *Ambiente & Sociedade* 20: 225–256.

Leinius, Johanna. 2024. "In the Defense of Life: The Existential Politics of Relating Body and Territory." In *Neoextractivism and Territorial Disputes in Latin America: Social-Ecological Conflict and Resistance on the Front Lines*, edited by Penelope Anthias and Pabel C. López Flores. Routledge.

Leroux, Darryl. 2019. *Distorted Descent: White Claims to Indigenous Identity*. University of Manitoba Press.

Moore, Donald. 2005. *Suffering for Territory: Race, Place, and Power in Zimbabwe*. Duke University Press.

Morphy, Howard, and Frances Morphy. 2013. "Anthropological Theory and Government Policy in Australia's Northern Territory: The Hegemony of the Mainstream." *American Anthropologist* 115 (2): 174–187.

Nadasdy, Paul. 2017. *Sovereignty's Entailments: First Nation State Formation in the Yukon*. University of Toronto Press.

Offen, Karl H. 2003. "The Territorial Turn: Making Black Territories in Pacific Colombia." *Journal of Latin American Geography* 2 (1): 43–73.

Poirier, Sylvie. 2005. *A World of Relationships: Itineraries, Dreams, and Events in the Australian Western Desert*. University of Toronto Press.
Poirier, Sylvie. 2008. "Reflections on Indigenous Cosmopolitics—Poetics." *Anthropologica* 50 (1): 75–85.
Poirier, Sylvie. 2013. "The Dynamic Reproduction of Hunter-Gatherers' Ontologies and Values." In *A Companion to the Anthropology of Religion*, edited by Janice Boddy and Michael Lambek. Wiley-Blackwell.
Poirier, Sylvie. 2017. "Nehirowisiw Territoriality: Negotiating and Managing Entanglement and Co-existence." In *Entangled Territorialities: Negotiating Indigenous Lands in Canada and Australia*, edited by Françoise Dussart and Sylvie Poirier. University of Toronto Press.
Poirier, Sylvie, and Clint Westman. 2020. "Living Together with the Land: Reaching and Honouring Treaties with Indigenous Peoples." *Anthropologica* 62 (2): 236–247.
Porto-Gonçalves, Carlos Walter. 2009. "De Saberes y de Territorios-diversidad y emancipación a partir de la experiencia latino-americana." *Polis: Revista latinoamericana* 22. http://journals.openedition.org/polis/2636
Postero, Nancy. 2017. *The Indigenous State: Race, Politics, and Performance in Plurinational Bolivia*. University of California Press.
Povinelli, Elizabeth. 2002. *The Cunning of Recognition: Indigenous Alterities and the Making of Australian Multiculturalism*. Duke University Press.
Povinelli, Elizabeth. 2011. *Economies of Abandonment: Social Belonging and Endurance in Late Liberalism*. Duke University Press.
Radcliffe, Sarah, and Isabella Radhuber. 2020. "The Political Geographies of D/decolonization: Variegation and Decolonial Challenges of /in Geography." *Political Geography* 78: 102–128.
Ricoeur, Paul. 1974. *The Conflict of Interpretation: Essays in Hermeneutics*. Northwestern University Press.
Rivera Cusicanqui, Silvia. 2012. "Ch'ixinakax utxiwa: A Reflection on the Practices and Discourses of Decolonization." *South Atlantic Quarterly* 111 (1): 95–109. https://doi.org/10.1215/00382876-1472612.
Rose, Deborah Bird. 2004. *Reports from a Wild Country: Ethics for Decolonisation*. University of New South Wales Press.
Ruiz-Serna, Daniel. 2023. *When Forests Run Amok: War and Its Afterlives in Indigenous and Afro-Colombian Territories*. Duke University Press.
Samson, Colin. 2016. "Canada's Strategy of Dispossession: Aboriginal Land and Rights Cessions in Comprehensive Land Claims." *Canadian Journal of Law and Society / Revue Canadienne Droit et Société* 31 (1): 87–110. doi:10.1017/cls.2016.2.
Scott, Colin. 2017. "The Endurance of Relational Ontologies: Encounters between Eeyouch and Sport Hunters." In *Entangled Territorialities: Negotiating Indigenous Lands in Australia and Canada*, edited by Françoise Dussart and Sylvie Poirier. University of Toronto Press.
Sempértegui, Andrea. 2021. "Indigenous Women's Activism, Ecofeminism, and Extractivism: Partial Connections in the Ecuadorian Amazon." *Politics & Gender*, 17 (1): 197–224.
Simpson, Leanne Betasamosake. 2011. *Dancing on Our Turtle's Back: Stories of Nishnaabeg Re-Creation, Resurgence, and a New Emergence*. Arbeiter Ring Publishing.
Simpson, Leanne Betasamosake. 2014. "Land as Pedagogy: Nishnaabeg Intelligence and Rebellious Transformation." *Decolonization: Indigeneity, Education & Society* 3 (3): 1–25.
Simpson, Leanne Betasamosake. 2015. "The Place Where We All Live and Work Together: A Gendered Analysis of 'Sovereignty.'" In *Native Studies Keywords*, edited by Stephanie Nohelani Teves, Andrea Smith, and Michelle H. Raheja. University of Arizona Press.
Simpson, Leanne Betasamosake. 2017. *As We Have Always Done: Indigenous Freedom Through Radical Resistance*. University of Minnesota Press.

Strathern, Marilyn. 2004. *Partial Connections*. Updated edition. AltaMira Press.
Sundberg, Juanita. 2014. "Decolonizing Posthumanist Geographies." *Cultural Geographies* 21 (1): 33–47.
TallBear, Kim. 2011. "Why Interspecies Thinking Needs Indigenous Standpoints." *Cultural Anthropology* 24: 1–8. https://culanth.org/fieldsights/why-interspecies-thinking-needs-indigenous-standpoints.
Tsing, Anna Lowenhaupt. 2004. *Friction: An Ethnography of Global Connection*. Princeton University Press.
Viveiros de Castro, Eduardo. 2004. "Perspectival Anthropology and the Method of Controlled Equivocation." *Tipití: Journal of the Society for the Anthropology of Lowland South America* 2 (1): 3–22.
Vizenor, Gerald. 1999. *Manifest Manners: Narratives on Postindian Survivance*. University of Nebraska Press.
Watson, Irene. 2015. *Aboriginal Peoples, Colonialism and International Law: Raw Law*. Routledge.
Watts, Vanessa. 2013. "Indigenous Place-Thought and Agency Amongst Humans and Non Humans (First Woman and Sky Woman Go On a European World Tour!)" *Decolonization: Indigeneity, Education & Society* 2 (1): 20–34.

1

Yamila Gutierrez-Callisaya
Translated by Mario Blaser

AYMARA WOMEN AND SOCIAL PRODUCTION DYNAMICS

CASE STUDY IN CANTAPA MARKA, BOLIVIA

INTRODUCTION

In the early 1980s, the Indigenous movement from the Andean region of Bolivia began what has been called the reconstitution of ayllus and markas. The ayllu can be understood as the basic Andean social unit, which includes humans and non-humans. Formed by several communities, the ayllu can extend over a territory that is occupied by various related families engaging in economic, cultural, political, and legal forms of organization based on their own cosmovision. They have their own structures of authority and territorial jurisdiction. The marka, in turn, is formed by several ayllus and has its own supra-ayllus authority. In Bolivia, we talk about reconstitution and not simply of recovery; it is understood that this form of territorial organization was dismembered during the colonial and republican period, and therefore, it must be re-unified and reconstituted from elements that have been disentangled. The process of reconstitution that began in the 1980s was promoted by different Indigenous leaders, authorities, and institutions, such as the

Andean Oral History Workshop, among others. The aim was to abandon the established union-based organizational model for rural communities and to undertake the reconstitution and strengthening of self-governing structures. Throughout this process, the movement demanded from the state the restitution of territorial titles under the legal figure of Communal Lands of Origin (or TCO in the Spanish acronym).

Given the government's refusal to embrace the concept of "Indigenous territories"—because it feared doing so would jeopardize the unity of the country—the term "Communal Lands of Origin" was proposed as an alternative and became incorporated into the national legal framework through the National Institute of Agrarian Reform Law of 1996 (INRA Law 1996). Colloquially, Communal Lands of Origin is understood as a synonym for Indigenous territory, including ownership rights over the land and its natural, renewable resources. During the constituent assembly in 2006–2008, the discussion of territory was reopened, but this time the political scenario was different and very favorable for Indigenous people. From the very first sessions and debates, it was made clear that the Indigenous Peoples' territorial rights acquired through Communal Lands of Origin titles would enter the constitution under the concept of "territory," although not precisely as "Indigenous territory." Different Indigenous representatives wanted either the concept of "originary" (native) or of "peasant" enshrined in the Constitution. The first term was a request of the representatives of the National Council of Ayllus and Markas of the Qullasuyu (CONAMAQ by its Spanish acronym), and the second was the request of representatives from Indigenous peasant communities belonging to the Unified Syndical Confederation of Peasant Workers of Bolivia (CSUTCB in its Spanish acronym). In response to these requests, the assembly created the term "Indigenous originary peasant territory." This new term gave collective rights to any human community that shared a cultural identity, a language, historical traditions, institutions, territoriality, and cosmovision, and whose existence predated the Spanish colonial invasion. However, the term also signals the complexities of the Indigenous movement in Bolivia and the various projects that are expressed in it, not all of which involve the notion of "territories of life" as presented in this volume's introduction.

What singles out the political project of reconstituting the ayllu within this complexity is its focus on decolonization and the search for a just society. It seeks freedom from racism and discrimination through rebuilding self-determined basic units of Andean sociality according to our own cosmovision. More than a simple return to the past, this project aims to rectify injustices and solve current problems that have been created by the dominant "colonial pattern" or coloniality (Quijano 2000). These problems are the sedimented result of policies that, building on a previous colonial and republican (i.e., post-independence from Spain) history of dispossession and destruction of Indigenous forms of organizing life, the Bolivian state has implemented since the National Revolution of 1952. The Agrarian Reform of 1953 ended the ayllus/markas system of vertical control of a maximum of eco-symbiotic niches (distributed from the highland down to the two slopes of the Andes) by prohibiting the double possession of lands in different provinces or departments into which the Bolivian territory was divided. Several "vertical" or "interzone" lands belonging to the ayllus of the highlands and those that were far from their main nucleus were turned into small independent plots of land, thus dissolving their belonging to a marka, for example. In addition, the revolution imposed the peasant worker's union as the form of organization through which communities should operate and, linking them to the new state as an arm to promote its nationalist political ideology, sought to uproot the deep political memory of the communities while imposing a Western mentality over an Andean mentality. Finally, the state implemented development projects designed to transform Indigenous ways of living into modern and Westernized ways of life (Guzman et al. 1999; Restrepo and Cusicanqui 1991)

State policies considered Indigenous and peasant forms of production as inefficient and outdated, and imposed agricultural technological packages in the form of "technical assistance" and programs of (un)training. In a civilizing role, economists introduced fertilizers, insecticides, enhanced seeds, and agricultural machinery, tools to achieve higher productivity in the communities. This process, promoted by the Agrarian Reform of 1953 and later by the INRA Law of 1996, slowly brewed problems such as the proliferation of pests, the decay of the organic layer of the soil, and, more recently, climate change. These issues have progressively complexified a land situation that was already marked by an aggressive parceling of land among family members (usually ending in inheritance and boundary conflicts). The result of these processes has been the out-migration of male workers and the concomitant overexploitation of the female workforce in agricultural activities.

Historically, temporary migration has always been part of the Aymara way of life as it was considered an opportunity to exchange products and technologies and to form bonds of community. Young men usually left the community in search of temporary employment, leaving the women and children behind under the care of their extended family. Nowadays, the situation is different: because there is not enough space for everyone to grow crops for exchange, men are forced to permanently migrate and work as wage labourers to earn a salary that will cover their basic needs. In the case of women, migration away from the community might initially be imagined as temporary, but for several reasons (including situations of violence and exploitation), they are frequently extended for long periods of time, often resulting in family abandonment. For women who remain in their communities, migration forces them to assume the labour of their migrant relatives in addition to their own. It is these kinds of concrete problems, among others, that the process of reconstitution of ayllus and markas seeks to address. In this chapter, I focus on one such process undertaken by Cantapa Marka, located in the central highland region of Bolivia within the jurisdiction of the Laja municipality, province of Los Andes, department of La Paz-Bolivia.

The work I present here is based on materials gathered during several periods of fieldwork, where I investigated issues of interest to the community. As an Aymara intellectual, I conceive of my work as a series of political acts oriented toward the defense of Indigenous rights. My work seeks to share knowledge and promote changes in public opinion and policy as well as to strengthen our identity and self-determination. I arrived in Cantapa in 2008, trying to follow the process of reconstitution of the ayllu. Since then, I have maintained a dynamic and mutually engaged exchange of ideas and analysis with the community, developed through frequent visits during different periods of time such as festivities, harvest seasons, and family events. This connection has promoted insightful conversations and long-standing friendships with the marka community members. Given that the authorities constantly change based on an annual rotation system of authorities formed by married men and women, to arrive at the topics I address here, we conducted a series of community meetings. Through these, we collaboratively determined the need to have some sort of evaluation of the process of reconstituting the ayllu, particularly regarding the progress of activities that bring life back to the territory. Within this topic, we also determined a special focus on how all of this affected women's roles.

I analyze two points from this experience: 1) how and to what extent the process of reconstituting the ayllu that began in Cantapa Marka almost two decades ago has generated solutions to the problems previously outlined; and 2) how such solutions have impacted the roles of Aymara women in their communities. Our interest in the role of women—as I will argue in more detail later—stems from the issue that coloniality has marginalized or rendered invisible the role of Aymara women in the politics of the ayllu and in the management of the territory. Yet, despite their disavowal of their role, Aymara women "(r)exist" through their work ethic and their cosmogony. Following Walter Porto-Gonçalves (2016), I understand "(r)existence" as a resistance that is not simply a reaction to the invader, but a form of (r)existence because it incorporates new horizons of meaning, reinventing its own circumstances. They resist because they exist; they (r)exist.

This chapter has three sections, in addition to the conclusion. The first part includes a historical background of the study area, to understand the disassembling of the ayllu and marka and its consequences. The second part focuses on the process of reconstitution to understand how people live in the community today and what "managing the territory" means within this process. Next, I analyze how the reconstitution of the ayllu is materialized through new social and productive initiatives, such as the strategic venture of the Agroecological Producers Association of Cantapa (APAECA in its Spanish acronym), that links local knowledge with new experiences to solve contemporary issues such as land scarcity, pollution, and the migration of women. In the conclusion, I connect the most salient points of each section to a discussion about the different forms of understanding (and doing) the territory, and the role of women in that.

HISTORICAL BACKGROUND

The ayllu, marka, and suyu were the units in which the pre-Colombian territorial structures were organized in the Andean region (this included groups that spoke both Aymara and Quechua). The ayllu was the basic unit regrouping the partialities aran/urin (higher/lower) within a marka. The marka is a territorial jurisdiction that hosted a group of ayllus of different sizes. The suyus were formed by a group of markas and made up the major structures that composed the Tawantinsuyu or Inca Empire. This structure and territorial organization articulated the topographic, socio-cultural, and ecological diversity of the area as part of a life strategy where the notions of constant flow and rotation, or muyu, were central.

The ayllus controlled and used a system of discontinuous territories between the (herding) highlands and other locations in the Inter-Andean mountain range. This system has been called "vertical control of ecological niches" or "logic of interzonal control of ecological floors" (Condarco and Murra 1987). Sections of the territory could be far away from the most populated centres of a marka, extending all the way to the Pacific as well as to the edges of the Amazonian forest. Olivier Dollfus (1981) defines the Andes geographically as "an ecological mosaic formed by geofacies," referring to the comprehensive characteristics of ecological floors formed by biotic, abiotic, and human systems. This other notion of territory also implies another conception of social space composed of a multiplicity of non-human entities—ranging from animals and plants to the sun, the moon, water, the winds, the mountains, and every element that constitutes the world— engaged in the effort to coexist in harmony and balance, in a relational and comprehensive manner. Thus, this notion of territory is not just about the geographical spatiality, but also the role that all human and non-human members play within it as their timelines and life forms intersect.

From the Aymara perspective, the territoriality of the ayllu or marka involves the permanent interconnection between the material and the immaterial. This interconnection is related to the different dimensions of being that the jaqi—the person—possesses: the ajayu, spirit of territorial belonging;[1] the sunaqi, cosmic vital energy;[2] and the qamasa, courage or force in the way of being.[3] In the same way, the territory has several dimensions of being or "spirits," such as the aynuqa, for collective farming; the sayaña, for family recreation; the uraqi, which integrates agricultural and non-agricultural aspects; and Pachamama, which includes the coexistence of the aka pacha (time-space of the social world), alax pacha (time and space of the world above, in the heavens), and manqha pacha (time and space of the world below). This is the "cosmo-experience" that the reconstitution of the ayllu and marka are trying to recover.

The attacks against the organization of markas, ayllus, and suyus began in the early colonial period, when the Spanish Crown imposed colonial institutions such as the "repartimiento" and the "encomiendas," which broke down the territorial units of the markas and suyus (see Bouyse Cassagne 1987). The invaders also dispersed and isolated (native) groups that had complemented each other by exchanging products from different ecological niches. The situation deteriorated further when the Republic of Bolivia was founded because new administrative units were created (e.g., departments, provinces, municipal sections, and cantons.) The new political-administrative units threatened the integrity of the markas, particularly its logic of interzonal control of ecological niches. In fact, this logic was replaced by a system of never-ending feuding over territorial limits between communities. Cantapa Marka was fragmented and expropriated; it became a private hacienda that was passed from one "owner" to the next, from the Spanish Don Eduardo Ferro at the beginning of the eighteenth century up to the Haus Soliz family in the twentieth century.

The memories of Doña Maria Quispe, almost eighty-nine years of age, are illustrative of the difference between living in the hacienda and living in a community of origin. This elder became an orphan at a very young age. When her mother died, she spent her childhood and adolescence under the care of her father and other family members. During her youth, she had to go live in Cantapa after being married, a displacement that was not exactly her choice:

> In my community we would work only as far as necessary, all of us would make chacras [agricultural plots] only for us, each family. We would all eat in the pampa [plains]; we would cook in big pots. It was always like this before, in

> carnivals and in the festivities of Espiritu, that is our celebration, we would cook together and eat together. We would go to a green pampa. I would bring my pot and we would eat and drink there.
>
> In the hacienda things were different, there was too much work; we were almost left without clothes. We only worked for the bosses, not for us. On Saturdays and Sundays, we would wash our clothes, but there was no time because at five o'clock in the wee hours, we had to go get fertilizer. I would carry three meals on my back, one child on me and the other one in my arms. I almost dropped the water; the road was long because the pampa was vast and we had to go around it. There were seven or eight herding places; from those pampas we would get fertilizer. It was the same when we threshed corn, we would go at dawn chacra by chacra [plot by plot] It was the same; we had to bring our meals while we were piling up the grain. We fertilized and plowed in the same way, we had to finish the row at five o'clock in the evening. One person would plant a seed, and another would plow, husband and wife working. We worked as slaves. (Interview in Cantapa, August 2019)

According to her testimony, the life of Doña Maria was essentially a form of exile from her own territory; she was a displaced person without rights. This memory reflects a life of near enslavement in the hacienda; a very different life to the one she had in her community, where work was done in a harmonious environment, for their own subsistence and to strengthen community bonds. The feeling produced could be described in Edward Said's words: "the crack that is impossible to heal imposed between a human being and the birthplace, between the ego and its true home: this essential sadness cannot be overcome" (2005, 593). During the republican period at the end of the nineteenth century and beginning of the twentieth century, the members of the community were not only separated from their territory but were also subjected to an explicit project of destruction of the ayllus, through the legal abolishment of any kind of community and in a state effort to extirpate their identification with the territory.

> During that time, the hacienda administrators would go from house to house and would whip those who wore coloured polleras [skirts]. They would destroy the tubs where the clothes were dyed. Nonetheless, we continued to wear our clothes. The administrator used to hit us, but we would run to hidden places and rivers, and there we would change our clothes. (Interview in Cantapa, August 2019)

For the Aymara, the colours of garments are an index of our identity because they relate to the topographic characteristics of the territory, thus each ayllu or community is identified with a particular colour. For this reason, a simple change in the colour of the garments has a bearing on how the subjectivity of women was imbricated with the territory.

These kinds of assaults on the deep relationship between the Aymara feminine subjectivity and the territory were concurrent with both the invisibilization of the former's roles in keeping the weft of relations that sustains the territory and the removal of Aymara women from decision-making spaces. To give a sense of the transformation, it is worth recalling that in pre-Hispanic times, women exercised political rights like men did; they led armies, enjoyed territorial rights and other privileges (Silverblatt 1991). However, with the arrival of the colonial process, these rights were systematically taken away, turning women into minors subject to the custody of men, erasing them from public space, and confining them to the domestic sphere. This control over women replicates control over nature, a relationship of inequality typical of colonialism, racism, and male chauvinism. From this perspective, the earth/nature is conceived as a woman's body and thus perceived as a sacrificial territory, subject to rape and conquest to render it into objects or merchandise. This expresses a culture of gender inequality that is reflected in day-to-day life, wherein feminine absence is underscored by the invisibility of women in post-colonial (i.e., republican) organization systems. An example of this absence was in the union's organizational structures that were imposed in Indigenous communities as appendages of the state since 1952. The highest positions of general secretary or director were always held by men while women—in the best-case scenario—could only participate in positions associated with household chores, such as secretaries or lower members in a council. To prevent the other worlds (so-called natural and supernatural) from being affected by the chaos and disorder generated by such policies—but mainly to keep in balance the worlds in the daily life of the territory—women resisted in their own ways through spiritual practices and rituals. These became the main path for women's political action, which would only re-emerge in the public space along with the reconstitution of the ayllu.

The Cantapa Marka carried the weight of nearly three centuries of the colonial hacienda. In 1957, within the Agrarian Reform framework, the people of Cantapa collectively recovered part of their lands. In 1967, they repurchased the remaining land of which they had been dispossessed for centuries (Gutierrez Callisaya 2015). Throughout all the periods of oppression and servitude, under colonial and republican rule, community members lost control of the self-governing structures that guaranteed their public-political rights. In this context, the Agrarian Reform presented itself as the recovery of territory and liberation of the people; however, what happened in reality was that the community fell under the rule of peasant unionism. The agrarian union became the main agent of (re)colonization because its foreign structure would favour the monopoly of politics by men at the expense of communal power based on the principles of complementarity and rotation, which was still present in the minds of its community members. In other words, unionism in Cantapa was simply another phase that allowed the destruction of the marka.

The process of reconstitution of the ayllu opened the possibility of recovering those principles that unionism disregarded. Several communities embraced a political process of reconstituting the ayllu and marka as a pachakuti, a process of internal change aimed at overcoming the chaos in which they found themselves.[4] They decided to return to a model of conviviality where the political rights of women were restored via the original authorities' model, where women and men have the same status, in complementarity or chacha-warmi. This is consistent with the Aymara jaqi principle, where parity or the need to complement masculine and feminine is essential to hold a position of authority, because being alone as a subject or as a person means dissonance.

THE PROCESS OF RECONSTITUTING THE CANTAPA MARKA

In 2003, Cantapa adhered to the reconstitution process and began to reorganize its political-administrative structure under the guidance of Aymara principles and cultural values. In parallel, the management of the territory is also beginning to be guided by Aymara cosmo-experience. Notably, women regain a leading role during the process through the reintroduction and enforcement of the principles of muyu and thakhi (rotation of position for a year term) and the chacha-warmi (male/female complementarity). The chacha-warmi principle implies that positions of authority are held as a couple formed by a Tata Jilaqata (male authority) and Mama T'alla or Mama Jilaqata (female authority).[5] Based on these principles, the political-administrative structure of the Cantapa Marka has been reorganized into four collegial bodies of authority that act in coordination with one another and the community in decision-making. These bodies of authority are the Yatichayir Kamanis, the council responsible for overseeing education; the Yapu Kamanis, the council for agricultural production; the Jilaqatas council formed by ayllu authorities responsible for the internal management of the community as well as for social and financial matters; and the Mallkus council, which includes the authorities that represent the marka in their interactions with state institutions, at a municipal, departmental, regional, national, or international level. The members of each council are internally sub-organized into specific boards. The positions of authority rotate among the families in the community; the families who own more properties have the duty to hold more positions of authority, the execution of which they must finance largely with their own means. That is why the positions of authorities are often referred to with the Spanish word "cargo," or weight, for it is a load one must carry for the community.

A very important component of the reconstitution process is that women's political status is respected and dignified and their role in activities that are vital to the community, such as agriculture, is made visible. For centuries, in Cantapa Marka, as in the Andean region in general, agriculture has guaranteed food security to its inhabitants through the practice of what some analysts call "interzone symbiosis" (Condarco 1987). Interzone symbiosis is characterized by the complementarity of plots of land located in different microclimates; this aynuqa lands system functions as an extension of the community's farmland. The system is formed by small parcels of land where each family participates individually. Each parcel is destined for single-crop farming, subject to rotation followed by several years of rest to promote pest control and elimination. The process involves stirring the soil and loosening the superficial layers, then turning over the remaining weed and using it as compost for the soil to supports the roots' growth. This process is a pre-Hispanic technology that was adapted to Andean soil conditions. Depending on the available cultivable space in the markas, there can be two or even twenty aynuqas, implying that it would take up to twenty years to return to the initial crop. As a result, the organic elements are recovered for a successful production.

However, managing the territory is not only a matter of using ancestral technology or natural or special ecological features of the environment; it also (and inescapably) implies a ritual dimension. This dimension operates as the link between the human and non-human world, meaning that production practices are not separated from spiritual practices, often called "Andean spirituality." On the contrary, they are so imbricated with each other that anything that happens on one side automatically affects the other side. Indeed, crops express this relationship between "worlds": if the relation is not good, the consequence will be a poor harvest or even catastrophe. If we forget about the powerful beings connected to the crops, pests or other adversities will manifest. This, in turn, would signify a discredit of the managing authorities, who might be seen as negligent, apathetic, or unable to carry the community on their backs, as good parents should do. What follows is a community member's expression of this dimension of territorial management:

> We produce potatoes, barley, fava beans, and mainly quinoa, those are the aynuqas that we have but there are always threats of hail and frost. There are specialized authorities such as the yapu kamanis who guarantee the production. They must ask in prayer to God, achachilas, wak'as, to the qut'a awichitas, supayas; sarawis and th'akis. This is led by irpiris or maestros, who recommend the best way to pray. You must invite them according to what the

> irpiri says, they are the ones who ask through the coca plant (Remigio Mamani, interview in Cantapa, January 2019)

Before the reconstitution, these practices were lost, and some community members spoke of a production crisis. Since the reconstitution, the practice of rituals in the chacras was re-established and extended to new agricultural practices, such as sown fields under solar tents that will be described in the following section. As mentioned, if these rituals are not performed, an accident may occur and even removing the soil becomes a difficult task. The participation of women is vital to the performance of these rituals. Doña Catalina Mamani states: "Once we had jilaqatas, mallkus, then we started to do more waxt'as, fasting. This helps to have a better harvest. Women always know how to do it. Men know as well, but they don't handle it like we do" (Interview in Cantapa, December 2018).

The reconstitution faced the challenge of how to work with formal education to consolidate the Aymara identity in new generations and to guarantee a thriving territorial management. A decade ago, we could clearly see that the school essentially un-educated children; not only was ancestral knowledge never taught there, but what children learned through their primary socialization processes in the home was attacked in the school (Gutierrez and Fernandez 2011). Nowadays, this situation has changed to some extent, as the Yatichayir Kamani, or the Education Council, are working with the teachers to encourage students to value their ancestral knowledge. A clear example is the Socio Production Project (PSP) of the Education Unit in Cantapa, that for the last few years has been focused on "Nayra achachilanakasana lurawipa amthpiñani," or recovery of ancestral knowledge. Within this framework, fourth-grade students recover knowledge about medicinal plants and their different uses as part of their school program (Interview in Cantapa, August 2019).

As mentioned in the introduction, these practices of territorial management are not a return to the past but instead a grounding in our own intellectual resources to face the challenges of the present and to endure into the future. As in other regions of Bolivia, Cantapa faces issues including a lack of farming land, the advance of agro-toxics, the exploitation of women, and migration to the cities. To face these challenges, the marka promoted the creation of producers' associations. We will focus on one of them, the Agroecological Producers Association, to show how the process of reconstituting the ayllu and the marka has sought to solve such problems by deepening the appreciation of our own resources and of women's political role.

AGROECOLOGICAL PRODUCERS ASSOCIATION OF CANTAPA

In Bolivia—and Cantapa is no exception—peasant families manage farmlands that extend over one to two hectares. These small sizes are due to the progressive parceling caused by population growth, and do not allow for a large production of agricultural goods directed to the market. As a result, most of the communities are abandoning the aynuqa tradition. Even so, it has become evident that developmentalist solutions that focus on increasing productivity through agro-technological packages (based on genetic engineering and agrochemicals) are of short duration. In fact, their use aggravates the situation by polluting and, in the long term, reducing the soil's fertility, in contrast to the aynuqas system, which allows permanent regeneration as well as the preservation of a diversity of native seeds.

Another indirect consequence of these developmentalist policies is the exploitation of women, a problem that becomes visible through migration numbers. Due to the lack of soil productivity, many young women are forced to migrate to the cities and become a source of cheap labour.[6] While they are not migrants in the usual sense—as are those who leave and do not return to their hometown—they are forced to (r)exist while facing countless adversities. When men leave for the city to work in temporary jobs such as construction or informal business activity, the women must fill in for the men in addition to their usual roles. The same is true when women migrate. However, this situation does not break families apart, mainly because the Indigenous principle of complementarity suggests that when a woman is absent her partner can replace her in those social or production roles and vice versa. Also, when a family member is absent, community members resort to family support or cultural kinship depending on what they need. Children participate actively in this process as well. This is how many families in the community travel between the city and the country in what is known as a dual residence phenomenon. In addition to work and traditional cooperation practices, such as the ayni and mink'a to cultivate the land, new practices have emerged, such as renting or sharecropping among extended family members or other people in the marka. Don Hilarion Quispe explains: "My brother works in the city, but he comes every weekend to see the land, especially when it's sowing and harvest time. His family also comes for that. What he earns is not a lot, and he helps himself with the crops. There was a year when he was unable to come, so we rented it among ourselves" (Interview in Cantapa, December 2018).

In addition to these strategies, the community members of Cantapa created the Agro-Ecological Producers Association of Cantapa (APAECA, in its Spanish acronym) with the purpose of encouraging ecological agricultural production and recovering ancestral knowledge to improve the quality of life among families in the community. The association's main activity is growing lettuce under solar tents.[7] Reportedly, the initiative was born because a young man studied agronomy at the Bolivian Catholic University in Tiwanaku where he learned about solar tents and how successful they can be for growing crops. The crespi lettuce was the most adaptable in the Tiwanaku region and in Cantapa Marka, and for that reason, it ended up being the main element for experimenting with a new model of family and community economy. This technique was attractive for the community because solar tents use space efficiently; as no special soil is required, spaces around the houses could be used for growing. This experience with lettuce has allowed some community members to imagine the possibility of farming a variety of crops such as onions and carrots. By showing them other streams of work, these experiments are "unañchas," a word that describes how through the successful crop new knowledge has been created.

The adoption of an associative system of production resonates with the Indigenous organizational logic based on the principles of unity, solidarity, and cooperation. There is a direct connection between the possession of land (or, in this case, the tents) and serving through cargos (authority positions), which guarantees them the right to remain a member of the producers association. Under the term "partner in charge" (socio responsable) the cargo is governed by the principle of thakhi, (a turn) that rotates through the list of partners. Any emerging conflict is solved through the Indigenous justice administration system. The nomination of the board of directors is guided by community values such as a person's demonstrated solidarity, a trait that signals their capacity to be irpiri, a guide or authority. These persons must assume a leading position, ensuring unity and the equal distribution of the activity benefits among the community. The irpiri must also assist the association's partners, giving them advice on any issue related to the production or sale of the product. During monthly meetings, partners share their experiences with the activity (good or bad) in order to help each other.

One of the association's main focuses was recovering ancestral agricultural knowledge. In that sense, the same protocols used for potato crops are implemented for crops in the tent, that is, they use the aynuqa technique. Primitiva Apaza de Huanca comments that "we renew the soil; after each production we must completely change the soil, it must be fertilized with fermented [organic] fertilizer, it cannot be done with just any fertilizer. You must gather the fertilizer, pile it up and then ferment it for about three months. That is the kind of fertilizer that we use; this is how we control the pests. We must always clean everything. We apply the aynuqa work as we do when we plant potatoes."

They have a rule: "We don't understand chemicals, we don't put them on things. It's better all-natural, it is better for ourselves; we sometimes eat from the tent, we do so confidently. We also have our own water" (Marcellino Mamani, interview in Cantapa, 2018). Nowadays, they are producing large amounts of lettuce without any kind of chemical or pesticide, this is extremely attractive to buyers who are interested in lettuces grown in Cantapa Marka. Their success is reflected in the establishment of more than fifty solar tents of about sixty square metres, each with a drip irrigation system.

As with other crops, lettuce is not exempt from a ritual dimension that, based on astronomical knowledge, has been transmitted from mothers to daughters through oral traditions. At the sowing time, a ch'alla, a libation of alcohol and coca leaves, is performed at the four corners of the solar tent while praising and showing signs of affection, courtesy, and attention to the crops. From that day on, the crops are greeted as a new productive member of the family. These practices allow the lettuce to become a lifeform or an entity that feeds the family and community's qullqa (a word meaning crop field, but which also connotes wealth), a key component of the Aymara territoriality (Yampara 2016, 109). According to the testimony of Mrs. Rosa Huito:

> We respect certain rules, for example, urt'a (full moon), jairi (new moon), during those lunar movements we don't touch the lettuce; it could be ruined. There are other secrets. Women in their period cannot enter the tent, this would ruin the crops. Much can be done with these little things. We apply our grandparent's knowledge. The same thing that we do with the potato aynuqa we do with the small plants; each morning we greet them as if they were people. We need to love them, talk to them as if they were people, give them a lot of affection, and not hurt them. In Aymara we call this "munart' añawa," we must love them as if they were our children or family members.

Raymunda Apaza affirms that although women are not the only ones working in the tent, they are responsible for the crops.

> Early in the morning, you need to water them. If weed is growing in some places, we need to remove it. At night we need to close the tent so that animals or dogs don't get inside. We always ch'allar [make an offering] to the Pachamama so that the lettuce will grow well and sell well. When we are menstruating, women cannot go inside the tent. During those days, our tatas or our children take over. But we are the ones that take the lettuce out to sell it, we are in charge of that, and of saving the profits. Women must always manage the money.

As an expert in non-traditional lettuce farming, she told me that she also participates in the bodies of communal power, accepting and respecting the turn system. When women are appointed, they participate at every level within the marka organization. It is through their knowledge and participation in these tasks that women exercise an important political role within the community. I will return to this point in the conclusion.

CONCLUSION

When reflecting on the Cantapa Marka, a series of problems arising from colonial policies—such as overlapping administrative units, developmentalism, and industrialization—have become evident. The poor results of high-performance agro-technological packages, the extreme parceling of land, and, more recently, climate change have resulted in the land's weakening. As a result, the population is being forced to migrate to the cities, but not in the traditional sense aimed at exchange; instead, men work in construction and women work as housekeepers or in the informal economy. In both cases, they are exposed to urban violence that affects their subjectivity. Considering the effort it takes, most youths prefer to exclude themselves from the traditional agricultural system, knowing that in most cases the crops' market value would not even cover production costs. In other cases, the situation often leads to family or even communal conflicts that erode unity in the community. Overall, these problems are both a cause and a symptom of deeper issues such as the dismemberment of the territory and relatedly, the marginalization of the role of women in the health of the territory.

From the Indigenous cosmo-experience, the interconnection between different beings and worlds that make up the territory are crucial. This means that when chaos and crisis arise in human society, there is also an existential crisis in the environment. The reconstitution of the ayllu entails an understanding that the world of humans is one of many that must coexist with other worlds. This cosmopolitical notion is an outrage to Western politics that only considers the relations between humans on the one hand, and their dominion over nature on the other. The dismemberment of the ayllu (and the marka) involved losing sight of the ayllu as a complex weft, binding human beings and non-human beings together. Consequently, ayllu politics must be understood as a whole in all its dimensions, a territory of life.

Once it is accepted that the ayllu has a form of understanding and organizing the territory "otherwise," it is also essential to establish the importance of women's political roles within this whole, even if—or especially because—they have been displaced and made invisible through their historical underrepresentation in political public life. The reconstitution of the ayllu has successfully reverted this situation by recognizing, giving visibility, and promoting the political roles of women. For instance, by being in charge of making the items that symbolize authority and that couples in positions of authority (cargos) within governing structures must wear, women impregnate these garments with the energies and potencies of alax pacha and manqha pacha. Similarly, the participation of women in ritual celebrations is vital, because they know how to better prepare the sacred elements and protocols that guarantee harmony and balance in the spiritual cosmos-biotic realm. Their authority within the family as givers of life, transmitters of knowledge, and household managers is also crucial. Women take care of their community as their own family. They care for and protect it by turning to the spiritual world and mobilizing their skills as keepers of harmony and balance in these reciprocal and mutual care relationships. It is based on these (cultural) elements, rather than on the notion of Western leadership, that the political role of the Aymara women must be understood.[8]

Lastly, the solar tents initiative with lettuce crops stands as an example of (r)existence that the process of reconstituting the ayllu generates in the face of a global crisis. The farmers resist by recovering their ritual protocols, such as the waxt'a (moon cycle) or o ch'allas (offerings), and they (r)exist by integrating this initiative within their traditional system of food crops in a counter-colonizing, productive system. This initiative began as an innovation envisioned from a university experience and was adapted under a holistic, cosmos-biotic philosophy that values nature over natural resources. The ayllus in Cantapa endure by reconstituting their form of living well, with the thakhi, the muyu, and the chacha-warmi as guiding principles of their organizational structures. They (r)exist on the face of a state that is indifferent to these attempts; a state that rather than encouraging these forms of productivity by guaranteeing a market with reasonable prices, allows the import of foreign products; a state that explicitly embraces an extractivist logic of production instead of promoting the use of native seeds, opening the door to technological packages based on GMOs. In the face of these challenges, the ayllu endures and (r)exists with dignity so that new generations are not forced to leave their hometown for an urban centre, deny their identity of origin, or submit themselves to various forms of violence away from their territories of life.

NOTES

1. This is represented by the children's umbilical cord after they are born. The umbilical cord is buried on the sayana or property where their home is located, fostering a kind of unspoken pact or telluric relation.
2. It implies that humans are the synthesis of the pluriverse.
3. It enunciates the historical memory that induces jaqui to fight for the ethics of respect.
4. Pachakuti is a very complex Ayamara/Quechua concept that can be translated as a knockdown, turning around, and putting things upside down, or a revolution, although the term has cosmological meaning that refers to cycles of changes where the order of things is re-sorted.
5. Generally, these authorities are married couples or chacha-warmi and hold their position as a couple for a one-year term. Their responsibilities are to take care of the territorial integrity of the community, to bring justice, to solve conflicts, to receive instructions from other governmental agencies, and to report intractable internal conflicts.
6. This is the result of the rural education system: individuals with unfinished education, semiliterate, with a precarious command of Spanish language and writing skills are precisely the only kind of people who qualify as cheap labour.
7. A solar tent has the structure of a greenhouse, with a ceiling made of a plastic material that lets in the sunlight, generating heat and humidity during the day and avoiding a drop in temperature at night. In Cantapa, the tents measure eight metres long, three metres wide, and two to three metres high; they use a maximum of four lateral windows and a rustic wooden door. To build them, low-cost materials are used such as adobe, rocks, clay, plastic material, wooden beams, and metal. Labour is typically done by family members or friends.
8. Nowadays women participate in almost every part of state power. While before it was thought that women could only work as housekeepers, nowadays they are councilwomen or mayors; they occupy various positions of power. They also participate in the legislative assembly and other high authority positions. And yet, these spaces are still imbued with the patriarchal matrix of male chauvinism.

REFERENCES

Bouysse Cassagne, Therese. 1987. *La identidad Aymara: Una aproximación histórica (Siglo XV y Siglo XVI)*. Hisbol CEPAL.

Condarco, Ramiro, and John Murra. 1987. *La Teoria de la complementariedad vertical eco-simbiotica*. Hisbol CEPAL.

Dollfus, Olivier. 1981. *El reto del espacio andino*. Instituto de Estudios Peruanos.

Porto-Gonçalves, Carlos Walter. 2016. "Lucha por la Tierra," *Polis* 45. http://journals.openedition.org/polis/12168.

Guitierrez-Callisaya, Yamila. 2015. "La reconstitución del Ayllu como política de descolonización." Tesis de Licenciatura, Universidad Mayor de San Andrés.

Guitierrez-Callisaya, Yamila, and Marcelo Fernandez. 2011. *Niñas (des)educadas: entre la escuela y los saberes del ayllu*. Programa de Investigaciones Estratégica en Bolivia.

Guzmán, G., M. González de Molina, and E. Sevilla de Guzmán. 1999. *Introducción a la agroecología como desarrollo rural sostenible*. Grupo Mundi-Prensa.

Quijano, Anibal. 2000. "Colonialidad del poder, eurocentrismo y América Latina." In *La colonialidad del saber: eurocentrismo y ciencias sociales. Perspectivas latinoamericanas*, edited by Edgardo Lander. CLACSO/UNESCO.

Restrepo, Iván, and Silvia Rivera Cusicanqui. 1991. "Pedimos la revisión de límites. Un episodio de incomunicación de castas en el movimiento de caciques-apoderados de los Andes Bolivianos. 1919–1921." In *Reproducción y transformación de las sociedades andinas siglos XVI–XX*, edited by César Foncesa Martel et al. Ediciones Abya Yala and Mlal.

Said, Edward. 2005. "Reflexiones sobre el exilio." In *Reflexiones sobre el exilio. Ensayos literarios y culturales*. Turolero.

Silverblatt, Irene. 1991. *Luna, sol y brujas: Género y clase en los Andes Prehispánicos*. Centro Bartolome de las Casas.

Yampara, Simón. 2016. *Suma qama qamaña: Paradigma cosmo-biótico tiwanakuta. Critica al sistema mercantil kapitalista*. Ediciones Qamañ Pacha.

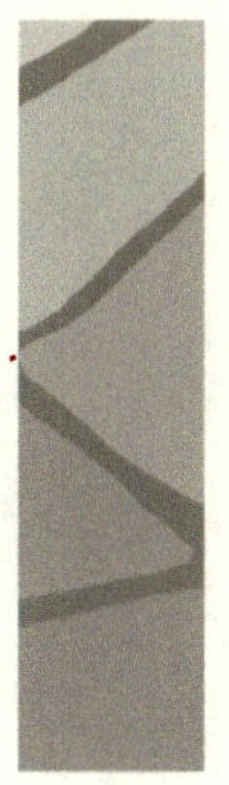

EQUIVOCATIONS

2

Lorna Quiroga

RECOVERING THE YRMO AND ITS ENTANGLEMENT IN PARAGUAY

In loving memory of Samaritana, Ita, Tito, and Veneto, who I imagine laughing somewhere in the Yrmo.

INTRODUCTION

The progressive recognition of Indigenous collective rights to land and territory in Latin America started in the 1980s and transformed the terms with which Indigenous demands were discussed. Until then, agrarian reforms were the framework for Indigenous land restitution. Emphasizing the redistribution of resources, this approach foregrounded a notion of land as property. However, around the late 1970s, Indigenous Peoples made clear that they were demanding more than lands as property, showing that they had a distinctive relationship with their territories of life (A. Escobar 2008), which legislation defined simply as soil (tierra) (Bauer 2016). In 1989, the International Labour Organization Convention No. 169 for Indigenous and Tribal Peoples framed this distinctive relationship in terms of cultural attachments and historical relations to a particular area. This convention was effectively mobilized in many countries, and it has become the dominant framework through which Indigenous movements and their supporters advance claims, and states understand and manage

Indigenous demands for territory as demands for the right to their own ways of living. This framework has been part of a regional context of neoliberal reforms and multicultural policies in many countries (Offen 2003; Wainwright and Bryan 2009).

However, Indigenous Peoples have been pushing against the limits of this approach, most recently foregrounding that their distinctive relationship to their territories is not simply a matter of culture. In this reframing, they try to bring into the conversation that living a good life with their territories is not a matter that can be defined and managed by humans alone but is rather defined in relation to other entities such as animals, spirits, stories, plants, sentient landscapes, and so on (Krenak 2019; Millan 2018). In that sense, their demands are revealed as a struggle for the right to exist as collectives—as assemblages of humans, non-humans, and more-than-human persons that take place in a specific space and from where their territories of (good) life are taking shape (A. Escobar 2014). Indeed, a territory of good life implies a conception and practice of the "Indigenous territory" that exceeds the usual meaning given by modern definitions of this term both as a form of (collective) private property and/or as cultural attachment to a place.[1]

These last two understandings of Indigenous territory are related to the modern nature/culture divide. In one view, territory is a natural environment that can be appropriated by humans through their labour (culture); in the other, territory is the superimposition of cultural perspectives on a piece of natural environment. In other words, this great divide orders the world enacted by the state and other agents of modernization.[2] This enactment is materialized through knowledges and practices, often through projects of development and modernization, and from which a particular space is delimited and organized exclusively by humans as a territory (Gudynas 2016). By this logic, the modern colonial nature/culture divide captures the heterogeneous ways that different entities live in relational reciprocity and reduces them into homogeneous binary categories classified in hierarchical, opposing terms (Blaser et al. 2004). Indeed, Indigenous territories of good life involve more than only human entities and their politics. They also involve fluid assemblages co-constituted by humans and non-human persons, entities with their own politics who are mutually linked by creation stories and are fundamentally relational (Ulloa 2016; Watts 2013). These territories are not organized according to the modern divide. Therefore, when Indigenous Peoples make "territory" the focal point of discussions about the right to exist as a collective, they are challenging the politics that delineate the organization of space, thereby disrupting the universality of modern conceptions of territory. However, this disruption is slow, complicated, and messy because, as the editors point out in the introduction, when Indigenous Peoples claim "territory," they engage in a field of equivocations. Eduardo Viveiros de Castro (2004) explains that an equivocation is not a misunderstanding or an inadequate translation, but rather something that happens when interlocutors use the same word to refer to two different things, without being aware of this referential difference. Marisol de la Cadena's (2015) paradigmatic example is Ausangate, a mountain that has minerals for the state, is a source of water for environmentalists, and is an ancestor for locals. While the last two might join forces against the first to impede mining efforts, what they are defending is not the same. The mountain is more than one but less than many, and this onto-epistemic multiplicity is similar to what happens with territory, as Carolina Tytelman explains in this volume with Nitassinan/Labrador. The "territory" that Indigenous Peoples claim is not the same as what the state imagines they are demanding; it is the traditional Indigenous territory *but not only*, as de la Cadena (2010) puts it.

This point is certainly not new. Scholars have indeed shown that behind the language of territory are the collectives that I mentioned above (Di Giminiani 2018; Landgraf 2022; M. Tola 2018). In many of these studies, the tendency is to present the equivocation as a problem. The category of "territory" imposes a limitation upon the expression of Indigenous practices and their cosmologies. In this chapter, I want to take a different approach to the issue of equivocations by attending to these limitations as sites of possibility for Indigenous movements to raise their own agendas. To do this, I propose paying attention to the kinds of challenges that Indigenous Peoples face and tackle by working through the equivocation inherent to the concept of territory (in any of its modern versions). The approach was suggested to me by the creative efforts of the Unión de Comunidades Indígenas de la Nación Yshir (UCINY), an Indigenous organization in Paraguay with which I have been working since 2011. UCINY is engaged in a "territorial" claim to recover their territory of good life, which they refer to as "Yrmo." The challenge for them seems to be how to make use of the equivocation (or control the equivocation, as Viveros de Castro puts it) implicit in the modern understanding of Indigenous territory while not getting the Yrmo trapped (captured) by the modern category in the process. Or to put it another way, the challenge is to keep in mind that claiming "territory" is an equivocation that enables Yshir people to keep on walking toward the recovery of the Yrmo. This is mostly an act of (r)existence, or as the editors argue, of endurance (see also Gutierrez-Callisaya in this volume).

It is important to highlight that this suggestion was made to me when I was recruited by UCINY in 2015 to collaborate with them as a non-Yshir facilitator in strengthening the practices and activities of a group of "women,"[3] self-identified as artisans, as part of its actions for recovering the Yrmo. The chapter reflects on "territory" as an equivocation and the challenges this implies, as I learned through walking the Yrmo with a group of artisans who shared with me their visions of good life in it. I have built the chapter from conversations with Yshir people, UCINY's representatives, and my participant observations of the daily life of artisans from three Yshir communities during four months in 2016. These methods were deployed as a collaborative research project (Coombes et al. 2014; Johnson et al. 2005) with UCINY as part of my master's thesis. My analysis is informed by a political ontology framework, a field of study that pays attention to power-laden relationships while focusing on "the inter-relations among different ontologies and conflicts that ensue as different ontologies strive to sustain their own existence in their interaction with other worlds" (A. Escobar 2016, 21). The chapter is organized into four parts. First, I contextualize the Yshir territorial claim. Second, I elaborate on the Yrmo as a territory of good life that exceeds a modern conception of the Indigenous territory, paying particular attention to the life project of this group of artisan "women." Then, I discuss the legal framework that sets up "territory" as a site of equivocation and describe how UCINY grapples with and moves through a field of equivocations to advance its agenda. The chapter ends with a reflection on the possible entanglements that emerge as a consequence of using equivocations as a means of communication between divergent worlds (de la Cadena 2019; Stengers 2013).[4]

CONTEXT

The Yshir people, also known as the Chamacoco or the Yshir Ebitoso people, are located at the northeast corner of the Chaco region in Paraguay.[5] They comprise about 2,500 individuals who currently live in seven communities with approximately 54,000 hectares of non-contiguous land (Basabe et al. 2021; Saurini 2021). However, according to a map drawn in 1928 with the collaboration of the Yshir people, at that time they inhabited an area of approximately one million hectares (Capdevila 2013).

In contrast to other parts of South America, the colonization of the Chaco occurred relatively recently, in the late nineteenth century. Since then, the Yshir people have lost access to this extended space in a gradual process that has accelerated in the last two decades. In the 1880s, the already-constituted Paraguayan state decided to privatize big extensions of land and rented other pieces to foreign enterprise to pay the debts contracted during the War of the Triple Alliance (when Argentina, Brazil, and Uruguay fought against Paraguay from 1864 to 1870). Over the following decades, intensive exploitation of the forest brought settlers to the banks of the Paraguay River.[6] Settlements were only established near the river, which enabled the Yshir people to continue with their way of living while engaging with foreigners for seasonal work in exchange for food and tools (Boggiani 1894). Most of the Chaco was still unexplored, but Bolivia and Paraguay claimed this region as part of their national territory (Pastore 1989). In the early 1920s, Bolivia began to assert its presence there, spurring its exploration. In the mid 1920s, General Juan Belaieff explored and mapped the Chaco for the Paraguayan state by recruiting Indigenous people, especially Yshir men who knew the area (Richard 2008a). [7] The Chaco War (1932–1935) between Paraguay and Bolivia introduced many soldiers to the area who carried diseases that decimated the Indigenous populations.[8] When the war ended, most Yshir people started to gravitate around camps near the river, close to potential piecemeal jobs that had become necessary as a source of livelihood (Cordeu 1989). The region was further parceled out and sold as private properties. However, this process did not necessarily mean that the Yshir people lost access to their territory, as most of the lands were bought by real estate speculators. In other words, after the war, the Yshiro resumed access to the Yrmo, moving through it to pursue their activities (Blaser 2010).

In this geographical area, this situation continued until the 1990s. Elsewhere, however, this was not the case, as Indigenous Peoples lost access to their territories and livelihoods in the wake of an advancing agricultural frontier (Villagra Carron 2018). This dire situation was the basis for state legislation in the 1980s that recognized Indigenous Peoples' rights to land (I will return to this point later). This legislation enabled the Yshir people to claim ownership of the lands they legally possess today. These lands were recovered between the mid-1980s and mid-1990s, not because the Yshiro lacked access to sources of livelihood but rather so they could establish independent communities away from the tutelage of missionaries, the military, and the patrones (bosses) who kept them in debt-bondage (Bedoya-Silva and Bedoya Garland 2005). From the mid-1990s onward, the Indigenous situation began to change, coinciding with the end of several decades of dictatorship (1954–1989).

The Chaco region, which until then had largely remained peripheral to the state's interests, became a central target of intervention for transnational actors and others who would reshape how this region was developed and managed (F. Vázquez 2005). Livestock production expanded, along with the infrastructures to support it, which meant a new wave of intense deforestation and fragmentation of the area. At the same time, environmental conservation projects established protected areas and private natural parks (Glauser 2009). Development projects also targeted Indigenous Peoples, aiming to teach them how to be productive in their recovered lands (veritable Indigenous islands amidst privatized or protected lands) and integrate with the progress taking place in the Chaco region. This context affected the Yshiro in many ways, as the vast majority depended on direct access to the forest and rivers beyond their community borders. Also affected were those who depended on wages or family-scale cattle-ranching and agriculture, because although they were not dependent on forest products, they had to nevertheless respond to the demands of helping their less fortunate relatives (Barras 2004). From within this context, the Yshiro created the Unión de Comunidades Indígenas de la Nación Yshir (UCINY) to represent the interests of all their communities. In 2010, as deforestation advanced and access to the forests and rivers became even more difficult, the communities decided that UCINY should pursue a strategy to recover the Yrmo. This strategy was presented to outsiders as a claim to traditional Indigenous territory, although it was not only that.[9]

RECOVERING THE YRMO

As explained earlier in the chapter, "Yrmo" is the word Yshir people use to refer to the space of a good life. Its meaning is expansive, ranging from the bush (monte) to the cosmos and, more recently, their traditional territory. The Yshir world, "according to several Yshiro elders, is governed by the principle of relationality—that is, the mutual dependence of all that exists. Reciprocity between all the entities that co-constitute it is fundamental to keep the flow of energy that sustains the *yrmo*" (Blaser 2009, 13; emphasis original). This world/cosmos emerges through the relations of different entities, and thus, it is not a pre-existent, abstract space container.[10] The Yrmo is co-constituted by unique and specific entities that co-emerge as Anabsero (mythical beings), doshipo (land animals), osasero (the rain), onota (the Paraguay river), monexne (stories), temxara (women), boshesho (children), wetere (almost men), nagarp (full men), to mention just a few. The relationship between these entities delineates the knowledges and practices that shape the contours of Yshir visions of a good life or life projects. Within those practices, these life projects cosmo-organize the space in which a unique and specific world, the Yrmo, is materialized.[11] In other words, the Yrmo is assembled as a complex collective by heterogeneous life projects.

Each life project is a thread that, from a particular standpoint, intertwines with others in the Yrmo. The term life project was coined by an Yshir intellectual and former community leader, Bruno Barras (2004), as distinct from practices implicit in development projects. Yshir life projects emerge from the specific ways Yshir members experience life and its challenges in the Yrmo (see Blaser 2004, 2010). They involve productive and affective practices that are not just about Yshir survival but also about maintaining the relationships with the entities that are unique and specific to the Yrmo. Yshir life projects are heterogenous because not every Yshiro relates with the various entities that constitute the Yrmo in the same way, and therefore, not everyone has the same experience of the

Yrmo.[12] Indeed, the practices and knowledge deployed in each life project entail profound familiarity and interactions with those entities who make each life project specific and distinctive. This specificity also entails particular responsibilities and obligations toward the entities that participate in their assemblage.

One of the life projects supported by UCINY for the recovery of the Yrmo is carried out by a group of "women" who identify themselves as artisans. I use the word "women" with quotes because it is usually understood that the word "temxara" in the Yshir language is equivalent to "women" in English. However, temxara are not simply women, whether the latter term refers to a biologically based difference or a culturally defined role contrasting with and referred to (the modern construction of) "men."[13] The category of temxara co-emerges with a multiplicity of other categories/entities that transcend the human/non-human divide.[14] In other words, temxara marks a difference that comes from a constellation of relationships and not from a binary classification of hierarchically opposing terms such as "men" and "women." In that sense, I find useful Rolando Vázquez's (2012) concept of relational difference to summarize the kind of difference the term "temxara" marks, one that exceeds modern classification. In sum, what makes temxara such—and what differentiates them from other entities—is the complex web of relations that transcends the human/non-human divide. Among the relations that give shape to temxara are those established with entities like plants and mythical beings, through the practical activities involved in crafting textiles and basketry for both ceremonial and commercial purposes.[15]

Sustaining the relations that make temxara implies passing on from generation to generation of temxara a set of both general and specific knowledge and practices. For those related to the crafting of textiles and basketry, temxara must learn how to walk in the bush; where to find plants used for their crafts; the precautions that must be taken to avoid the dangers of encountering certain animals or spirits; the signs that communicate what the entities of the Yrmo want and expect; and how to avoid private property and men from outside their communities. In addition, artisans must gain specific knowledge of the plants they use, which includes knowing how to engage the plants' spirits, when to cut them, how to clean them, and how to weave objects that are effective for different tasks or for commercial purposes.[16] Of course, along with the experiential learning come stories and responsibilities that many of the entities they engage with have passed on to temxara (see T. Escobar 2007; Susnik 1995). In short, the knowledges that inform temxara's practices come from communications and interactions with the entities that co-constitute them and, by extension, that co-constitute the Yrmo. Thus, weaving bags and baskets is not only a practice concerned with livelihood; it also contributes to prolonging and sustaining the relationships that weave the Yrmo as a collective, a territory of (good) life.

It is from the experience of these relations that the artisan's visions of a good life or a life project take shape, including their expectations for the recovery of the Yrmo. In contrast, other life projects, for example those of teachers, are of a different shape. Teachers spend years training in institutions away from their communities and then work most of the time at the schools in the settlements. Their daily practices involve relations with entities such as education ministry officers, formal education curricula, and so on. These entanglements shape the teachers' visions of a good life and inform their expectations about what the practice of recovering the Yrmo should entail for them. To put it simply, while artisans might expect the territorial claim to preserve their relationships with plants and mythical beings, teachers might expect that the claim would bring more land and new opportunities for Yshir communities, such as more space for small livestock.

None of these life projects are more important than another; all are tightly connected, and as a result, the strategy of recovering the Yrmo must meet everyone's expectations. All life projects together and simultaneously constitute the Yrmo, but none of them can recreate it or sustain it alone. In that sense, heterogenous life projects emerge from those relational differences in which entities (and their practices)—including the Yshiro themselves—become distinctive and specific. However, they are also entangled with each other through mutual obligations and responsibilities (some toward plants, mythical beings, and animals; others toward Yshir human relatives; and others still toward institutions like schools or UCINY itself). All of their life projects, directly or indirectly, are affected by what is taking place in the Yrmo; this was the main reason why Yshir communities decided to pursue a territorial claim.

The task of UCINY, then, is to satisfy, at least to some extent, all these heterogenous visions of a good life that constitute the Yrmo, through the strategy of its recovery. If some or many life projects are not accomplished to some extent, the strategy—and the Yrmo itself—could fall apart. In fact, the importance of sustaining these life projects is reflected in how UCINY takes a particular interest in supporting actions that, from an outsider's perspective, might seem unrelated to the territorial claim, such as sponsoring football teams, ceremonies, small cattle ranching projects, language strengthening projects, scholarship programs, food assistance in droughts, and more. In that sense, UCINY's main challenge is to sustain the heterogeneity of practices that constitute the Yrmo while leading a strategy that is framed in terms of a demand for an Indigenous territory to ensure its legibility to the state and other agents of modernity (Scott 1998). This implies that UCINY must navigate through a field of equivocations by claiming territory.

CLAIMING TERRITORY IN PARAGUAY

The space for UCINY to advance the Yshir life projects through a territorial claim is largely framed by two pieces of standing legislation that pertain directly to Indigenous rights, namely Law 904/81 and the International Labour Organization (ILO) Convention No. 169 for Indigenous and Tribal Peoples (1989). Each was adopted in different historical moments, and each carries a series of assumptions about what is at stake for Indigenous rights to land and territory, informing all kinds of practices and interventions promoted by the state and other agents of modernization. In effect, the assumptions in these pieces of legislation cast their shadows upon and inform initiatives that range from educational curricula to agricultural advisory services, and from women's health promotion to workshops for land management planning (planes de ordenamiento territorial), and with which UCINY must grapple in its strategy to recover the Yrmo.

Law 904/81: Land as (Collective) Property

In the mid to late 1970s, when many dictatorial governments in South America were under scrutiny by the administration of United States President Jimmy Carter for their human rights violations, the dictatorship of General Stroessner (1954–1989) came under intense international and local pressure to recognize Indigenous collective rights (Horst 2011). Stroessner had promoted an expansion of the agricultural frontier that encroached upon and pushed Indigenous Peoples away from their territories of life. Limited access to their ancestral territories gradually forced Indigenous Peoples to work for food and goods offered by markets, eventually making them dependent on relationships of overexploitation (Villagra Carron 2011). Indigenous allies were concerned about these conditions and the scarce possibilities for survival they spelled (Chase-Sardi et al. 1990). Thus, they took advantage of the international context to push for a law that could be accepted by the regime. In 1981, Law 904 was passed, establishing the right of Indigenous communities to land. It set up the procedures and conditions through which Indigenous rights could be realized and created the Instituto Nacional del Indígena (INDI) to regulate the entire process.

The law recognized as a claimant any Indigenous community formed by more than twenty nuclear families and represented by their own leader, who should be selected through an election recognized by the state. The law also established a minimum quantity of land to be granted by the state through a calculation that considered the region where the claimant community was from (either the Eastern or the Chaco region) and the number of families comprising it. In the Chaco region, for instance, the calculation was that each family would require one hundred hectares to sustain itself; in the Eastern region, each family would require twenty hectares (Tierraviva 2013).[17]

Nowhere does the law mention Indigenous Peoples' right to a territory, only Indigenous communities' right to land. By defining Indigenous Peoples as communities and their territories of life as portions of land that could be held in property by those communities, the law sought to include Indigenous Peoples in the established status quo. In this way, the categories used by the law made Indigenous Peoples and their claims legible to the state; it also set up the scenario for a variety of practices that would intervene in Indigenous communities and their relationships with the entities that made up their territories of life. For instance, the law's way of calculating the quantity of lands to be granted to petitioning communities was predicated on assumptions about the main economic activity, at that moment, for each region of the country. The hundred hectares per nuclear family in the Chaco region assumed that Indigenous Peoples would raise cattle; and the twenty hectares per nuclear family in the Eastern region assumed that people would engage in intensive agriculture as peasants (Blaser 2010). But it assumed something more, too: it defined the family as a basic productive unit. In practice, this reflected a heteronormative ideal that informed the organization of a space in ways amenable to capitalist production (not to mention the religious morals embedded in the assumption).[18] By doing this, the law projected and materially began to cement a particular kind of territory, composed of productive heteronormative nuclear families that cultivate/transform/work the land, the natural world.[19]

This version of Indigenous territory emerged from a particular context and a set of situated knowledges. Many of the allies, men, and women who helped draft the law had participated in the agrarian leagues and religious missions that had pushed for relatively successful land tenure reforms (agrarian reform) in the 1960s and 1970s. This affected how they understood the challenges that Indigenous Peoples faced and how the law could address them. Of course, the law was also shaped by concerns about its approval by a conservative, patriarchal, and violent ruling government that did not leave Indigenous supporters much margin for debate. Thus, as a reflection of what the state could recognize, the law ended up de facto inscribing the colonial situation in which Indigenous Peoples were forced to live. It reduced Peoples to communities; spaces of good life to plots of land; social bonds and attachment to different entities (other-than-humans) into property relations; and different ways of conceiving and organizing space into the heteronormatively gendered divisions of modern space. This scenario shifted in some ways when ILO Convention 169 became part of Paraguay's legal framework.

ILO Convention 169: Land as Culture

By the beginning of the 1990s, with the waning of the Cold War, various Latin American countries began transitioning to democratic regimes. These transitions often took shape under the tenets of neoliberal reforms that were demanded by the International Monetary Fund and the World Bank as conditions for refinancing the debts incurred by the previous dictatorial governments.[20] In accordance with these neoliberal prescriptions, many of the tasks involving the organization of space and society were thus transferred from the state to other agents such as private companies providing public services; NGOs (with the support of financial institutions such as the World Bank) providing social services; and the judiciary, which became further entangled with supranational institutions, such as the Inter-American Court of Human Rights or the United Nations. This reconfiguration of the state also included a new ordenamiento territorial (land planning) that enabled the clarification of property rights, including those of Indigenous communities, and made it possible to foster various development projects, particularly infrastructure and conservation initiatives (Bryan 2011). After the end of the Stroessner regime in 1989, Paraguay followed the regional trends—particularly with regards to the influx of new actors giving shape to a post-dictatorial order—including those that considered the role that Indigenous Peoples and the (underdeveloped) lands that they inhabited would play. Extant and newly created state institutions were joined by NGOs, international financial agencies, ecologists, conservationists, and private investors, among others, all trying to realize their own projects to integrate Indigenous populations into the emerging order. In this context, ILO Convention 169 came to play an important role.

ILO Convention 169 understands Indigenous territories as the total area *traditionally* owned, used, or *currently* occupied by Indigenous and Tribal Peoples. This implies that Indigenous Peoples have a say in those areas, regardless of whether they have legal property rights or not. The convention proposes a cultural notion of territory that stresses the subjective and historical relation Indigenous Peoples have with a particular area, a relation that enables the reproduction of life and culture. In this way, justifications for Indigenous claims in legal procedures tend to focus on the special bonds (historical and cultural) that communities have and sustain in a particular area of the nation-state territory (Wainwright and Bryan 2009). This grounds scholars' attention to culture as the crucial distinction that differentiates Indigenous territories from the territory of a nation-state (Bryan 2012; Radcliffe 2017). This difference highlights a particular way of being and living in the world, a culture that develops from the special relationship an Indigenous group has established with a particular place.

Paraguay signed the convention in 1996, but there is no regulation to organize its application, and thus, territorial restitutions still follow Law 904/81. However, Indigenous allies and other agents of modernization constantly cite the convention in their demands, creating precedents for its application. In particular, the convention's emphasis on cultural difference has been a part of how land claims through Law 904/81 are argued to prove the authenticity of claims. Moreover, most international agencies of cooperation operating in Paraguay are usually bound to follow Convention 169 to lend support to the state for modernization projects in various fields. Currently, any project financed by international sources must respect it. This requirement induces its implementation by the state and other actors, making this cultural version of Indigenous territory important and entangled with land as collective property. Nonetheless, actual implementation does depend on Indigenous capacities and understandings of how international cooperation projects work, so that they can demand the convention as a right. UCINY quickly understood that most of the financial aid for development projects in the area must conform to the convention's injunctions, and Indigenous Peoples therefore must have at least a say in what goes on in the traditional territories, leading UCINY to demand that this principle be respected.[21]

However, this cultural version of territory is not fully aligned with the Yshir agenda of recovering the Yrmo and what it entails, a point that has been raised in the literature that analyzes legal land claims processes and their impacts upon other cases. In effect, the application of the convention (more than the convention itself) inscribes a version of the Indigenous territory as a culturally homogeneous place with fixed boundaries that are static in space–time, rendering it a differentiated unit (place) of the national territory. In legal procedures, the place being demanded therefore appears as bounded and authentic (because it is traditional) as well as homogeneous; territories are "defined by their difference from other places which lay outside, beyond their borders," and thus seem to be disconnected from inter-relations and from the conflicting encounters between different stories and experiences (Massey 2005, 64). A territory appears static because the main category that defines it, culture, is constructed by knowledges and practices supposedly grounded in the past, rooted in pre-colonial or pre-nation-state times. The cultural attribute of the Indigenous territory must produce a difference from other territories to be legible to the state and other parties, because ultimately, in this difference lies the *authenticity* of a *true* Indigenous claim. This cultural difference tends to render the Indigenous territory as culturally homogeneous, underpinned by the assumption that everyone's experience and relation with it is the same, which, as we have seen, is certainly not the case for the Yrmo.[22] Beyond not quite aligning with how the Yrmo is constituted through dynamic and heterogenous practices, the cultural perspective that makes Indigenous territory different can be, and often is, easily dismissed by subordinating the Indigenous perspective to the greater common good of the nation—in the case of Paraguay, the need to transform this isolated area into a productive region for the nation (Correia 2018). We have seen this subordination in many conflicts about resources in Bolivia and elsewhere in Latin America (Anthias 2018; Rojas 2016) as well as in North America (Voyles 2015; Yates et al. 2017).

Navigating Equivocations

As I have pointed out, Law 904 and ILO Convention 169 shape—to a large extent, albeit not totally—the terrain in which UCINY persists with the strategy of recovering the Yrmo, which involves sustaining the heterogenous life projects that compose this territory of good life. For many external observers, however, recovering the Yrmo as a territorial claim is fundamentally about possessing, controlling, and/or having access to a certain area of land and its resources, an understanding that is certainly reinforced by the standing legal framework. This perspective creates a situation in which UCINY must enact homonymic actions, such as legally claiming a portion of lands for the Yshir peoples' survival, while attempting to recover the Yrmo. We see this when looking at some aspects of the legal actions of the claim.

As a territorial claim, the project of recovering the Yrmo is unique and pathbreaking in Paraguay. The claimants are an Indigenous nation who are demanding not just portions of lands, but access to and participation in decisions made about their "territory." However, because ILO Convention 169 is not fully regulated, proceedings follow Law 904 for Indigenous land-related claims in Paraguay. In this context, UCINY advances its actions by, for example, demanding the land where a third party has established a ranch called Puerto Ramos, in a space known by Yshiro as Eshma. This private property separates the communities of

Inishta and Karcha Bahlut from a third one, Puerto Diana. Yshir people keep going to Eshma to recreate the bonds and obligations they have with the entities that inhabit that space. Indeed, not so long ago, they were able to hunt, fish, gather plants for making handicrafts, or walk through it, perhaps by using the same trail their ancestors once walked (Cordeu 1989). Many Yshir people talk about Eshma as a site of abundance to which they kept returning in hard times. In addition, artisans from the Puerto Diana community told me that the plants they need to make handicrafts are abundant in Eshma. Today, Yshir people can only go through that area by a public dirt road, not the trails more suitable for year-round walking; they cannot fish, hunt, or gather inside the property, as they could be shot by the employees of the ranch. Because of these restrictions, artisans depend on their relatives to bring them plants from other communities. The restitution of Eshma is extremely important for Yshir people and, in particular, for artisans from the Puerto Diana community. UCINY is aware that Eshma is more than the private property at stake for the state and the owner of the land title. However, it is through disputing this private property that UCINY could reclaim Eshma. In effect, in the affidavits and justification for the claim, UCINY argues that the restitution would give Yshir people access to important resources (plants, game, and fish) for their livelihoods, and it includes stories that demonstrate the people's historical and cultural bonds to this place (Basabe et al. 2021).[23] In other words, UCINY makes use of the state's version of Indigenous (collective) lands by performing the equivocation in which Puerto Ramos, the private property, is the land at stake in the claim for Eshma.

For some observers, the restitution of this private property to Yshir people would help to produce a territory, as they would connect several communities' lands, creating a big area of contiguous Indigenous lands. However, recovering the Yrmo goes beyond that. It involves the capacity to intervene in the kinds of relations that shape it. Right now, Yshir movements and access have been restricted due to monocrops, intensive cattle ranching, and infrastructure megadevelopment projects that have expanded to the region. At the same time, other projects that intend to protect the ecosystem of the region have been gaining traction, also preventing Yshir people from moving through the Yrmo. In this context, mobilizing the right to have a say in what goes on in the traditional territory, as enshrined by ILO Convention 169, involves Indigenous creativity and effort. For example, UCINY demands different forms of participation in all kinds of initiatives from which it continually draws resources to support the life projects that constitute the Yrmo. This has enabled them, for instance, to be part of a UN-REDD (United Nations Reducing Emissions from Deforestation and Forest Degradation) project that purchased lands from a third party for the purpose of producing carbon credits for twenty years, after which the lands will fully revert to UCINY.[24] Likewise, UCINY is constantly invited to participate in a variety of projects funded by international cooperation organizations in the region. UCINY is aware that in many cases, these invitations are pro forma and intended to lend legitimacy to the projects, yet they often negotiate their participation to draw resources to support the life projects.

It is challenging to make use of equivocations that make sense to external supporters or associates and, at the same time, enable life projects to operate at more subtle levels in the everyday practices of UCINY. In effect, one of the challenges UCINY routinely faces is responding to the categories (and associated expectations) that are relevant to the institutions they relate with in the process of the territorial claim. A good example is the one through which I met UCINY's representatives while working for a local human rights NGO, Tierraviva, which provides legal and logistical support for the territorial claim. I was tasked with helping UCINY's representatives to draw up a proposal to gain funding from international financial agencies. The funds were directed to Indigenous organizations' actions. The form we were following was designed as a guide to elucidate the activities to be funded, and it included questions about numbers of participants and percentages in terms of age and gender.[25] The request for percentages was odd to UCINY representatives. As they explained to me, recovering Yrmo could not be divided in that way; life projects would not map onto those categories. For UCINY, it was not possible to estimate or fragment the experiences of Yshir people in those terms. They agreed with the funding agency about the general objective of such activities: these should be oriented toward the recovery and protection of the territory, and this type of project needed everybody to be on board. But the agency approached it by aggregating groups of peoples according to criteria that were irrelevant to the life projects. Nevertheless, the leaders wanted the financial aid as it would allow them to carry on with legal actions in the capital city and foster some life projects in the communities. After pondering for a while, they proposed a series of activities that were apparently oriented toward the subjects of inclusion targeted by the financial agency (see A. Escobar 1995). The activities centred on elders, youths, and women and were described as supporting different aspects of Yshir culture that would strengthen the bonds with the ancestral territory. For me, this was a strange moment; only later did it dawn on me that what I had witnessed was the purposeful staging of a controlled equivocation (see the introduction of this volume). Instead of regarding the categories of the external agency as an obstacle that placed limitations on their life projects, UCINY described activities that would sustain those life projects in terms that would better fit the agency's agenda.

One of the activities proposed was presented as being exclusively for young and adult women who produced handicrafts. They said that it was aimed at supporting their livelihoods and was a token of female Yshir culture. The activity thus included the keywords "women," "livelihoods," and "culture," coinciding in general terms with the multicultural and feminist agenda of inclusion and equity that the leaders read as an equivocation. Making use of this equivocation enabled them to support the life projects of temxara. Indeed, the support for women's livelihoods came to sustain the practices through which temxara and their relatives—plants and mythical beings—co-emerge in relational difference as unique and specific entities in the Yrmo. It has been from within these experiences that temxara see the actions of UCINY as aligned with their life projects.

FINAL REFLECTIONS

In this chapter, I have sought to bring into the conversation on Indigenous territorial struggles the way in which the Yshir Nation in Paraguay sustains and seeks to recover the Yrmo by staging it as a territorial claim. I have tried to illustrate that these are not the same. While the former implies supporting heterogenous life projects that weave the Yrmo as a collective (transcending the human/non-human or nature/culture divide and the succession of binaries that proceed from there), the latter is tied to a series of assumptions that remit back to this divide. However, to recover the Yrmo, UCINY must navigate the terrain of territorial claims, which is largely shaped by Paraguay's legal framework. This implies challenges, which UCINY addresses by making use of equivocations. Doing so has enabled UCINY to support heterogenous life projects that sustain the Yrmo.

By working through equivocations, UCINY is not only moving toward recovering the Yrmo, it also has established partial connections with the modern/colonial project (Strathern 2004). I have analyzed the equivocations in very schematic ways to point out what, for me, are some of the most interesting sites of possibilities for the Yshiro's own agenda. However, equivocations are never stable; they are moving targets and do not provide any certainty about how things really are (de la Cadena 2015). The challenge is to make use of the equivocation as effectively as possible, in a way that enables Yshir people to continue with their worlding practices. For instance, state officers have been introducing ILO Convention 169's cultural emphasis when applying Law 904. Thus, to make the equivocation effective for state officers, UCINY, like many other Indigenous organizations, has a double task: making the relationships that co-constitute the Yrmo legible in terms of cultural and historical bonds (for example by public performances of ritual singing and dancing) and presenting their life projects in terms of economic potentialities for livelihoods (Blaser 2009).[26]

Looking at UCINY's actions in this way implies understanding that they are not fully determined by the dominant practices of the state and other agents of modernization, while remembering, as the political ontology framework proposes, that neither are they fully disconnected from the modern/colonial projects (Blaser 2014; de la Cadena 2010; A. Escobar 2018). Indeed, navigating the equivocations entails partial connections between divergent worlds (de la Cadena 2019, 478; Strathern 2004), and such an encounter has the potential to generate unexpected and unpredictable new entanglements.

For example, the life projects of temxara are becoming entangled with modern practices, producing new sets of relations. Temxara's practice of making cords with plants from the forest and weaving bags and other artefacts for their group was a part of everyday life in the past. Nowadays, temxara make basketry with a plant more abundant near the communities, and the objects they produce are exclusively for commercial purposes. This is a new way of weaving the Yrmo, in which temxara are entangled with women's modern practices. Ethnographer Branislava Susnik (1995) has argued that part of the "domestication" of temxara by missionaries involved the introduction of basketry as a proper practice for women. Through this concrete practice, missionaries attempted to render temxara into women suitable for Paraguayan society. Basketry materials were near the community, which made it possible to displace temxara to the domestic sphere, where they could carry on with other reproductive tasks considered suitable to women instead of going around in the forest, encountering mythical beings, plants, and animals, singing, and weaving bags for the annual ceremony, and thus, participating in the cosmopolitics of the Yrmo. Missionaries were not the only ones that attempted to "domesticate" temxara, and the trend has been continued by diverse interventions that conceive of women and temxara as pertaining to the domestic sphere. It is not difficult to see why UCINY described the life project of temxara artisans as artisan women; their description was intended to resonate with the place that has been assigned to women in Paraguayan society, even though that is not the same place that temxara have in the Yrmo, as expressed in UCINY leaders' discomfort in thinking of the communities in terms of percentages. Paying attention to this life project as a relational difference in which unique and specific entities are co-constituted, thereby delineating the Yrmo, raises questions about what might be at stake in struggles that extend beyond Indigenous territories; the challenges Indigenous organizations like UCINY navigate to sustain their territories of life; and the unexpected entanglements that might co-emerge if these practices are considered as enacted by women, but not only.

NOTES

1. Specifically, "territories of good life" refers to Arturo Escobar's (2008, 2014) concept of "territories of difference," and to "life projects," coined by Yshir intellectual Bruno Barras (2004). Both are connected to Indigenous ideas of buen vivir in Latin America and thus, overall, to the editors of this book's concept of territories of life.
2. This modern order has a presumption of universality that was made possible through the colonization of the Americas by Europeans who imposed their own way of doing *a* world (Mignolo 2005), classifying everything that exists into these two realms (Descola 2013). From there, nature and everything associated with the reproduction of life are conceived of as passive and in a subordinate position because they lack what (some) humans have, i.e., culture. Some humans are therefore associated with Western, heterosexual white men, who are bestowed with culture—a capacity for creating, transforming, producing, organizing, knowing, or managing nature (Lugones 2010; Segato 2016).
3. I explain in a later section (Recovering the Yrmo) why I have placed the word "women" in quotes. I am not troubling the individuals' self-identification, rather, I am drawing attention to the term as a modern/colonial category.
4. In this chapter, my use of the term "entanglement" derives from the concepts of Ch'ixi (Rivera Cusicanqui 2012) and cyborg (Haraway 1991), as well as entangled territorialities (Dussart and Poirier 2017). Broadly speaking, these terms describe encounters, fusions, or connections in which deep involvement between entities occurs in such a way that it is neither possible to describe them as independent from each other nor as completely merged; although they mutually affect each other, they remain distinctive entities (Dussart and Poirier 2017).
5. The Chaco region occupies half of Paraguay, parts of Bolivia, and northern Argentina. After Amazonia, this is South America's most biodiverse ecosystem.
6. It is important to highlight that while lands were sold, the colonization process of the Chaco region was quite different in other parts of Paraguay (Bonifacio 2013; Kidd 1997; Villagra Carron 2011) and in other countries (Combès et al. 2009; Gordillo 2006; F. Tola 2013). The encounter between missionaries, Mennonites, foreign capital, military, obrajes, and cattle ranchers and different Indigenous Peoples, their subgroups, and network of relationships (Ferreira 2018) shaped those entanglements and spaces in particular ways. Each of these unique encounters produced different narratives about the colonization processes and its effects, despite the fact that the whole region was effectively occupied around the same time by similar agents of modernization.
7. He was searching for places near sources of freshwater to establish military posts, as one of the main problems colonizers encountered in the Chaco was water scarcity during the long dry seasons (Belaieff 1928).
8. Some of them contracted sexually transmitted infections through being raped or having sex with soldiers (Baldus 1931). Within their communities, most Indigenous women could choose their sexual partners, and they were not used to men treating them with violence, as soldiers and other colonizers frequently did (Chase-Sardi 1983; Kalish and Unruh 2018; Richard 2008b).
9. De la Cadena's (2015) refrain "but not only" is useful to mark the excess produced by radically different worlding practices at play, while also highlighting the onto-epistemic multiplicity that emerges when radical divergent worlds partially connect with each other through a field of equivocations. In that sense, the refrain signals that there is more than one (entity) but less than many at stake.
10. Many critical geographers have made similar arguments showing that space is a social construct embedded in power-laden human relationships. In that sense, territory as a political space—whether this refers to the national or not—is approached as socially organized by the politics of human beings and it is thus no longer an abstract, pre-existent space that contains a society (see Agnew 1994; Brenner and Elden 2009). While these

remarks are still valid, in this chapter I refer to Indigenous relational ontologies rather than to the modern and colonial political arrangements of space.

11. The term "cosmo-organize" connects with de la Cadenas's (2015, 2010) use of Isabelle Stengers's (2005) concept of cosmopolitics, wherein more-than-humans participate in the constitution of worlds as spaces of good life.
12. A similar point regarding how space is embodied and experienced differently has been made by several feminist geographers (Massey 1994; McDowell 1999) and more recently by Latin American feminist and Indigenous scholars (Cabnal 2019; Gago 2019; Leyva and Icaza 2019).
13. Argued in different ways by Plumwood (1993), Haraway (1991), Lugones (2010), or Canova (2020).
14. Similar remarks were made by de Almeida Matos et al. (2019), Maizza (2017), McGregor (2014), and Strathern (1988), among others, who have shed light on my approach to the relational difference that might co-constitute temxara.
15. The group produces two main sets of artesano, or crafts. One is mainly woven for ceremonial purposes, with the fibers of a thorny plant known in Yshir ahwoso as nekur (Bromelia hieronymi), a plant from the Bromeliaceae family popularly known in Paraguay as karaguata and chaguar in the north of Argentina (Arenas 1997, 2004; Montani 2013). The other type of craft is produced exclusively for commercial purposes; they use palm tree leaves (mainly of the Copernicia alba) to produce all sorts of basketry, hand fans, hats, and other household ornaments. This is an abundant tree found near the current location of the communities.
16. Tim Ingold (2002) points out that this type of knowledge is more than a means to an end and that it requires an attentive perception of the environment; development framed this knowledge as ecological traditional knowledge and Indigenous scholars from Turtle Island have been problematizing this term (see for example McGregor 2014; Pierotti and Wildcat 2000), showing connections with the kind of endurance that the editors of this book explain. More locally, using other terms around textiles, this traditional knowledge has been explained within the long-term collaboration project between Denise Arnold and Aymara women in Bolivia (see Espejo and Arnold 2018).
17. A community formed by twenty families in the Chaco would receive 2,000 hectares versus 400 hectares in the Eastern region.
18. In a personal conversation with one of the experts involved in drafting the law, I was told that family was thought of in relation to the household composition or whatever Indigenous communities considered family. In practice, however, this category is usually translated as nuclear family.
19. This is a utilitarian and hierarchical relationship with the land; a very modern and Lockean understanding of it.
20. Reforms included the reconfiguration of the state to attract capital (e.g., dynamization of bureaucracy, decentralization, privatization of public services, and so on) and, at the same time, the recognition of long-neglected rights (e.g., human rights and Indigenous collective rights).
21. In Paraguay since 2018, this is usually translated in terms of free, prior, and informed consent, without much consultation, in accordance with Presidential Decree number 1.039/2018. In practice, consultation and consent are done in one step or visit, and the area is reduced to the land that Indigenous communities legally possess, rather than their territories.
22. This sense of homogeneity creates a presumption of generality that describe most modern categories. Donna Haraway (1991) argues that knowledge is always situated and that the presumption of generality in modern science often reflects that the practices and points of view represented are those of men. While this has changed over time with the active participation of Indigenous People in the process of representing the cultural and

historical bonds with a particular place, of which women are always part (present or not), the way other knowledges and practices are included in modern projects tends to reproduce the men/women binary, as if this were a universal truth. An example of this is provided by Miriam Tola (2018), who describes how Pachamama in Bolivia has been rendered as Mother Earth, epitomizing the heteronormative reproductive tasks of women and nature for the modern/colonial project.

23. For instance, they mention ethnographic accounts about Eshma, such as the beginning of the fight between the Anabsero and Yshir ancestors that ended in Karcha Bahlut (Susnik 1995). This is part of the story about where Yshir men, as we know them today, have emerged (Cordeu 1989; T. Escobar 2007). While this type of story is presented as demonstrating cultural and historical bonds from past times, most of the legal and political actions UCINY is engaged in to recover the Yrmo begin or end with a ceremony whereby those mythical beings are once again present to ensure good life for Yshir people (Blaser 2009, 2010).
24. See the project description at https://guyra.org.py/tobich/.
25. It was not mandatory to include percentages or women, but they were asked to add a brief justification if they decided not to include one of these.
26. It is important to highlight that similar cases with similar arguments from the same Indigenous Nation made at almost the same time had different outcomes (Tierraviva 2013). In one case, the equivocation was effective, while in the other, it was not. UCINY seems to be aware that equivocations might not work on all occasions, and the organization sometimes changes its emphasis, depending on the entity it is dealing with.

REFERENCES

Agnew, John A. 2005. "Space: Place." In *Spaces of Geographical Thought: Deconstructing Human Geography's Binaries*, edited by Paul Cloke and Ron Johnston. SAGE Publications.

Anthias, Penelope. 2018. *Limits to Decolonization: Indigeneity, Territory, and the Hydrocarbon Politics in the Bolivian Chaco*. Cornell University Press.

Arenas, Pastor. 1997. "Las bromeliáceas textiles utilizadas por los indígenas del Gran Chaco." *Parodiana* 10: 113–139.

Baldus, Herbert. 1931. "Os índios Chamacocos." *Revista Do Museu Paulista* XV (2): 5–63.

Barras, Bruno. 2004. "Life Projects: Development Our Way." In *In the Way of Development: Indigenous Peoples, Life Projects and Globalization*, edited by Mario Blaser, Harvey A. Feit, and Glenn McRae. Zed Books.

Basabe, Claudio, Marcos Glauser, and Rodrigo Villagra Carron. 2021. *El territorio Yshir: una cartografía de su economía y ecología humanas*. Centro de Estudios Antropológicos de la Universidad Católica.

Bauer, Kelly. 2016. "Land versus Territory: Evaluating Indigenous Land Policy for the Mapuche in Chile: Evaluating Indigenous Land Policy for the Mapuche in Chile." *Journal of Agrarian Change* 16 (4): 627–645. https://doi.org/10.1111/joac.12103.

Bedoya Silva-Santisteban, Alvaro, and Eduardo Bedoya Garland. 2005. *Servidumbre por deudas y marginación en el Chaco de Paraguay*. International Labour Organization.

Belaieff, Juan. 1928. *Informe del General Juan Belaieff: viaje de reconocimiento a Bahia Negra*. Ministerio de Defensa Nacional; Museo Andres Barbero.

Blaser, Mario. 2004. "Life Projects, Indigenous Peoples, Agency and Development." In *In the Way of Development: Indigenous Peoples, Life Projects and Globalization*, edited by Mario Blaser, Harvey A. Feit, and Glenn McRae. Zed Books.

Blaser, Mario. 2009. "The Threat of the Yrmo: The Political Ontology of a Sustainable Hunting Program." *American Anthropologist* 111 (1): 10–20.

Blaser, Mario. 2010. *Storytelling Globalization from the Chaco and Beyond*. Duke University Press.

Blaser, Mario. 2014. "Ontology and Indigeneity: On the Political Ontology of Heterogeneous Assemblages." *Cultural Geographies* 21 (1): 49–58.

Blaser, Mario, Harvey A. Feit, and Glenn McRae. 2004. *In the Way of Development: Indigenous Peoples, Life Projects and Globalization*. Zed Books.

Boggiani, Guido. 1894. *I Ciamacoco: Conferenza tenuta in Roma alla Società geografica italiana, il giorno 2 giugno, 1894, ed in Firenze alla Società antropologica, il 24 dello stesso mese*. Presso la Società romana per l'antropologia.

Bonifacio, Valentina. 2013. "Building Up the Collective: A Critical Assessment of the Relationship between Indigenous Organisations and International Cooperation in the Paraguayan Chaco." *Social Anthropology* 21 (4): 510–522.

Brenner, Neil, and Stuart Elden. 2009. "Henri Lefebvre on State, Space, Territory." *International Political Sociology* 3 (4): 353–377. https://doi.org/10.1111/j.1749-5687.2009.00081.x.

Bryan, Joe. 2011. "Walking the Line: Participatory Mapping, Indigenous Rights, and Neoliberalism." *Geoforum* 42 (1): 40–50.

Bryan, Joe. 2012. "Rethinking Territory: Social Justice and Neoliberalism in Latin America's Territorial Turn." *Geography Compass* 6 (4): 215–226.

Cabnal, Lorena. 2019. "El relato de las violencias desde mi territorio-cuerpo-tierra." In *En tiempos de muerte. Cuerpos, rebeldias, resistencia*, edited by Rosalba Icaza and Xochitl Leyva. CLACSO: 113–123.

Canova, Paola. 2020. *Frontier Intimacies: Ayoreo Women and the Sexual Economy of the Paraguayan Chaco*. University of Texas Press.

Capdevila, Luc. 2013. "Colonialismos nacionales en acción: Experiencias militares en Chaco boreal en vísperas de la guerra, 1920/1930." *Nuevo mundo mundos nuevos*, February. https://doi.org/10.4000/nuevomundo.65031.

Chase-Sardi, Miguel. 1983. "Pequeño Decamerón Nivaclé: Literatura oral de una etnia del Chaco paraguayo." *Suplemento antropológico* 18: 15–252.

Chase-Sardi, Miguel, Augusto Brun, and Miguel Angel Enciso. 1990. *Situación sociocultural, económica, jurídico-política actual de las comunidades indígenas en el Paraguay*. Centro Interdisciplinario de Derecho Social y Economía Política, Universidad Católica.

Combès, Isabelle, Kathleen Lowrey, and Diego Villar. 2009. "Comparative Studies and the South American Gran Chaco." *Tipití: Journal of the Society for the Anthropology of Lowland South America* 7 (1): 69–102.

Coombes, Brad, Jay T. Johnson, and Richard Howitt. 2014. "Indigenous Geographies III: Methodological Innovation and the Unsettling of Participatory Research." *Progress in Human Geography* 38 (6): 845–854.

Cordeu, Edgaro J. 1989. "Los chamacoco o ishir del Chaco Boreal: Algunos aspectos de un proceso de desestructuración étnica." *América Indígena* 49 (3): 545–580.

Correia, Joel E. 2018. "Indigenous Rights at a Crossroads: Territorial Struggles, the Inter-American Court of Human Rights, and Legal Geographies of Liminality." *Geoforum* 97: 73–83.

de Almeida Matos, Beatriz, Julia Otero dos Santos, and Luisa Elvira Belaunde. 2019. "Corpo, terra, perspectiva: o gênero e suas transformações na etnologia." *Amazônica: revista de antropologia* 11 (2): 391–412.

de la Cadena, Marisol. 2010. "Indigenous Cosmopolitics in the Andes: Conceptual Reflections beyond Politics." *Cultural Anthropology* 25 (2): 334–370.

de la Cadena, Marisol. 2015. *Earth Beings: Ecologies of Practice across Andean Worlds*. Duke University Press.

de la Cadena, Marisol. 2019. "An Invitation to Live Together: Making the 'Complex We.'" *Environmental Humanities* 11 (2): 477–484.
Descola, Philippe. 2013. *Beyond Nature and Culture*. University of Chicago Press: 57–88.
Di Giminiani, Piergiorgio. 2018. *Sentient Lands: Indigeneity, Property, and Political Imagination in Neoliberal Chile*. University of Arizona Press.
Dussart, Françoise and Sylvie Poirier, eds. 2017. *Entangled Territorialities: Negotiating Indigenous Lands in Australia and Canada*. University of Toronto Press.
Escobar, Arturo. 2008. *Territories of Difference: Place, Movements, Life, Redes*. Duke University Press.
Escobar, Arturo. 2014. *Sentipensar con la tierra: nuevas lecturas sobre desarrollo, territorio y diferencia*. Primera ed. Ediciones Unaula.
Escobar, Arturo. 2016. "Thinking-Feeling with the Earth: Territorial Struggles and the Ontological Dimension of the Epistemologies of the South." *Revista de Antropologia Iberoamericana* 11 (1): 11–33.
Escobar, Arturo. 2018. *Designs for the Pluriverse: Radical Interdependence, Autonomy, and the Making of Worlds*. Duke University Press.
Escobar, Ticio. 2007. *The Curse of Nemur: In Search of the Art, Myth, and Ritual of the Ishir*. University of Pittsburgh Press.
Espejo, Elvira, and Denise Y. Arnold. 2019. *Ciencia de las mujeres: experiencias de la cadena textil desde los ayllus de Challapata*. Instituto de Lengua y Cultura Aymara.
Ferreira, Andrey C. 2018. "Societies 'Against' and 'In' the State—from Exiwa to the Retakings: Territory, Autonomy and Hierarchy in the History of the Indigenous Peoples of Chaco-Pantanal." *Vibrant: Virtual Brazilian Anthropology* 15 (2). https://doi.org/10.1590/1809-43412018v15n2a408.
Gago, Verónica. 2019. *La potencia feminista: o el deseo de cambiarlo todo*. Tinta Limón.
Glauser, Marcos. 2009. *Extranjerización del territorio paraguayo*. Fundacion Rosa Luxemburgo.
Gordillo, Gastón. 2006. *En el Gran Chaco: antropologías e historias*. Prometeo Libros.
Gudynas, Eduardo. 2016. "Beyond Varieties of Development: Disputes and Alternatives." *Third World Quarterly: Rising Powers and South-South Cooperation* 37 (4): 721–732.
Haraway, Donna. 1991. *Simians, Cyborgs, and Women: The Reinvention of Nature*. Routledge.
Horst, René. 2011. *El régimen de Stroessner y la resistencia indígena*. Centro de Estudios Antropológicos de la Universidad Católica.
Ingold, Tim. 2002. *The Perception of the Environment: Essays on Livelihood, Dwelling and Skill*. Routledge.
Johnson, Jay T., Renee Pualani Louis, and Albertus Pramono. 2005. "Facing the Future: Encouraging Critical Cartographic Literacies in Indigenous Communities." *ACME: An International Journal for Critical Geographies* 4 (1): 80–98.
Kalish, Hannes, and Ernersto Unruh, eds. 2018. *No llores! La historia enlhet de la guerra del Chaco*. Nengvaanemkeskama Nempayvaam Enlhet, Museo del Barro.
Kidd, Stephen William. 1997. *Love and Hate among the People Without Things*. St. Andrews.
Krenak, Aílton. 2019. *Ideias para adiar o fim do mundo*. Nova edição. Editora Companhia das Letras.
Landgraf, Luciana. 2022. "Ontologies de la terre et activités extractives: le cas de la Terre Indigène Yanomami au Brésil." *Revue International Des Études Du Développement* 2 (249): 89–119.
Leyva, Xochitl, and Rosalba Icaza, eds. 2019. *En tiempos de muerte: cuerpos, rebeldias, resistencias*. CLACSO.
Lugones, María. 2010. "Toward a Decolonial Feminism." *Hypatia* 25 (4): 742–759.
Maizza, Fabiana. 2017. "De mulheres e outras ficções: contrapontos em antropologia e feminismo." *Ilha Revista de Antropologia* 19 (1): 103–35. https://doi.org/10.5007/2175-8034.2017v19n1p103.

Massey, Doreen B. 1994. *Space, Place, and Gender*. University of Minnesota Press.
Massey, Doreen B. 2005. *For Space*. Sage Publications.
McDowell, Linda. 1999. *Gender, Identity, and Place: Understanding Feminist Geographies*. University of Minnesota Press.
McGregor, Deborah. 2014. "Traditional Knowledge and Water Governance: The Ethic of Responsibility." *AlterNative: An International Journal of Indigenous Peoples* 10 (5): 493–507.
Mignolo, Walter. 2005. *The Idea of Latin America*. Blackwell.
Millan, Moira. 2018 "Organización social y territorios: formas alternativas para la defensa del derecho a la Salud." Presentation at the II Congreso Nacional, Pluri e Internacional del movimiento por el derecho a la salud, Facultad de Ciencias Sociales de la Universidad de Buenos Aires, Buenos Aires, December 5-7.
Montani, Rodrigo. 2013. "Los bolsos enlazados wichis: etnografia de un agente ergologico." *Suplemento Antropológico* XLVIII (2): 7–144.
Offen, Karl. 2003. "The Territorial Turn: Making Black Territories in Pacific Colombia." *Journal of Latin American Geography* 2 (1): 43–73.
Pastore, Carlos. 1989. *El Gran Chaco en la formación territorial del Paraguay: etapas de su incorporación*. Criterio-Ediciones.
Pierotti, Raymond, and Daniel Wildcat. 2000. "Traditional Ecological Knowledge: The Third Alternative (Commentary)." *Ecological Applications* 10 (5): 1333–1340.
Plumwood, Val. 1993. *Feminism and the Mastery of Nature*. Routledge.
Radcliffe, Sarah A. 2017. "Geography and Indigeneity I: Indigeneity, Coloniality and Knowledge." *Progress in Human Geography* 41 (2): 220–229.
Richard, Nicolás. 2008a. "Los baqueanos de Belaieff. La mediación indígena en la entrada militar al Alto Paraguay." In *Mala guerra: los indigenas en la Guerra del Chaco (1932–1935)*, edited by Nicolás Richard. ServiLibro, Museo del Barro, CoLibris.
Richard, Nicolás, ed. 2008b. *Mala guerra: los indigenas en la Guerra del Chaco (1932–1935)*. ServiLibro, Museo del Barro, CoLibris.
Rivera Cusicanqui, Silvia. 2012. "Ch'ixinakax utxiwa: A Reflection on the Practices and Discourses of Decolonization." *South Atlantic Quarterly* 111 (1): 95–109. https://doi.org/10.1215/00382876-1472612.
Rojas, Cristina. 2016. "Contesting the Colonial Logics of the International: Toward a Relational Politics for the Pluriverse." *International Political Sociology* 10 (4): 369–382.
Saurini, Lila. 2021. *Informe del Instituto Paraguayo de Artesania, diagnostico comunitario y fortalecimiento regional con enfasis en la actividad artesanal de las comunidades Yshir*. Instituto Paraguayo de Artesania.
Scott, James C. 1998. *Seeing Like a State: How Certain Schemes to Improve the Human Condition Have Failed*. Yale University Press.
Segato, Rita Laura. 2016. "Patriarchy from Margin to Center: Discipline, Territoriality, and Cruelty in the Apocalyptic Phase of Capital." *South Atlantic Quarterly* 115 (3): 615–624.
Stengers, Isabelle. 2005. "The Cosmopolitical Proposal." *Making Things Public: Atmospheres of Democracy*, edited by Bruno Latour and Peter Weibel. MIT Press.
Stengers, Isabelle. 2013. "Introductory Notes on an Ecology of Practices." *Cultural Studies Review* 11 (1): 183–196.
Strathern, Marilyn. 1988. *The Gender of the Gift: Problems with Women and Problems with Society in Melanesia*. University of California Press.
Strathern, Marilyn. 2004. *Partial Connections*. Updated ed. AltaMira Press.
Susnik, Branislava. 1995. *Chamacoco 1: cambio cultural*. 2a ed. [1969]. Museo A. Barbero.
Tierraviva. 2013. *Situación de los derechos a la tierra y al territorio de los pueblos indígenas en Paraguay*. Coordinadora de Derechos Humanos del Paraguay.

Tola, Florencia. 2013. "Introducción. Acortando distancias. El Gran Chaco, la antropología y la antropología del Gran Chaco." In *Gran Chaco: ontologias, poder y afectividad*, edited by Florencia Tola, M. Celeste Medrano, and Lorena Cardin. Rumbo Sur.

Tola, Miriam. 2018. "Between Pachamama and Mother Earth: Gender, Political Ontology and the Rights of Nature in Contemporary Bolivia." *Feminist Review* 118 (1): 25–40.

Ulloa, Astrid. 2016. "Feminismos territoriales en América Latina: defensas de la vida frente a los extractivismos." *Nómadas* 45: 123–139.

Vázquez, Fabricio. 2005. "La mundialización y los nuevos territorios del Alto Paraguay." In *Enclave sojero: merma de soberanía y pobreza*, edited by Ramon Fogel and Marcial Riquelme, 183–216. CERI.

Vázquez, Rolando. 2012. "Towards a Decolonial Critique of Modernity: Buen Vivir, Relationality and the Task of Listening." *Capital, Poverty, Development, Denktraditionen Im Dialog: Studien Zur Befreiung Und Interkulturalität* 33: 241–252.

Villagra Carron, Rodrigo. 2011. *The Two Shamans and the Owner of the Cattle: Alterity, Storytelling and Shamanism amongst the Angaité of the Paraguayan Chaco*. Centro de Estudios Antropológicos de la Universidad Católica.

Villagra Carron, Rodrigo. 2018. "Diagnóstico socio-jurídico de tierras y territorios indígenas en Paraguay." *Suplemento antropológico* 53: 129–182.

Viveiros de Castro, Eduardo. 2004. "Perspectival Anthropology and the Method of Controlled Equivocation." *Tipití: Journal of the Society for the Anthropology of Lowland South America* 2 (1): 3–22.

Voyles, Traci Brynne. 2015. *Wastelanding: Legacies of Uranium Mining in Navajo Country*. University of Minnesota Press.

Wainwright, Joel, and Joe Bryan. 2009. "Cartography, Territory, Property: Postcolonial Reflections on Indigenous Counter-Mapping in Nicaragua and Belize." *Cultural Geographies* 16 (2): 153–178.

Watts, Vanessa. 2013. "Indigenous Place-Thought and Agency Amongst Humans and Non-Humans (First Woman and Sky Woman Go On a European World Tour!)" *Decolonization: Indigeneity, Education & Society* 2 (1): 20–34.

Yates, Julian Sebastian, Leila Harris, and Nicole J. Wilson. 2017. "Multiple Ontologies of Water: Politics, Conflict and Implications for Governance." *Environment and Planning D: Society and Space* 35 (5): 797–815.

3

Carolina Tytelman

TERRITORIALITY AND CO-MANAGEMENT IN NITASSINAN/LABRADOR

INTRODUCTION

How are territories produced in colonial contexts? How do Indigenous and colonial territories become entangled and with what results? In this chapter, I consider the territory of Nitassinan/Labrador and the relations between the Innu Nation and the Canadian province of Newfoundland and Labrador to investigate these questions. I argue that Nitassinan (the Innu territory) and Labrador (the provincial territory) are not just different names for the same thing, but different entities that are constituted by different practices, and even, one could argue, different realities. Furthermore, the points of encounter (geographical and otherwise) between these realities constitute sites of what the editors of this volume (following Eduardo Viveiros de Castro) call equivocations and entanglements.[1] Neither Nitassinan nor Labrador are enclosed, complete, or self-coherent places; they both involve heterogeneous practices, often either in tension with or enabling each other, but always shaping distinctive patterns that are nevertheless entangled. Entanglement is a useful concept because it allows us, as Sylvie Poirier argues, "to inquire into the dialectical and the dialogical dimension of the encounters and the coexistence of Indigenous and non-Indigenous worlds" (2017, 215). In this case, the practices of place (i.e., those that contribute to the production of a place) of Nitassinan and Labrador are entangled by more than five hundred years of colonial encounters and occur within a colonial context characterized by unequal degrees of access to power.[2] The specific question I ask is: How are the entanglements that extend from the equivocal site of Nitassinan/Labrador articulated in a forest co-management process?

Why focus on a co-management process to analyze these entanglements in the first place? In Canada, co-management processes and their institutions distill some of the characteristics of the current relationship between Indigenous Peoples and different levels of the state; a relationship that, while still colonial, is in a process of reconfiguration (Nadasdy 2003; Stevenson 2006; Natcher and Davis 2007; White 2020). Co-management processes are, for the different parties, a form of adaptation to the changing conditions of the Indigenous/state relationships. The state's participation in these processes can be understood as an adaptation to the demands of those who challenge its claim to sovereignty,[3] such as Indigenous Peoples. For Indigenous Peoples, participation in these processes can be understood, in turn, as a strategy of survival and self-determination in a colonial context (Snook et al. 2018; Willow 2016; Scott C. 2001). In this specific case, it is possible to see the Innu People's participation in the co-management process as part of their endurance or creative adaptability to protect their territory of life, as discussed by Mario Blaser, Sylvie Poirier, and Penelope Anthias in the introduction to this volume. Innu participation is hence the "hard work" required to maintain and reproduce their territory and the practices that sustain and create their territory; that is, their core values and their responsibilities toward multiple social relationships, including those with other-than-human beings and with the land in a hostile modern/colonial context. This context, as the editors discuss, tends to voraciously swallow everything, like a relentlessly rising ocean flooding those territories that cannot resist or adapt. One could ask how effective this strategy is for the Innu Nation, if—keeping with the metaphor—their adaptation depends on taking wet elements from the ocean? This is not a minor issue, considering the significant literature on co-management that identifies the inherent limitations of adaptations that play by the state's rules (i.e., the use of wet materials to protect their territories of life from the rising ocean).

The co-management process analyzed here is centred on the so-called Forest District 19a in Labrador. It was established by a series of legal arrangements between the Innu Nation and the Newfoundland and Labrador Government that started in the early 2000s: the 2001 Forest Agreement and the 2003 Interim Forest Agreement. The latter agreement established the Forest Management Committee (FMC), a co-management body composed of two representatives from the Innu Nation, two representatives of the Provincial Government, and a non-voting committee chair. While forest plans for the district continue to be based, although with modifications, on the plan originally developed between the Innu Nation and the provincial government, the co-management process currently only works nominally, and the FMC does not meet regularly.

In the following sections, I examine several aspects of this co-management process, including the conceptualizations of the territories, the type of language and other symbolic elements used in the co-management process, and the conceptualization of time and ideas of accountability to explore this moment and expression of the complex entanglement between Nitassinan and Labrador. This co-management process was the focus of my doctoral research, based on over two years of ethnographic fieldwork in Labrador between 2007 and 2010.[4] During this time, I lived with my family (my husband, a fellow graduate student, and our two children) in Nitassinan/Central Labrador. Since then, and upon my move to St. John's, I have remained actively involved in various collaborative projects with Innu Nation and regularly travel to Nitassinan/Labrador.

NITASSINAN AND LABRADOR

Nitassinan is the Innu territory. Often translated as "our land" or "our territory," Nitassinan refers to the entirety of the Innu People's ancestral land (most of the Quebec-Labrador Peninsula) or the territory associated with a particular Innu group (Mailhot 1997). The Innu are

Algonquian-speaking people formerly known as Naskapi-Montagnais Indians. They developed a successful way of life based on hunting and fishing, living in nomadic bands that moved through and had an intimate knowledge of Nitassinan. Since the 1600s, but more markedly since the mid-1800s, the colonial advancement progressively interfered with Innu Peoples' access to Nitassinan. Their territory was divided into two colonial jurisdictions: Quebec and Labrador (part of the province of Newfoundland and Labrador). In Labrador, the colonial government imposed destructive policies of forced settlement, cultural assimilation, and territorial appropriation for development projects without consent from the Innu and without treaty negotiations. In the 1960s, the Innu were settled in Sheshatshiu and Davis Inlet (relocated to Natuashish in 2002). The Innu People reacted to the colonial advancement by protesting, organizing their own institutions, and taking legal actions to protect their rights and territory[5] (Arbour et al. 2018; Henriksen 1973; Leacock 1954, 1969; Loring 1998; Samson 2003;). Currently, most of the Innu live in nine communities in the province of Quebec and have their own political organizations, while around three thousand people live in the two Innu communities in Labrador: Sheshatshiu and Natuashish. Each of the two communities has a band council—the Sheshashiu Innu First Nation and the Mushuau First Nation, respectively—while the Labrador Innu Nation represents the two communities.

The underlying understanding that the Innu hold regarding Nitassinan is that this is their territory and always has been (Loring and Ashini 2000, 175). The Innu received their territory from Tshishe-Manitu, the Great Spirit and it is "the root of their culture. It is here that the world-view and the philosophical concepts which are part of the [Innu] intellectual culture were formulated" (Vincent and Mailhot 1983, 21; quoted in Armitage 1990).

Nitassinan is produced by multiple constellations of social relationships, which include human and non-human persons. A fundamental part of Innu conceptualization of Nitassinan is that animals, animal masters, and other non-human persons are constitutive of the territory (Armitage 1992; Castro 2015). Different spheres of reality that include the people's social world, the social world of animals, that of animal masters, and other spirits compose Nitassinan. A complex web of social relationships connects these spheres. In this sense, Nitassinan includes several

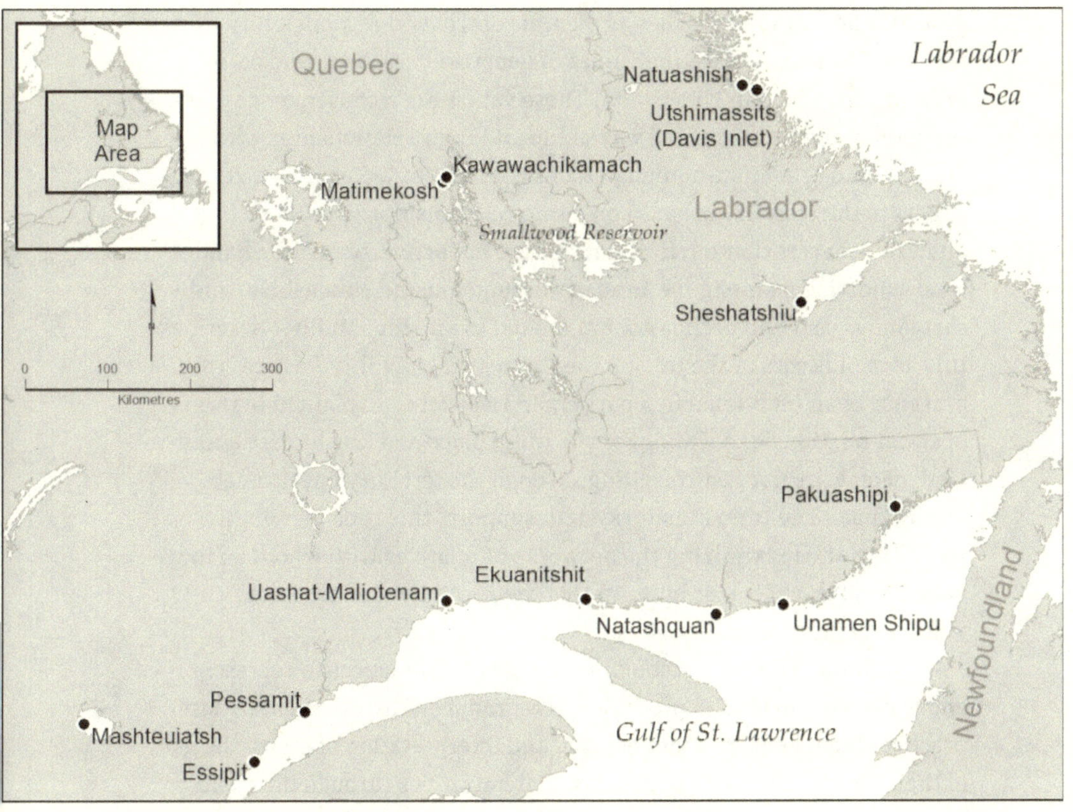

MAP 3.1 | Innu Communities.
(Created by the author.)

timescapes (Halbmayer 2004) that intercept each other. The terms of engagement between human and non-human persons include friendship, sexuality, and competition as well as kinship. There are possibilities for crossings between the human, animal master, and animal worlds, with humans visiting or becoming animals or animal masters themselves, like the Caribou Man, an Innu man who married a female caribou (Armitage 1992; Castro 2015; Henriksen 2009).

In this web of social relations, where humans and non-human persons are linked, the Innu see themselves as having a warden role. Innu conceptualizations of their territorial rights are not associated with the Western conception of property rights but with the exercise of what

José Mailhot (1986) describes as mental control and responsibility over the land.[6] Fundamental Innu values of generosity, respect, and autonomy are embedded in Nitassinan. These values are a consequence and a function of the Innu hunting way of life and their relationships with the animals and other non-human persons (Castro 2015; Henriksen 2009). Access to the territory is based on social relationships.[7] Mailhot's (1997) analysis suggests that territorial rights are collective, but with a band-level subdivision among the Innu of Sheshatshiu and Natuashish, and that land access and occupancy are related to kinship. Mailhot describes this form of access to the territory as "structural mobility," where "the presence of an individual in a particular area can be explained in terms of social relationships" (102). For the Innu, place and kinship are entangled: people are not just travelling through the territory but through family lanes. The Innu kinship system supports this type of mobility, by stretching and maximizing the networks of relatives with whom an individual can travel, live, or hunt. In this way, both the definition of family and the territory are open.

Innu People use a combination of social practices to represent and express—and thus to produce and reproduce—their territory. These practices include the production, use, and interpretation of maps; the use of their toponymic systems, dreams, and narratives through different mediums (including stories, songs, and drumming); and the production of textile drawings and rock art. Historically, Innu represented their knowledge of Nitassinan in maps of travel routes, usually outlined in birch bark or sandy superficies, based on personal memories (Loring 1987; Samson 2003, 78; Speck 1977 [1935], 148–149). Today, most Innu are familiar with Western-style cartography as well as with the colonial toponymic system. The interpretation of these tools, however, is based on Innu ideas about Nitassinan and animal agency (Castro 2015). Dreaming is another way to represent and conceptualize Nitassinan and the social relationships among its inhabitants. Dreams are considered a form of communication with animal masters (Armitage 1992, 27; Henriksen 2009) and a way to represent and understand their land (Samson 2003, 78). Innu-aimun, the Innu language, still the first language for most Innu People of Labrador is key to the way Nitassinan is produced in place names, stories, and songs. Toponyms work in this way as "rich evocative symbols" (Basso 1996) that connect people, non-human persons, place, and time. The Innu place-name system has developed through time based on various elements, sometimes in combination with one another, including references to people, animals, and notable events; it expresses a specific relation with their territory.

On the other hand, Labrador is a product of colonial expansion. It encroached onto the places of the Inuit and the Innu. While Labrador was, until recently, the only place that the state recognized,[8] these other places continue to exist as Indigenous People continue to deploy practices that produce them, even as these become increasingly entangled with those that produce Labrador.

The colonial conceptualizations of the territory (and of Indigenous People) were imagined, created, and recreated at a great geographical remove from Nitassinan, and the settlers and travellers who arrived there brought with them their own set of conceptions about place. The European and Euro-North American "imaginative geographies" (Said 1978) of Labrador are multiple and sometimes contradictory, constructed through the narratives of missionaries, explorers, and traders, as well as doctors, scientists, researchers, and later, settlers.[9] In conjunction with the deployment of state construction tools—maps, census, etc.—these narratives produce "Labrador" as a particular entity. This entity is conceptualized as part of the imperial economic and political interests in the New World, as part of Newfoundland, and finally, as part of Canada (Newfoundland became a Canadian province in 1949). With a population of about twenty-six thousand people in an area of 294,330 square kilometres, Labrador is currently the continental part of the Canadian province of Newfoundland and Labrador.

Multiple practices and ideas—some complementary, some contradictory—are embedded in the production of Labrador as a place. Labrador has been conceptualized, among other things, as a wilderness: a place for adventures and scientific inquiries, a place in need of evangelization, and a place for military expansion and industrial development. Most of these notions included call for some type of external intervention, ultimately presented in terms of progress: to bring civilization, scientific knowledge, or economic development to Labrador. For settlers, Labrador also became home and a place associated with their identities.

Labrador is no exception to well-known colonial tropes. The land was conceived as an empty and pristine wilderness in which the explorers and settlers were the first to arrive; a place unknown and virtually untouched by human presence (Denevan 1992; Sluyter 2001). The Indigenous inhabitants of Labrador were viewed almost as part of the natural landscape, and therefore unproductive and inferior to the Europeans in their cultural expressions and uses of the territory (Hinton 2002; Moore et al. 2003, 12). Labrador was also conceptualized as a land of resources to be exploited, attracting fishers, whalers, traders, settlers, and speculators. Breton and French Basques started fishing on the Strait of Belle Island in the sixteenth century. Seasonal Basque whaling operations took place in the Strait of Belle Island during the mid-to-late sixteenth century, based in Red Bay. Soon thereafter, French, Portuguese, Spanish, Basques, and English—and then, Newfoundlander—fishing vessels visited the coast annually during the summer and then later established year-round colonies there. French fur traders were established in central Labrador in 1743, and the Hudson's Bay Company arrived in 1836. The perceived potential for forestry exploitation originated speculative activity in Labrador and competitive ownership claims from Quebec and Newfoundland. The Canadian Geological Survey confirmed the potential for mining activities in 1892 with the discovery of iron ore deposits in Labrador and Quebec, and although development projects would not start until the 1950s and 1960s, its prospects informed ideas of Labrador and development policies long before that. In all these cases, Labrador was viewed as a source of raw material to be used elsewhere, and development was (and is) understood as the deployment of extractive industries (Burke 2003; Procter 2012). Linked to the expansion of global capitalism, the role of Labrador was—and continues to be—centred on the exploitation and exportation of natural resources. Labrador is constantly recreated as a frontier space that must be open to progress, but whose inhabitants rarely see its benefits. Industrial development further encroached upon Indigenous territories in Labrador.

The practices that produce Labrador are grounded in colonial claims of sovereignty, based on colonial legal artefacts, principally the Doctrine of Discovery, a type of legal self-referential claim based on self-authorizing power. The Doctrine of Discovery is an international doctrine based on ethnocentric ideas of European superiority. It asserts that Europeans acquired legal property rights over Indigenous land, as well as governmental, political, and commercial rights over its inhabitants without requiring knowledge or agreement from them, just by arriving and "discovering" the "new" land by performing rituals like planting flags, displaying religious symbols, painting signs, or burying plates and coins. England and France added to the Doctrine of Discovery the principle of occupation to justify their rights. They were in competition with Portugal and Spain, who had the advantage of receiving papal bulls in support of their rights over the so-called New World.

As in other colonial spaces, Western cartographic representations have been a key practice in the production of Labrador. Maps are creative and constitutive of the reality that they are supposed to reveal (Harley 1989, 2009), conceptualizing "unfamiliar space in Eurocentric terms, situating it within a culture of vision, measurement, and management" (Harris 2004). Explorers, fishers, merchants, missionaries, and scientists contributed to cartographic representations that, becoming hegemonic, added to the invisibility of Nitassinan and other Indigenous places. In most cases, these cartographic representations were only possible because of Indigenous guides' knowledge, maps, and help. The advancement of the cartographic project in Labrador was produced as part of a set of technologies—census, scientific reports, and Royal Commission's reports—that helped to produce a colonial space. It also involved the imposition of new toponyms over the existing Innu and Inuit place names (some of which they also recognized).

NITASSINAN AND LABRADOR IN THE CO-MANAGEMENT PROCESS

Since the arrival of Europeans and their practices of production of Labrador, Nitassinan and Labrador have been territories in tension, coexisting in complex, sometimes messy ways, with different levels of mutual acknowledgement. How are these two different places interacting in the context of forest co-management? How does the process of co-management allow for the creation and maintenance of these two places? To understand their intersections in the process of co-management, this section analyzes the "object" under co-management, its place, and its conditions. It looks at the conceptualization and representation of the territory and the territorial practices that it facilitates or hinders.

Co-Management of What?

While the focus of this co-management process is on forestland, this concept is never defined. It may appear self-evident, but the idea of the forest requires attention: what exactly is a forest, and how and by whom was the forest land of Labrador conceptualized as such? There are more than 720 written definitions of forest in usage in different parts of the world, ranging from legal and administrative considerations to types of land or types of use, with various legal implications (Lund 2006). Newfoundland and Labrador's administrative definition of forestland is "land upon which are growing or standing trees or shrubs and includes dry marsh, bogland and land commonly known as 'barrens'" (Department of Natural Resources 2010). This provincial definition refers to particular ways of producing the forest, focusing on specific aspects and elements (e.g., trees and shrubs).

The forest in Labrador as a distinctive land category was, like Labrador, a creation of the colonial process, based on a Western ontology of nature, what Philippe Descola (2013) calls "naturalism," which in turn supports particular ideas of development and land ownership. The Labrador forest was perceived as a distinctive type of wilderness, as a separate, natural entity typical of Western conceptualization. As in other parts of North America (Nash 2014 [1967]), the forest was either conceptualized in utilitarian terms, as a resource with market value, or in romantic terms, as a place for adventures. The creation of the forest as a resource in Labrador was linked to the creation of the forest as a resource in Newfoundland (and to a lesser degree, in Quebec). It took place in a colonial context that assumed ownership over the territory. The realities and perceptions of the forestry sector in Newfoundland, as well as Newfoundland's need for economic diversification, influenced the conceptualization of the Labrador forest and its legislation.

In opposition to the colonial construction of the forest, the Innu People see the forest as integrated with the territory and social relations. Trees, rivers, ponds, and their inhabitants are partly constitutive of Nitassinan and their social relationships. The Innu language distinguishes forest and other areas: for example, minashkuau can be translated as forest or wooded area, and ishku-minashkuau as the place where the forest ends. However, this distinction does not imply that the value of the forest can be separated from the value of Nitassinan and from the well-being of a whole set of persons—human and non-human—that live there.[10] During my fieldwork, I cannot recall a single conversation about the forest that did not include references to Nitassinan or the non-human persons dwelling there; discussions about forest and forestry practices typically turned into discussions about caribou, which occupy a central role in Innu culture. The co-management process, however, focuses on the forest as a particular entity with market value, not as a social place. The focus of the co-management process is thus a Western forest, a colonial forest.

Co-Management Where?

The co-management process was limited to a particular section of a forest district as defined by the provincial government: Forest District 19a, encompassing 2,270,000 hectares. The limited scope of the co-management process was agreed upon by the Innu Nation early in the process even though the Innu land claim, which was under negotiations at the time, claimed a much bigger extension of the territory. The Land Claim Agreement-in-Principle (signed in 2011), which resulted from those negotiations but is yet to be ratified, is more limited in scope than the Innu Nation's original pretensions. However, it covers a bigger, albeit different, area than the forest co-management process analyzed here. The Land Claim Agreement-in-Principle establishes different types of areas, with different levels of Innu control and capacity to exercise their rights. The Labrador Innu Settlement Area, over which a co-management board similar to the FMC would have authority, encompasses 3,643,600 hectares. However, during the FMC meetings that I observed, the provincially defined administrative scope of the co-management process was never under discussion.

Innu participation in the co-management process introduced, at least initially, changes in the conceptualization of the forest district's location. Its extent was, however, rather limited: only in the title of the 2003 forest plan (Forsyth et al. 2003) the district is located as being within "Labrador/ Nitassinan." In the forest plan's content, there is only one mention of Nitassinan and Innu culture, while "Labrador" is used extensively.

During the FMC meetings that I attended, the place under co-management was referred to following the provincial bureaucratic nomenclature as District 19a, although sometimes the Innu representatives mentioned Nitassinan. However, in the Innu Nation's reports, newsletters, and presentations, the space was always referred to as Nitassinan, and in the cases when Labrador was included, Nitassinan was always presented first (i.e., Courtois 2008).

Cartographic representations of the territory under co-management also follow the constitutive logic of Labrador. In the forest plans and other documents, there is extensive use of Western cartographic representation. For example, the 2003 forest plan includes twelve maps. In them, Labrador is presented according to its colonially imposed boundary and out of context, floating on a white page. There are maps showing Labrador forest districts and forestry offices, and "Labrador eco-regions," illustrating different types of forests classified according to their composition. The Innu communities of Natuashish and Sheshatshiu are not represented, although Sheshatshiu appears on a map in the 2018 version of the plan. Other maps exemplify the different scales used to define the protected areas inside District 19a, as well as the location of such areas. As pointed out before, maps are not just a technical resource but also a particular representation and expression of imperial expansion and the configuration of national conscience (Anderson 1991). In this particular case, Colin Samson, an anthropologist who works with the Innu People, points out how these government maps replaced the Innu presence and experience (2003, 78). In the context of co-management, all maps and documents predominantly used colonial place names. There is an almost complete absence of Innu toponyms, except for those under common usage. At the toponymic and cartographic level, the place under co-management is neither Nitassinan nor Labrador/Nitassinan; it is simply the colonial place of Labrador.

The Languages of Co-Management

English is almost exclusively the language of the co-management process. All of the co-management documents, including agreements, forest plans, FMC agendas, and budgets are written in English. Although the executive summary of the first forest plan was translated into Innu-aimun, a translation is not included in the last version of the plan. All the FMC meetings were conducted in English (although some public consultations with Innu community members early in the 2003 forest plan planning process were conducted in Innu-aimun). This language use is naturalized and, to my knowledge, never openly contested during the co-management process. When, during a meeting, I asked the FMC representatives about the possibility of provincial officials learning Innu-aimun, everyone, Innu and non-Innu, laughed at the idea. An Innu Nation representative said: "That is never going to happen." However, during an interview, one provincial representative recognized that nobody in the provincial government being able to speak Innu-aimun was a limitation, and although they were not open to learning the Innu language, this representative suggested that it would be nice to have an Innu employee among the provincial staff. While Innu representatives are forced to know English to participate in negotiations and in co-management meetings, other stakeholders need not reciprocate by learning Innu-aimun. In the same sense, while Innu People must know the English name of geographic features, government officials do not need to learn, or use, Innu-aimun names (except when these are the official names recognized by the government).

The use of colonial languages in co-management processes limits Indigenous participation. The imposition and naturalization of colonial languages, an integral part of colonization processes, expresses the symbolic power of the dominant group, which can legitimate its own domination by making it invisible (Bourdieu 1991). This is a common occurrence in co-management processes in Canada and around the world: to participate in negotiations and co-management institutions with the state, Indigenous Peoples must not only learn the colonial language but new ways of communicating and thinking.[11] The use of English restricts Innu participation by naturalizing colonial relationships, reducing the pool of possible Innu representatives to those able and willing to communicate in English, and assuming that there is congruence in words' meanings without considering core cultural differences of understanding or the impossibility of some translations. The Innu Nation accepted this limitation in the context of unequal power relationships with the provincial government.

Besides the use of English, the technical language used in the co-management process further entrenched this imbalanced situation.

The use of forestry lingo made FMC meetings difficult to follow or boring for anyone without specific forestry knowledge. While some of the Innu representatives have a solid background in forestry, for others the meetings were difficult to follow. These Innu representatives were uncomfortable or bored, and following a pattern that I also observed on other occasions, did nothing to dissimulate this: they kept moving in their chairs or around the room, and looked for excuses to abandon the meetings, spending time in corridors around the boardroom. The provincial representatives perceived this type of behaviour as a lack of interest or collaboration; however, I consider this an everyday form of resistance (Scott 1985).[12]

Technical forestry lingo used in the co-management process is also associated with a paradigm of resource development, which supports the exploitation of the forest as an economic resource and links its value to the market. For example, "management" is a term that crystallizes a particular vision of nature and humankind's relationship with nature "developed in the service of a utilitarian, exploitative, domination-over-nature worldview of colonialists and industrial developers" (Berkes 2012, 266), but it is presented in the forest plan as a technical, neutral term. The possibility of another view, where humans can be "embedded in rather than outside and above ecological relations" (Howitt 2001, 157) is in fact negated by the management approach because its premises are incongruous with it.

In addition, the co-management process privileged the provincial government's style of communication over the Innu one, which seems to be a problematic characteristic of co-management processes (Greskiw and Innes 2008; Nadasdy 1999). Most of the Innu communication is based on speaking and listening with extensive sharing of stories. Ideas are often expressed in indirect or metaphorical terms. The government, on the other hand, favors forms of communication that emphasize literacy and the production of documents that address ideas in direct, non-metaphorical ways. The co-management process tended to reproduce this government preference, imposing literacy requirements on communication, with the production of plans, agendas, documents, and agreements. The Innu Nation's various failures to accommodate such requirements were perceived by the government as a lack of accountability.

In the colonial context in which the Innu People live, accountability is not a minor issue. Practices of accountability have been part of the colonial apparatus throughout history (Buhr 2011; Neu 2000; Neu and Graham 2004, 2006). Embedded in and limited to financial accounting practices, accountability ethnocentrically links notions of answerability and enforcement with the use of money and resources. Indigenous ontologies, on the other hand, link accountability to wider ideas of responsibility. Indigenous knowledges and ontologies are based on reciprocal relationships with the natural world, including animals, plants, forests, waters, and other entities, ancestors, and future generations (Larsen and Johnson 2017; McGregor 2021; Rose 1999).

In the case of the FMC, accountability is demanded and understood in terms of criteria set by the provincial government. When non-Innu members of the FMC referred to the Innu Nation's lack of accountability, they added to a recurrent issue in the relations between the Innu Nation and the federal and provincial governments (Alcantara 2007; Backhouse and McRae 2002). They also reproduced a perception of deficient accountability among First Nations that is embedded in Euro-Canadian society.[13]

PLANNING LANDSCAPES

An important part of the co-management process involves planning for the uses of the forest (even though much of the planned forest exploitation failed to materialize). Planning is a tactic that contributes to the constitution of a place marked by the colonial state, and a factor in the creation of wilderness or natural places that then are open for colonial development. Western planning practices are constructed as rational and neutral, hiding the role of the ideologies that sustain them. These practices, in turn, "constitute some ways of thinking, some ways of being-in-place, as irrational" (Howitt 2001, 156). In consequence, those groups whose rationality does not adjust to this epistemological model (Porter 2007, 467) are not considered "legitimate knowers" (Sandercock 2003). Indeed, "the rational-comprehensive paradigm" (Howitt 2001, 157) central to the planning epistemology marginalizes Indigenous perceptions of their land because their perspectives are incongruent with the basic premises that support planning. In the co-management planning process, Innu practices are considered, if not directly irrational, "cultural," and Innu People are not considered legitimate knowers of their territory.

A characteristic of this planning process is the use of the concept of "landscape" in the forest plans. The territory is organized into three different landscapes: ecological, cultural, and economic. There is no superimposition among these landscapes. This requires clarification regarding the relevance of particular practices to any of the above categories (e.g., is hunting part of the economic or the cultural landscape?), and thus impacts several issues, including ideas of culture and knowledge, the conceptualization of animals and other non-human persons, and gendered perceptions of economic activities.

Forest plans are based on a concept of natural ecosystems that are defined as those "functioning prior to, or in the absence of human industrial activities" (Forsyth et al. 2003, 18). Forest District 19a is characterized as "a relatively undisturbed tract of boreal forest" (18) which "has experienced relatively little impact from human industrial activities" (24). This characterization repeats earlier perceptions of the territory as pristine or empty, contributing to the creation of Labrador and the invisibility of Nitassinan and its inhabitants. It also naturalizes the presence of Indigenous People (and even early settlers), making invisible Indigenous roles as agents in landscape changes in Labrador, repeating a tendency that has been observed in other Western perceptions of place (Porter 2007).

Paradoxically, Innu presence, as well as that of other ethnic groups, is included in the cultural landscape chapter that describes the historical conformation of the social relations in the forest district (which dedicates two paragraphs to archaeology and six to "European history") and provides a reference to what it calls "Innu culture and the natural economy":

> The Innu believe that the foundation of Innu culture and the natural economy are the ecosystem of Nitassinan, "our land." The Innu believe that "everything depends on everything" an insight that inter-related forest ecosystems support wildlife, fish, plants, fresh water and air. From an Innu perspective, protecting the natural composition,

> structure, and function of forest ecosystems is the highest priority. (Forsyth et al. 2003, 40)

Ultimately, the forest plan uses what it has framed as an Innu perspective to justify the use of the Western forestry paradigm. The paragraph quoted above, for example, sets Innu "beliefs" (not knowledge, as discussed below) in an ecological reductionist view of their own culture. Western categories such as wildlife (see below), are presented as components of the Innu's holistic beliefs, and furthermore, it argues that the Innu believe in the existence of a "forest ecosystem" whose protection is the Innu's highest priority.

While there is no explanation of what constitutes the "natural economy," the economic activities of the Innu and other Indigenous and non-Indigenous inhabitants of Labrador are included in the cultural landscape chapter. On the other hand, the plan's economic landscape "is intended to describe forest-based activities which have a direct market value either as a product or as a service" (Forsyth et al. 2003, v). The forest plan itself recognizes that these activities currently have marginal market value. Nevertheless, in the 2003 and subsequent forest plans, these marginal economic activities are considered "economic" while the Innu activities that the plan itself describes as "a large and important part of the Labrador economy" (v), and which operate over the same territory but on a domestic scale, are not part of the economic landscape chapter.

By excluding the domestic economy from the economic landscape chapter, the forest plan does not consider the economic value of this sector. While the market value of the domestic economy of the Innu People of Labrador is difficult to quantify because of a lack of data, the value of the domestic production around the Canadian North has been estimated to be equivalent to 30 to 60 percent of the area's total income (Elias 1995). Besides, there are social, economic, and nutritional benefits of Innu participation in domestic economic activities (Castro 2015; Samson and Pretty 2006). Finally, this division between economic and cultural activities also has gender-specific implications, as the domestic economy is often based on female work, which tends to be invisible. By framing all domestic economic activities as "cultural," the forest plan perpetuates the invisibility of women's work in the domestic sector.

TIME

Planning conceptualizes and reinforces particular ideas not only of place but also of time. Planning assumes and imposes a linear conceptualization of time (Howitt 2001, 155), which presupposes that the future can be thought of in advance, and that time can be bound and separated into blocks (e.g., five years, twenty years), while Indigenous conceptions of time are often organized around concepts of circularity and patterned cycles (McNab 1999; TenHouten 1999). Moreover, an aversion to making overly specific plans for the future appears to be a common trait in Indigenous societies, related to an ontology that does not give human beings a prominent role over other entities.

During my fieldwork, I was insistently told, "You don't know what is going to happen." Plans tended to be general, open, and flexible, and nothing was set until a particular action, or task was about to take place, or actually taking place. It seems that, after making general plans, Innu People make decisions regarding the concrete form a plan might take according to the contextual circumstances. These circumstances might involve things such as weather conditions but are also dependent on their networks of social relationships, including the decisions and desires of other people and non-human persons about particular events—something that was also noted by other authors (Samson 2003; Wadden 2001). Thus, the type of rigid planning developed by the state, based on assumptions about time and human persons' capacity to control all the variables, is considered by the Innu to be pretentious and a little naïve.

ANIMALS, WILDLIFE, ANCESTORS

An elder told me the history of the Caribou Man, an Innu man who married a caribou mare and became the caribou master. Caribou Man is one of the most powerful animal masters, a leader and protector of many animals, who gives the Innu permission to hunt and can withhold the animals if the Innu People fail to show respect. When he finished telling the history, he added; "My aunt told me that Caribou Man is our ancestor."

While attending FMC meetings or reading documents related to the co-management process, I keep thinking about this elder and others like him who told me similar histories of family bonds with animals and animal masters. Besides expressing generalities about Innu values, the co-management process does not consider this aspect of Nitassinan. This is one of the ways of being in the land that planning considers irrational. The rational construction of place in the co-management process is based not on an entanglement of social relationships but on a careful separation of nature and culture—particularly visible in the forest plan's division of the different landscapes (ecological, cultural, and economic) discussed above.

This orientation is also evident in how animals are conceptualized. In the co-management process, animals appear as resources, as wildlife, or as a threat, not as strands in the webs of social relationships. When animals are named in forest plans, they are part of the "ecological landscape" and are referred to simply as "animals," "wildlife," "species at risk," or "endangered species," and, usually in a different category, "fish." The forest plans list the animals following Western zoological categories (mammals, birds, etc.). It presents wildlife as part of the ecological characteristics of the forest district (Forsyth et al. 2003, v, 37) and, alongside fish, as forest resources.

Innu's characterizations of animals are not included, even when there are some resemblances between their zoological knowledge and Western science. The Innu organize non-domestic animals in different categories, which include "four legged animals, waterfowl, birds, fish and insects," with "an additional classification of animal species into kingdoms (tipentamun)...superimposed upon the category of Innu animals" (Armitage 1992, 68). As in other examples of co-management where Indigenous categories are not considered (Asch 1989b) and "the notion of wild is rarely addressed" (Suchet 2002, 146), this co-management process overlooks the existence of the Innu system and only considers and validates the knowledge coming from the Western sciences, as further analyzed below.

BELIEF, KNOWLEDGE, AND CAPACITY BUILDING

As in other co-management processes, the Nitassinan/Labrador forest co-management process entails the extensive use of Western-style scientific knowledge, while the Indigenous knowledge is either dismissed, misunderstood, or considered supplementary to the scientific knowledge (Spak 2005; Nadasdy 2005). Important aspects of Indigenous systems of knowledge, including Indigenous ethics of care, reciprocity, connection, and respect toward the territory and its inhabitants, are excluded (Berkes 2012; Muller et al. 2019; Whyte and Coumo 2016). Moreover, by presenting Indigenous knowledge as belief, it becomes, as Viveiros de Castro points out, "a species of theological dogmatism" (2014, 195). In contrast, scientific knowledge is presented as objective and value-free (Howitt 2001; Poirier 2013), and therefore is the type of knowledge that sustains the planning process and forms the basis of the forest plans. An example of the forest plans giving preeminence to scientific knowledge is the ecosystem landscape chapter that focuses on ecological land classification systems for District 19a. These classifications and their associated maps, tables, and aerial and satellite pictures produce a particular knowledge about the Labrador forest. This is a type of knowledge that "seeks to simplify nature and render it legible for state intervention" (Porter 2007, 471). It is the only "real" knowledge presented in the forest plans, as the Innu People's knowledge of their territory is presented as "beliefs" or "perspectives." Contrary to how the scientific knowledge appears, there is no systematic presentation of these "beliefs," only vague references, principally in the cultural landscape chapter.

During FMC meetings, Western scientists, some of them provincial employees, were invited to discuss topics related to their areas of expertise. In none of the meetings I observed were elders invited to expound on their knowledge. That does not mean, however, that there was no interest in Innu concepts. To the contrary, there was a lot of interest, but also a lack of understanding of non-Western ideas. A project funded by the FMC, for example, was supposed to systematically present Western and Innu knowledge together, organized in a book where a Western concept would be followed by the Innu equivalent. As proposed, this project was unrealizable, as not only did it imply an oversimplification and de-contextualization of Innu knowledge, but it also assumed a level of compatibility between the systems of knowledge that allowed for easy translation and the adaptability of the Innu concepts to the structure of Western science. This project was never completed.

Because the Innu are not considered legitimate knowers of their territory, they are required to engage in "capacity building." Originally linked to notions of development in underdeveloped countries, capacity building has expanded to situations of internal colonialism in developed countries. Gary Graig (2007) argues that capacity building is constructed over a "capacity deficit model," which defines groups by what they are lacking, failing to recognize groups' existing capacities and knowledge and obscuring the structural reasons of poverty and inequality. In the context of Indigenous capacity building in relation to the forest sector in Canada, Mark Stevenson and Pamela Perreault (2008) also question the capacity deficit model that presumes that Indigenous groups need capacity building, and which ignores that they have been managing their territories for millennia. In this context, Stevenson and Perreault argue that it is not appropriate to refer to capacity without questioning for whom and for what this capacity is required. Consequently, I believe that is important to question why the Innu People need to build capacity.

During an interview, a provincial official stated that "a lot of money from the FMC is directed to capacity building for the Innu Nation." When I asked what the Innu needed to build capacity for, the official replied, "to manage the forest." However, the Innu have been "managing" Nitassinan, including the "forest," for a long time. Why do they need to build capacity now? An Innu Nation official provided the answer to this question during an interview: the reason for capacity building was "to participate in the co-management." Thus, the Innu Nation needs to capacitate its members to be able to function in a Western-style institution. In other words, for the co-management process to resemble a balanced institution, it is necessary that the Innu participants "build capacity" to function in what is, basically, an alien process defined by Western parameters. Building capacity is, therefore, the state's response to its own need for Indigenous interlocutors to be able to engage in dialogues and negotiations whose terms are defined exclusively by the state.

What about the state's capacity building? Had the provincial government taken any initiative to build up its own capacity to deal with the other party in the co-management process of Forest District 19a? Although the provincial government has attempted to capacitate its officials to work in a diverse cultural environment, these attempts have been very limited. For instance, one of the provincial representatives in the FMC mentioned that he had attended a one-day seminar about

"Aboriginal sensitivity" sponsored by the provincial government. During interviews, some provincial officials expressed their frustration with this situation, talking about their own initiatives to learn more about the Innu culture, including reading about the Innu and talking with more experienced colleagues. Beyond that, the meagre institutional initiatives of the provincial government reaffirm a capacity deficit model that works "within the constellation of existing economic, technical, social and political relationships, institutions and systems" (Stevenson and Perreault 2008, 7).

STRATEGIC PARTICIPATION

At this point, it is clear that Innu ways of knowing and conceptualizing Nitassinan, as well as the practices that produce Nitassinan, are marginalized in the co-management process of Forest District 19a. Since its inception, this process has responded to the logics and necessities of Labrador, reproducing and facilitating its practices of place. Considering the differences in the recognition of place in the co-management process, one must ask why the Innu Nation continues to participate in it. The Innu Nation's participation in this process is part of a wider strategy toward self-government. Although this goal has yet to be reached, the co-management process offers access to symbolic and material resources through which the Innu could continue to produce and reproduce Nitassinan.

The forest co-management process implies recognition of the Innu Nation's claims over Nitassinan, and, at the same time, it gives visibility to such claims. The co-managament process started after the Innu People protested, demanding the right to participate in forest decisions in their territory. Thus, this process is based on the provincial government's recognition of its obligation to consult with the Innu Nation. This positions the Innu Nation as the Indigenous government with legitimate claims over this part of the territory vis-à-vis claims from other groups.[14] As such, the co-management process legitimated Innu claims over their territory.

The forest co-management process gives the Innu Nation access to funds and opportunities that would not be available to the Innu People otherwise. The Innu Nation uses these according to its own necessities and goals. By participating in the forest co-management process, the Innu Nation expands its capacity to determine the agenda of issues related to the forest. At the planning level, this is reflected in specific measures linked to the protection of caribou, including the extension of protected areas, the establishment of corridors, and the subsequent diminution of the area available for exploitation. At the research level, this allowed for the establishment of specific programs, such as the Climate Change Monitoring program.

Innu participation in the co-management process allowed the Innu Nation to partially support its Environment Office and offer capacity-building opportunities to its members. However, these opportunities are useful beyond the co-management process, for example, in terms of expertise in support of land claim negotiations. It also allows for the development of communication channels with provincial officers and a better understanding of the state's bureaucratic operations. Finally, Innu participation in the co-management process allows them to exercise specific Nitassinan practices of place. For example, the co-management process injected money into the community. This money, available mostly in the form of salaries, is incorporated into the mixed economy of the community (that combines subsistence and market elements), stretching people's capacities to sustain trips to nutshimit (the country/the bush), thus spending time in their territory.[15]

This forest co-management process began because the Innu People protested to protect their rights. The existing option—the status quo before the co-management process—had been that the provincial government would manage this forest district as any other provincial forest district, doing the minimum amount of required consulting with various community stakeholders and continuing to act as if its sovereignty over the territory was unchallenged.[16] The Innu participation in the co-management process is a way to establish and to practice their sovereignty over Nitassinan.

CONCLUSION

At the beginning of this chapter, I posed the question of how the entanglement of Nitassinan and Labrador is articulated in the co-management process of Forest District 19a. This is a pertinent question because co-management processes have become a common practice in the relationships between Indigenous and state governments in Canada and internationally. As I have shown, the co-management process was built over an equivocation (i.e., the governmental assumption that Nitassinan and Labrador are just different names for the same place rather than two different yet entangled places). What happened to this equivocation and these places in the co-management process? Were the practices that produce Nitassinan and Labrador equally recognized or sustained through this process? The short answer is no. Nitassinan and Labrador as places were unevenly reflected, recreated, and recognized. Labrador's practices of place were (and are) fully acknowledged and reproduced, while Nitassinan's practices of place are marginalized. This happened in several ways, including the definition of the object and the scope of the co-management process, the language of the co-management process, and the forms of representation and types of knowledge considered valid through it.

Underlying all aspects of the co-management processes is a Western division between nature and culture that allows for and recognizes some, but not all, practices of place. Marked by the colonial creation of Labrador, the co-management process is based on the conceptualization of the forest as a type of wilderness containing resources (whether pulp, carbon credits, or any other component of the forest) with market value and available for development. The relation between the parties (and their practices of place) is unbalanced: to participate in this process, the Innu People must learn the language and the practices of the state (i.e., "capacity building") and its accountability practices, but it is never the other way around. In other words, the practices of reciprocity and respect that are paramount to the Innu People's social relations are completely absent in the relationship with the provincial government.

The Innu People continue to be in a colonial situation, which requires multiple strategies to defend their existence as people and their access to Nitassinan, their territory of life. Negotiations with governments and participation in co-management boards are part of the Innu Nation's repertoire of strategies. Their participation in the forest co-management process, even when it followed the rules imposed by the state, allows the Innu Nation access to some symbolic and economic resources to continue the production of their own territory, and it provides a template for future participation in other institutional arrangements that simultaneously legitimate Innu claims over their territory vis-à-vis the provincial government and other Indigenous and non-Indigenous groups in Labrador.

In the colonial context, participating in the co-management process is a form of defence of their territory, a form of endurance. It could be argued that this defence is sustained on the wet material of the ocean of colonialism, and is therefore severely limited. However, adapting these wet materials—the imperfect process of co-management and other instruments such as land claims and court cases—may be the only means available to defend Nitassinan, the territory of life, at this point in the colonial process. What other avenues need to open to allow for more promising futures is the big question that faces us today.

NOTES

1. While an extensive discussion about this is not possible in this chapter, it must be noted that the Innu Nation representatives that took part in the process, and Innu People in general (and this could be easily be extended to other Indigenous groups), are well aware of the existence of this and other equivocations, as they are obligated to participate in the colonial society on colonial terms. They are familiar, thus, with the differences between concepts, because they forcedly live with (and within) them. These equivocations, however, are often unrecognized by the provincial representatives.
2. There are other practices of place in this area, as the Inuit population have also inhabited part of Labrador and have their own claims in different stages of recognition. In 2005, the Labrador Inuit and the provincial and federal governments signed the Labrador Inuit Land Claims Agreement. This created Nunatsiavut (Our Beautiful Land in Inuktitut) in Northern Labrador. In 2019, the NunatuKavut Community Council (NCC) (formerly the Labrador Métis Association) signed a Memorandum of Understanding with the Federal Government of Canada toward its recognition. NunatuKavut Community Council land claims overlap with those of the Innu Nation. The legitimacy of NunatuKavut Community Council's claims have been disputed by both the Nunatsiavut Government and the Innu, as well as the President of the Inuit Tapiriit Kanatami (ITK), Canada's Inuit national organization. The Memorandum of Understanding is being legally challenged by Nunatsiavut and Innu Nation.
3. While The Royal Commission on Aboriginal People (Dussault and Erasmus 1996) suggests that co-management processes are a potential way to resolve long-standing conflicts between Indigenous Peoples and state governments, some authors argue that

co-management processes have structural limits that restrict the scope and type of Indigenous participation (Asch 1989a, 1989b; Nadasdy 2003, 2005; Rose 1999; Young et al. 2020).

4. This chapter is based on my doctoral dissertation (Tytelman 2016), particularly on chapter 3.
5. For a discussion of the resistance during the low-level flight crisis, see Wadden (2001).
6. Other authors described the relation to the land as stewardship (Armitage 1990, 119; Lacasse 2004, 249).
7. Hunting territories, the system prevailing among most hunting peoples of Northwest North America, is not found among the Innu of the Northwestern area of the Quebec-Labrador Peninsula or the central Labrador region (Mailhot 1997).
8. Besides the Indigenous claims, the province of Quebec also claims ownership over parts of Labrador.
9. See for example Cabot (1920); Hind (1863); Holme (1888); Hubbard (2004 [1908]); Prichard (1911); Wallace (1907); Wallace 1977 [1905]); and Watkins (1930) among the explorers and traders, as well as doctors Grenfell (1929, 1933) and Paddon (2003), and settlers such as Baikie (1983) and Goudie (1973).
10. This conceptualization of forest is similar to the conceptualization of dgiyaq discussed by Scott Simon (this volume). In both cases, Indigenous Peoples understand the forest not as a collection of trees, but a network of interacting humans and non-human beings.
11. For further discussion about this issue in Canada and beyond, see Howitt 2001; Nadasdy 2003; Poirier 2001; and Rose 1999.
12. This can be linked to the strategy of existence in an inhospitable context of modernity/coloniality discussed by Blaser, Poirier, and Anthias in the introduction to this volume.
13. The conflicting understandings of accountability and responsibility in the context of this co-management forest have been discussed in more detail elsewhere (Tytelman 2014, 2021).
14. Including claims by the NunatuKavut Community Council.
15. In a similar fashion as Lorna Quiroga describes in her chapter of this volume for the Yshiro People in Paraguay.
16. This is particularly relevant in relation to the NunatuKavut Community Council Claim.

REFERENCES

Alcantara, Christopher. 2007. "Explaining Aboriginal Treaty Negotiation Outcomes in Canada: The Cases of the Inuit and the Innu in Labrador." *Canadian Journal of Political Science* 40 (01): 185–207.

Anderson, Benedict. 1991. *Imagined Communities: Reflections on the Origin and Spread of Nationalism*. Verso.

Arbour, Chelsee, Napes Ashini, Anthony Jenkinson, and Stephen Loring. 2018. "Pour ramener l'été: à la recherche d'une concordance entre l'histoire innue et l'archéologie." *Recherches amérindiennes au Québec* 48 (3): 31–44.

Armitage, Peter. 1990. *Land Use and Occupancy among the Innu of Utshimassit and Sheshatshit*. Innu Nation Naskapi Montagnais Innu Association.

Armitage, Peter. 1992. "Religious Ideology Among the Innu of Eastern Quebec and Labrador." *Religiologiques* 6 (4): 63–110.

Asch, Michael. 1989a. "To Negotiate into Confederation: Canadian Aboriginal Views on Their Political Rights." In *We Are Here: Politics of Aboriginal Land Tenure*, edited by Edwin N. Wilmsen. University of California Press.

Asch, Michael. 1989b. "Wildlife: Defining the Animals the Dene Hunt and the Settlement of Aboriginal Rights Claims." *Canadian Public Policy/Analyse De Politiques* 15 (2): 205–219.
Backhouse, Constance, and Donald M. McRae. 2002. *Report to the Canadian Human Rights Commission on the Treatment of the Innu of Labrador by the Government of Canada.* Canadian Human Rights Commission.
Baikie, Margaret. 1983. *Labrador Memories: Reflections at Mulligan.* Them Days.
Basso, Keith H. 1996. *Wisdom Sits in Places: Landscape and Language among the Western Apache.* University of New Mexico Press.
Berkes, Fikret. 2012. *Sacred Ecology.* Routledge.
Bourdieu, Pierre. 1991. *Language and Symbolic Power.* Harvard University Press.
Buhr, Nola. 2011. "Indigenous Peoples in the Accounting Literature: Time for a Plot Change and some Canadian Suggestions." *Accounting History* 16 (2): 139–160.
Burke, Rhonda Carol. 2003. "Land, Resources and Discourse of Development in Central Labrador." MA thesis, Memorial University of Newfoundland.
Cabot, William Brooks. 1920. *Labrador.* Small, Maynard.
Castro, Damián. 2015. "Meating the Social: Atikut-euiash Sharing in Sheshatshiu, Labrador." PhD diss., Memorial University of Newfoundland.
Courtois, Valerie. 2008. "Sustaining Nitassinan: Facing Climate Change—An Innu Perspective." In *Climate Change and Renewable Resources in Labrador: Looking toward 2050*, edited by T. Bell, J.D. Jacobs, A. Munier, P. Leblanc, and A. Trant. Proceedings and Report of a Conference held in NorthWest River, Labrador, 11–13 March. Labrador Highlands Research Group, Memorial University of Newfoundland.
Denevan, William M. 1992. "The Pristine Myth: The Landscape of the Americas in 1492." *Annals of the Association of American Geographers* 82 (3): 369–385.
Department of Natural Resources, Government of Newfoundland and Labrador. 2010. *Forestry.* http://www.nr.gov.nl.ca/nr/forestry/index.html#1.
Descola, Pierre. 2013. *Beyond Nature and Culture.* University of Chicago Press.
Dussault, René and Georges Erasmus. 1996. *Report of the Royal Commission on Aboriginal Peoples: Looking Forward, Looking Back.* Indian and Northern Affairs Canada. Canada Royal Commission on Aboriginal Peoples.
Elias, Peter Douglas. 1995. *Northern Aboriginal Communities: Economies and Development.* Captus Press.
Forsyth, Jay, Larry Innes, Keith Deering, and Leen Moores. 2003. *Forest Ecosystem Strategy Plan for Forest Management District 19 Labrador/Nitassinan.* Innu Nation and Newfoundland and Labrador Department of Forest Resources and Agrifoods, Northwest River.
Goudie, Elizabeth. 1973. *Woman of Labrador.* P. Martin Associates.
Graig, Gary. 2007. "Community Capacity-Building: Something Old, Something New...?" *Critical Social Policy* 27 (3): 335–359.
Grenfell, Wilfred T. 1929. *A Labrador Doctor.* Library of Alexandria.
Grenfell, Wilfred T. 1933. *Forty Years for Labrador.* Hodder and Stoughton.
Greskiw, G. and John L. Innes. 2008. "Comanaging Communication Crises and Opportunities between Northern Secwepemc First Nations and the Province of British Columbia." *Canadian Journal of Forest Research* 38 (7): 1935–1946.
Halbmayer, Ernst. 2004. "Timescapes and the Meaning of Landscape: Examples from the Yukpa of Northwestern Venezuela. Kultur, Raum, Landschaft. Zur Bedeutung Des Raumes in Zeiten Der Globalität." *Revista ArtifaraAtención! Jahrbuch Des Österreichischen Lateinamerika-Instituts* 6: 136–154.
Harley, John Brian. 1989. "Deconstructing the Map." *Cartographica: The International Journal for Geographic Information and Geovisualization* 26 (2): 1–20.
Harley, John Brian. 2009. "Maps, Knowledge, and Power." In *Geographic Thought: A Praxis Perspective*, edited by George Henderson and Marvin Waterstone. Routledge.

Harris, Cole. 2004. "How Did Colonialism Dispossess? Comments from an Edge of Empire." *Annals of the Association of American Geographers* 94 (1): 165–182.
Henriksen, Georg. 1973. *Hunters in the Barrens: The Naskapi Indians on the Edge of the White Man's World*. ISER.
Henriksen, Georg. 2009. *I Dreamed the Animals: Kaniuekutat: The Life of an Innu Hunter*. Berghahn Books.
Hind, Henry Youle. 1863. *Explorations in the Interior of the Labrador Peninsula: The Country of the Montagnais and Nasquapee Indians*. Longman, Green, Longman, Roberts, & Green.
Hinton, Alexander Laban. 2002. "The Dark Side of Modernity." In *Annihilating Difference: The Anthropology of Genocide*, edited by Alexander Laban Hinton. University of California Press.
Holme, Randle F. W. 1888. "A Journey in the Interior of Labrador, July to October, 1887." Paper presented at the *Proceedings of the Royal Geographical Society and Monthly Record of Geography* 10 (4): 189–205.
Howitt, Richard. 2001. *Rethinking Resource Management: Justice, Sustainability and Indigenous Peoples*. Psychology Press.
Hubbard, Mina. 2004 [1908]. *A Woman's Way through Unknown Labrador*. McGill-Queen's University Press.
Innu Nation, the Government of Newfoundland and Labrador and the Government of Canada. 2011. *Labrador Innu Land Claims Agreement-in-Principle*.
Lacasse, Jean-Paul. 2004. *Les Innus et le territoire: Innu tipenitamun*. Les éditions du Septentrion.
Leacock, Eleanor. 1954. "The Montagnais "Hunting Territory" and the Fur Trade." *American Anthropologist* 56 (5): 1-59.
Leacock, Eleanor. 1969. "The Innu Bands of Labrador." In *Native People, Native Lands: Canadian Indians, Inuit and Metis*, edited by Bruce Cox. Carleton University Press.
Loring, Stephen. 1987. "William Brooks Cabot (1858–1949)." *Arctic* 40 (2): 168–169.
Loring, Stephen. 1998. "Stubborn Independence: An Essay on the Innu and Archaeology." In *Bringing Back the Past, Historical Perspectives on Canadian Archaeology*, edited by Pamela Smith and Donald Mitchell. Canadian Museum of Civilization.
Loring, Stephen, and Daniel Ashini. 2000. "Past and Future Pathways: Innu Cultural Heritage in the Twenty-first Century." In *Indigenous Cultures in an Interconnected World*, edited by Claire Smith and Graemer K. Ward. UBC Press.
Lund, H. Gyde. 2006. "Definitions of Forest, Deforestation, Afforestation, and Reforestation." Forest Information Services.
Mailhot, José. 1986. "Territorial Mobility among the Montagnais-Naskapi of Labrador." *Anthropologica* 28 (1): 92–107.
Mailhot, José. 1997. *The People of Sheshatshit: In the Land of the Innu*. ISER.
McGregor, Deborah. 2021. "Indigenous Environmental Justice: Towards an Ethical and Sustainable Future." In *Routledge Handbook of Critical Indigenous Studies*, edited by Brendan Hokowhitu, Aileen Moreton-Robinson, Linda Tuhiwai-Smith, Chris Andersen, and Steve Larkin. Routledge.
McNab, David T. 1999. *Circles of Time: Aboriginal Land Rights and Resistance in Ontario*. Wilfrid Laurier University Press.
Moore, Donald S., Anand Pandian, and Jake Kosek. 2003. "The Cultural Politics of Race and Nature: Terrains of Power and Practice." In *Race, Nature, and the Politics of Difference*, edited by Donald S. Moore, Jake Kosek, and Anand Pandian. Duke University Press.
Muller, Samanta, Steven Hemming, and Daryle Rigney. 2019. "Indigenous Sovereignties: Relational Ontologies and Environmental Management." *Geographical Research* 57 (4): 399–410. https://doi.org/10.1111/1745-5871.12362.

Nadasdy, Paul. 1999. "The Politics of TEK: Power and the 'Integration' of Knowledge." *Arctic Anthropology* 36 (1–2): 1–18.
Nadasdy, Paul. 2003. *Hunters and Bureaucrats: Power, Knowledge, and Aboriginal-State Relations in the Southwest Yukon*. UBC Press.
Nadasdy, Paul. 2005. "The Anti-politics of TEK: The Institutionalization of Co-management Discourse and Practice." *Anthropologica* 47 (2): 215–232.
Nash, Roderick F. 2014 [1967]. *Wilderness and the American Mind*. Yale University Press.
Natcher, David and Susan Davis. 2007. "Rethinking Devolution: Challenges for Aboriginal Resource Management in the Yukon Territory." *Society and Natural Resources* 20 (3): 271–279.
Neu, Dean. 2000. "Accounting and Accountability Relations: Colonization, Genocide and Canada's First Nations." *Accounting, Auditing & Accountability Journal* 13 (3): 268–288.
Neu, Dean and Cameron Graham. 2004. "Accounting and the Holocausts of Modernity." *Accounting, Auditing & Accountability Journal* 17 (4): 578–603.
Neu, Dean and Cameron Graham. 2006. "The Birth of a Nation: Accounting and Canada's First Nations, 1860–1900." *Accounting, Organizations and Society* 31 (1): 47–76.
Paddon, H. 2003. *Labrador Memoir of Dr Harry Paddon, 1912–1938*. McGill-Queen's University Press.
Poirier, Sylvie. 2001. "Territories, Identity and Modernity among the Atikamekw (Haut St-Maurice)." In *Aboriginal Autonomy and Development in Northern Quebec and Labrador*, edited by Colin Scott. UBC Press.
Poirier, Sylvie. 2013. "The Dynamic Reproduction of Hunter-Gatherers' Ontologies and Values." In *A Companion to the Anthropology of Religion*, edited by Janice Boddy and Michael Lambek. John Wiley & Sons.
Poirier, Sylvie. 2017. "Nehirowisiw Territoriality: Negotiating and Managing Entanglement and Coexistence." In *Entangled Territorialities: Negotiating Indigenous Lands in Australia and Canada*, edited by Françoise Dussart and Sylvie Poirier. University of Toronto Press.
Porter, Libby. 2007. "Producing Forests: A Colonial Genealogy of Environmental Planning in Victoria, Australia." *Journal of Planning Education and Research* 26 (4): 466–477.
Prichard, H. Hesketh. 1911. *Through Trackless Labrador*. Sturgis & Walton Company.
Procter, Andrea. 2012. "The Prospects of Culture: Resource Management and the Production of Difference in Nunatsiavut, Labrador." PhD diss., Memorial University of Newfoundland.
Rose, Deborah Bird. 1999. "Indigenous Ecologies and an Ethic of Connection." In *Global Ethics and Environment*, edited by Nicholas Low. Taylor and Francis.
Said, Edward W. 1978. *Orientalism: Western Conceptions of the Orient*. Penguin.
Samson, Colin. 2003. *A Way of Life That Does Not Exist: Canada and the Extinguishment of the Innu*. Verso.
Samson, Colin, and Jules Pretty. 2006. "Environmental and Health Benefits of Hunting Lifestyles and Diets for the Innu of Labrador." *Food Policy* 31 (6): 528–553.
Sandercock, Leonie. 2003. "Out of the Closet: The importance of Stories and Storytelling in Planning Practice." *Planning Theory & Practice* 4 (1): 11–28.
Scott, Colin, ed. 2001. *Aboriginal Autonomy and Development in Northern Quebec and Labrador*. UBC Press.
Scott, James C. 1985. *Weapons of the Weak: Everyday Forms of Peasant Resistance*. Yale University Press.
Sluyter, Andrew. 2001. "Colonialism and Landscape in the Americas: Material/Conceptual Transformations and Continuing Consequences." *Annals of the Association of American Geographers* 91 (2): 410–429.
Snook, Jamie, Ashlee Cunsolo, and Aaron Dale. 2018. "Co-management Led Research and Sharing Space on the Pathway to Inuit Self-determination in Research." *Northern Public Affairs* July: 52–56.

Soren, Larsen and Jay Johnson. 2017. *Being Together in Place: Indigenous Coexistence in a More Than Human World*. University of Minnesota Press.
Spak, Stella. 2005. "The Position of Indigenous Knowledge in Canadian Co-management Organizations." *Anthropologica* 47 (2): 233–246.
Speck, Frank G. 1977 [1935]. *Naskapi: The Savage Hunters of the Labrador Peninsula*. University of Oklahoma Press.
Stevenson, Mark G. 2006. "The Possibility of Difference: Rethinking Co-management." *Human Organization* 65 (2): 167–180.
Stevenson, Mark G., and Pamela Perreault. 2008. *Capacity for What? Capacity for Whom?: Aboriginal Capacity and Canada's Forest Sector*. Knowledge Exchange and Technology Program (KETE), Sustainable Forest Management Network, Edmonton, Alberta.
Suchet, Sandie. 2002. "'Totally Wild'? Colonizing Discourses, Indigenous Knowledges and Managing Wildlife." *Australian Geographer* 33 (2): 141–157.
TenHouten, Warren D. 1999. "Text and Temporality: Patterned-Cyclical and Ordinary-Linear Forms of Time-Consciousness, Inferred from a Corpus of Australian Aboriginal and Euro-Australian Life-Historical Interviews." *Symbolic Interaction* 22 (2): 121–137.
Tytelman, Carolina. 2014. "Natural Resources and Cultural Understandings: The Comanagement of Forest District 19A, Labrador/Nitassinan." In *Papers of the Forty-Second Algonquian Conference: Actes du Congrès des Algonquinistes*. SUNY Press.
Tytelman, Carolina. 2016. "Place and Forest Co-management in Nitassinan/Labrador." PhD diss., Memorial University of Newfoundland
Tytelman, Carolina. 2021. "Carpas e insectos en Labrador/Nitassinan: Ideas de responsabilidad en el proceso de comanejo forestal entre el pueblo Innu y el gobierno de Terranova y Labrador (Canadá)." *Cuadernos de antropología social* (54): 29–46.
Viveiros De Castro. Eduardo. 2014. *Cannibal Metaphysics*. University of Minnesota Press.
Wadden, Marie. 2001. *Nitassinan: The Innu Struggle to Reclaim Their Homeland*. Douglas & McIntyre.
Wallace, Dillon. 1907. *The Long Labrador Trail*. FH Revell Company.
Wallace, Dillon. 1977 [1905]. *The Lure of the Labrador Wild: The story of the exploring expedition conducted by Leonidas Hubbard, Jr.* Breakwater Books.
Watkins, Henry George. 1930. "River Exploration in Labrador by Canoe and Dog Sledge." *The Geographical Journal* 75 (2): 97–116.
White, Graham. 2020. *Indigenous Empowerment through Co-management: Land Claims Boards, Wildlife Management and Environmental Regulation*. UBC Press.
Whyte, Kyle, and Chris J. Cuomo. 2016. "Ethics of Caring in Environmental Ethics: Indigenous and Feminist Philosophies," in *The Oxford Handbook of Environmental Ethics*, edited by Stephen M. Gardiner and Allen Thompson. Oxford Handbooks.
Willow, Anna. 2016. "Boreal Forest Prospects and Politics: Paradoxes of First Nations Participation in Multi-Sector Conservation." *Conservation and Society* 14 (2): 86–99. www.jstor.org/stable/26393232.
Young, Nathan, Steven J. Cooke, Scott G. Hinch, et al. 2020. "'Consulted to Death': Personal Stress as a Major Barrier to Environmental Co-management." *Journal of Environmental Management* 254: 109820. https://doi.org/10.1016/j.jenvman.2019.109820.

4

Benoit Éthier
and Sipi Flamand

ATIKAMEKW NEHIROWISIW OTIPERITAMO[SO]WIN

INDIGENOUS TERRITORIALITIES, RELATIVE AUTONOMIES, AND ENTANGLED SOVEREIGNTIES

INTRODUCTION

For several decades now, Indigenous Peoples throughout the world have been advancing claims for the recognition of their ancestral rights and their inherent rights to self-determination at the national and international levels (Bellier 2019; Gagné 2020; Forest and Rodon 1995; LaBeau 1996). These claims find support in the 2007 United Nations Declaration on the Rights of Indigenous Peoples,[1] which recognizes the right of Indigenous Peoples to be autonomous and to administer themselves in all matters relating to their internal and local affairs (UN 2007, articles 3 and 4).

In conjunction with these Indigenous mobilizations and movements, a whole literature has been developed by Canadian Indigenous scholars and activists who reflect on Indigenous quests and claims for self-determination, autonomy, decolonization, and resurgence by engaging the concept of sovereignty (see, notably, the work of Taiaiake Alfred 1999, 2005; Glen Sean Coulthard 2014; Ladonna Harris et al. 2011; Audra

Simpson 2014; and Leanne Simpson 2011, 2017, among others). The use of the concept of sovereignty can pose some dilemmas of equivocation to the extent that it largely refers to a state-based political structure, and to a very specific logic of political power, territorial ownership (borders), and time (Nadasdy 2017). As Paul Nadasdy clearly points out in his book *Sovereignty's Entailments* (2017), modern treaties negotiated between Indigenous Peoples and the Canadian government have resulted in some Indigenous autonomy, which is overseen and limited by the federal, provincial, and territorial governments. These treaties allowed for the creation of semi-autonomous political structures modelled on those of the state, which Nadasdy identifies as "state-like entities," or structures integrated into the Canadian state that do not have most of the powers associated with independent states. This point is echoed in the metaphor of "nested sovereignties," introduced by the Mohawk researcher Audra Simpson (2014), whereby approaches to Indigenous sovereignties cannot be freed from the sovereignties of colonial states.

It is, however, interesting to note that the use of the concept of sovereignty by Indigenous Peoples in different colonial contexts can vary and suggest something other than sovereignty based on the state model (Blaser et al. 2010; Gagné 2020). In effect, although different Indigenous nations share a common desire for greater autonomy, the political structures, principles, and forms of authority governing territorial activities may vary from one Indigenous nation to another. That is why we make the effort to indicate the plural form of "Indigenous sovereignties" to express the fact that Indigenous approaches and aims are plural, corresponding to the socio-political and cultural diversity of the various Indigenous nations (Blaser et al. 2010; Gagné 2020). Moreover, in the approaches and claims of Indigenous sovereignty, there remains a form of equivocation in the use of a single concept to refer to models, logics, and political practices that are quite distinctive. In fact, to extend Eduardo Viveiros de Castro's (2014) analysis, the equivocation resulting from a dialogue between two distant universes of meaning suggests the presence of a deep ontological and epistemological misunderstanding, despite the use of a common conceptual referent—the concept of sovereignty in this case.

This chapter deals with the equivocation between state institutions and the Atikamekw Nehirowisiw Nation[2] in the context of land claims. A significant part of the chapter is devoted to describing the negotiating context and the Atikamekw Nehirowisiwok visions of "territorial sovereignty" (tiperitamowin aski).[3] The Atikamekw Nehirowisiw sovereignty project (nehirowisiw otiperitamo[so]win) revolves around a set of values, principles, and practices that guide ontological and political relations within a sociality in which the territory of origin and belonging (notcimik) plays a central role. We argue that, given the specificities of Atikamekw Nehirowisiw history and context, nehirowisiw otiperitamo[so]win involves the constant exercise of balancing contradictory forces of interdependence/independence in the search for regenerating a form of sovereignty into nitaskinan (unceded ancestral territory claimed).[4] This form of sovereignty diverges from the one promoted by the colonial state (i.e., premised on neoliberal economic development and a centralized power structure). Like other Indigenous Peoples, we see here a form of endurance—a "transformative continuity" and a "creative adaptability"—to the centralized and hierarchical power structures proposed by state models (Clastres 2011; Graeber 2006; Scott 2009; L. Simpson 2017; see also the introduction of this volume).

The first section of the chapter provides an overview of the discussions conducted by Canadian Indigenous researchers on the issues of sovereignty, self-determination, and decolonization. This will allow us to contextualize and relate the specific approach, vision, and practice of the Atikamekw Nehirowisiwok in the next three sections. After describing the history of the Atikamekw Nehirowisiwok self-determination process and claims in section two, we present values and conceptions of sovereignty in local terms in section three. Finally, in section four, we discuss the politics of consensus that is favoured by community members and how this practice is performed and applied today.

"SOVEREIGNTIES" IN INDIGENOUS DECOLONIAL LITERATURE

Issues surrounding sovereignty, self-determination, and Indigenous recognition are prominent in the work of Canadian Indigenous scholars. Some, like A. Simpson (2014), point to the effective limitations of Indigenous sovereignties within a colonial state such as Canada. Simpson uses the metaphor of a net to represent the limits and tensions in terms of legitimacy and competences, which necessarily arise because Indigenous nations remain subject to the laws and political structures of the state.

Faced with this crucial issue, other authors, such as Leanne Simpson (2011, 2017), an Anishnabekwe from the community of Michi Saagig Nishnaabeg (Alderville First Nation, Ontario), highlight Indigenous visions and practices of sovereignty in their own terms and concepts. Without denying the limitations of Indigenous powers in the face of a controlling colonial state, these works highlight the need to rethink the very terms of Indigenous sovereignty outside of Western etymology, epistemologies, and colonial politics.

These Indigenous scholars' perspectives on sovereignty emphasize the primacy of territory in Indigenous approaches and aspirations. The occupation and transmission of ancestral territory is described as an inseparable aspect of Indigenous language and political, legal, and cultural identity (Borrows 2010, 2016; Coulthard 2014; Harris et al. 2011; L. Simpson 2011, 2017) As noted by John Borrows (2010, 2019), an Anishinabe lawyer and professor, Indigenous self-determination is specifically based on Indigenous legal values and traditions in relation to Indigenous territories of life—territories of politics, endurances, and modes of existences.

L. Simpson emphasizes the importance of the link and access to ancestral territory in maintaining Indigenous political and legal principles and practices. To borrow L. Simpson's (2017) words, Anicinabek legal knowledge represents a "grounded normativity," suggesting that ethical and practical frameworks of several Anicinabek Peoples are grounded in the territory and emanate from it. For L. Simpson, cultural endurance and resurgence based on values, practices, and political knowledge anchored in territories of life is a requisite part of Indigenous self-determination:

> *Biiskabiyang*—the process of returning to ourselves, a reengagement with the things we have left behind, a reemergence, an unfolding from inside out—is a concept, an individual and collective process of decolonization and resurgence. To me, it is the embodied processes as freedom. It is a flight out of the structure of settler colonialism and into the process and relationships of freedom

> and self-determination encoded and practiced within Nishnaabewin or grounded normativity. (2017,17)

The concept of biiskabiyang is the art of making a retrospective evaluation that is both personal and collective, which implies a return to oneself, to one's history, to one's principles of collective life, and to one's social and territorial relations. For Glen Coulthard, this self-recognition is intended as a critical re-evaluation process of the creativity and implementation of Indigenous principles and normative practices in a context of negotiation with state institutions (2007, 456). Finally, according to Betasamosake Simpson (2014) and Coulthard (2007, 2014), this introspective process is an essential step in Indigenous endurance, resurgence, decolonization, and collective affirmation. In particular, it aims to adapt and recreate political structures that are in line with culturally and geographically rooted values.

The literature about Indigenous resurgence developed by Indigenous authors emphasizes a form of Indigenous endurance based on the affirmation of Indigenous philosophies as a transformative praxis, as a mediating force and a political alternative. This Indigenous endurance in claims of sovereignty implies that Indigenous people position themselves as "creators of the terms and values by which they are to be recognized" (Coulthard 2007, 450). Indigenous sovereignties are grounded in Indigenous historicities, traditions, epistemologies, and ontologies. They thus entail an affirmation and a regeneration of the language, of the oral tradition, and of the ancestral territorial authorities. In this respect, some Indigenous scholars (e.g., Coulthard 2007; Simpson 2011) see the political approaches of self-determination and Indigenous sovereignties as offering alternatives to the neoliberal (post-)colonial project and to the state structure of centralized power. These approaches involving resurgent and novel political forms represent, in the words of Mario Blaser (2004), the expression of "Indigenous life projects," based on Indigenous epistemological and ontological principles and meaningfully involved in daily practices—in Indigenous mobilizations around the recognition of their rights and in ongoing relationships with ancestral territories.

The endurance of Indigenous political forms and thought also strive to establish consensual and egalitarian modes of decision-making, respecting traditional modes of authority. For instance, aside from Coulthard (2014) and L. Simpson (2011, 2017), other Indigenous authors like Taiaiake Alfred (1999, 2005) and Ladonna Harris et al. (2011) emphasize the importance of an Indigenous leadership based on consensus, a form of leadership practised in societies with decentralized power (Clastres 2011). Overall, Indigenous decolonial literature demonstrates the importance of reappropriating a form of leadership and a decision-making process that is more in tune with Indigenous philosophical and political foundations, grounded within their territories of life. Finally, the Indigenous decolonial literature suggests that, despite the various forms they may take, the approaches to Indigenous sovereignties share at least three central aspects: 1) the special relationship to the communal ancestral territory to which they belong and have been inhabiting for many generations; 2) collective introspection aimed at identifying common values and a common history; and 3) the application of a consensual political practice respecting a decentralized power model. These aspects identified by Indigenous researchers working to lay the reflexive and practical bases of the approaches to Indigenous resurgence and self-determination closely match the reflections and approaches carried out by the members of the Atikamekw Nehirowisiw Nation in their project of sovereignty (nehirowisiw otiperitamo[so]win). In their efforts and strategies toward this goal, the Atikamekw Nehirowisiwok exercise, in their own way, a practice of collective introspection and of self-recognition (nisitoweritcikewin) through a series of internal consultation practices between the members of the Nation in their mother tongue (nehiromowin), which is still the dominant language in the three communities of Wemotaci, Manawan, and Opitciwan. These steps are part of a politics of consensus (orocowewin), which aims to bring together the members of the Nation around a common societal project, namely the application of governmental and territorial sovereignty (nehirowisiw otiperitamo[so]win). In the following section, we offer a summary description of the steps taken by the members of the Nation, which sheds light on the way in which nehirowisiw otiperitamo[so]win is conceived, performed, and put into practice by the members of the Nation. This will enable us to better understand the areas of friction and misunderstanding—the equivocation that remains uncontrolled[5]—relating to the negotiations for territorial autonomy ("sovereignty") conducted by the Atikamekw Nehirowisiwok with both levels of government (federal, provincial) for the past several decades.

THE ATIKAMEKW NEHIROWISIW'S SOVEREIGNTY AND STEPS TO SELF-DETERMINATION

In 1973, the Canadian government implemented the Comprehensive Land Claims Policy, aimed at concluding final agreements on lands claimed by various Indigenous communities in Canada that had not signed any treaty to date (Charest 1992, 2016; Crown-Indigenous Relations and Northern Affairs Canada, 2024; Dupuis 1993; Grammond 2013; Lacasse 2004). The Canadian government's objective in pursuing this policy was to legally assert its title of sovereignty over Canadian territory, which would then be freed from ancestral rights held by Indigenous Peoples (Charest 1992, 2016; Cleary 1993; Dupuis 1993). The latter are then encouraged to negotiate fixed and bounded territorial areas over which they will obtain specific modern rights. In exchange, Indigenous Peoples are expected to definitively cede their ancestral land title (the extinction clause) to the said territories and to other territories that they inhabited at the time of the signing of the Royal Proclamation of 1763 (Asch 2008; Dupuis 1993).

In 1975, two years after the establishment of the Canadian Comprehensive Land Claims Policy, the members of the Atikamekw Nehirowisiw and Innu Nations combined their efforts and resources to create their own political organization, the Conseil Atikamekw-Montagnais (CAM), whose main mission was to promote and defend the rights of their members and to act as a political representative vis-à-vis their state interlocutors (Charest 1992; Dupuis 1993). In 1979, the CAM initiated the comprehensive land claims process and adopted a resolution to take over all programs and services currently provided by Indian Affairs Canada and/or other federal and provincial agencies (CAM 1979; Charest 1992). All these steps were taken in an effort to acquire more power for the management of their own territories of life. In April 1979, the CAM submitted to Canada's Department of Indian Affairs a statement of claims which included eleven proposals which were to serve as a basis for negotiations (CAM 1979, 181–182; our translation):

1. As culturally autonomous peoples before the arrival of Europeans, we want to be recognized as peoples with the right to self-determination.

2. As Indigenous Peoples, descendants of the first inhabitants of the territories located to the east of the Quebec-Labrador Peninsula, we also ask that our sovereign rights be recognized on these lands.
3. We refuse to allow the final extinction of these rights to become a prerequisite for any agreement with the governments of the dominant society.
4. We demand compensation for all past and current violations of our territorial rights.
5. We oppose any new project to exploit the resources of our territories by members of the dominant society as long as our rights have not been recognized.
6. We want to control the future exploitation of our lands and their resources.
7. We want to prioritize the development of renewable resources on our land over that of non-renewable resources.
8. We want the economic foundation provided by control over the use of our lands to ensure our economic, social, and cultural well-being for generations to come, as was the case before we were invaded by the traders, settlers, and industrial enterprises.
9. We want to take our development in hand from every point of view and no longer leave it in the hands of members of the dominant society.
10. We want to orient our development according to our values and traditions handed down by our ancestors and which have been developed over millennia in harmony with our natural and social environment.
11. In the future, we want to be treated as equals with the governments of the dominant society and no longer be seen as inferior peoples.

In October 1979, a few months after the filing of this statement of claim, the federal government agreed to begin comprehensive land negotiations. The Government of Quebec moved in the same direction in January 1980 (Charest 1992). Throughout the negotiation process, the CAM carried out important work, such as the CAMROUT project[6] (Brassard and Castonguay 1983) (also known as the Grande Recherche), aimed at documenting territorial knowledge as well as the occupation and use of the claimed ancestral territories (Brassard and Castonguay 1983; Castonguay 1983; Charest 1992, 2005, 2016; Dandenault 1983; Léger 1983). The CAM also set up various organizations and associations to continue this work and promote the dissemination of information to its members. For example, in 1980, the CAM created the Société de Communication Atikamekw-Montagnais (SOCAM), a radio station whose role it is to disseminate a wide range of information related to Indigenous political issues to all the Innu and Atikamekw Nehirowisiwok communities on a daily basis (Charest 1992). This radio station also promotes the transmission of ancestral knowledge—owing to the significant participation of the elders in its programs—the transmission of the Innu and Nehiromowin language—the language of the Atikamekw Nehirowisiwok, given that the majority of radio programs are produced in these languages—and, finally, the dissemination and promotion of Innu and Nehirowisiw music, which has an important place in the station's musical programming. To this day, SOCAM is broadcast to the majority of Innu and Atikamekw Nehirowisiwok homes, thus contributing to the identity and political affirmation of the members of these Nations.

In 1982, the Atikamekw Nehirowisiwok created their own political organization, the Conseil de la Nation Atikamekw-Atikamekw Sipi (CNA), which represents the three Atikamekw Nehirowisiw communities, namely Wemotaci, Manawan, and Opitciwan. The managing board is made up of the three band chiefs, a president, and later, the title of elected Grand Chief[7] and a general manager (Charest 1992; CNA 2012; Dupuis 1993). When it was created, the CNA was a coordinating committee for the development of services offered to the Atikamekw Nehirowisiwok communities. The body therefore had a mandate to ensure the implementation of decisions taken during the general assemblies of the Nation's representatives concerning issues common to the three communities (Charest 1992). In 1994, when the CAM was dissolved,[8] the CNA immediately took over as a spokesperson in the comprehensive territorial negotiations led by the Atikamekw Nehirowisiwok with the governments of Quebec and Canada (Charest 2016; CNA 2012). Subsequently, the Atikamekw Nehirowisiwok set up various organizations within the CNA with the aim of developing its self-government and supporting the various social and educational programs for the three Atikamekw Nehirowisiwok communities. These organizations include the Territory Secretariat; Educational, Linguistic and Cultural Services; and Onikam Social Services.

Other self-determination approaches and strategies include the 1998 creation of the Commission on the Atikamekw Constitution, whose main objective was to submit a first draft of a constitution that would put forth the governmental mechanisms specific to the Nation (Conseil de la Nation Atikamekw, 1998, 1). As part of this work on elaborating a written constitution, a series of consultations took place among members of the Nation, in which the elders and territorial leaders had an influential voice and a form of authority. These in-house political consultation sessions create space for sharing experiences and knowledge and offer guidance to the elected political representatives of the Nation, both for the CNA and for the band councils. Throughout the process of designing a constitution and to this day, the Atikamekw Nehirowisiw Nation has succeeded in maintaining the most important relationships between elected politicians and traditional authority figures. In this process, the elected leaders recognize the political and territorial roles, responsibilities, and authorities of the territorial leaders (ka nikaniwitcik) and extended families (witcicanak) for the management of family hunting territories (atoske / natoho aski) (Éthier 2017; Éthier and Poirier 2018; Houde 2014). In this case, the role of the elected leaders is to provide a structure for consultation and to endorse the words, conceptions, and visions of the elders and ka nikaniwitcik regarding territorial management practices and values (Éthier et al. 2019). Such consultation with the elders and territorial leaders and the recognition of their voices and perspectives—which are grounded in notcimik, the territories of origin and belonging—are somehow the expression of an Atikamekw Nehirowisiw form of sovereignty (nehirowisiw otiperitamo[so]win).

In 2002, the CNA and the members of the Nation adopted the Political Memorandum of Understanding (Protocole d'entente politique), thereby establishing the political title of Grand Chief elected by universal suffrage by all the members of the Atikamekw Nehirowisiw Nation. The memorandum stipulates, among other things, that the Grand Chief's responsibilities are to:

> represent the Nation as a whole in its relations with governments and other First Nations at the level of the United Nations; be the guarantor of the respect of the constitution and the independence of the judiciary; oversee the negotiation in view of the signing of the final text of the treaty and the maintenance of its proper functioning. (CAN 2002; our translation)

The Political Memorandum of Understanding reinforces the political authority of the CNA and legitimizes its role as the official representative of the Nation for territorial negotiations. The Memorandum thus confirms the CNA's mandate to prepare the structures of an autonomous government and to watch over the integrity, completeness, and indivisibility of nitaskinan, the claimed and non-ceded ancestral territory (CNA 2012). Nitaskinan itself is subdivided into thirty family territories (natoho / atoske aski) that are under the responsibility of family institutions (witcicanak) and territorial leaders (ka nikaniwitcik) (Éthier and Poirier 2018). Finally, the Political Memorandum of Understanding aims to maintain the unity of the Nation, while maintaining partial or relative autonomy for each of the communities and families in the management of activities recognized in their fields of jurisdiction, one of those being the family territories.

The balance regarding jurisdictions between different institutions—namely extended families (witcicanak), the band councils (imposed structure), and the council of the nation (a relatively recently created structure)—is a perpetual challenge that characterizes the Atikamekw Nehirowisiwok political relationships both internally (intra-systemic) and externally (extra-systemic) (Morissette 2004; Poirier 2001). Internally, for the Atikamekw Nehirowisiwok members, the responsibilities and jurisdictional authorities between these three main institutions need to be clarified on a regular basis, as some issues (such as land, education, and health) concern all institutions. The ambiguity and entanglement of jurisdictional powers (also well known in the Canadian government in regard to provincial, territorial, and federal jurisdictions) sometimes leads families to ask for the departure of a chief or certain band councillors, or can lead to band councils withdrawing their support for the council of the nation.

Despite their political efforts, the CNA faces recurring difficulties in rallying all the elected representatives of the band councils in the three communities, an effort that creates divisions and tensions at the political level, which in turn may provoke fatigue among those who feel that their elected leaders should work together for the sake of the Nation and not against one other. These divisions, alongside the quest for community and family autonomies, in turn cast doubt on the very essence of the political objective inscribed in the Political Memorandum of Understanding (CNA 2016, 53). However, despite these divisions between elected representatives, community members take advantage of certain ad hoc opportunities to engage in their own initiatives outside of official political organizations (CNA, band councils) to protect and preserve their territories of life from external and industrial encroachment. This was the case in recent years (2012 and 2020–2023) when Atikamekw Nehirowisiwok families rallied against over-logging by organizing blockades on logging roads, preventing the logging industry from accessing nitaskinan. This popular mobilization prompted the Government of Quebec to act quickly, and immediately initiated bilateral negotiations on the management and development of natural resources over the contested territory (CNA 2016; Poirier 2017, 220).[9]

In the years that followed the 2002 Political Memorandum of Understanding, there were several calls for unity in the Nation, by both elected representatives and by actors involved in grassroots bodies, such as community youth councils. Among the most striking calls were the Declaration of the Unity of the Nation made in Wemotaci in 2012 and the Declaration of Sovereignty of Atikamekw Nehirowisiw made on September 8, 2014, at the National Assembly of Quebec. These two declarations were made by all the elected representatives of the three band councils and the Grand Chief of the Atikamekw Nehirowisiw Nation. They aimed to consolidate alliances between band councils and extended families, while firmly asserting their right to self-determination as a People and as a Nation.

Drawing on Benedict Anderson's analysis of the development of modern nationalism in his seminal work *Imagined Communities* (1991), Sylvie Poirier highlights the ambiguous relationship to the concept of "nation" among the Atikamekw Nehirowisiwok:

> Thus, for the Atikamekw, the ambiguity of the concept "nation" does not lie in how they are represented to the Other but, rather, in how they represent themselves to themselves. Actually, all the ambiguities relating to "nation" reveal the present-day persistence and pervading influence of a mode of individual and collective identification that is constructed according to a social organization within which affiliation with the family group and ancestral territory, coupled with responsibility for this territory, takes precedence over an "imagined" political entity. There is in fact, no nationalism that is devoid of these ambiguities. However, the Atikamekw are dealing with both non-modern and modern modes of identity. And therein lies one of the original features of their cultural dynamic, authenticity, and resistance. (2001, 103).

The concept and idea of a nation as a political entity born out of modernity has been the subject of discussion and debate among the Atikamekw Nehirowisiwok, notably throughout the process of elaborating an Atikamekw Nehirowisiw constitution. Poirier highlights the Indigenous appropriation of the concept from the public assemblies conducted for the establishment of an Atikamekw Nehirowisiw self-government. In the dialogue and negotiation processes with modernity and colonial governments, the Atikamekw Nehirowisiwok have carried out the exercise of trying to find equivalences between modern concepts, such as "nation," and the Atikamekw Nehirowisiwok concepts and visions of "living together." Among the equivalents mentioned at the Aski [territory] Summit (1996), we note Ei nictweikisinanok or Ei nictokweisinanok (three joined communities); nicto otenaw Atikamekw (three Atikamekw Nehirowisiwok communities); and Mamo Itiwin (all experiences and events shared) (CNA 1996). The first two proposals emphasize the necessary alliance between the communities (Wemotaci, Manawan, and Opitciwan) to establish a balance of power. The third proposal, used to define the unifying concept for Atikamekw Nehirowisiwok families, suggests putting forward a way of being and living that is culturally shared and that is distinct from the way of life and values conveyed by colonial society. As clearly emphasized in the 1979 statement and thereafter, the rights and responsibilities related to cultural and territorial practices are at the heart of Atikamekw Nehirowisiwok sovereignty processes and claims.

In the 2014 Atikamekw Nehirowisiw Declaration of Sovereignty, Atikamekw Nehirowisiwok elected officials highlight the persistence of "Atikamekw Nehirowisiw otiperitamowin," which is translated in the declaration as "Atikamekw governance," that is, their sovereignty, their way of life, and their right and duty to occupy and protect their territory: "The protection of nitaskinan, the defense of its way of life and its aspirations will at all times drive the actions of Atikamekw Nehirowisiw and its current and future institutions. In this regard, Atikamekw Nehirowisiw will use all the means they deem appropriate to defend their rights and interests" (CNA 2014).

The Atikamekw Nehirowisiwok elected representatives who orchestrated this declaration were clear. This was an affirmation of an established fact, given that the Atikamekw Nehirowisiwok have never ceded their territorial sovereignty. This declaration recalls one made twenty years earlier by Elder César Néwashish, a hunter who was recognized and respected by members of the three communities. It read: "Tell them that we have never ceded our territory, that we have never sold it, that we have never traded it, nor that we have ever ruled otherwise with regard to our territory" (April 7, 1994; our translation). This quote was collected a few days before César Newashish's death, when members of the Nation's negotiation table went to the hospital where he lay with the objective of hearing his words and visions regarding the life project and self-determination of the Atikamekw Nehirowisiwok. Since then, this quote—displayed in band councils, in schools, and in CNA offices—has become a kind of collective saying that is constantly repeated in the various political proclamations emphasizing nehirowisiw otiperitamo[so]win, the sovereignty of the Atikamekw Nehirowisiw as a united People sharing similar values and a common structure of government. This might lead some observers to assume that the CNA is replicating the colonial state form of sovereignty at a lower scale, as Nadasdy has argued. However, this is not as straightforward as it might seem. In fact, and as will be shown in the next section, nehirowisiw otiperitamo[so]win necessarily includes maintaining a balance between different relative autonomies: between families, clans, and communities (intra-systemic autonomy) as well as between peoples and nations (inter-systemic). This balance, which is difficult to maintain in relationships of interdependence, reciprocity, and contextual alliances between extended families (witcicanak) and communities, is therefore at the heart of the Atikamekw Nehirowisiw's territories of life and their definition of sovereignty. We refer to these alliances as contextual because they are, as Jean Dennison (2017) reminds us, in a complex dynamic of renegotiation, validation, and adjustment.

NEHIROWISIW OTIPERITAMO[SO]WIN

Among the Atikamekw Nehirowisiwok, witcicanak (the plural form of witcican) are political entities representing extended families related to a common ancestor. Wicican is described as the first institution or society (peikw otenam—literally, the first village or the first heart [peikw otehinam[10]]) (Christian Coocoo, personal communication, 2018). In Atikamekw Nehirowisiw customary law, territorial rights and responsibilities are under the aegis of witcican and territorial leaders (ka nikaniwitcik). Ka nikaniwitcik is the representative of the members of extended families and has responsibility and authority over the management of their family hunting territories (atoske / natoho aski). With the authorizations and suggestions of the other members of their extended family, territorial leaders will subdivide these family hunting territories according to the demographic and environmental contexts and the needs of the members of witcicanak (G. Ottawa, personal communication, 2018).

The ka nikaniwitcik have a voice of influence and responsibility to maintain social cohesion within witcican. Their words are more concerned with ensuring harmony and meeting the needs of the extended family (witcican) members. Ka nikaniwitcik plays an important role as a mediator in the case of conflict in the management of territorial resources between members of his extended family when the conflict is limited to the family hunting territory, or with members from other witcicanak when the conflict involves members of other extended families, which may also include members of other Nations, such as the Eeyouch (Cris), Innu, or Anicinabek (Éthier 2017; Houde 2014; G. Ottawa, personal communication, 2018).

The forms and status of power, authority, and sovereignty of witcicanak are strongly rooted in Atikamekw Nehirowisiw territories of life. In nehiromowin, the term "nehirowisiw otiperitamo[so]win" is used to describe this territorial authority, responsibility, and sovereignty. In this section, we will further flesh out the meaning of this expression.

First, the term "nehirowisiw," placed at the beginning, is used as an ethnonym to identify members of the Atikamekw Nehirowisiw Nation. However, the term refers more to a way of being than to an ethnic identification. The term "nehirowiṣiw" emphasizes a way of being based on fundamental moral principles that are known and valued culturally. Nehirowisiw includes values such as balance, autonomy (nehi-), and those of experience, action, movement, and dynamism (rowi). The ending -siw (singular) or -siwok (plural) indicates that these qualities are attributed to a particular living entity (CNA, online). Being a Nehirowisiw implies the maintenance of intimate relationships with the ancestral territory, particularly in terms of the mastery of practices and the application of rules of conduct favouring, for example, the preservation and respectful use of territorial resources and equitable sharing of hunting, fishing, and gathering products. Here is how Cécile Mattawa, a linguistics specialist from Manawan, defines the term:

> Nehirowisiw: The one who comes from the land, one's food is also described there, one's tools and equipment, the fact, and the way of using resources. A being independent of all (*wir tipirowe* or autonomous). One's identity also encompasses beliefs, territory, way of life (*Onehirowatcihiwin*), one's innate right as an "Indian" or as a Nehirowisiw, the resources and elements that one adapts to one's life (for example: an "Indian" can relate or tell about the benefits of a medicinal plant only if this plant grows on one's territory). (Mattawa 2024)

As this quote underlines, the term "nehirowisiw" emphasizes the concept of personal autonomy, an autonomy that takes place in relation to a balance and reciprocity with other autonomous entities, including territorial entities or resources. The term thus refers to a form of territorial authority based on occupation, use, knowledge, and relationships with the resources of the ancestral territory. This logic is even more explicit when we put the terms "nehirowisiw" and "tiperitamowin" together.

In a report submitted to the Atikamekw-Montagnais Council, José Mailhot and Sylvie Vincent (1980) analyze the use of the term "tiperitamowin"[11] based on testimonies from Innu hunters. The morphological analysis of the term carried out by Mailhot and Vincent (1980, 1982) echo the translations made by Atikamekw Nehirowisiwok linguists. According to their morphological analysis, the concept tiperiten [tipenitam] would be formed by the morpheme tip- and the morpheme -enit. The tip- morpheme can be translated as "measure," "compare," or "match" and the -enit morpheme refers to the "subject's thought," to "mental activity." From Mailhot and Vincent's (1980) analysis, we can see that the concept of tiperitamowin is mainly used by Innu and Atikamekw Nehirowisiwok hunters to talk about the influence, control, or mastery that a person exercises. From the Atikamekw Nehirowisiw perspective, it is this influence and mastery that gives the person not only rights and powers but also responsibilities. There is a direct link here between the influence or control of the person over a thing or in a particular domain, and their powers, authority, rights, and responsibilities, particularly in relation to the ancestral territory. According to Atikamekw Nehirowisiwok linguists, the addition of the particle -o at the beginning of the word and the particle -so before the suffix -win in the verbal noun are a reference to an internalization, to a self-reflection: "to oneself" or "to self." Thus, the expression "nehirowisiw otiperitamo[so]win" could be translated as "responsibility for oneself," "sovereignty," or "autonomy of the person." Nehirowisiw otiperitamasowin emphasizes the process of interiorization, a return to one's values, one's history, and one's commitments. In addition, nehirowisiw otiperitamasowin inspires a philosophical and pragmatic approach, naming not only individual and collective introspection, but a process of relating to and balancing with the environment, with notcimik, the Atikamekw Nehirowisiw territories of life, literally "the place where I and my ancestors come from."

Atikamekw Nehirowisiwok territories of life support mnemonic, political, experiential, multi-generational, and multi-species dimensions. Territories of life are also marked by the relationships and history of extended families who interact with each other in political dynamics of relative autonomy, reciprocity, and interdependence. As emphasized in Cécile Mattawa's quote, families have developed expertise in certain areas relating to the resources they find within their family hunting territory, a territory which has been passed down from generation to generation. Atikamekw Nehirowisiw customary law also puts forward a complex system and network of exchanges between families who have to share the fruits of their activities or share access to territorial resources. Beyond the networks of solidarity often extended between Nations through marriage, the practices of inter-family exchanges and reciprocities favour the creation of ad hoc alliances as well as a form of political unity, both of which have been formalized by the members of the Atikamekw Nehirowisiwok communities in the creation of the CNA.

As mentioned earlier, the CNA was formed with an objective of decolonization and self-determination in relation to state institutions and with the goal of realizing the projects of Indigenous "good life," which provide visions and models for resource management that diverge from neoliberal development practices. In their efforts, the Atikamekw Nehirowisiwok, like other Indigenous Peoples, work to create alliances or interconnections between different levels of autonomy and authorities.

To understand these different levels of autonomy (extended families, communities, and nation) and their relations to different levels of authority, we draw on the concepts of relative autonomy (Morphy 2011; Morphy and Morphy 2013) and entangled sovereignty (Dennison 2017). Relative autonomy refers to these forces of interdependence/independence and the plays of alliances and dissension, which are at the heart of political relationships, both within local institutions and systems (intra-systemic) and between local and exogenous institutions and systems (inter-systemic). Within the nation itself, one can thus see different levels of intertwined autonomies and political cohesion which come from this fragile balance ensuring respect and non-interference between the different structures of authorities/responsibilities.

The analytical concept of entangled sovereignties, put forward by Dennison, an anthropologist and member of the Osage First Nation (in Oklahoma), emphasizes this practice of continuous negotiation between levels of authority and autonomy and thus the need for a balanced compromise that allows social cohesion (2017). Rather than conceiving these negotiations and compromises as a constraint or limit on sovereignty, as Simpson (2014) proposes with her analysis of nested sovereignty, Dennison emphasizes the shared or mutual benefit of negotiation between actors and authority structures. This ties in with Viveiros de Castro's (2004) proposal for controlled equivocation: a genuine recognition on the part of interlocutors of the presence of an equivocation, and the exercise of translation carried out in an open, egalitarian dialogue.

The Atikamekw Nehirowisiwok work at creating and maintaining contextual alliances produced in dialogue and negotiation processes with other Indigenous Nations, but also within their own Nation and institutions (formal and informal). As described in the following section, this exercise is complex and difficult and is guided by the search for and the politics of consensus—a political practice that responds closely to central cultural values, such as reciprocity, the autonomy of families, and the complementarity of knowledge and expertise. This political and democratic mode is certainly an avenue worth exploring for rethinking intercultural dialogue and moving toward this desire for controlled equivocation.

OROCOWEWIN: POLITICS OF CONSENSUS IN THE PROCESS OF SOVEREIGNTY

The political steps taken by the CNA concerning land claims, the development of a constitution, and the elaboration of an autonomous government are carried out through consultation sessions and with the commitment of families, territorial leaders, and elders. In these assemblies or public consultation sessions, all members are invited to share their points of view, their experience, their concerns, and their visions. Speeches during these consultation sessions are aimed at the common good, especially for future generations, and are not intended for the individual good or interest. In collective decisions, we ensure that the voice of each witcican (extended family) is respected (Ottawa 2014; Éthier et al. 2020). The concept used in Nehiromowin to emphasize this form of collective decision-making is orocowewin. Orocowewin could be translated literally as "what is decided together." Some 1998 CNA documents drawn up to support claims for self-government and the drafting of the nitaskinan Constitution translate this concept as "decision," "regulation," "law," "resolution," "judgment," or "decree." This concept can also refer to a major collective project, political or otherwise, or to a direction to be taken (a life project).

In the projects they develop, the members of the CNA regularly work in committee with the elders and the heads of family territories (ka nikaniwitcik). As we saw earlier, the work resulting from these committees is then discussed in seminars or assemblies, bringing together representatives of the band councils, the CNA, and the territorial leaders. There are also youth representatives and other community members present. The aim of these assemblies is to take the plurality of experiences into account to work on the construction of a shared project that respects the plurality of perspectives. Some of the members involved in the organization of these gatherings stress that, to be carried out, collective projects must necessarily be the result of a consensus. Otherwise "people will immediately reject it [the collective project]. People must feel that it is coming from them."[12]

The form that these symposia and assemblies take is itself quite flexible. As one of the organizers of the 2014 regional conference on territorial issues held in Wemotaci emphasized:

> When you organize gatherings, you don't write all the programming. We talk about topics that we would like to discuss with people, why we want to organize a gathering, but we don't really do a definitive program. It's not improvisation, but we trust people. We are confident that everyone can contribute something. There are leaders [among the Atikamekw Nehirowisiwok]. We trust the leaders. They will bring something. We informally approach subjects that we would like to discuss, to put into practice, but each brings their own contribution. It is not me who decides what people will do or say, but I trust, and things are done by themselves and in the right way. (Charles Coocoo, August 2014; our translation)

In nehiromowin, the concept of natokiskeritamowin is used to give notice of a consultative assembly aimed at bringing together a diversity of points of view and experiences. The term "natokiskeritamowin" could be translated as "pooling of knowledge" or even "inventory of knowledge."

Atikamekw Nehirowisiw brings together diverse points of view, experiences, and family knowledge. In recent articles (Éthier et al. 2019; Éthier et al. 2020), we have described how this diversity is essential in the maintenance of the bonds of reciprocity, autonomy, and interdependence between Atikamekw Nehirowisiw extended families (witcicanak), which are their central and primary institutions (peikw otenam). With respect for the autonomy, roles, and social status of family members, the Atikamekw Nehirowisiw's consensual approach aims to work on a societal project that respects the relative autonomy of each extended family. The Atikamekw Nehirowisiw's approach to sovereignty and a collective self-determination project is therefore defined by these dynamics of alliance and interdependence as well as by the historic desire to ensure decentralized power and a territorial authority initially maintained by the family clans. The entangled Atikamekw Nehirowisiwok sovereignty necessarily implies internal alliances within political structures that are imposed (band councils under the Indian Act) or created locally (the CNA), which are intermediaries between family political structures (family clans) and Western state structures. Indigenous *unnested* sovereignties are formulated in their own terms, without interference from the colonial state institutions, but in a constant dialogue and relationship, in relative autonomy. In this process, the phenomenon of equivocation is inevitable. To control it, the decentralization of powers and epistemological and ontological openness are required. Much remains to be done to achieve this, but we hope that this chapter, in drawing up a portrait of Atikamekw Nehirowisiwok visions, relations, and political knowledge, may facilitate this passage toward controlled equivocation in negotiations between the state and Indigenous Peoples.

CONCLUSION

This chapter presented different forms of relative autonomy within the Atikamekw Nehirowisiw Nation, which asserts and negotiates its sovereignty (nehirowisiw otiperitamo[so]win) both as a united People and as a plurality of interdependent and autonomous entities (as witcisanak). Through this dynamic, the text promotes the concepts of entangled sovereignties (Dennison 2017) and relative autonomies (Morphy 2011; Morphy and Morphy 2013), which clearly present this complex entanglement and interconnection of negotiated sovereignties.

By relying on the concept of relative autonomy, the analysis shows that at least two levels of autonomy overlap and occur daily in contemporary political structures and processes among the Atikamekw Nehirowisiwok, especially in their efforts toward self-determination. On the one hand, there is an intra-systemic autonomy that characterizes the powers, responsibilities, and rights of family clans and band councils. On the other hand, there is an extra-systemic autonomy claimed by the Nation as an ethnoterritorial political unit. The two forms of relative autonomy are nested, the first (intra-systemic) being systematically involved in the processes of the second (extra-systemic). Therefore, family representatives and elected representatives of band councils are directly mobilized in the self-determination initiatives led by the CNA, such as land claims, the development of a constitution, code of practice, and self-government. The CNA's self-determination initiatives aim to recognize and give more power to traditional decision-making structures—and therefore to family clans—for the management of territorial resources, which remains the central issue in Atikamekw Nehirowisiw sovereignty.

When we refer more directly to the sovereignty initiatives carried out by the Atikamekw Nehirowisiwok, we quickly realize that these are developed from practices, values, and precepts that do not correspond to the model of power and territorial management of colonial states. It turns out that there remains a certain uncontrolled equivocation, a deep ontological and epistemological misunderstanding that the conditions and definitions of Indigenous and state sovereignty must be read as being at once intricate, dynamic, ambivalent, and uncertain (Blaser 2009).

As a life project, the Atikamew Nehirowisiw's approaches to sovereignty are part of political practices and models that are territorially anchored. Atikamekw Nehirowisiw sovereignty initiatives put forward common aspirations for future generations to have a better lifestyle and for families to have greater autonomy in the management of their family territories. Territories of life as political, relational, mnemonic, and interspecies modes of existence play a prominent role in the application of Atikamekw Nehirowisiw sovereignty. The roles and responsibilities of extended families (witcicanak), which are the primary institutions, are directly related to the management, preservation, and balanced sharing of territorial resources. These obligations and responsibilities also constitute their rights, authorities, and sovereignty (nehirowisiw otiperitamowin). Like other Indigenous Peoples, Atikamekw Nehirowisiwok sovereignty is an essential part of a complex relationship of interdependence with the territory. In turn, territories of life are the political, ecological, and identity core from which the rights, responsibilities, status, and relative autonomy of persons and families are derived. Here, we are quite far from the logic of state sovereignty and the idea of creating "state-like entities," which is neither conceivable nor desirable for members of several Indigenous Nations, such as the Atikamekw Nehirowisiwok.

NOTES

1. Canada only agreed to sign this declaration in 2010.
2. The Atikamekw Nehirowisiwok live mainly in three communities nested in the boreal forest, namely Wemotaci, Manawan, and Opitciwan, and number over eight thousand members.
3. Sipi Flamand is chief of the Atikamekw Nehirowisiw community of Manawan and a master's student at the School of Indigenous Studies at the Université du Québec en Abitibi-Témiscamingue. Benoit Éthier is a professor at the School of Indigenous Studies and director of the Laboratoire de cartographie participative at the Université du Québec en Abitibi-Témiscamingue. Sipi Flamand and Benoit Éthier have been collaborating on various projects related to Indigenous political and territorial self-determination since 2008.
4. A distinction is made here between the territory of origin and belonging (notcimik), family territories (natoho aski and atoske aski), and the unceded territory claimed by the nation (nitaskinan). Each of these concepts reveals a precise aspect of Atikamekw Nehirowisiw territoriality. For a detailed explanation of these concepts, and the various Atikamekw Nehirowisiwok territorial systems, see Éthier and Poirier 2018 and Poirier 2001.
5. By borrowing and modifying Viveiros de Castro's (2014) term, "controlled equivocation," Blaser (2009) underlines the uncertainty and ambivalence caused by the phenomenon of equivocation, particularly in a context of territorial negotiation between state institutions and Indigenous Peoples. The concept of uncontrolled equivocation suggests the presence of a misunderstanding arising from the use of the same term (e.g., the concepts of sovereignty and territory), but with two completely different meanings. These two meanings are linked to the coexistence of two different worlds that are in asymmetrical power relationships, where one of the interlocutors imposes its world and vision without taking the other into account (Blaser 2009). Controlled equivocation, on the other hand, suggests a recognition of alterity and a dialogue held in egalitarian power relationships (Viveiros de Castro 2014; see also the introduction of this volume).
6. Conseil Atikamekw Montagnais, Recherche sur l'Occupation et l'Utilisation du Territoire (CAMROUT).
7. The first election of a Grand Chief by universal suffrage among the Atikamekw Nehirowisiwok dates back to 2002. This political authority is a special initiative and therefore does not come under the Indian Act, unlike band councils.
8. This dissolution occurred when the members of the Atikamekw Nehirowisiw and Innu Nations decided to conduct the comprehensive land claim process separately.

9. As a result of these negotiations, a framework agreement was reached on August 1, 2012, between the CNA and the Government of Quebec. This agreement was to be the source of a new nation-to-nation relationship with the provincial government in terms of natural resource management, specifically logging. A few months later, however, the incumbent Quebec Liberal Party led by Jean Charest, whose government had signed this framework agreement, lost the elections. No formal agreement followed this framework agreement (Conseil de la Nation Atikamekw 2016, 52).
10. The morpheme ote- is a locative ("here"). Peikw Otehinam (the "first heart") refers to the institution of the extended family (witcicanak), which remains at the centre of Atikamekw Nehirowisiw sociality.
11. Tipenitamun in the Innu language. See also Lacasse (2004), who resumes the linguistic analysis of Mailhot and Vincent.
12. This quote comes from an interview conducted in the summer of 2014 with an elder from Wemotaci involved in comprehensive land claims and in the development of an Atikamekw Nehirowisiw government since the early 1980s.

REFERENCES

Alfred, Taiaiake. 1999. *Peace, Power, Righteousness: An Indigenous Manifesto.* Oxford University Press.

Alfred, Taiaiake. 2005. *Wasase: Indigenous Pathways of Action and Freedom.* Broadview Press.

Asch, Michael, ed. 2008. *Aboriginal and Treaty Rights in Canada: Essays on Law, Equality, and Respect for Difference.* UBC Press.

Bellier, Irène. 2019. "La reconnaissance des peuples autochtones comme sujets du droit international: Enjeux contemporains de l'anthropologie politique en dialogue avec le droit." *Clio@Thémis: Revue électronique d'histoire du droit.* https://hal.archives-ouvertes.fr/hal-02304596/document.

Blaser, Mario. 2004. "Life Projects: Indigenous Peoples' Agency and Development." In *In the Way of Development: Indigenous Peoples, Life Projects and Globalization*, edited by Mario Blaser, Harvey Feit, and Glenn McRae. Zed Books.

Blaser, Mario. 2009. "The Threat of the Yrmo: The Political Ontology of a Sustainable Hunting Program." *American Anthropologist* 111 (1): 10–20.

Blaser, Mario, Ravi De Costa, Deborah McGregor, and William D. Coleman. 2010. *Indigenous Peoples Insight for a Global Age and Autonomy.* UBC Press.

Borrows, John. 2010. *Canada's Indigenous Constitution.* University of Toronto Press.

Borrows, John. 2016. *Freedom and Indigenous Constitutionalism.* University of Toronto Press.

Borrows, John. 2019. "Earth-Bound: Indigenous Resurgence and Environmental Reconciliation." In *Resurgence and Reconciliation: Indigenous–Settler Relations and Earth Teaching*, edited by M. Asch, J. Borrows, and J. Tully. University of Toronto Press.

Brassard, Denis, and Daniel Castonguay. 1983. *Nitaskinan: Rapport sur l'occupation du territoire par les Attikameks.* Conseil Atikamek-Montagnais, Québec.

CAM (Conseil Attikamek-Montagnais). 1979. "Nishastanan Nitasinan (Notre terre, nous l'aimons et nous y tenons): Revendications territoriales des bandes attkamèques et montagnaises adressées au Ministre des Affaires indiennes et du Nord, Représentant du gouvernement du Canada." *Recherches amérindiennes au Québec* 9 (3): 171–182.

Castonguay, Daniel. 1983. *Manouane: Rapport sur l'occupation et l'utilisation du territoire.* Conseil Atikamek-Montagnais.

Charest, Paul. 1992. "La prise en charge donne-t-elle du pouvoir? L'exemple des Atikamek et des Montagnais." *Anthropologie et sociétés* 16 (3): 55–76.

Charest, Paul. 2005. "Les assistants de recherche amérindiens en tant que médiateurs culturels: expériences en milieux innu et atikamekw du Québec." *Les Cahiers du CIÉRA* 29 (1–2): 115–129.
Charest, Paul. 2016. "De la prise en charge à l'autonomie gouvernementale pour les Innus: Un projet de société réduit face à des nouveaux obstacles." *Les Cahiers du CIÉRA* 14: 8–32.
Clastres, Pierre. 2011. *La société contre l'État: Recherches d'anthropologie politique.* Les Éditions de Minuit.
Cleary, Bernard. 1993. "Le long et difficile portage d'une négociation territoriale." *Recherches amérindiennes au Québec* 27 (1): 49–60.
CNA (Conseil de la Nation Atikamekw). 1996. *Sommet Aski.* Conseil de la Nation Atikamekw.
CNA (Conseil de la Nation Atikamekw). 1998. *E Nehiromonaniwok ka aicinikateki Atikamekw iriniw kitci masinahikan ka wi orasinahikatek / Termes de référence en Atikamekw pour la Commission sur la Constitution Atikamekw.* Conseil de la Nation Atikamekw.
CNA (Conseil de la Nation Atikamekw). 2002. *Protocole d'entente politique.* Conseil de la Nation Atikamekw.
CNA (Conseil de la Nation Atikamekw). 2012. *Commission territoriale atikamekw, 29–30 octobre 2012.* Conseil de la Nation Atikamekw.
CNA (Conseil de la Nation Atikamekw). 2014. *Déclaration de souveraineté atikamekw.* Conseil de la Nation Atikamekw.
CNA (Conseil de la Nation Atikamekw). 2016. *Rapport Synthèse: La Constitution atikamekw.* Conseil de la Nation Atikamekw.
Coulthard, Glen Sean. 2007. "Subjects of Empire: Indigenous Peoples and the 'Politics of Recognition' in Canada." *Contemporary Political Theory* 6: 437–460.
Coulthard, Glen Sean. 2014. *Red Skin, White Masks: Rejecting the Colonial Politics of Recognition.* University of Minnesota Press.
Crown-Indigenous Relations and Northern Affairs Canada. "Renewing the Comprehensive Land Claims Policy: Towards a Framework for Addressing Section 35 Aboriginal Rights." rcaanc-cirnac.gc.ca/eng/1408631807053/1544123449934.
Dandenault, André. 1983. *Weymontachie: Rapport sur l'occupation et l'utilisation du territoire.* Conseil Atikamek-Montagnais.
Dennison, Jean. 2017. "Entangled Sovereignties: The Osage Nation's Interconnections with Governmental and Corporate Authorities." *American Ethnologist* 44 (4): 684–696.
Dupuis, Renée. 1993. "Historique de la négociation sur les revendications territoriales du Conseil des Atikamekw et des Montagnais (1978–1992)." *Recherches Amérindiennes au Québec* XXIII (1): 35–48.
Éthier, Benoit. 2017. "Orocowewin notcimik itatcihitowin: Ontologie politique et contemporanéité des responsabilités et des droits territoriaux chez les Atikamekw Nehirowisiwok (Haute-Mauricie, Québec)." PhD diss., Université Laval.
Éthier, Benoit, Christian Coocoo, and Gérald Ottawa. 2019. "Orocowewin notcimik itatcihowin: the Atikamekw Nehirowisiw Code of Practices and the Issues Involved to its Writing." *Potchefstroom Electronic Law Journal*, 22. https://doi.org/10.17159/1727-3781/2019/v22i0a7593.
Éthier, Benoit, Gérald Ottawa, and Christian Coocoo. 2020. "Redefining the Lexicon of Power, Envisioning Indigenous Future: The Atikamekw Nehirowisiw Nation and Comprehensive Land Claims Negotiations." *Anthropologica* 62 (2): 262–275.
Éthier, Benoit, and Sylvie Poirier. 2018. "Territorialités et territoires de chasse familiaux chez les Atikamekw Nehirowisiwok dans le contexte contemporain." *Anthropologica* 60 (1): 106–118. https://www.utpjournals.press/doi/10.3138/anth.60.1.t11.
Forest, Pierre-Gerlier, and Thierry Rodon. 1995. "Les activités internationales des autochtones du Canada." *Études internationales* 26 (1): 35–57.
Gagné, Natacha, ed. 2020. *À la reconquête de la souveraineté: Mouvements autochtones en Amérique latine et en Océanie.* Presses de l'Université Laval.

Graeber, David. 2006. *Pour une anthropologie anarchiste*. Lux Editeur.
Grammond, Sébastien. 2013. *Terms of Coexistence: Indigenous Peoples and Canadian Law*. Thomson Reuters.
Harris, Ladonna, ed. 2011. *Re-creating the Circle: The Renewal of American Indian Self-Determination*. University of New Mexico Press.
Houde, Nicolas. 2014. "La gouvernance territorial contemporaine du Nitaskinan: Tradition, adaptation et flexibilité." *Recherches amérindiennes au Québec* 44 (1): 23–33.
Labeau, Pierre-Christian. 1996. "Le droit des peuples à disposer d'eux-mêmes: son application aux peuples autochtones." *Les Cahiers de droit* 37 (2): 507–542.
Lacasse, Jean-Paul. 2004. *Les Innus et le territoire: Innu Tipenitamun*. Les éditions du Septentrion.
Léger, Yves. 1983. *Obedjiwan: Rapport sur l'occupation et l'utilisation du territoire*. Conseil Attikamew-Montagnais.
Mailhot, José, and Sylvie Vincent. 1980. *Discours montagnais sur le territoire*. Conseil Atikamekw-Montagnais.
Mailhot, José, and Sylvie Vincent. 1982. "Le droit foncier montagnais." *Interculture* 15 (2–3): 65–74.
Mattawa, Cécile. 2024. "Nehirowisiw." Fondements et Identités. https://atikamekwsipi.com/fr/la-nation-atikamekw/fondements/identite.
Morissette, Anny. 2004. "De la forêt à la réserve, la mosaïque politique d'une bande autochtone: L'exemple des Atikamekw de Manawan (Québec)." Master's thesis, Université de Montréal.
Morphy, Frances, and Howard Morphy. 2013. "Anthropological Theory and Government Policy in Australia's Northern Territory: The Hegemony of the 'Mainstream.'" *American Anthropologist* 115 (2): 174–187.
Morphy, Howard. 2011. "'Not Just Pretty Pictures': Relative Autonomy and the Articulations of Yolngu Art in Its Context." In *Ownership and Appropriation*, edited by Veronica Strang and Mark Busse. Routledge.
Nadasdy, Paul. 2017. *Sovereignty's Entailments: First Nation State Formation in the Yukon*. University of Toronto Press.
Néwashish, César. "Personnalités célèbres." http://atikamekwsipi.com/fr/la-nation-atikamekw/personnalites-celebres.
Ottawa, Eva. 2014. "Construire notre avenir en misant sur notre héritage ancestral." *Recherche amérindienne au Québec* 44 (1): 115–117.
Poirier, Sylvie. 2001. "Territories, Identity, and Modernity among the Atikamekw (Haut St-Maurice, Québec)." In *Aboriginal Autonomy and Development in Northern Quebec and Labrador*, edited by Colin Scott. UBC Press.
Poirier, Sylvie. 2017. "Nehirowisiw Territoriality: Negotiating and Managing Entanglement and Coexistence." In *Entangled Territorialities: Negotiating Indigenous Lands in Australia and Canada*, edited by Françoise Dussart and Sylvie Poirier. University of Toronto Press.
Scott, James. 2009. *The Art of Not Being Governed: An Anarchist History of Upland Southeast Asia*. Yale University Press.
Simpson, Audra. 2014. *Mohawk Interruptus: Political Life Across the Borders of Settler States*. Duke University Press.
Simpson, Leanne. 2011. *Dancing on Our Turtle's Back: Stories of Nishnaabeg Re-creation, Resurgence, and a New Emergence*. Arbeiter Ring Publishing.
Simpson, Leanne. 2017. *As We Have Always Done: Indigenous Freedom through Radical Resistance*. University of Minnesota Press.
Viveiros de Castro, Eduardo. 2004. "Perspectival Anthropology and the Method of Controlled Equivocation." *Tipiti: Journal of the Society for the Anthropology of Lowland South America* 2 (1): 3–22.
Viveiros de Castro, Eduardo. 2014. *Cannibal Metaphysics*. University of Minnesota Press.

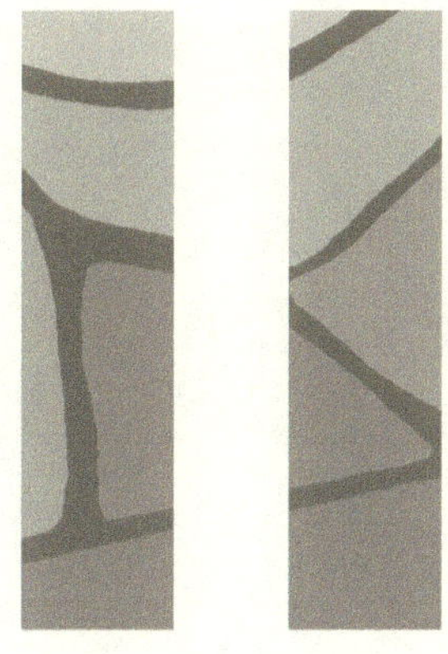

ENTANGLEMENTS

5

Scott E. Simon

ENTANGLED ROOTS

INDIGENOUS LIFE PROJECTS AND THE STATE ON FORMOSA

INTRODUCTION

Formosa ("beautiful island") was named by Portuguese sailors who admired the island's high mountains and luxuriant vegetation while sailing between Macau and Japan around 1542. Better known as Taiwan, a name derived from the ethnonym of a group indigenous to the area of what today is Tainan City, Formosa and an archipelago of other islands (Baldacchino and Tsai 2014) are now governed by the Republic of China (ROC), a state with only fourteen official diplomatic allies in the world. Taiwan receives international attention for geopolitical tensions because the People's Republic of China (PRC) routinely threatens to annex the islands by force if necessary, although it has never governed there. Taiwan is inhabited not only by settlers of Chinese descent but also by 580,000 Indigenous people belonging to sixteen legally recognized "Indigenous groups" and 746 "Indigenous communities." To make sense of these entanglements, I distinguish between *Formosa* as an island or country, "home to the living things whose lives come and go in that place"

(Rose 2011, 17), *Taiwan* as the emergent (but contested) nation, and the *Republic of China* as the state with its bureaucracy and institutions. Just as Carolina Tytelman and Paul Wattez argue (this volume), different place names are not synonyms. They represent distinct, yet entangled, coexisting political and spatial configurations. Unfortunately, amidst all of the media attention to geopolitical tensions, the perspectives of peoples indigenous to Taiwan are usually ignored. And yet, these perspectives are central to the current processes of reconciliation (with hopes for decolonization) in Taiwanese society (Simon et al. 2023).

Formosa has a long history in the imaginations of Western explorers, geographers, natural historians, and ethnographers. The name is evocative because it refers to the landscape, animals, plants, and diverse non-Chinese peoples in the high mountains, but it is awkward because of its colonial connotations. The conundrum is that the peoples who are indigenous to the place do not have their own name for the island—more than thirty-five thousand square kilometres of mostly steep mountains and fertile valleys—as a distinct place. Only on Pongso no Tao (Orchid Island) do the Yami (Tao) people have the perspective of looking across water to the island, which they call "Ilaod." The peoples indigenous to Formosa have their own spatial and geographical ontologies, and this chapter explores one of them. I focus on the local, grounded world that the sejiq truku people (literally "mountain people") call "dgiyaq": the mountain-forests inhabited by animals and ancestors that are most intimately known by hunters and trappers. If Formosa can be understood as a meshwork of peoples and other non-human inhabitants—that is, as territories of life—then dgiyaq is the mountain dweller's way of giving sense to those entangled lives. A focus on territories of life, as we see in the introduction to this volume, allows us to take seriously the entangled worldings of humans, other living entities, and spirits. It highlights how different collectives struggle to maintain their own particular sympoietic worlds as they affirm their radical heterogeneity. Formosa is fascinating precisely because of the diversity of worldings present in such a small geographical space.

Peoples indigenous to Formosa have, over six millennia, emerged from the same populations that spread throughout the Pacific and Indian Oceans as Austronesians (Liu 2022, 65). They have maintained their languages and ways of life as peoples distinct from the later Chinese arrivals, who only began settling the island following the establishment of a Dutch trading post in 1624 at place called Tayouan (Andrade 2008). As Chinese settlers expanded across the island plains, often intermarrying with local Austronesian peoples and becoming what is now an ethnic group of "native Taiwanese" or "Hoklo Taiwanese," the place name "Tayouan" was transformed into "Taiwan" as the name of that frontier society. From the perspective of those who preceded the arrival of Chinese settlers, the expansion of Taiwan on their territories was a genocide and the beginning of a racist society in which the dominant groups from China treated the locals as savages. The existence of peoples who are indigenous to Formosa seems to be overshadowed by geopolitical conflicts emanating from China, but they still endure today. Since 1984, they have demanded to use the internationally recognized label "Indigenous Peoples" to foreground the plight of their territories of life. The state has accepted and used the legal term of "Indigenous" since 1994. I will subsequently use the term "Indigenous Peoples" with the caveat that this is a relatively recent self-designation, one that makes possible certain negotiations with the state, but that also carries with it some traps.

Taiwan's indigeneity was shaped in the crucible of colonial rule. During the Japanese period (from 1895 to 1945), the military pacified the island's Indigenous Peoples and placed them under state sovereignty for the first time in history. The people remember their armed resistance against Japan, and their modern identities were formed by these experiences (Simon 2015).[1] Japanese administrators created what Paul Barclay (2018) calls "bifurcated sovereignty" when they endowed Chinese settlers with modern property rights but managed Indigenous Peoples as property-less wards of the state. The arrival of the ROC (under the aegis of a US-led Cold War) after 1945 did not end the colonial situation. To the frustration of the Indigenous Peoples, the ROC took control of the lands nationalized by the Japanese for their own purposes rather than return them to Indigenous communities. The ROC state even executed Indigenous leaders who advocated for the creation of a pan-Indigenous autonomous district (Harrison 2001).

In the democratization of the 1980s, an Indigenous social movement was born (Allio 1998), which brought Indigenous groups in Taiwan into contact with those of other countries, including at United Nations events and in relations with the Mohawk, the Cree, and other colonized peoples in Canada. The same efflorescence of social movements also enabled Taiwanese nationalists to found the Democratic Progressive Party (DPP) which, when in power, has actually upheld the ROC as a way of avoiding conflict both within Taiwan and with China. In today's electoral system, Indigenous voters tend to reject the DPP and have formed an alliance with Mainlanders (those who came in the 1940s from China) and the Chinese Nationalist Party (Kuomintang, KMT) (Rudolph 2003; Simon 2010). Their main goals are to affirm their particular relations with mountains, forests, and non-human entities—goals which they sometimes pursue through public political claims about recovery of the lands and the sovereignty they enjoyed before the Japanese period. At other times, they affirm the same goals through more informal arrangements made with the colonizers. China claims Taiwan internationally, but it has never ruled the island, remaining to most people a remote threat beyond the horizon. All the above social and political changes brought Indigenous groups into new entanglements with other human groups, creating new arenas for conflict and strategic cooperation with external colonizers.

The goal of this chapter is to explore the political ontologies of the peoples known today as the Truku and the Sediq, amidst their entanglements with other peoples and with non-human others. I explore how they view the island, their place in the mountain forests, and the good life. I focus on how Indigenous claims are dealt with in both state law and in traditional law, which they call "Gaya." I look at how people I worked with claim and enact sovereignty through practices of storytelling, law drafting, and everyday practices of trapping. My examinations are framed by the following questions: How do Sediq and Truku Peoples inhabit the mountain-forests they inherited from their ancestors, and how do they try to protect their lifeworlds through negotiations with the state?

BACKGROUND: TAIWANESE INDIGENEITY AND MY RESEARCH

Ever since democratization, an Indigenous social movement has demanded the return of lost land, control of the names used to describe them, and political reform, all based on what social movement leaders call "inherent" or "natural sovereignty." The mountain groups alone already had what the state called "self-government" in thirty mountain townships, but the Indigenous Peoples wanted more, and on their own terms. Indigenous people, as citizens, obtained a quota of Indigenous lawmakers in the Legislative Yuan as soon as direct elections began in 1992, using the two legal categories of "plains" versus "mountain" Indigenous people. In 1996, the cabinet-level Council of Indigenous Peoples was founded. In 1997, the term "Indigenous Peoples" was included in constitutional revisions. In 1999, Indigenous activists convinced Democratic Progressive Party (DPP) presidential candidate Chen Shui-bian to sign a promise of a "New Partnership Agreement" between the state and Indigenous Peoples based on sovereignty, autonomy, and territory (Awi and Huang 2021). To everyone's surprise, Chen won the 2000 and 2004 elections. He continued to promise "quasi-nation-to-nation relations," and in 2005, the Legislative Yuan passed the Basic Law on Indigenous Peoples (Republic of China 2018 [2005]). A legal framework subsequently emerged as legislators, including Indigenous lawmakers, sought to reconcile Indigenous demands with vested interests. In 2016, newly elected President Tsai Ing-wen (DPP) apologized for four hundred years of colonialism and established the Presidential Office Indigenous Historical Justice and Transitional Justice Committee. However, by 2025, not a single Indigenous autonomous government has been established and no traditional territory has been returned. Indigenous activists are aware that their interests are often subordinated to state needs even under the label of Indigenous rights, as often happens in other neoliberal states engaged in what Elizabeth Povinelli (2002) famously called the "cunning of recognition."

I have dedicated most of my adult life to working with the closely related Truku and Sediq peoples. I first met Truku Indigenous rights activist Igung Shiban during my five-year residence in Taiwan from 1996 to 2001, and wrote an article at her request about cement mining in her community. When I left to take a job at the University of Ottawa, moving closer to my parents, I promised her that I would return annually and continue to do research with her and her community. Until the COVID-19 pandemic, which made travel to Taiwan impossible for two years, I was able to conduct three to six months of research most years, with funding from either Canada or Taiwan. I also made personal visits and have taken Canadian students with me for three field research courses. I followed the advice of Igung and her brother to do fieldwork in her hometown in Fushi, as well as in related communities in both Hualien and Nantou Counties. As Igung identified as Truku and her brothers as Sediq, they encouraged me to immerse myself in the community life on both sides of what were emerging political and ethnic identities. Their hope was that my writing would bring international attention to their ways of life, and maybe even become a resource that their groups could use in negotiations with the state. I thus became fully entangled with their concerns. We remained in touch daily through social media even during my absences.

It was because of Igung that land disputes served as my point of entry into a study of Indigenous issues, beginning in 2000. My first and most frequent fieldsite is Bsngan (Fushi in Chinese). Fushi is Taiwan's largest village, a state-led amalgamation of Truku communities over an area of 1040 square kilometres, including most of the Taroko National Park. The most densely populated area is between the National Park and the Asia Cement quarry and factory. Based on written documents and oral narratives, I documented how Asia Cement had leased Indigenous reserve land from Hsiulin Township amidst a controversy about consent documents from landholders that may have been forged (Simon 2002). I soon learned that local people had even more acute conflicts with the Taroko National Park, which after its reestablishment in 1986, allowed the Truku People to maintain usage rights to their land but placed severe restrictions on their activities, including a complete ban on hunting and trapping.

In 2000, the Truku Peoples were still legally classified as Atayal. In fiercely contested processes of "name rectification," the communities in coastal Hualien County gained state recognition as Truku in 2004. In 2008, the closely related peoples in highland Nantou County gained recognition under the name Sediq as politically independent from both the Atayal and the Truku. In a complex set of entanglements, both the Truku and the Sediq are composed of people who speak Toda, Tgdaya, and Truku languages that write, respectively, the word "human" as "Sediq," "Seediq," or "Seejiq." However, the Council of Indigenous Peoples uses the Toda variant as the name of the whole "tribe" in English-language publications. In March 2025, state statistics enumerated 35,791 Truku and 11,686 Sediq. The point is not merely that there are disagreements within Indigenous communities and even families about identity. Rather, these identities are the foundation of Indigenous claims to sovereignty, but paradoxically are created, not from Indigenous senses of belonging, but from the imperatives of modern statecraft to identify and enumerate populations to pave the way for dispossession, occupation, and extraction.

While hanging out with people during field work, I began to meet hunters and trappers who encouraged me to study their land-based rituals and practices, knowledge, and understandings of territory. Some of them told me that they wanted to work with a foreign anthropologist so that local state actors would perceive them as representatives of an internationally recognized and valourized hunting culture, rather than as poachers. Hunters and trappers taught me about the entanglements of different animals and plants, the existence of spirits, and practices of negotiating land use within their communities and with outsiders. They impressed upon me the notion that identifying large tracts of land—marked as polygons on maps—as belonging to a state (or even to a large-scale Indigenous autonomous zone) is foreign to their customary Gaya. Instead, they drew my attention to the proper rituals regarding ancestral spirits, ethical relations with mammals, birds that convey messages, and the face-to-face relations with other hunters and trappers along their traplines (Simon 2013, 2015, 2023a, 2023b). These are the most salient entanglements in their lives, the ones that constitute what we articulate in this volume as territories of life.

THEORETICAL FRAMEWORK: POLITICAL ONTOLOGY AND ENTANGLEMENTS

To understand how Indigenous People engage with external forces, from states and corporations to politicians speaking in their name, two concepts are useful. The first is entanglement. As Sylvie Poirier notes, "the concept of entanglement allows us to inquire into the dialectical and the dialogical dimensions of the encounters and coexistence between Indigenous and non-Indigenous worlds, ontologies, and actors" (2017, 215). The second concept is political ontology, which brings together both worlding practices and ontological work. These are power-laden negotiations, and conflicts "ensue as different worlds or ontologies strive to sustain their own existence as they interact and mingle with each other"

(Blaser 2009a, 11). Ontology, as an understanding of local theories about what exists in the world or being-in-the-world, dovetails with Gaya, a word usually translated as "sacred law."[2] Gaya, a cosmology derived from particular ontological and epistemological principles, is the central moral compass that people use as they negotiate different forms of entanglements, including with the state, corporations, and social movements.

Ontological principles are rendered apparent in embodied, everyday practices. Let us say, for example, that parents from the Truku community of Skadang take their children out of school—themselves taking unpaid leave from work—to hike the mountain path to their ancestral homes and along the Skadang River, explaining on the way the flora, fauna, and sites of historical events. They enter entanglements; tightening nodes of connection along pathways with other organisms, with spirits discerned in the physical landscape, and with humans, including park officials and tourists. Political ontology reveals the conflict or cooperation that can occur as parents negotiate with schools and bosses, as well as with officials of the National Park or other authorities that claim to manage rivers and forests according to the state's law. It is ontological work when people affirm an identity as being from Alang Skadang (for which Skadang "community" is a barely adequate approximation, see below), rather than from Fushi Village, or according to other scales as Truku or Sediq, or as citizens of Taiwan or the Republic of China. The alang is the basic unit of their territories of life. It is also ontological work when they insist on maintaining hunting territories, traplines, and gardens according to their own laws, even when punished by park officials for doing so. It is also ontological work when people speak in Truku and seek ways to keep the language alive in modern life.

Behind each village in Hualien are steep and verdant mountains, formerly inhabited by stateless mountain dwellers, but now managed by state actors including the Taroko National Park and the Council of Agriculture Forestry Division or leased to private companies. One of the first Truku words people taught me was "dgiyaq" for mountain-forests, a word they glossed in Chinese as shanshang ("on the mountains"). I eventually grasped that dgiyaq is neither a landform rising above its surrounding area (a mountain) nor a collection of trees (a forest). In fact, the word "truku," which local people gloss as "terraces in the mountains," is closer to the sense of the English word "mountain." Dgiyaq is rather a meshwork of human and non-human lives that would reveal its secrets to me only over years of walking through them. One word people did not teach me was a Truku word for "state." When I inquired, people told me they use the Japanese "kokka," because they never had a state before the Japanese arrived. These mountains, despite being nominally under state control, are still the territories of life for Indigenous Peoples.

Political ontology is also revealed through the words of Indigenous thinkers and activists. Truku leader Tera Yudaw, for example, took the issue of Indigenous hunting in the Taroko National Park to the United Nations Permanent Forum on Indigenous Issues in 2007. Because Taiwan is not a member of the UN, Tera would not normally have access to such venues, but he had integrated himself into the Panamanian delegation, with their permission.[3] He assumed ignorance on the part of UN officials, including Chinese diplomats (who had the power to turn off the microphone) about the location of the Taroko National Park. Only when he had finished speaking did he turn around his nameplate, marked "Panama," to reveal that he had hand-written "Truku from Taiwan" on the other side. More importantly, he said: "The land is our blood. The mountain forest is our home. Only with hunters do we have land. Only with hunters do we have wild animals" (Simon and Awi 2015, 21). He expressed an ontology in which humans, plants, and animals are mutually entangled; land mixes with blood, and the well-being of each depends on that of the others. True to the political ontology of an autarkic people, he challenged the premise of the international system that only states can legitimately represent peoples. Noting the irony of doing international work when their own state is barely recognized, some of his fellow travelers in the Indigenous social movement boast that they get a better hearing from the UN than does their state (Simon 2020a). But Tera could not escape entanglement with a state, even if it was a temporary relationship of convenience with Panama. Tera bravely spoke back to a world in which, according to Mario Blaser's argument, Indigenous rights are conceived within a modern ontology that reduces Indigenous lifeworlds to cultures forced to fit into small recesses (2009b, 891). It encapsulates Indigenous peoples within states, even if they offer the world alternative ontologies that do not legitimize the existence of states.

Political ontologies and entanglements emerge as people seek a good life, malu kndsan in Truku (Shen 1998, 27). People seek the good life with the group of people they call the alang, a social unit that is kin-based and thus similar to a clan but with greater options for the integration of outsiders. This was the main political unit before colonialism. Japan tried to break up the power of the alang by resettling peoples of the mountain-forests into permanent villages where they adopted modern agriculture under police surveillance (Simon 2015). They forced people from different alang, even those with violent histories of feuds and vendettas, to live in the same village (Simon 2020b). This is why Fushi is composed of people who identify with at least five different alang. Some people dispute (even among siblings) whether they should be called Truku or Sediq. Despite this local diversity, the state obliges them towork together and elect a local government as a single village. Some people refute the state entirely as a colonial imposition while others embrace its existence and seek to occupy places within it to represent their communities. This situation leads to many political controversies.

A good life, revolving around alang and sapah (family), is rooted in the land of the ancestors. It involves hard work, which people describe with a trope of men hunting and women weaving, and generosity while sharing the fruits of one's labour with alang and sapah. A morally upstanding person who follows Gaya will be rewarded with hunting success or prosperity in this life, have a good death (holding the hand of a loved one), and cross a Rainbow Spirit Bridge (Hakaw Utux) to enter the realm of the ancestors. Those who violate Gaya—for example those who sell their ancestors' land to outsiders for cash, monopolize financial or political resources for private gain, or violate norms of sexual propriety—will face immediate repercussions in this life. In the next section, I will show how people reflect on Gaya and the good life through spoken memories of historical and recent events.

STORYTELLING AND CONVERSATION

While gathering around a fire on a winter evening, giving a sermon in church, or driving from village to town, people tell stories to each other and to visitors. Sharing stories is ontological work because the moral lessons reinforce the importance of Gaya. In Truku, people refer to some stories as tminun kari ludan sbiyaw ("weaving together the words of the elders of the past"). In a worlding process of storied performativity, there is a deep connection between stories and practices (Blaser 2013, 552).

Origin myths are one way in which Indigenous Peoples affirm a place in the world. High up in the central peaks of Formosa, a giant stone emerges from the forest canopy. Known as Pusu Qhuni, it is spoken of as the most mystical place in the forest and the place of sejiq (human) origin. In the 2011 film *Seediq Bale*, Pusu Qhuni is invoked twice as the origin of the Seediq people, as half-stone, half-tree, from which emerged the first girl and the first boy (Sterk 2020, 136). Hunters told me about this taboo abode of the ancestral spirits, which is best avoided, and where hunting is strictly forbidden. One hunter told me about a naïve youth who failed to perform the necessary rituals, propped his rifle against the stone and slept under its shelter, waking up to find that his rifle had disappeared. He walked into the forest to look for his rifle, only to look back and see his rifle where he had left it. When he returned, the rifle disappeared again. Back and forth he went, the rifle disappearing as he neared Pusu Qhuni and re-appearing as he distanced himself from it. Only after making oblations to the ancestral spirits could he retrieve his rifle and continue on his way. Hunter and scholar Huang Chang-hsing (Lowsi Rakaw) tells how Christians in the 1950s tried to tame Pusu Qhuni's powers by placing crosses there, only to have their community devastated by a decade of natural disasters in ancestral retribution (Huang 2000, 68–69). Pusu Qhuni is rich in ontological and cosmological significance, a source of knowledge and philosophy, as well as a physical emanation of Gaya. It reminds people that, regardless of political affiliation as Truku or Sediq, they are rooted in the forest.

Pusu means "root, stem, origin"; qhuni means "tree" (Sterk 2020, 135). A derivation of pusu, tnpusu ("from the root, rooted") can mean "Indigenous" as in the song "SEDIQ/SEEDIQ/SEEJIQ ku tnpusu tndxral Taiwan" (I am Sediq/Seediq/Seejiq, Indigenous from the territory of Taiwan) (Watan Diro 2017, 24). However, these roots are not just any roots; they are the origins of human life. In both Hualien and Truku, people recall stories about their ancestors after emerging from Pusu Qhuni, as human populations flourished on three peaks in the central mountains. Eventually, small groups broke away and left in search of animals to hunt and gardens to till, some making their way toward the Pacific Ocean along three different rivers. For Hualien Truku, a decisive moment in their historiography is when their ancestors crossed the mountains and saw the glare of the sun reflecting from the sea for the first time. In Nantou, one person showed me three different mountain peaks from which originated the Truku, Tgdaya, and Toda peoples. Truku anthropologist Masaw Mowna documents how these different groups arrived in Hualien by following the Takili, Mugua, or Toda rivers, respectively (Masaw 1998, 25).

The main ontological claim is that small autarkic groups of people have inhabited these mountain-forests since the beginning of time. They recall life without states, before chiefs, and when no one tried to dominate anyone else. They had great respect for ludan (elders) who demonstrated skills and knowledge through practice and could be followed on hunting or ritual expeditions. Important decisions were made through consensus among brothers and their wives. Those who upheld Gaya were praised by their peers as "sejiq balay," which literally means "real people." These memories complement sparse Chinese historical records that until the seventeenth century described a far-away island to the east inhabited by savages (Zheng 1995), and confirm the 1592 record that Japanese envoys sent by Hideyoshi Toyotomi were repudiated on their quest to establish tribute relations with Formosa, on the grounds that there is no state with which to negotiate any agreement (Clulow 2013, 5–6). Each alang was autonomous; there was no state to interfere in their lives.

One of my key informants likes to tell a story he learned from his father. Surprised to see a strangely uniformed man on his trapline, a hunter demanded, "What are you doing on my hunting territory?" The uniformed man replied, "What right do you have to enter the forests of the Japanese Empire?" The lesson, says the storyteller, is that the Indigenous People were not consulted when China's Qing Dynasty ceded Formosa to Japan in 1895 and that the Indigenous People have never ceded sovereignty of their forests to any state. This is a powerful political ontological claim. From the hunter's perspective, all states represent claims made by outsiders to exercise power over the Indigenous Peoples; but in the end, none of those state claims are as powerful as Gaya, with the ultimate reality of the ancestors. The uniformed officer was surely from the Bureau of Pacification and Development, or Bukonshō, a Japanese word that took an unexpected and ironic turn in local language development, as we will see below.

People tell stories about how the Japanese forced them to surrender, about anti-Japanese resistance and rebellions, and about how the Japanese imposed on them an American model of reserves, chiefs, and band councils. Not without contradiction, they also show pride in the fact that they or their elders served in the Japanese military. In Nantou, the Japanese police made a dictionary to help officers communicate with local people. They translated the Japanese kijun (submission) as snegul. Sediq nationalist and Presbyterian minister Watan Diro explained that snegul means "to follow," as in the way that a younger man would follow an experienced hunter. From the Sediq perspective, this was a new form of interpersonal entanglement, but was never understood as a transfer of sovereignty.[4] All of these stories emphasize how the Indigenous Peoples are still the hosts; all states are recent arrivals and, usually, unwelcome guests on their territory. Speaking in Mandarin, they embrace the Chinese word for sovereignty, zhuquan, which literally means "host power" (Martin 2019, 16). They use it, for example when protesting for hunting rights in the Taroko National Park, to emphasize that they have always been there, whereas other peoples are merely guests passing through.

People tell stories about the post-war arrival of the ROC as a second wave of colonialism. There are few stories about the 1947 island-wide uprising against the ROC, known in Taiwanese nationalist narratives as the "2:28 Massacre," but since Indigenous people usually distrust Taiwanese nationalism, they use such stories to distance themselves from the majority Taiwanese. In the Seediq village Gluban, where survivors were relocated by the Japanese military after the 1930 anti-colonial Musha Incident, people related how some men accepted guns from the rebels, went hunting, and only learned about the crackdown when they came down the mountains weeks later and surrendered their weapons to the Chinese police officers. "The Chinese did not punish them," explained one man, "because they knew we fought against the Japanese. They admired us for that." In this story, the Seediq refused to join a Taiwanese rebellion, but instead sought a new form of entanglement with Chinese Mainlanders and with the ROC state. Most importantly, this relationship allowed them to hunt. In the early years, the township offices even helped them market bushmeat.

Modern stories reveal entanglement with contemporary Taiwan, as in accounts about elections, social movements, or the Presidential

Justice Committee. Very often, stories draw distinctions between the nation-state—with its relations of exclusion, extraction, and sale of resources—and the alang-based Gaya, with its relations of sharing and equilibrium with the spirits and other dwellers of the mountain-forests. People relish stories of how they extract concessions from the dominant society to maintain their sovereignty, as when they convinced Asia Cement to permit hunting on the hills behind the mine or the National Park to let them establish eco-tourism lodges on their land. They tell stories about how they convinced authorities to give them official house numbers, rather than accuse them of being squatters; and how they carried solar panels up the mountains on their backs so that they could finally have electricity. They love to claim authority that bypasses or transcends the state. However, in dealing with the state, they must also learn to speak in the language of law.

WRITING LAW: STATE FRAMEWORKS AND A TRUKU RESPONSE

The Indigenous Peoples Basic Law, first promulgated in 2005, was inspired by draft versions of the United Nations Declaration on the Rights of Indigenous Peoples (UNDRIP). Article 1 states, "This Law is enacted for the purposes of protecting the fundamental rights of indigenous peoples [sic], promoting their subsistence and development and building inter-ethnic relations based on co-existence and prosperity" (Republic of China 2018 [2005]).[5] Article 2 defines Indigenous land as "traditional territories" or "reservation land." Article 4 promises that self-government and autonomy will be implemented "in accordance with the will of indigenous peoples [sic]." Articles 5 and 6 provide details about implementing autonomy. Articles 7 to 9 are about Indigenous education, local government responsibilities, and language development. Article 10 takes a neoliberal approach to culture, requiring the government to "give guidance to the cultural industry and incubate professional talent." Many articles, including those that outline the protection of biological knowledge and intellectual property rights (Article 13), the use of natural resources, including fauna (Article 19, which legalizes non-profit Indigenous hunting), and the co-management of forests, land, etc., are derivative of Article 4 and require the establishment of self-governance for effective implementation (Simon and Awi 2015). Activists argue that the Basic Law, secondary only to the Constitution, takes precedence over other laws. Police and judges, in case of conflicts between different laws, usually argue that laws drafted prior to the Basic Law take precedence.

Hunting regulations have been especially contentious. Since 2012, revisions to the Wildlife Conservation Act permit Indigenous People to legally hunt non-endangered wildlife in unrestricted territories for cultural and ritual reasons. To do so, hunters must apply for permission twenty days in advance at the township office with information about the identity of the hunter, the precise time and location of the planned hunt, and details about the species and number of animals to be caught. However, hunters say that they cannot predict the species, location, or time, because the ancestors decide the outcome of the hunt and, in the words of one person, "animals don't make appointments." They are only permitted to hunt with homemade rifles. Such laws entangle Indigenous Peoples with the state but impinge upon their sovereignty. Hunters say that these regulations are a direct violation of Gaya because the process and outcome of the hunt is determined by the relationship between the hunter and the ancestors, not between the hunter and the state. It is not surprising that people try to take the law into their own hands, one way or another. The state has recently created Indigenous court hearings intended to incorporate Indigenous perspectives into issues such as hunting, but it is still unclear what benefit these attempts at legal pluralism will bring to Indigenous hunters (Upton 2022).

Truku nationalists, immediately after legal recognition in 2004, took the approach of writing their own law. As a political faction based on Hualien Presbyterian networks (Hara 2003), they turned their attention to creating a Truku autonomous government. In July 2005, they founded the Taroko National Autonomy Promotion Committee.[6] One of their first tasks was to draft the Taroko Autonomy Law (TAL). In 2006, the Committee revised the TAL into a national "constitution" with 10 articles and 101 clauses. The leaders hoped to establish an autonomous government during the DPP Chen Shui-bian presidency (from 2000 to 2008) but had meetings at various government levels up to the premier without result. They continued lobbying during the first years of the KMT Ma Ying-jeou presidency (from 2008 to 2016) and were initially encouraged by supportive public remarks made by KMT politicians.

They finally abandoned their efforts after being told that the TAL has no validity under constitutional law. Nonetheless, their attempts to put Gaya into written law reveal much about the difficulty of reconciling Indigenous ontologies with the nation-state.

The TAL responds to the Basic Law, beginning with the declaration: "In order to respect the natural sovereignty and the spirit of traditional Gaya of the Taroko people, and to protect its independent development, according to the [ROC] Constitution and the Basic Law on Indigenous Peoples, this establishes the Taroko Autonomy Law." The first article establishes legal definitions, notably that Taroko (tailuge) would include the Toda, Tgdaya, and Truku groups. Clause 5 declared that sovereignty belongs to all Taroko people. Clause 6 claimed all resources on Taroko territory. Clause 7 said that no law would be valid on Taroko territory without approval by the Taroko National Council. Article 2 included an anti-discrimination clause regarding gender, sexual orientation, religion, race, class, and political party. Article 3 established a National Council with representatives from four geographical areas in Hualien and Nantou. Article 4 established an elected leader (bukung) as head of the executive to represent the Taroko externally. Article 5 created a Council of Elders. Article 6 guaranteed local autonomy to different geographical areas. Article 7 defined the jurisdiction of the autonomous government. Article 8 provided guidelines for elections. Article 9 outlined basic policies of external affairs (including the need to sign a treaty with the ROC), economics, social welfare, education, and culture. Article 10 had provisions for implementation and revisions of the law.

The process of drafting this law enabled local leaders to deliberate on the relationship between Gaya and ROC law. Retired school principal Tera Yudaw, the one who would eventually visit the UN, began public hearings by saying that their ancestors were from Nantou's central mountains and arrived at the shores of Hualien about four hundred years ago. Gaya is in the first clause of the TAL, giving it priority over ROC law. The autarkic spirit of Gaya is evident in the autonomy granted to all sub-regions, and to the power given to a Council of Elders. This movement was led by people who knew both Gaya and state law, and wanted to find a way for them to coexist. Seeking to combine two legal traditions, but on their own terms, their goals somewhat resembled the Australian Aboriginal notion of living by "two laws" (Austin-Broos 1996).

Despite the good intentions of its authors, the TAL was like all laws in that it became an arena for conflict. This was partly because it was an innovation to transcribe orally transmitted Gaya based on the model of state-centric constitutional law, and people perceived those efforts as self-contradictory. Never in history had these different alang, which in some cases had lived for generations in violent conflict, tried to unite and create formal institutions of collective governance on their own initiative. Leaders in Ren'ai Township of Nantou, refusing to identify with the geographical zone that TAL drafters called Qilai (klbiyun), renewed their own movement for recognition. Self-proclaimed representatives of the Hualien Toda protested publicly and on television against what they called "Truku hegemony." Interestingly, most people seemed to pay little or no attention at all, as if it were merely a competition between elites for a place in the state system (Rudolph 2003).

My fieldwork began amidst these debates. On June 4, 2005, I attended the public hearing in the Fushi village hall. Tera Yudaw, the mayor, and a Presbyterian pastor took their places at the front, under a portrait of Sun Yat-sen, founder of the ROC. That was a rather ironic image because "Sun Yat-sen thought" has been an ideology since the 1950s, used as justification for "local autonomy" that includes thirty mountain townships in which only Indigenous people can be elected as magistrate. The Truku had to explain why their version of local autonomy was superior to that model. An hour after the scheduled beginning, only nine women and six men had arrived. After Tera's opening remarks, the pastor spoke about the name rectification movement, the discrimination that urban Indigenous people suffer, the need to regain lost territory, and why autonomy offers them an opportunity to live according to Gaya. As he spoke, the mayor left to recruit others, coming back with four other men and five women. Tera explained that other Indigenous groups have sought autonomy but failed due to the lack of internal consensus. He said that their successful name rectification movement had proven that the Taroko can unite. He fielded questions about how the autonomous region would be funded, how they would find skilled cadres, etc. When asked about the budget, he explained that they would receive the same royalties from Asia Cement and others that Hsiulin Township now receives.

Over the next several years of field research, I realized that everyone, even those who refused to attend such meetings, was judiciously deliberating about the relationship between Gaya and state law. Gaya had always been diffused through society, the basic unit of which was the face-to-face alang. In what had always been a "society against the state" (Clastres 1977), they resisted not only colonial forces but also internal innovations that might allow individuals to accumulate power or wealth. During the summer of 2005, ordinary people accused Tera of trying to crown himself "King of the Taroko." Some described attempts by local elite to map territory and claim "autonomy" as "colonialism from within," an argument picked up by local sociologists, including Professor Chi Chun-chieh and his Truku graduate student (Chi and Chin 2012). People were very aware that those promoting (and opposing) autonomy are caught up in other entanglements at the national level, accusing them of collaborating with either the KMT (stalwarts of the ROC) or the DPP (proponents of an independent Taiwan). Some people expressed disappointment that they had not been invited to public hearings, with suspicions that grassroots people were intentionally excluded. People criticized the TAL as being more inspired by the ROC Constitution than by Gaya, which never had written articles and clauses. They questioned why this "autonomy" was different from existing laws. Especially when leaders discussed mining royalties, it appeared as if the project were little more than one faction of elites trying to seize power from another. A Seediq nationalist pointed out the irony that the word "bukung," used in Article 4 of the TAL as the name of the elected leader, was derived from the name of a Japanese colonial institution, the Bukonshō (which patrolled the forests). With a dismissive chuckle, he said people got accustomed to calling anyone who must be obeyed "bukung," and now mistake it as tradition. In their critiques, people drew attention to the project as foreign to their traditional ontologies. The very attempt to take a living, oral tradition and translate it into written law represented a major ontological rupture. Although I think that the TAL was a sincere attempt to align Gaya with state law, what I describe in the next section provides a contrasting practice of sovereignty.

ENTANGLEMENTS OF ON-THE-GROUND AUTONOMY

Looming above the villages where these debates took place is dgiyaq, the mountainous habitat of wild animals and home to some more marginal people who have different perspectives on Gaya. Although people had told me about their hunting institutions and even taken me with them to inspect traps or hunt, I did not fully understand how well hunters and trappers implement Gaya until, in the fall of 2012, I spent a fortnight in a distant area high in the mountains with an elderly hunter (to whom I refer by the pseudonym Gasil) and two younger men in their forties (both now deceased). None of these men had permanent employment or incomes, nor the means to marry and have a family. Instead, they barely eked out a living by selling meat and by occasionally taking day jobs that nobody else wanted, like killing pigs and cleaning up the blood at wedding sacrificial rituals (Lin 2011). Because Gaya requires people to share, they also rely on the kindness of others to provide them with food and even money for rice wine. Most villagers dismiss such people as "drunken ghosts," but I have found them to be among the most knowledgeable people about Truku language and lifeworlds. Even in the absence of legalized, state-recognized autonomy, they have carved out independent spaces for themselves in the mountain-forests. Amidst all the local diversity, they are the people who have the strongest entanglements with non-humans and do the most to protect the territories of life that have been cultivated and nourished by their ancestors for generations.

The first indication that I was entering a de facto autonomous zone was when, observing state law, I went to the police station to apply for a mountain permit. The officer looked incredulous when I told him my plans to spend two weeks there and said, "Even we don't dare to go there. There are drunken aborigines with rifles." From the perspective of the Indigenous People, the mountain permit system was a constant irritant and one that *should* be resisted. An elder said to me on another occasion in frustration, "You don't need anyone's permission to visit my house." He was upset that I would even consider that the state could legitimately intervene in his power to host me. In retrospect, I see resistance to mountain permits as an effective practice of autonomy. From the state's perspective, these spaces are not too anomalous. Even in Taiwan's urban areas, there are marginal spaces in which non-state actors stake out territory and keep the police at bay (Martin 2019, 70–73).

In the mountain-forests, all hunters know the limits of their own territories; only a limited number of hunters are permitted in each territory. This is why, when people protest against National Park prohibitions and officials ask why they don't just hunt elsewhere, local people sigh in exasperation as they explain that other forests already belong to other people. Within the borders of each alang-based territory, trappers carve out traplines through the dense vegetation. With permission, younger men walk along their paths to shoot flying squirrels at night. If an elder hunter catches a heavy mammal, such as a boar, he will arrange for a younger man to help carry it, with an understanding about how they will share the meat or the proceeds of the sale. Since Gaya is highly egalitarian, there is an expectation that each person will get an equal share. There may be conflicts about Gaya, just as there are about state law, but they can usually be resolved through local mediation. What is important is that Gaya continues to exist. The hunters think they are already living well, even in the absence of state-recognized autonomous zones, which they fear would be a new form of exclusion. For such hunters, the notion that people down in Bsngan could interfere in their hunting management is scarcely better than taking orders from Taipei, Tokyo, or Beijing.

Even in the absence of legal Indigenous autonomy, for most of the year and across most of the Central Mountain Range of Formosa, hunters, police, and conservation officers have come to coexist, informally negotiating distinct ontologies amidst lines of entanglement. This informal understanding is why people told me that they are able to trap, carry guns, and even sell meat, as long as they do so discreetly. They say that police usually only arrest and fine people at special moments in the year, such as before the Lunar New Year, when officers have quotas to meet. In most communities, police and conservation officers are also local, with ties of kinship to the hunters. One local Truku person told me that they maintain good relations with both Truku and ethnically Taiwanese officers;[7] the officers who arrest and fine them are from the coastal Amis Indigenous group. He remembers very well that the Amis once helped the Japanese suppress the Truku. From the Taiwanese police officers' perspective, such flexibility in law enforcement mobilizes sentiment (qing) as policing and governance through mediated compromise at the local level (Martin 2019, 61). Even when officers have no choice but to intervene, as when a hiker calls their attention to the presence of a trap or the sound of gunshot, police in Taiwan maintain a certain degree of flexibility through deflective practices of "eating cases" (chi'an), or simply not filing them (76). Such practices make Indigenous-state entanglements tolerable to most Indigenous people, even in the absence of legal Indigenous autonomy. Tolerance is not legalization, however, which explains why there are regular protests for hunting rights. The Indigenous seek stronger forms of resilience, even resurgence, as they seek to protect themselves and keep their entangled relations with other entities intact, even amidst ongoing colonialism.

CONCLUSION

This essay has explored the experience of the sejiq tnpusu (the rooted people), their political ontologies, and their ways of negotiating entanglements with foreign states over the past 120 years. In storytelling, they recall a pre-colonial past without a state, when each alang was an autonomous political entity. The telling of these stories is ontological work. People know that their entanglement with the state began when they were coerced by the Japanese to accept state rule, yet they have never renounced their sovereignty. Ontological conflicts emerged between the peoples of Gaya, who have their ways of inhabiting the forests in equilibrium with non-human animals and spirits, and a new nation-state ontology that includes land cadastres, classifications of ethnic groups, and state appropriation of mountain-forests for extraction of "natural resources." As their entire territory came under the control of Japan and then the ROC, they had no choice but to enter into relations with outsiders.

After Taiwan evolved into a liberal democracy, the Indigenous rights movement started proposing new forms of legal recognition. State actors and Indigenous activists agreed in principle that territory must be returned and sovereignty recognized. However, there is disagreement about how to do that. The state, in a logic of multicultural biopolitics, imagines Indigenous groups based on modern ideas of ethnicity and exclusive territories. As the Truku and Sediq obtained recognition in the 2000s, individuals and communities had to choose which side to join. People had difficult decisions to make, which they did through their interpretations of Gaya. Because their decisions were about collective entanglements with the state, it was inevitable that conflicts would arise. The Truku Autonomy Law was a local innovation but had at best a tepid reception among the Truku people, as they found it difficult to understand how it fit into Gaya or how it differed from prior written documents that promised autonomy while actually subordinating them to the state. There is a fundamental ontological disagreement between the modern logic of the map, which includes attempts to define ethnic groups and boundaries via polygons drawn on paper, and that of the itinerary, which imagines Gaya as lines emanating from Pusu Qhuni along paths literally carved by trappers. As Poirier points out in regard to similar dynamics in Australia, "maps are fixed, whereas itineraries are open-ended, forever unfolding" (2004, 78). Indigenous Peoples do not entirely reject the possibility of forming alliances with outsiders they meet along those pathways, whether those outsiders be Japanese, Chinese, or Taiwanese. However, ceding land or sovereignty is a serious violation of Gaya.

From a purely legal perspective, in a state system, groups must be recognized as legal persons if land is to be returned and sovereignty exercised. An example would be the right for the Truku to provide or withhold from the state their consent for development projects, a right that was not recognized when the Taroko National Park and Asia Cement were established. For ordinary people merely trying to make a living, including as employees of the park and the cement company, these issues can seem distant from daily concerns. The urgency is even more difficult to perceive when even hunters have found informal ways to manage their traplines according to their own institutions. They are still the real masters of the mountain-forests and Gaya, the ontology that defines their existence, still exists. The hunters claim it will continue to exist no matter which external state holds control of Taiwan. They evoke the presence of a reality that will outlive all states as long as sejiq truku roam the mountain forests.

Human activities, from telling stories around a fire to drafting laws about a Taroko Autonomous Region, to wandering in the forest, reveal that political ontologies are always emerging entanglements. The Indigenous Peoples may not have chosen the arrival of either Japan or the ROC, and they have not yet been recognized by those powerful forces as political equals. Nonetheless, whether they attempt to negotiate with the state or to hide from it while implementing their own hunting institutions in the forests, the real people are still inspired by Gaya and able to live by it. In a sense, modernist written laws, with vocabularies of autonomy, sovereignty, territory, and rights—all inspired by encounters with Indigenous Peoples internationally—are similar to the crosses that Christian Indigenous converts placed at Pusu Qhuni. They are attempts to shape entanglements with others in a way that they themselves find meaningful. As noted in the introduction to this volume, territories of life may appear in association with the legal category of "Indigenous Peoples," but in fact transcend that notion. In the highlands of Formosa, as long as the people remember Pusu Qhuni, they remain rooted in the land, with Gaya as the centre of their various ontological and political entanglements.

NOTES

1. The Japanese classified the Indigenous populations into nine groups, based on linguistic and cultural criteria. Among the Atayal, they further sub-classified three groupings, including the Sediq, which are then further categorized into three main groups, each with its own dialect. The Truku are those who, over four centuries, migrated along the Takili (Liwu) River toward the Pacific Coast. Unable to pronounce "Truku," the Japanese transformed the name of the people into Taroko (タロコ), which was used to name the Taroko Gorge and the Tsugitaka-Taroko National Park.
2. It is the same word in Truku and Tgdaya. In Toda, it is "Waya."
3. Until 2017, Panama was one of the few countries that had formal diplomatic relations with the ROC on Taiwan.
4. Private communication with Darryl Sterk and Watan Diro.
5. The term "indigenous peoples" is uncapitalized in the official translation.
6. The Chinese ethnonym is Tailuge zu. At first, some people preferred to romanize it as Taroko. Although the spelling "Truku" prevailed and became the official English version, "Taroko" reflects local written usage at the time.
7. Here, "Taiwanese" is an ethnic group, referring to speakers of Taiwanese, or the Hoklo language. They are the majority in Taiwan, and usually disliked by Indigenous people, who describe them as settlers prone to taking their land and exploiting their labour.

REFERENCES

Allio, Fiorella. 1998. "La construction d'un espace politique austronésien." *Perspectives chinoises* 47 (May–June): 54–62.

Andrade, Tonio. 2008. *How Taiwan Became Chinese: Dutch, Spanish, and Han Colonization in the Seventeenth Century*. Columbia University Press.

Austin-Broos, Diane J. 1996. "'Two Laws,' Ontologies, Histories: Ways of Being Aranda Today." *Australian Journal of Anthropology* 7 (3): 1–20.

Awi Mona (Tsai Chih-wei), and Huang Chia-yuan. 2021. "Conflict and Reconciliation Between

Civil Law and Indigenous Legal Traditions: The Case of Land Governance in Taiwan." In *Taiwan's Contemporary Indigenous Peoples*, edited by Chia-yuan Huang, Daniel Davies, and Dafydd Fell. Routledge.

Baldacchino, Godfrey, and Huei-Min Tsai. 2014. "Contested Enclave Metageographies: The Offshore Islands of Taiwan." *Political Geography* 40: 13–24.

Barclay, Paul. 2018. *Outcasts of Empire: Japan's Rule on Taiwan's "Savage Border," 1874–1945*. University of California Press.

Blaser, Mario. 2009a. "The Threat of the Yrmo: The Political Ontology of a Sustainable Hunting Program." *American Anthropologist* 111 (1): 10–20.

Blaser, Mario. 2009b. "Political Ontology: Cultural Studies without 'Cultures'?" *Cultural Studies* 23 (5–6): 873–896.

Blaser, Mario. 2013. "Ontological Conflicts and the Stories of People in Spite of Europe: Toward a Conversation on Political Ontology." *Current Anthropology* 54 (5): 547–568.

Chi, Chun-Chieh, and Hsang-Te Chin. 2012. "Knowledge, Power, and Tribal Mapping: A Critical Analysis of the 'Return of the Truku People.'" *GeoJournal* 77 (6): 733–740.

Clastres, Pierre. 1977. *Society Against the State*. Translated by Robert Hurley. B. Blackwell.

Clulow, Adam. 2013. *Statecraft and Spectacle in East Asia: Studies in Taiwan-Japan Relations*. Routledge.

Hara, Eiko 原英子. 2003. "Taiyaru Sedekku Taroko o meguru kizoku to meishō ni kan suru undo no tenkai (1)—Taroko ni okeru dōkō o chūshin niタイヤル・セデック・タロコをめぐる帰属と名称に関する運動の展開（1）——タロコにおける動向を中心に" ["The Development of the Identity Movement of the Atayal, Sediq, and Truku: Focused on Truku Trends (1)."] *Taiwan Genjūmin Kenkyū* 台湾原住民研究 [*Taiwan Indigenous Research*] (7): 209–227.

Harrison, Henrietta. 2001. "Changing Nationalities, Changing Ethnicities: Taiwan Indigenous Villages in the Years after 1946." In *In Search of the Hunters and Their Tribes: Studies in the History and Culture of the Taiwan Indigenous People*, edited by David Faure. Shung Ye Museum of Formosan Aborigines.

Huang, Chang-xing 黃長興. 2000. "東賽德克群的狩獵文化" ["Hunting Culture in Eastern Seediq Groups."] 民族學研究所資料彙編 [*Field Materials of the Institute of Ethnology*] (15): 1–104.

Lin, Ching-Hsiu. 2011. "The Circulation of Labour and Money: Symbolic Meanings of Monetary Kinship Practices in Contemporary Truku Society, Taiwan." *New Proposals: Journal of Marxism and Interdisciplinary Inquiry* 5 (1): 27–44.

Liu, Yi-chang. 2022. "Taiwan Prehistoric Maritime Trade Networks and Their Impacts." In *Taiwan Maritime Landscapes from Neolithic to Early Modern Times*, edited by Paola Calanca, Liu Yi-chang, and Frank Muyard. École française d'Extrême-Orient.

Martin, Jeffrey. T. 2019. *Sentiment, Reason, and Law: Policing in the Republic of China on Taiwan*. Cornell University Press.

Masaw Mowna 廖守臣. 1998. 泰雅族的社會組織 [*Atayal Social Organization*]. Hualien: Tzu Chi University Research Center on Aboriginal Health. 花蓮：慈濟醫學院暨人文社會學院原住民健康研究室.

Poirier, Sylvie. 2004. "Ontology, Ancestral Order, and Agencies among the Kukatja of the Australian Western Desert." In *Figured Worlds: Ontological Obstacles in Intercultural Relations*, edited by John Clammer, Sylvie Poirier, and Eric Schwimmer. University of Toronto Press.

Poirier, Sylvie. 2017. "Nehirowisiw Territoriality: Negotiating and Managing Entanglement and Coexistence." In *Entangled Territorialites: Negotiating Indigenous Lands in Australia and Canada*, edited by Françoise Dussart and Sylvie Poirier. University of Toronto Press.

Povinelli, Elizabeth A. 2002. *The Cunning of Recognition: Indigenous Alterities and the Making of Australian Multiculturalism*. Duke University Press.

Republic of China. 2018 [2005]. "The Indigenous Peoples Basic Law." Taipei: Ministry of Justice.

https://law.moj.gov.tw/ENG/LawClass/LawAll.aspx?pcode=D0130003.
Rose, Deborah Bird. 2011. *Wild Dog Dreaming: Love and Extinction*. University of Virginia Press.
Rudolph, Michael. 2003. *Taiwans multi-ethnische Gesellschaft und die Bewegung der Ureinwohner: Assimilation oder kulturelle Revitalisierung?* LIT Verlag.
Shen, Ming-ren 沈明仁 (Pawan Tanah). 1998. 崇信祖靈的民族賽德克人 [*A People Who Believe in Ancestral Spirits: Sediq People.*] Haiweng.
Simon, Scott. 2002. "The Underside of a Miracle: Industrialization, Land, and Taiwan's Indigenous Peoples." *Cultural Survival Quarterly* 26 (2): 64–67.
Simon, Scott. 2010. "Negotiating Power: Elections and the Constitution of Indigenous Taiwan." *American Ethnologist* 37 (4): 726–740.
Simon, Scott. 2013. "Of Boars and Men: Indigenous Knowledge and Co-management in Taiwan." *Human Organization* 72 (3): 220–229.
Simon, Scott. 2015. "Making Natives: Japan and the Creation of Indigenous Formosa." In *Japanese Taiwan: Colonial Rule and its Contested Legacy*, edited by Andrew D. Morris. Bloomsbury.
Simon, Scott. 2020a. "Yearning for Recognition: Indigenous Formosans and the Limits of Indigeneity." *International Journal of Taiwan Studies* 3 (2): 191–216.
Simon, Scott. 2020b. "History of the Conquered: Rethinking Historiography with Indigenous Peoples on Formosa." In *Connaissons-nous la Chine?* edited by Paul Servais. Academia-L'Harmattan.
Simon, Scott E. 2023a. "Hunting Rights, Justice, and Reconciliation: Indigenous Experiences in Taiwan and Canada." In *Indigenous Reconciliation in Contemporary Taiwan*, edited by Scott E. Simon, Jolan Hsieh, and Peter Kang. Routledge.
Simon, Scott E. 2023b. *Truly Human: Indigeneity and Indigenous Resurgence on Formosa*. University of Toronto Press.
Simon, Scott, and Awi Mona. 2015. "Indigenous Rights and Wildlife Conservation: The Vernacularization of International Law on Taiwan." *Taiwan Human Rights Journal* 3 (1): 3–31.
Simon, Scott E., Jolan Hsieh, and Peter Kang, eds. 2023. *Indigenous Reconciliation in Contemporary Taiwan*. Routledge.
Sterk, Darryl. 2020. *Indigenous Cultural Translation: A Thick Description of Seediq Bale*. Routledge.
Upton, J. Christopher. 2022. "From Thin to Thick Justice and Beyond: Access to Justice and Legal Pluralism in Indigenous Taiwan." *Law & Social Inquiry* 47 (3): 996–1025.
Watan Diro. 2017. *Sediq/Seediq/Seejiq Nation* 賽德克族群區會7020母語朗讀演講詩歌競賽. Puli: Sediq Mother Language Promotion Team.
Zheng, Chantal. 1995. *Les Austronésiens de Taïwan à travers les sources chinoises*. L'Harmattan.

6

Hernán Ruiz Fournier
Translated by Eleanor Douglas

DISPOSSESSION OF THE GUARANÍ TERRITORY OF KARAPARÍ

CONTRADICTIONS WITHIN THE PLURINATIONAL STATE OF BOLIVIA

INTRODUCTION

The Chaco Region in the department of Tarija, located in the extreme southeast of Bolivia, borders on the Republic of Paraguay and the Republic of Argentina. It belongs to the Bolivian Chaco macro region which, in turn, constitutes part of the South American Gran Chaco, a homogeneous biogeographical area of more than one million square kilometres, shared with Argentina, Paraguay, and Brazil. The Chaco constitutes the second largest forested area in all of Latin America, after the tropical forests of the Amazon (PNUD 2013). The Chaco Tarijeño possesses great natural wealth, revealed by its ecosystems, biodiversity, and large natural resource reserves, including hydrocarbons (the most important in Bolivia).

In recent decades, the discovery and exploitation of natural gas in this region have generated substantial royalties and taxes. This income has been directly invested and managed by regional institutions, thanks to the new system of autonomies, making the Chaco Tarijeño

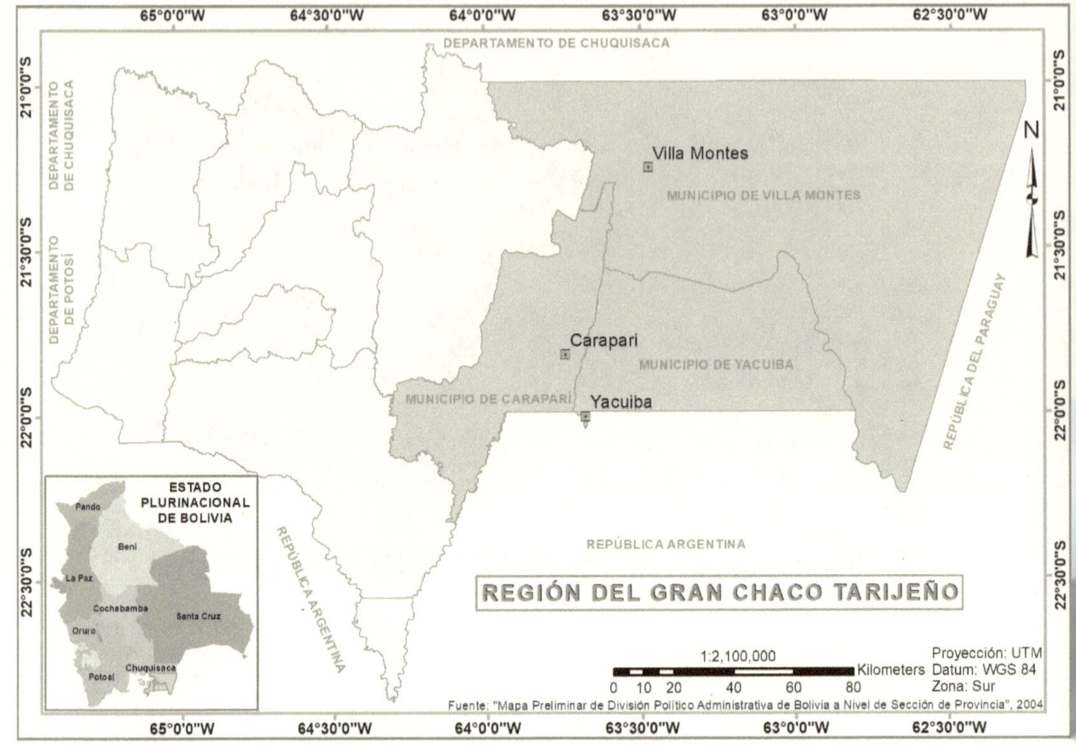

MAP 6.1 | Gran Chaco Region (also known as Gran Chaco Province) within Tarija Department.

(Source: "Mapa Preliminar de División Político Administrativa de Bolivia a Nivel de Sección de Provincia," State Service of Bolivian Autonomies, 2004. Open source.)

one of the fastest-growing economic regions in the country. However, Indigenous Peoples ancestrally inhabiting this region—the Guaraní, the Weenhayek, and the Tapiete—representing more than 10 percent of the Gran Chaco population, have not received meaningful benefit from this income despite their territories and way of life being drastically affected. According to official data, public investment in projects and programs favouring Indigenous Peoples between 2006 and 2015, on average did not exceed 2 percent of the annual budgets of the Gran Chaco Region.

In 1996, relying on Law 1715 of the National Institute of Agrarian Reform (INRA in its Spanish acronym), the Guaraní People demanded from the Bolivian state the reconstitution of their ancestral territory and the titling of Native Communitarian Lands (TCO in the Spanish acronym) for all their communities located in the Bolivian Chaco. However, after more than twenty years of "saneamiento" (the legal land titling process) in various Guaraní areas of the Chaco, results for Indigenous Peoples have been negligible. Only 10 percent of the original territorial demand favoured by the Bolivian Guaraní Peoples' Assembly (APG in its Spanish acronym),[1] was titled to the Guaraní as TCO land, while remaining land was left in the hands of third parties (former landowners and current migrant owners from other regions of the country) and the state itself, with its public lands, which have been defined to a large extent as priority areas for hydrocarbon exploration or exploitation.

The subject of this chapter, Guaraní communities constituting the Zonal Captaincy of Karaparí in the Gran Chaco Region of the Department of Tarija, suffer the most intense socio-economic difficulties, resulting from a long history of patronage and servitude within the hacienda regime, which prevailed until recently. The Indigenous population was plunged into a situation of extreme vulnerability, due to the violation of their human and collective rights, territorial dispossession, and socio-cultural discrimination (CCGT 2010).

The state's postponement and neglect of the Karaparí Guaraní People's demand for recognition of their Native Communitarian Lands as well as the expansion of the agriculture frontier, changes in Indigenous Peoples' traditional use of the land due to increased occupation by new actors and activities, and the discriminatory socio-economic and political context directly threaten the Guaraní People's cultural survival and hinders their life project based on the reconstitution of their ancestral territory. Given this situation, the question addressed in this chapter is: What are the fundamental reasons the Bolivian state systematically denies the Guaraní People of the Karaparí Captaincy their right to communitarian lands and ancestral territory, even though the new constitution enshrines the notion of a "plurinational state," which includes Indigenous Peoples' rights? The state's refusal to recognize the rights of the Guaraní is not only evident in the process and outcome of saneamiento, which itself displayed many deficiencies and uncertainties regarding ownership of claimed communitarian lands; it can also be observed in the non-compliance with and obstruction of the exercise of the Guaraní People's collective rights, which include prior consultation in industrial hydrocarbon projects and political and economic participation in local governments and resource administration.

The goal of this chapter is to demonstrate, based on facts and testimonies from the actors involved, that the current situation of the Guaraní People is due to the dominance of a developmentalist economic model based on extractivism, present throughout the state's administrative structure and defined as the intensive exploitation and exportation of nature valorized as primary commodities. Extractivism is characterized by the violent expansion of extractive territories and the subordination, suppression, and denial of pre-existing territories (Gudynas 2015; Svampa 2019). In the Bolivian Chaco, this model has imposed a rentier logic within public administration, which is then exploited by local power elites, involving family groups owning lands and haciendas as well as migrant groups with emerging economic clout. Extractivism thus reproduces colonial logics of territory and the state in ways that condition and constrain the struggles to reclaim territories of life (see also Anthias 2022; Gustafson 2020; Prada 2011).

Karaparí is a prime example of what the editors of this volume call entanglement—the co-presence of multiple ontologies in the same territory. Guaraní communities in Karaparí are entangled with the nation-state's territory, which imposes political-administrative boundaries and a modern property regime that favours non-Indigenous claimants. They are also entangled with transnational networks of hydrocarbon investment and production, which frame subterranean matter as commodities that can be extracted and sold and rely on the state's monopoly on violence and law to secure access to these resources. While difference is not extinguished, the reproduction of Guaraní ways of being (Ñande Reko) is profoundly constrained by these territorial entanglements.

To support this central argument, the first section provides a brief historical overview of the Guaraní people, noting significant life-altering events and then situating them within the current territorial and organizational context. The second section addresses the problematic of territorial dispossession of Bolivia's Guaraní People and their claim on the state for communitarian lands, as well as contradictions generated between extractivism and the so-called Plurinational State of

Bolivia. The third section engages with the Guaraní Peoples' community struggles for the recovery of their lands and the exercise of their rights in the case of the Karapari Zone. Finally, the fourth section draws some relevant conclusions.

This chapter is based on materials from several months of fieldwork conducted between 2018 and 2019, which include my participation in activities organized by the Guaraní People in Karapari, as well as group interviews with key community leaders. The analysis of the material is informed by my more than twenty years of association and solidarity support with Guaraní organizations, as a researcher at the Tarija Centre for Regional Studies (CERDET in its Spanish acronym), and as a researcher, project coordinator, and advisor to the Tarija Council of Guaraní Captains (CCGT in its Spanish acronym) and to Guaraní representatives in the Assembly of the Autonomous Regional Government of the Gran Chaco.

HISTORY OF THE TERRITORY AND ORGANIZATION OF THE BOLIVIAN GUARANÍ PEOPLE

The Guaraní People of Bolivia ancestrally inhabit the macro region of the Bolivian Chaco, which extends in the southeast to three departments: Santa Cruz, Chuquisaca, and Tarija, encompassing a total of sixteen municipalities that collectively represent approximately 130,000 square kilometres, more than 13 percent of the national land mass. As an ethnic group, the Guaraní are considered one of the largest in the country, along with the Aymara and Quechua. The Tupi Guaraní linguistic family also includes other Indigenous Peoples in Bolivia, such as the Guarasuwe, Guarayu, Sirionó, Tapiete, and Yuki, among others, located in various departments of the Lowlands (Díez 2012).

The Guaraní People's history in Bolivian territory begins with three migratory processes: from Mato Grosso (Brazil) through Chiquitano territory to the Río Grande; from Central Chaco (Paraguay) to the Cordillera; and from the Paraná River (Argentina) by way of the Pilcomayo River. These migrations might have been motivated by the search for the "Ɨvɨ Maraëi" (Land without Evil), which, in the Guaraní imaginary, represents the ideal territory of abundance and peace. It is estimated that these influxes occurred toward the end of the fifteenth century, before the arrival of the Spanish (Pifarré 1989).

Upon their arrival in the Chaco, the Guaraní met and culturally mingled with other ethnic groups, such as the Chané of Arawak origin, giving rise to the current Bolivian Guaraní identity (Saignes and Combès 2007). The Guaraní resisted conquest by the Inca Empire, and later, the Spanish invasion. However, the religious Jesuit missions of the seventeenth century and the Franciscan missions of the eighteenth managed to penetrate Indigenous territory to evangelize and prevent military aggression by the Spanish (Melia 1988). Gradually, Indigenous resistance gave way to the establishment of missions and haciendas throughout the Chaco region. Slowly, relations of exchange developed between Guaraní communities and settlers, but always to the disadvantage for the former. Later, the Bolivian War of Independence (1809–1825) engaged several Guaraní chiefs as protagonists who enlisted their warriors in the liberation armies of Juana Azurduy and Manuel Belgrano (Saignes and Combès 2007).

During the Bolivian Republic, relations between Guaraní communities and the karai (white or non-Indigenous) haciendas became increasingly tense, due to the haciendas' encroachment on Indigenous territories. In 1892, President Aniceto Arce ordered the Republican Army to take Guaraní leaders—among them the mythical Apiaguaiki Tüpa—by force in an effort to crush remaining Indigenous resistance and to seize their lands. The infamous Kuruyuki Massacre resulted in the annihilation of more than five thousand warriors and their families, as well as the dispersal of Indigenous survivors, mainly women and children, fleeing military atrocities (Saignes and Combès 2007).

Despite this calamity, the Guaraní effectively contributed to the Bolivian Army during the Chaco War against Paraguay (1932–1935), even while being unjustly accused as traitors for speaking the same "enemy" language. The war not only ignored the Guaraní regional presence on the Bolivian side, but it also helped consolidate state presence within—and sovereignty over—Indigenous territories. The result was the dispossession of Guaraní lands, which were distributed among remaining troops after the cessation of hostilities (Richard 2008).

Subsequently, some remaining Guaraní families in the Chaco set up small communities, while others were forced to migrate to different areas—to the urban peripheries of Santa Cruz and even to Argentina. Many Indigenous families were subjected to regimes of servitude on the region's cattle ranches, where, until a short time ago, landowners leveraged their labour and stripped away their small remaining plots. Some suffered extreme conditions of semi-slavery, since they were transferred for generations as part of the landholders' patrimony, deprived of their fundamental rights and subsisted for decades on a daily plate of food as exploitative payment for their labour.[2] At the same time, through schools, the health and justice systems, and a monocultural bureaucracy, the Republican state displayed its indifference to and dismissal of Indigenous identity, institutionalizing a contemptuous attitude of racism and discrimination toward the Guaraní culture that persists to this day in the Chaco (CCGT 2010).

Chaco regional history is similarly identified with the extraction of natural resources. Extraction primarily occurs in a peripheral area but extends its tentacles to political and economic power centres, which are mainly located in western Bolivia. Huge quantities of wood extracted from Chaco forests were used to sustain mining exploitation centres and railway construction (Ardaya et al. 1998), and many of these forested areas formed part of the Chaco Indigenous Peoples' ancestrally occupied territories. It goes without saying that the resulting devastation in Indigenous communities is notable.

Gas and oil exploitation began in the Chaco in the 1920s, making it one of the country's first areas of production. It started after an initial discovery in the Indigenous community of Mandiuti, thanks to stories from individuals who were already using oil as a medicinal resin and a source of energy (Orgáz 2002). According to accounts by Indigenous elders, the overlapping of hydrocarbon exploration and exploitation and Indigenous territories—especially those of the Guaraní—resulted in territorial dispossession and the violation of their rights. Currently, intensification of the extractivist logic in these territories continues to generate an increasingly negative impact on the social, cultural, and economic structures of the decimated Guaraní population.

Organizing efforts by the Bolivian Guaraní People originate in community struggles to restructure their territory after the Kuruyuki Massacre in 1892 and the spread of a cattle ranching system throughout much of the twentieth century in the entire Bolivian Chaco (Caurey 2012).

Indigenous families gradually reorganized into communities, forming a communal captaincy, which, in turn, associated with others in the same region or jurisdiction to form a zonal captaincy. Currently, the Bolivian Guaraní People are organized in twenty-seven zonal captaincies in three departments: Santa Cruz, Chuquisaca, and Tarija, which incorporate a total of more than three hundred Guaraní communities throughout the Bolivian Chaco (APG 2008).

THE STRUGGLE FOR RECONSTITUTION OF GUARANÍ TERRITORY AND CONFLICTS WITH THE STATE

Land and Territory in the Guaraní Imaginary

In Bolivia, the terms "land" and "territory" are used together because legislation refers to each concept with a distinct purpose, as Yamila Gutierrez-Callisaya points out (this volume). Before the new constitution came into effect, conservative governments resisted using the term "territory," due to the unfounded fear of a possible rupture of the territorial integrity of the nation-state; therefore, the term "land" was imposed as a collective land ownership category, leaving no doubt about its agrarian scope. However, with the subsequent promulgation of the new constitution of the Plurinational State of Bolivia in 2009, the concept of "territory" was recovered, used along with the term "land," to signify all historical, legal, and social implications that both terms reflect. The modifications to the Political Constitution of the State (CPE in its Spanish acronym) that occurred in 1994 were followed by agrarian reform through the INRA Law (No. 1715) of 1996, which included the category of Community Lands of Origin, in response to the Indigenous demand for territories. Subsequently, the national dialogue of 2000 convened to discuss public policies for the eradication of poverty, and various social sectors formalized their proposal for a Constituent Assembly to completely reform the CPE and give way to a state that recognizes the cultural plurality of the Bolivian people and their various political, social, and economic expressions.

As members of the Confederation of Indigenous Peoples of Eastern Bolivia and of the Unity Pact, Bolivian Guaraní People have an important presence in and impact on the constituent process[3] and were direct participants in the Constituent Assembly (2006–2007). According to some analysts, the Bolivian constituent process began with the "First Indigenous March for Territory and Dignity" in 1990, in which Guaraní people participated. The march signified the first direct challenge to the Bolivian Republic and its constitution as a monocultural nation-state, due to the state's exclusion of the country's ethnic diversity and Indigenous Peoples' rights. With this mobilization and subsequent actions, modifications to the CPE were pushed to the fore. Later, in 2000, different social sectors formalized their proposal for a Constituent Assembly to completely reform the CPE and make way for a plurinational state that would recognize the Bolivian peoples' cultural plurality and their political, social, and economic diversity. This message was embraced by the Movement toward Socialism (MAS in its Spanish acronym) as part of its governmental program when it assumed power in 2005 under Evo Morales, who ultimately convened the 2006 Constituent Assembly.

The proposal from the APG, presented during public hearings, clearly expresses Indigenous concerns regarding the dismantling of their territory, reduction of their communitarian lands, and the overlaying of state political-administrative structures over their own:

> Currently, [I]ndigenous territories are experiencing an overlaying of responsibilities and competencies based on our country's political-administrative division. On the one hand, we are divided into provinces, and within these, sections and cantons further fragment our traditional administrative units. With municipal territorialization extending from urban boundaries into rural areas, based on the section, not only territorial but also political jurisdiction has been affected, since it generated a duality of authorities, which, until this day, has not been resolved in certain communities and captaincies.
>
> On the other hand, with the 1996 National Institute of Agrarian Reform Law of 1715, Native Communitarian Lands, a form of collective ownership, was recognized. However, unrealistic limitations are placed on the domain of traditional property, since our initial demands had been reformulated by several governments,

> according to third-party interests. The goal is to avoid our lands being considered as part of the legal regularisation of ownership rights in Native Communitarian Lands. In other words, our traditional territorial units have been affected and reduced by the TCOs themselves.
>
> Subsequently, Indigenous Districts and Municipalities are created within captaincies, establishing Presidents of Base Territorial Organizations and Deputy Mayors; likewise, we have authorities in the cantons and the provinces and departments that further fragment the Guaraní TËTAGUASU ["big house," capitalization in original] and with this, Guaraní territorial integrity. (APG de Bolivia 2008, 12)

The above excerpt describes the way in which Guaraní territory has been fragmented by colonial violence, the Bolivian Republic's political-administrative divisions, natural resource extraction, and even, contradictorily, by the saneamiento process itself, as implemented under the INRA law. The result, over time, is the assignment of differing territorialities to the same space, so that Guaraní territory and culture is subsumed into a Chaco identity, minimizing and rendering inferior that which was originally Indigenous (see Quiroga and Tytelman, this volume).

During this history of Indigenous struggles for the reconstitution of their territory and recovery of their communitarian lands, the intrinsic value and meaning for Indigenous Peoples' life projects must be highlighted. The Bolivian anthropologist Sarela Paz explains the concept of Indigenous territory from a socio-political perspective, pointing out that "the concept of [I]ndigenous territory constitutes a certain type of law, a category of historic vindication, a unit of natural resources, and a discursive practice that interweaves issues of citizenship with [I]ndigenous identity mobilization" (1998, 1). This wide-ranging and complex concept of what territory signifies for Indigenous Peoples reaches beyond the legal category of the TCOs. This would explain why contradictions appeared when the INRA law was applied during processes of saneamiento of agrarian property, because the definition of collective land tenure was based on state positivist law as opposed to concepts of traditional access determined by customary norms, kinship relations, social affinities, and family loyalties to local powers, which also enshrine concepts of rights.

Despite gaps and contradictions in the law and its application, Paz points out that Indigenous territories constitute a political practice that generates discourse and builds identity, denoting the symbolic nature and political transcendence of collective forms of land ownership:

> Native Communitarian Lands provide not only a pragmatic proposal of concession or land-granting on the part of the state, but—and fundamentally—a subjective sense of the constitution of [I]ndigenous citizenship as a function of territory, which when projected to society in general, creates relationships not only between the state and [I]ndigenous people, but also between [I]ndigenous people and the "others." (8)

For Indigenous Peoples in general, and in this particular case the Guaraní People, the TCO constitutes a motive for mobilization and a principal demand on the state and its administrative bodies because it is the fundamental anchor for their reconstitution as political and social subjects. In the same vein and based on research in the Guaraní territory of Itika Guasu (O'Connor province, department of Tarija) Penelope Anthias (2022) points out that, despite contradictions in the formulation of the concept and implementation of saneamiento processes, the TCOs, within the framework of the INRA Law No. 1715 and its subsequent modifications (Law No. 3545), were the main axis of Indigenous claims. Moving beyond just one category of land tenure, the TCOs are a vehicle for a wider proposal of "territorial demand," which pushes the limits of state cartography and Bolivian agrarian law.

Furthermore, as explained by Alba Van der Valk et al. in their (2011) exploration of the coloniality of power in Caraparí, the current notion of territory that underlies the Guaraní imaginary has more to do with a historical claim to a right and an issue of identity than with a concrete definition of space: "Territory for Guaraní communities more clearly represents a longing than a definite idea or statement; it is a condition for defining their Indigenous identity. Territorial reconstitution is a political struggle (a vindication) for a right to identity, which is vetoed or denied by the non-Indigenous and the state" (Interview in Tarija, 2018).

In the words of a Guaraní leader, mburuvicha (chief) Víctor Barrios, from the Karaparí Zone, territory was the big house that protected the source of life and allowed the Ñande Reko to survive: "If we wanted food or needed medicine, we could get it from the hillsides; we could raise our animals with no problems and our crops produced well; we lived in peace with our culture. But now we have to request permission and we don't have the TCO; we are already ceasing to be Guaraní" (Interview in Caraparí, 2019). In the Guaraní People's worldview, territory is strongly linked to the ideal of Ɨvɨ Maraëi, understood to be the land where full potential is realized according to Ñande Reko and where Iyambae (being free without an owner), Mbaeyekou (spiritual or material wealth), and Yerovia Katu (collective happiness) are possible (Siquier and Caurey 2017).

Limitations of the Plurinational State Facing Extractivism

A central axis of economic policy during the MAS government (2006–2019) was the recovery of surplus rents and state control over the hydrocarbon industry, which involved charging higher production taxes as well as signing new operational contracts controlled by the state company Yacimientos Petrolíferos Fiscales Bolivianos (YPFB). Thanks to the considerable public income generated (more than thirty-seven billion USD between 2006 and 2019 [YPFB 2019]), it was once again possible to expand state bureaucracy, infrastructure construction, and social policy based mostly on direct cash transfer programmes and poverty alleviation.

The mining and hydrocarbon industries contributed significantly to the growth of Bolivia's GDP during this period. For several years, Bolivia obtained first place in the region, displaying growth indicators that were unprecedented in its economic history. However, a growing dependence on the export of these commodities and their international market variances gave rise to a rent-seeking state, demonstrated not only by the distribution of surplus but also by its public spending priorities. The result was the intensification of a tertiary and informal economy, with certain privileged sectors maintaining the logic of capital (Arze 2016).

From his standpoint, former Vice President of Bolivia, Alvaro García Linera summarizes the essence of the political, economic, and social model as a social system under construction, with advances and setbacks; one which empowers the state to act as a mechanism for wealth creation and redistribution in society, especially among the poorest and most needy. However, the former official also recognizes that this model generates a series of negative consequences for the environment, which then also affect people. Unlike capitalist logic, the project of communitarian socialism, or living well, is based on the use value of natural resources and incorporates a relationship of interdependence between community and nature (2011, 67).

It should be clarified that the "living well" concept originates from a translation of Suma Qamaña (Aymara), Sumaj Kawsay (Quechua), and Yaiko Kavi (Guaraní) in an attempt to establish equivalence and comparison between Indigenous concepts and the term "development," typical of the Western ideal of a good life and understood as progress derived from material growth. The comparison allows for the observation of different logics within both propositions about "ideal" conditions and ways of life, as well as of roots in totally different and even conflicting premises (Prada 2011). Starting with state transformation processes, engendered by the new constitution, an attempt was made to internalize the living well paradigm—which proposes, as a fundamental condition, the harmonious relationship between what modernity conceives as "human beings" and "nature"—as the new civilizational frame of reference for government plans. However, subsequent public policy continued to deepen the extractivist model, justified by the need to socially distribute part of the surplus, generating a logic of increasing dependence on rents.

Based on several countries' experiences, including that of Bolivia, the researcher, ecologist, and social scientist Eduardo Gudynas describes how surpluses generated by extractive industries cause a serious contradiction for redistributive policies as they relate to the benefits:

> A considerable part of these surpluses is possible as long as governments and significant social sectors continue to agree to tolerate social and environmental externalities and to settle for collecting taxes and royalties, in certain situations. Readjusted conservative extractivist regimes estimate that part of the surplus can be poured into social benefits, while progressives try to capture a larger proportion thereof, justifying this is necessary to finance

> monetized social assistance. In one way or another, the promotion of economic compensation is the result.
>
> Gradually, extractive activities generate a spill-over effect where the struggle for surpluses becomes increasingly important. Disputes turn their focus to income or economic compensation and are no longer about the phenomenon of surpluses or even about their origin in extractivism. (2015, 229–230)

This is the central contradiction ensconced in the Bolivian model, which finally came to light with the 2011 conflict of the Isiboro Secure National Park and Indigenous Territory and the Aguaragüe Park in the Chaco. Three breaking points in the political project of the new Plurinational State reveal themselves: the violation of the right to prior consultation as a principle of Indigenous Peoples' self-determination, because it allegedly contradicts the "national" interest (Paz 2012); the intensification of the extractivist model to sustain a rentier state; and a project of identity-related, economic, territorial, and political recolonization (Makaran and López 2018).

It is worth highlighting that one of the most important achievements of Bolivian Indigenous Peoples in terms of collective rights is, without doubt, the prior, free, and informed consultation by states when administrative or legislative measures may directly affect communities and their territories, the goal being to reach an agreement or obtain consent (ILO Convention 169). Through the existence of several laws, this right is recognized as having been established in Bolivia since 1991 and later incorporated into the existing constitution of the Plurinational State in 2009.[4]

According to the umbrella organizations of Indigenous Nations and Peoples in the Bolivian lowlands and highlands, especially those affected by mining and hydrocarbon extraction, prior consultation has not been carried out as established in the law or the results of that consultation have been ignored by state administrators. A variety of factors are cited, such as the complexity of its application, ignorance of the scope of the norm, and contradiction with the prevailing economic model and the political priorities of sectors close to government (Aylwin and Tamburini 2015).

Prior consultation is the effective materialization of the right to Indigenous Peoples' self-determination, as well as the path for states to sincerely demonstrate their pluralist and non-colonial orientation, leaving behind the tutelage of and domination over Indigenous Peoples and territories (Yrigoyen 2013). Consequently, the plurinational nature of the Bolivian state is focused on this right, and its violation implies a denial of its ethos. During the second Morales government (2010–2014), there was an attempted agreement to a specific regulatory law regarding prior consultation, resulting principally from conflicts with Guaraní people in the Chaco. However, it was dismissed because of a lack of agreement between Indigenous and government interlocutors on the scope of the bill. Subsequently, the MAS government chose to pass contradictory laws, such as The Law of Mother Earth, with a merely developmentalist perspective, as well as Supreme Decrees limiting prior consultation and compensation for socio-environmental impacts and opening the doors to hydrocarbon exploration and exploitation in protected areas and TCOs.

Such measures clearly revealed the decision to limit and roll back major advances in rights achieved by Indigenous Peoples in recent times to guarantee the economic model. In the words of Morales himself, during the inaugural ceremony of a seismic exploration project in Camiri-Santa Cruz: "It is impossible so much time is wasted on these so-called consultations, this is our state's great weakness" (qtd. in "Evo" 2015).

DISPOSSESSION AND RECONSTITUTION OF THE GUARANÍ TERRITORY OF KARAPARI

Reorganization of Karaparí Guaraní Communities and their Struggle for Land

The Karaparí Zonal Captaincy was one of the last to reorganize and join the APG, due mainly to their subjugation to the hacienda system and their vulnerability to the hostile and exclusionary environment of discrimination toward Indigenous People, which had resulted in the denial of their fundamental rights. According to various leaders, the reunification of the Guaraní families and the rearticulation of the communities in the APG during the late 1990s and early 2000s resulted when national Guaraní and local leaders broadcast information about Indigenous rights and presented the APG as their parent organization for the first time.

Román Gómez Lopez, Regional Assemblyman of the Guaraní People, previously the Mburuvicha Guasu (Grand Captain) of Karaparí,[5] recounts that between 1990 and 1992, initial attempts to reorganize communities produced limited results. However, after 1998, a few communities began organizing thanks to new leaders trained through their participation in national APG assemblies. Later, according to Mburuvicha Víctor Barrios Segundo,[6] APG leaders arrived from Camiri to publicize the existence of the Indigenous organization and to promote a new appreciation of Guaraní culture. Popular reporters were trained and radio programs aired to inform communities who were unaware of the organization and were losing their culture.

Karaparí Guaraní communities organized as a Zonal Captaincy long after other sectors of Bolivian Guaraní People. It was only in 2005 that community articulation began through members of the Zonal Captaincy of the Karaparí Guaraní People. According to leaders, community members were unaware of how to establish the organization and were therefore unprepared when legal land titling clearing procedures were enacted. From the beginning of the Guaraní communities' reorganization process, opposition and violence emanated from municipal peasant and ranching sectors, who considered Guaraní organization a threat to their ownership over lands claimed by Indigenous People. The Mburuvicha Barrios explains:

> One of the first to promote Indigenous organization was the Mburuvicha Benito Díaz; in 2004, he participated in meetings of the Bolivian APG and brought the initiative to our communities. The bosses beat him, burned down his house, and tried to get him off their land. He was a farm worker and wanted a small plot for his family, and that's why they beat him, tied him up, and whipped him. He denounced the situation to another Guaraní Captaincy and support was forthcoming so that further abuses could be prevented and to start organizing. (Interview in Caraparí, 2019)

According to Guaraní leaders, this slow and fragile process of community reorganization was related to the Guaraní majority's lack of knowledge about their rights, a determining factor working against their claims for land. Subsequently, these claims were presented to the Bolivian state by the APG but were poorly executed in the field phase by the National Institute of Agrarian Reform.

For his part, the Mburuvicha Roman Gomez explains why the organization was unable to establish itself earlier, due to fears of repression by bosses and discrimination from the general public:

> Leaders were afraid of the organization becoming visible to the bosses. Most of the men in the Guaraní communities were working for the boss and could only work for themselves and their families on Sundays. Some young people no longer wanted to be Indigenous; they did not want to be recognized as Guaraní in order to avoid discrimination. At school we were discriminated against, even teachers called us ava, chawanko,[7] and other disparaging names. (Interview in Caraparí, 2019)

In the municipality of Caraparí, Guaraní identity was hidden for many years, including by Indigenous people themselves, to avoid discrimination from bosses. Migrants arriving from the valleys displaced Guaraní families from their lands and subjugated them economically to maintain them in conditions of servitude. This is how the Mburuvicha Verónica Roca[8] tells it: "It was as if we were enclosed; we were ashamed to admit we were Guaraní. Our grandparents and parents had no knowledge of laws and rights. Many went to Argentina to work when the bosses arrived. Families arriving from Tarija settled in the area and remained as owners in my community" (Interview in Santa Rosa community, 2019).

Another factor preventing Guaraní organizational resurgence was the imposition of a new territorial structure in rural Bolivia, created by the 1994 Popular Participation Law No. 1551, during the Government of Gonzalo Sánchez de Lozada. This regulation provided for a different type of municipal organization, incorporating rural areas of provincial sections previously administered at the departmental level into municipal jurisdiction, and creating OTBs[9] as community or neighbourhood units. OTBs acquired legal status and were incorporated into mechanisms of social control, thereby empowering non-Indigenous community organizations to exercise territorial hegemony.

In the case of Caraparí Municipality, considering the situation of territorial dispossession of the Guaraní, the OTBs consolidated peasants' and ranchers' political and social power to the detriment of Indigenous communities. The Mburuvicha Gomez confirms this experience in Guaraní communities in the municipality, clarifying that the initial weakness of the Indigenous organization allowed OTBs to be controlled by peasants and ranchers who subjugated Indigenous families and communities. As a result, this newly established land tenure system excludes the Indigenous territorial presence, while a political and social state structure subjugates the Indigenous organization, thereby limiting, to a large extent, the exercise of individual and collective rights.

Due to the power of hacienda owners and their influence over INRA officials—as illustrated in the research of Van der Valk et al. (2011)—the saneamiento process over legal land ownership in the municipality of Caraparí ignored the existence of Indigenous families and communities and consolidated the rights of peasants and ranchers. In the words of Mburuvicha Román Gómez:

> In the beginning of saneamiento , INRA ignored the APG Karaparí because it lacked legal status and coordinated only with the Territorial Base Organizations [OTBs], that is, with peasants and hacienda owners. If communities did not have legal status, they were not taken into account; as far as INRA was concerned, no Guaraní organization existed. Besides, peasant OTBs, already benefitting from territorial recognition, were superimposed over Indigenous communities. When the APG requested legal status for Guaraní communities from the Caraparí Municipal Council, it was denied, given that councilors linked to the haciendas or peasant communities didn't want Guaraní communities to have their own space. (Interview in Caraparí, 2019)

As a result, most families in this area still do not have the right to their own space, or they live on reduced pieces of land adjoining haciendas, peasant communities, or urbanized areas, which are insufficient for the development of individual productive activities.

Additionally, in response to the many complaints and social conflicts, originating with the saneamiento process executed by the state, the Bolivian ombudsman issued a report in 2004 which, regarding the municipality of Caraparí in the Gran Chaco of Tarija, says: "INRA has prioritized land ownership clarification processes in areas where oil companies are operating, noting that they even finance the institution's work in order to receive preferential treatment" (Defensor del Pueblo 2004). According to accounts from Karaparí Guaraní leaders, INRA technicians carried out their field work solely in coordination with oil company representatives and private landowners, deliberately ignoring the existence of Indigenous families and minimizing the ancestrally occupied territory of the Guaraní communities.

In 2011, once a consolidated captaincy of the APG Karaparí was in place, a petition was presented to the Bolivian state for the endowment of TCOs throughout the entire municipality of Caraparí, due to the exclusion of Indigenous families and communities from the prior, simplified land ownership clarification procedure. As a result, the saneamiento process was modified to meet the Indigenous demand, but with an adverse reaction from municipal peasants and cattle ranchers, who undertook a misinformation and intimidation campaign against the APG. The Mburuvicha Roca recounts how this scenario played out and describes its consequences:

> In 2011, Guaraní leaders analyzed the result of the saneamiento process and the situation of the majority of families who were left without land. A claim was presented to the Land Vice Ministry—the request for a TCO having been formulated in consensus with the Captaincy—demanding all identified municipal public land be granted to Guaraní communities. Later, all communities received a visit, which included representatives from ranchers, peasants, the ombudsman's office, and a report was filed. There was enormous resistance and pressure, especially from peasants who even had support from the mayor himself. (Interview in the Santa Rosa community, 2019)

Due to this pressure, and without having been able to effectively verify the TCO saneamiento process, peasants and the Karaparí APG reached an agreement that identified public lands would be apportioned equally to both plaintiffs. Despite the unfavorable treatment of the Guaraní People, to date the agreement has not been fulfilled. INRA does not provide data about available public lands nor about reductions to unused lands on individual properties (haciendas) when they do not comply with the "social economic function" as defined by law.

Additionally, according to official 2008 reports from the Ministries of Justice and Labour, many Guaraní families remained captive on haciendas in the municipality of Caraparí, paying off unjust debts incurred over generations. These debts accumulated as bosses underpaid their Indigenous workers, exchanging food and clothing for their undervalued labour.[10]

Lawyer Juan Carlos Aróstegui, former consultant to the International Labour Organization, describes this problem:

> With participation from the Ministry of Labour, extreme situations of servitude and slave-like conditions of Guaraní families in Caraparí were identified. They found cases in which Guaraní workers, who had served employers for more than twenty years, were denied fair remuneration and social benefits stipulated by law. Some bosses dared to laugh (when they were sued) because the debt they would have to pay to compensate Indigenous peons' labour rights was extremely high and they argued workers had been paid with food and clothing for their families. Some of these cases were resolved favorably, but others were not effectively followed up by the Ministry and leaders themselves. (Interview in Tarija, 2018)

This subjugation of Guaraní communities to cattle ranches was aggravated by their exclusion from essential state services, such as health and education. When Indigenous communities did not exist as territorial units, local governments did not provide services in accordance with their respective cultural orientation, thereby fomenting the assimilation of the Indigenous population into consistently disrespectful conventional systems. It came to the point where Guaraní parents would prohibit children from speaking their language so they would not be discriminated against in public schools, while Indigenous women avoided receiving care in health centres for fear of mistreatment by staff.

The Denial of Indigenous Rights Today

The Guaraní People of the Karaparí Zone are currently organized into twenty-one communities scattered throughout six districts, both rural and urban, of the Caraparí Municipality of the Tarijeño Gran Chaco Region. These communities are composed of families of Guaraní Indigenous origin, as well as those of criollo or peasant origin, who—mainly due to family relationships or social affinity—have joined the Guaraní organization. It should be noted that in the municipality, there are a total of forty-five communities in the rural area, meaning communities with an Indigenous presence represent 47 percent (Asamblea Regional del Gran Chaco Tarijeño 2015).

According to the census prepared by the Indigenous organization in 2015, with the support of the NGO CERDET, 510 families in 21 Guaraní communities (for a total of 1,399 people) had been registered. In comparison with previous data provided by the Diagnostic of Guaraní People in the Department of Tarija, published by the Tarija Council of Guaraní Captains and the Ministry of Justice in 2009, it is clear there was relative growth in the number of communities as well as affiliated families. Taking these data into account in the current municipal context, it is clear that the Indigenous organization has been strengthened by a larger demographic presence, which effectively promotes increased political and social empowerment of the Guaraní identity. However, living conditions for most Guaraní families have not changed significantly with respect to indicators of past administrations. For example, 40 percent of Guaraní families do not have safe drinking water in their homes and only 50 percent of families have electricity. A total of nearly 500 cultivated hectares in all 21 communities amounts to an average of one hectare per family, an insufficient amount of land to generate surpluses, according to traditional practices and the area's agroecological conditions. Likewise, data regarding other productive activities for Guaraní family sustenance, such as livestock, hunting or fishing, harvesting, or the sale of their labour, reveal an economic situation of mere survival.

Currently, a woman directs the Assembly of the Guaraní People of the communities of the Karaparí Zone, the Mburuvicha Justina Suarez. She describes the Indigenous families' situation in the following terms:

> We do not have sufficient land; our families suffer many unmet needs—there is not enough for our children; the authorities have taken our land. Before we could hunt, now everything is closed and prohibited. Now we cannot even get a log [wood] to build our houses. Besides, oil companies have arrived in our territory and destroyed everything. Some families only have a quarter hectare of land and it's not enough. In my community, Arorenda, we are five families living in a single house and we have no land. There are families with ten or more children and it's very hard. Peasants arriving from other places have more land. (Interview in the Arorenda community, 2019)

These structural conditions produce an extremely precarious reality for Guaraní families and communities, considering their limited access to land and their dependence on temporary work on local farms and in oil companies. In the words of the Mburuvicha Roca, this Indigenous reality continues to be ignored by local authorities and undermined by state political changes:

> The authorities say that (Karaparí) is Guaraní territory, but it is only talk. Many say the Guaraní do not exist. It is contradictory that some authorities recognize the Guaraní people but deny them their rights. The Bolivian constitution recognizes our rights as an Indigenous People, but the state officials [who work in local governments] refuse to attend to us. (Interview in Santa Rosa community, 2019)

Likewise, exclusion is manifested in the systematic neglect of Indigenous Peoples' legitimate demands for participation in public planning and budgeting. This exclusion reveals a policy of subordination despite regulations that exist to protect the rights they have achieved and despite changes incorporated into the political structure such as the declaration of a plurinational state. The Mburuvicha Gabriel Baldiviezo, current Director of the Guaraní in the Regional Autonomous Government of Carapari, summarizes this situation as follows:

> Support from the municipality is not sufficient; doors are closed to us. We are not taken into account in the Annual Operational Plans of the Carapari Municipal Government. The mayor says assistance reaches all mixed communities, but it only reaches peasants; the peasants exclude us from their meetings and we don't know which benefits arrive. With the Regional Government, things are improving somewhat; a little help arrives for the communities, but resources are lacking. (Interview in the Guabiyurenda community, 2019)

By contrast, lawyer Miguel Gallardo, legal advisor to INRA in the legal clearing of land titles in the municipality of Caraparí, former cabinet coordinator for the Caraparí municipal mayor, and former representative of the ombudsman in Chaco, describes his experience:

> Projects executed by the mayor's office respond to the common good: for example, local roads. But racism and discrimination of the Guaraní still exist, in both urban and rural areas, although it is gradually becoming less, thanks to favorable regulations regarding Indigenous People. Programs and projects must respond to certain public investment criteria; for example, in the case of latrine construction for basic sanitation or drinking water infrastructure, home ownership (legal papers) must be demonstrable, and the system is not set up to identify beneficiaries as Indigenous or peasants, in order to differentiate. Besides, situations of internal conflict in mixed communities arise between Indigenous and peasant families, making public investment difficult. (Interview in Caraparí, 2018)

Gallardo highlights that state structures and public servants at the local level continue to operate according to a monocultural logic, as evident in the content of municipal plans and the way they are drawn up: the vision of development planning continues to be very general and does not allow differentiation according to cultural characteristics in the municipality. The first steps are still being taken to change these planning and public management models, but guidance from planning technicians in drawing up plans is missing.

In addition to territorial dispossession suffered by Guaraní families and communities during colonization, and the municipality's deficient land titling clearing process, there is also hydrocarbon exploration and exploitation in particular areas, which results in repeated rights violations (though these are denied by the state). Mburuvicha Barrios clarifies that oil companies do not take Indigenous communities into consideration in their studies and projects; they limit jobs for Guaraní families and ignore Indigenous rights such as prior consultation and compensation:

> Indigenous communities are never taken into account; only a few non-Indigenous families and communities receive or negotiate compensation with the oil companies. In 2012, interested persons (of the Guaraní People) in accessing a job had the endorsement of our organization, but the companies operating in the area would not accept it and requested endorsement from the OTBs, which rejected Indigenous people. Only since 2015 has the company [REPSOL] recognized the APG as an organization representing the communities of the Guaraní People of Karaparí. (Interview in Caraparí, 2019)

In February 2019, a leaders' meeting of the Karaparí APG was organized in the community of Santa Rosa to discuss the ways in which one REPSOL project was violating their rights. Company representatives explained the guidelines under which the industry operated, based on the current regulations and conditions imposed by the Bolivian State:

> REPSOL respects all Guaraní communities in the area, as well as their organization, the APG and its leaders. It has always tried to maintain good relations with communities in its areas of operation. If prior consultation about the project was not carried out, it is because the Guaraní communities or the TCO are not directly affected. Even so, based on company policy, an agreement has been reached with the Municipal Government [of Caraparí] to transfer resources for the development of communities adjacent to the project, among which is [only] one Guaraní community. But other benefits cannot be granted to additional Guaraní communities in the Zone because they do not fall within the area of influence nor are they considered to be a TCO. Therefore, the one commitment the company can assume is to provide information of public knowledge concerning its operations in the municipality. Only in the event that construction or a project affects an Indigenous community will a prior consultation procedure go ahead. But, even in this case, the operational leader is the state company, YPFB, while REPSOL is only the field operator. Therefore, additional information should be provided by YPFB or the Ministry of Hydrocarbons. (Personal notes from the APG-REPSOL meeting, February 15, 2019, Santa Rosa Community, Caraparí)

As can be seen by these statements, the company refuses to recognize that Guaraní communities are affected by its activities and likewise denies their right to prior consultation and compensation, based on its interpretation of the norm. This refusal occurs despite the fact that, in its Environmental Impact Assessment, the entire area is explicitly recognized as forming part of the Guaraní People's ancestral territory (Tarija Eco Gestión S.R.L. y REPSOL 2016, Chapter 2). In addition, the company's stance illustrates that the state—through the YPFB and the sector ministry—adopts the role of facilitator for the industrial sector, all the while refusing to entertain a meeting with the Indigenous organization, despite leaders' repeated attempts at communication.

Currently, the intensification of this extractivist logic in Indigenous territory, compounded by the permanent denial of their rights, is leading to further deterioration of the social, cultural, and economic structures of the decimated Guaraní population and is directly threatening the territorial demand of the Guaraní People and their life project.

CONCLUSION

The history of the Guaraní People is one of territorial dispossession, echoing conditions endured by many Indigenous Peoples at different times and under different socio-political conditions. The particular case of Guaraní communities of the Karaparí Zone in the Gran Chaco is a paradigmatic example of colonial violence reproduced in the republic and maintained even in the new Plurinational State, despite structural changes to public regulations and institutions. Colonial thinking persists at all levels of state administration, sustaining an anti-Indigenous perspective and systematically denying the collective rights of Indigenous Nations and Peoples who constitute and provide meaning to the ethos of the new social pact. At the same time, this thinking, typical of modernity, promotes a developmental perspective based on an extractivist and rentier model, which, in practice, contradicts the Guaraní worldview of harmony and balance in the Ɨvɨ Guasu (Guaraní territory/world), even though official discourse proclaims the opposite.

Territorial dispossession of Guaraní communities in the Karaparí Zone was achieved through the plundering of community lands and the establishment of the hacienda regime, under which Indigenous families were subjected to generations of indentured servitude, both before and after the creation of the Republic of Bolivia. Even in the new Plurinational State, access to land is denied to the Guaraní people, while their collective right is subordinated to economic priorities based on hydrocarbons, thereby promoting internal recolonization of their ancestral territory. This historic process of dispossession and denial of rights has led to the exclusion of Indigenous identity in the municipality, to the extent that the state denies the existence of Indigenous communities and minimizes their cultural legacy. The intent is to mobilize colonial entanglements to conceal diversity and homogenize Chaco identity under the image of the modern creole product of colonial heritage.

Deliberate discriminatory behaviour against the Karaparí Guaraní People is promoted by local power elites who enact not only a pattern of inherited coloniality but also a new mestizo social hegemony, originating with migrants linked to central government power structures. The struggle of the Guaraní People of Karaparí is the struggle for inclusion in the Plurinational State to exercise their collective rights to land and self-determination, reconstituting their territory, and practicing their traditional way of life.

NOTES

1. This is the umbrella organization representing all communities of the Guaraní People of Bolivia.
2. Several factors shed light on the case of Guaraní families living in a state of servitude—that is, in forms of forced labour in which individuals perform labour without remuneration and under coercion to pay off a debt. These included: the articulation of Indigenous communities with their parent organization the APG (1987), the intervention of the Catholic Church, social investigations, and ILO reports, which culminated in the ratification in Bolivia of ILO Convention 29 through Law 3031 in April 2005 and the subsequent Supreme Decrees (Sánchez and Miranda 2014).
3. The modifications to the CPE that occurred in 1994 were followed by agrarian reform through the INRA Law (No. 1715) of 1996, which included the category of Community Lands of Origin, in response to the Indigenous demand for territories. Subsequently, the national dialogue of 2000 convened to discuss public policies for the eradication of poverty, and various social sectors formalized their proposal for a Constituent Assembly to completely reform the CPE and give way to a state that recognizes cultural plurality of the Bolivian people and their various political, social, and economic expressions.
4. The new political constitution of the Plurinational State of Bolivia attempts to reflect the plurality and diversity of the composition and origin of the Bolivian people, their cultural expressions, practices, and political forms. It also reflects types of economic organization based on the recognition of the pre-existence of the Indigenous Nations and Peoples to the state itself. For this reason, one of the central parts of the new Mother Law is the Charter of Collective Rights of these pre-existing Nations and Peoples.
5. He was a zonal leader of the Guaraní People (former Great Captain of the Karaparí Zone 2010–2012). Current or former leaders and officers are called Mburuvicha (authority) or Captain even if they no longer hold a position in the Guaraní organization.
6. He was a zonal leader of the Guaraní People (former Captain Grande of the Karaparí Zone 2016–2018).
7. "Ava" is a Guaraní word meaning Indigenous man, but non-Indigenous people use it with contempt to identify Guaraní people. "Chawanko" or "chaguanco" is of Quechua origin, meaning "skinny legs," alluding to the physical appearance of Indigenous people who worked as farm labourers.

8. Roca is the current Head of Land and Territory of the APG Karaparí. Previously she was Mburuvicha Zonal from 2012 to 2014.
9. The Popular Participation Law No.1551 of 1994, established the Territorial Base Organizations as a form of recognition of the existence of community organizations that represented the population of a certain territory within the urban-rural municipalities, granting them legal status and accrediting their right to participate in the redistribution of tax sharing resources at the subnational level.
10. Until 2000, more than 50 percent of the Guaraní population of the communities in the Karaparí Zone did not own a Bolivian state-issued personal identification document, which was like saying "they did not exist" (CCGT 2010).

REFERENCES

Asamblea Regional del Gran Chaco Tarijeño. 2015. *Plan de desarrollo regional del Gran Chaco Tarijeño 2013–2017*. ARGCH.

Anthias, P. 2018. *Limits to Decolonization: Indigeneity, Territory and Hydrocarbon Politics in the Bolivian Chaco*. Cornell University Press.

Anthias, Penelope. 2022. *Límites a la descolonización: Territorios indígenas y política de hidrocarburos en el Chaco boliviano*. Plural Editores.

APG de Bolivia. 2008. *Plan estratégico de la Nación Guaraní: situación y plan de vida*, edited by Daniel Zapata. IBIS Dinamarca.

APG-ZK and CERDET. 2017. Plan de gestión territorial indígena de la capitanía Zona Karaparí. Oxfam.

Ardaya, Gloria, Mónica Moraes, and Carlos Toranzo, eds. 1998. *Tarija. Pobreza, género y medio ambiente*. Muela del Diablo Ed.

Arze Vargas, Carlos. 2016. "Una década de gobierno ¿Construyendo el Vivir Bien o un capitalismo salvaje?" CEDLA, Revista fiscal 17. https://cedla.org/publicaciones/pfyd/revista-fiscal-17-una-decada-de-gobierno-construyendo-el-vivir-bien-o-un-capitalismo-salvaje/

Asamblea del Pueblo Guaraní (APG) de Bolivia. 2006. "Propuesta hacia la Asamblea Constituyente." Chaco Boliviano: APG.

Aylwin, José, and Leonardo Tamburini, eds. 2015. *Convenio 169 de la OIT: los desafíos de su implementación en América Latina a 25 años de su aprobación*. Grupo Internacional de Trabajo sobre Asuntos Indígenas.

Caurey, Elías. 2012. *Nación Guaraní: ñamae ñande rekore—una mirada a nuestro modo de ser*. Imp. Preview-Gráfica.

CCGT (Consejo de Capitanes Guaraní de Tarija) and Ministerio de Justicia de Bolivia. 2010. "Diagnóstico Socioeconómico del Pueblo Guaraní del Departamento de Tarija." COSUDE; Imp. Ed. Bellas Artes.

Defensor del Pueblo. 2004. *Informe especial: los derechos a la propiedad, la tenencia de la tierra y el proceso de saneamiento*. Ed. Presencia.

Defensoría del Pueblo. 2016. *Informe: sin los Pueblos Indígenas no hay estado plurinacional*. Editorial GRECO.

Díez Astete, Alvaro. 2012. "Estado del arte sobre la cultura Guaraní en Bolivia." *Inventario del universo Guarani*. CRESPIAL-UNESCO.

Estado Plurinacional. 2009. *Constitución política del estado*. Gaceta Oficial de Bolivia.

"Evo: en la consulta previa se pierde mucho tiempo." *Correos del sur*, 13 July 2015. https://correodelsur.com/politica/20150713/evo-en-la-consulta-previa-se-pierde-mucho-tiempo.html.

García Linera, Alvaro. 2011. *Las tensiones creativas de la revolución: la quinta fase del Proceso de Cambio*. Vicepresidencia del Estado Plurinacional de Bolivia.

Gudynas, Eduardo. 2015. *Extractivismos: ecología, economía y política de un modo de entender el desarrollo y la naturaleza*. CLAES—CEDIB. Imp. Sagitario.

Gustafson, Bret. 2020. "La política del gas natural y los límites de la autonomía guaraní en Bolivia: reflexiones sobre la época de Evo Morales." *Etnografías contemporáneas* 6 (11): 114–132.

Makaran, Gaya, and Pavel López. 2018. *Recolonización en Bolivia: neonacionalismo extractivista y resistencia comunitaria*. Universidad Nacional Autónoma de México—Centro de Investigaciones sobre América Latina y el Caribe, Bajo Tierra Editorial.

Melia, Bartomeu. 1988. *Ñandereko, nuestro modo de ser*. CIPCA y Imp. Popular.

Orgaz García, Mirko. 2002. *La guerra del gas: nación versus estado transnacional en Bolivia*. OFAVIN.

Paz Patiño, Sarela. 1998. "Los territorios indígenas como reivindicación y práctica discursiva." *Revista nueva sociedad* 153 (January–February 1998): 120–129. https://nuso.org/revista/153/pueblos-indigenas-y-democracia/.

Pifarre, Francisco. 1989. *Historia de un pueblo*. CIPCA, Imp. Popular.

PNUD (Programa de las Naciones Unidas para el Desarrollo), George Gray Molina, coord. 2013. *Informe temático de desarrollo humano: la otra frontera: usos alternativos de recursos naturales en Bolivia*. PNUD. https://hdr.undp.org/en/content/la-otra-frontera.

Prada Alcoreza, Raúl. 2011. "El vivir bien como modelo de Estado y modelo económico." In *Más Allá del Desarrollo*, edited by Grupo Permanente de Trabajo sobre Alternativas al Desarrollo-Fundación Rosa Luxemburgo/Abya Yala. Imp. WA-GUI.

Richard, Nicolás. 2008. *Mala guerra, los indígenas en la Guerra del Chaco (1932–35)*. CoLibris Editions y Asunción: ServiLibro.

Saignes, Thierry, and Isabelle Combès, eds. 2007. *Historia del pueblo Chiriguano*. Plural Ed.

Sánchez, Miranda, and Ian Sergio. 2014. "El caso de las comunidades cautivas del Chaco chuquisaqueño: una mirada desde los organismos internacionales." *Barataria Revista Castellano-Manchega de Ciencias Sociales* 17: 165–176. https://revistabarataria.es/web/index.php/rb

Siquier, Gabriel, and Elías Caurey. 2017. *Ñanderu tüpa regua ñande reko rupi (Teología Guaraní)*. Porticus; Charagua—Iyambae.

Svampa, Maristella. 2019. *Las fronteras del neoextractivismo en América Latina: conflictos socioambientales, giro ecoterritorial y nuevas dependencias*. Bielefield University Press.

Tarija Eco Gestión S.R.L. and REPSOL. 2016. *Estudio de evaluación de impacto ambiental: analítico específico; perforación exploratoria del Pozo Boyuy X2, área Caipipendi*. REPSOL.

Van der Valk Tavera, Alba, Blanca Montaño Marquez, Silvia Flores Villca, et al. 2011. *Colonialidad del poder en carapari: estudio de la disputa por la tierra, relaciones de trabajo y autoridad*. Plural Ed.

Yrigoyen, Raquel. 2013. "Hacia una nueva relación del estado con los pueblos: autonomía, participación, consulta y consentimiento." *Revista Justicia y Democracia* 11. http://repositorio.amag.edu.pe/handle/123456789/191.

7

Paul Wattez

IYIYIWCH TERRITORIALITIES OF INTIMACY

WALKING, PADDLING, AND HUNTING ON NOCIMIC AND IYINIW ASTCHEE

INTRODUCTION

It is commonly observed that ancestral lands are constantly being (re) positioned and (re)affirmed by Indigenous Peoples as the central reference of their worlds. Working with the Iyiyiwch[1] in Northern Quebec, I have learned that they are no exception. Over the last fifteen years, I have been working with the Iyiyiwch on various issues, such as forestry management, socio-cultural transformations, local modes of transferring and protecting iyiyiw knowledge, and the heritage debate, and I continue to do collaborative educational feedback and work on conceptions of well-being. Through my interpersonal work-related activities with the Iyiyiwch, I have come to grasp that their manifold relationship to their ancestral territory has been maintained in various ways to adapt to the challenges, dilemmas, and impacts of colonialization on their lifeworld: first, through the fur trade and, in recent decades, through Canadian and Quebec state policies and the intensification of the presence of extractive industries and a non-Iyiyiw population (Feit 2004, Morantz 2002;

Scott 1986, 2018; Tanner 2004, 2007, 2014). Through these adaptations, the Iyiyiwch have managed to reproduce slightly different experiences with their land while, at the same time, generating new ones. Thus, while all the following words—nocimic and iyiniw astchee, on the one hand, and nhodo istchee and iyiyiw istchee, on the other—refer to the ancestral territory, from the perspective of the Waswanipi Iyiniwch, among whom I have conducted extensive fieldwork since 2008,[2] each emphasizes slightly different experiences of it.

This chapter takes, as a starting point, the slight difference between the various terms the Iyiyiwch use to speak of their ancestral land to explore the equivocality inherent in the concept of territory as used by the Iyiyiwch and the state respectively, and how this equivocality has played out in unexpected ways since the 1975 signing of the James Bay and Northern Quebec Agreement (JBNQA). One of the effects I highlight here is how the concept of territory becomes multivocal based on the various and intimate ways the Iyiyiwch continue to engage with the iyiyiw world (see chapters by Simon and Ruíz Fournier, this volume).

The JBNQA is considered the first modern treaty in Canada. At its heart were the recognition of the Indigenous title to the land and a clear demarcation of the rights associated with such title within a territory, as the latter is conceptualized by the state. In other words, a key issue for the Canadian/Quebecer colonial state was, through the delimitation of territorial jurisdictions, establishing regimes of property and rights within a perimeter of land. This would allow orderly negotiations needed to proceed with planned economic developments. For the Iyiyiwch, on the other hand, the major consideration in the negotiation of the JBNQA was to continue to live with the land and to practise their traditional activities, i.e., hunting, fishing, and trapping. Their main concern at the time was the state's refusal to recognize the vitality and endurance of a way of life that was far from vanishing. With the signing of the agreement, the "James Bay's Cree territory" (the perimeter of land with clearly stipulated rights and jurisdiction) was created. Simultaneously, an equivocal sense (Viveiros de Castro 2004) of "territory" was established as well: while the representatives of the Iyiyiwch and of the state governments both referred to the land, they were indeed affirming their own different territorial realities, with the former having a better understanding of what was at play than the latter, i.e., creating "multiple realities" and a "basic mode of articulation that constitutes heterogenous modes of existence and collectives" (Blaser, Poirier, and Anthias, introduction of this volume).

My contention is that this equivocation has had a domino effect on the practical meaning of all the terms that express the Iyiyiwch experience of their ancestral territory. An important consequence has been what I call the institutionalization of experiences of the land, meaning the involvement of Iyiyiwch regional and local administrations in the creation and organization of land-based activities. Such institutionalization has had an impact on the kinds of intimacies that the participants of these activities establish with the land. This process can be better understood by considering two other iyiyiw concepts: iyiyiw iituun, which means literally "iyiyiw ways of doing," and miyuu pitamtisiwn, which means literally "well-living/being" or "being well." More precisely, the ways in which the Iyiyiwch mobilize iyiyiw iituun during the land-based activities provide a hint as to how their relationship with the land is associated with its institutionalization or, on the contrary, with the kind of intimacy better expressed by miyuu pitamtisiwn. In that sense, the Iyiyiwch maintain a relationship with their ancestral territory that, as I propose in this chapter, is constructed through manifold territorial intimacies.

I begin by introducing the various terms the Iyiyiwch use to refer to their ancestral territory and discussing how responses to the challenges that colonial conceptions of territoriality posed to their way of life (including intimacy with their territories) resulted in entangling the latter with the former (Dussart and Poirier 2017). I then discuss how, coupled with the impacts of Indigenous colonization in Canada, this entanglement led to the institutionalization of the experiences of intimacy with the land. In the following sections, I focus on two instances of this institutionalization—hunting breaks and land excursions[3]— to illustrate how, even if they still enable intimate relations with the land, participants and the larger community perceive these practices ambivalently. My examination of institutionalization and the resulting ambivalence exposes the various results of the articulations, negotiations, and adjustments generated by the entanglements of territories within the Iyiyiw world.

EXPERIENCING THE ANCESTRAL TERRITORY

Since the negotiation of the JBNQA, the term "James Bay" was assumed to be equivalent to iyiyiw istchee or the ancestral territory of the Iyiyiwch, although there is much more to iyiyiw istchee, as the terms "nocimic" and "iyiniw astchee" are used in reference to it.

Nocimic emphasizes the experience of family-like relationships (Tanner 2004) between human persons and the "other-than-human persons" (Hallowell 1992, 64) who make up the Iyiyiw world. These notably include animals, winds, rivers, lakes, mountains, thunder, ice, and spirit beings, whether tutelary or not (Feit 2000, 141–143 and 1995, 184; Scott 2006, 1989; Tanner 1979). Iyiniw astchee, on the other hand, emphasizes the experience of inter-family (human) relationships enabled by current and historical types of political and social groupings: the community and the band. In other words, iyiniw astchee refers to the area of ancestral territory shared by a particular community. These experiences with and within their territory are closely associated with the values of reciprocity, mutual aid, and solidarity, fashioning closeness and intimacy between all persons (human and other-than-human) of the Iyiyiw world.

Aside from nocimic and iyiniw astchee, the Iyiyiwch use two further concepts to refer to their ancestral territory, but rather than being associated with experiences of intimacy with the land, they are associated with what would appear to an outsider as political claims of ownership. The concepts are nhodo istchee, the family hunting territory,[4] and iyiyiw istchee, the Cree Nation territory (the aggregate of all nhodo istchee). For the moment, let us say that these four concepts comprise the Iyiyiw land tenure system in its contemporary coexistence with Quebec and Canadian land tenure systems (Chaplier and Scott 2018, 51). In effect, nhodo istchee and iyiyiw istchee were enshrined as the Iyiyiwch's cultural and political territorial reference in the 1970s negotiation of the JBNQA between Iyiyiw decision makers grouped in the Cree Nation Government (CNG)[5] and the Quebec government, for whom James Bay was the cultural and political territorial reference. Iyiyiw istchee is composed of a multitude of nhodo istchee. The regional sum of each community's family hunting territories delineates iyiyiw istchee as the national territory of the Iyiyiwch. The local sum of the family hunting grounds of a community delimits the territory of this community and establishes iyiyiw istchee as its territory, which in the case of the Waswanipi Iyiniwch is iyiniw astchee in the southern and inland dialect.

According to JBNQA stipulations, nhodo istchee and iyiyiw istchee are the units that comprise the basis for territorial negotiation with the federal and provincial states and the non-Iyiyiwch for whom these same units are the central reference to conceptualize the Iyiyiwch ancestral land and rights. In other words, since that agreement, these units have become increasingly relevant for the Iyiyiwch because they constitute the crucial interface for negotiations with governments and extractive industries (forestry, mining, and hydroelectricity) operating on their land.

IYIYIWCH'S RESPONSES FOR MAINTAINING THE INTIMACY WITH THEIR ANCESTRAL TERRITORY

In the wake of the 1975 signing of the JBNQA, the Iyiyiwch created two institutions of Iyiyiw governance to pursue the traditional way of life: the Cree Trappers' Association (CTA) and the Cree Hunters and Trappers Income Security Board (CHTISB).[6] Through them, the Iyiyiwch established the Income Security Program (ISP) with the objective of encouraging Cree families and individuals who wish to pursue hunting, fishing, and trapping as a way of life (thereby establishing the status of "permanent hunters" living off the land). In order to mobilize entire families—including workers and school children—toward the goal of occupying the land, in the 1980s the Iyiyiwch created two institutionalized hunting breaks to be undertaken during two of the six seasons of the Iyiniwch[7]: the "goose break" in meuskumin (spring thaw), from late April to mid-May, and the "moose break" in wastebekun (first falls), between early and late October. Although these initiatives contributed to the continuation of the Iyiyiw way of life through steady occupation and valorization of the land, the number of active Iyiyiw hunters/trappers/fishermen has since progressively declined. The transmission and acquisition of local knowledge have not been able to prevent this ongoing decline, which was further intensified by the intergenerational impact of the settlement of the Iyiyiwch in the 1930s and the schooling of their children in the 1960s.

Between 2017 and 2018, among the Waswanipi Iyiniwch, the population of "permanent hunters, trappers, and fishers," i.e., those enrolled in the ISP, represented 18 percent of the community population (CHTISB 2018, 52). Their settlement became permanent with the creation of the reserve in 1976.[8] Schooling for children began as early as 1931 (Marshall et al. 1987, 55), following the 1920 amendment to the Indian Act that made schooling for First Nations children mandatory (Bousquet and Hele 2019, 25). The decrease in the transmission and acquisition of Iyiniw knowledge can be gauged by the local valorization of the practice and knowledge of traditional activities, although within the framework of the ISP these activities are institutionally evaluated according to whether they are permanent or occasional (during hunting breaks, extended stays, weekends, or holidays). Among the so-called "permanent hunters," there are different profiles based on their respective knowledge of traditional activities (hunting, fishing, and trapping techniques, skinning, and butchering of animals or preparation of hides), knowledge of the land (hunting, fishing, and trapping sites, knowledge related to lakes, rivers, rapids, islands, marshes, mountains, or portages), and their values of mutual aid and solidarity (distribution of meat, treatment of leftovers, or management of the occupation of non-Indigenous people).

Promoting the transmission and the acquisition of local knowledge is thus the current priority and a supplementary objective to the occupation of the territory. Therefore, in the 2000s, the CNG created two excursions, mostly for the younger generations, to address this new priority: the "canoe brigades" and the "winter journeys" (henceforth "land excursions"), whose traveling across the territory replicates the nomadic character of traditional activities practised during hunting breaks. The hunting breaks and the land excursions implemented in every Iyiyiw community constitute two institutional strategies dedicated to the protection of the Iyiyiw way of life through the promotion of land-based activities. In addition, the CNG supported this community effort to enhance the transmission and the acquisition of local knowledge by participating in the 2008 public consultation conducted by the Quebec government on the reformulation of Quebec's provincial heritage legislation, which was implemented in 2012 as the Cultural Heritage Act

(Loi sur le patrimoine culturel; CNG 2008). For that purpose, the CNG produced a definition of what heritage is or could be for the Iyiyiwch based on the concept of iyiyiw iituun. Through this equivocal term (iyiyiw iituun for heritage), the Iyiyiwch repositioned and reaffirmed their ancestral territory as the central reference of their world. It was also a means to pursue and further improve some of their existing or future initiatives and projects, such as the hunting breaks and the land excursions. This is part of what I call the Iyiyiw *self-heritagization strategy*, which defines the fact that the Iyiyiwch take charge, with or without the heritage tools available in Quebec, of the heritage-making process of their own culture. This includes the actualization, transmission, and protection of the Iyiyiw knowledge according to Iyiyiw epistemological, ontological, and political principles, with the primary goal of meeting their own objectives, needs, and concerns (Wattez 2024).

The analysis of interpersonal relations within the Iyiyiw world during the hunting breaks and the land excursions brings to light the epistemological, ontological, and political stakes involved in the maintenance of intimacies with the land and of their transformations through the institutionalization of their territorial experience. My analysis of these transformations reveals the coexistence of family and community intimacies in the maintenance of the relationship with the ancestral territory (see also the chapters in this volume by Tytelman, Simon, Éthier and Flamand, and Gutierrez-Callisaya). My analysis exposes in detail the results of articulations, negotiations, and adjustments generated by entanglements within the Iyiyiw world, such as the dynamics of the standardization of knowledge, practices, and relationships. They are part of either homogenization and particularization at work during hunting breaks and land excursions or the exclusion or inclusion of local conceptions of iyiyiw iituun, whether or not these are excluded or included by the political definition of iyiyiw iituun proposed by the CNG (Wattez 2024).

HUNTING ON NOCIMIC

Among the Waswanipi Iyiyiwch, the geographic scope of nocimic is matched only by the scope of its users' territorial experience. Nocimic, whose boundaries are not mapped, can cover all or part of a family hunting territory whose boundaries are mapped with or without overlap. As Adrian Tanner proposes, nocimic among the Iyiyiwch and Innu can be defined as follows:

> Nocimic is often translated as the bush and refers to the relatively familiar landscape beyond the limits of the settlements and the hunting camps where hunting activities occur. It is a realm where every lake, stream and hill is named, either in relation to its history or as a recognizable geographic landmark from the hunter's perspective, an area criss-crossed with named and familiar old trails, portages, and former campsites ... this is an environment that is socially constructed by the East Cree and the Innu, every bit as much as is the farming landscape in Western societies. *Nocimic* is thus familiar territory, domesticated in the sense that its animal occupants, like humans, live in domestic family groups, have leaders, act with intentions, want to deal with respectfully, and follow rules of reciprocity. (2004, 207)

Although Tanner minimizes the importance of hunting camps in the Iyiyiwch relationship to nocimic, the Waswanipi Iyiniwch tend instead to view them as part of the continuity of the social and cosmological intimacy between themselves and the other-than-human persons. This intimate relationship is not exclusive to the hunters. Other members of extended families experience it as well when animals are brought back to the camp. This closeness is experienced through relationships of respect and reciprocity during the hunt, the sharing of harvests, and certain rituals. The institutionalization of these experiences through the goose break and the moose break do not run counter to territorial intimacy. Rather, they help foster it by encouraging people to engage in the iyiyiw way of life on and off the land. However, the institutionalization of practices does have effects on this intimacy, such as the standardization and reduction in scope of local knowledge and practices.

During hunting breaks, extended families gather for two to three weeks at their main hunting camps during meuskumin for goose hunting and wastebekun for moose hunting. Main hunting camps may have several cabins housing a nuclear family and its extended family members. Some nuclear families have multiple cabins at various locations in nocimic. These are usually old main hunting camps that have been deserted because of a territorial reorganization of hunting on nocimic. These camps remain an important place for hunting groups regardless of their state of conservation and equipment. Since hunters can travel great distances to hunt moose and geese, they may stay there for one or more days, depending on the location of their current main hunting camp.

Life at the main camps is very active. Preparations for the hunt are the responsibility of all members of the hunting groups. Each member is responsible for their own equipment (guns, cartridges, bullets, clothing, means of transport and communication, and food) and for contributing to the collective preparation of the hunt by making sure that nothing is missing. The women are responsible for the daily stewardship of the camps (cutting firewood, cleaning the cabins, and cooking), as well as for the children and elders who remain in the camp. Men contribute to the maintenance of the camps and their surroundings by repairing the cabins, maintaining the access roads, and supplying equipment once they are back from hunting.

Iyiyiw hunters organize themselves into one or more hunting groups within the extended family of the ndoho uchimaau,[9] the head of the family's hunting territory whose authority is based on an equitable sharing of the territory and resources that the Iyiyiwch can draw from,[10] and on a "strong egalitarian ethic" between human and other-than-human persons (Scott 1997, 38–39). These groups are composed almost exclusively of men.[11] The moose and goose hunts, in which I participated as a guest apprentice hunter, were carried out by motorboat along waterways, which include lakes, rivers, and streams—though sometimes through swamps and muskegs—to reach certain places of nocimic renowned for moose and goose hunting. Hunting groups were composed of three to ten hunters divided into one to three boats depending on the places of nocimic chosen to go hunting. Most of the hunters know every lake, river, stream, swamp, and muskeg, as well as every mountain, hill, beach, shore, historic gathering place, and old camp.

The choice of the hunting spots and routes is discussed between the ndoho uchimaau and the other members of the hunting group before departure. Nonetheless, to allow themselves time to gain knowledge of the land and the animals through dreams (Feit 1995; Scott 2006), hunters often make up their minds only shortly before leaving. Departures, early in the morning, are marked by propitiatory offerings made in the water or on the shores. They are made to show respect to the other-than-human persons who could interfere during trips to prevent any danger, such as that from winds when hunters must navigate on lakes, rivers, and streams. Navigation is differently challenging during these two seasons because the water level is high during meuskumin (because of the melting of snow and ice), and low during wastebekun. Hunters update their hunting and forest knowledge of nocimic according to these seasonal characteristics as well as others, such as weather conditions, topographical settings, and anthropogenic transformations, not to mention climate changes. Hunters also update their knowledge according to adaptations by animals to these conditions, and to observations from previous hunts. Thanks to such updates, one hunter guided the group I was part of for moose hunting through a channel on very shallow waters, avoiding every rock and stick and preventing us from getting stuck in the mud while navigating. Following moose tracks spotted at several places along a stream, we found a group of seven moose and killed two.

Three "first-time rituals" are popular among the Iyiniwch hunters: ooscheh minhoo niskah ("first goose killed"), ooscheh minhoo moosah ("first moose killed"), and ooscheh minhoo gagoosah ("first bear killed"). They acknowledge the first relationship between a hunter and the animal that he will bring to share with his family. To confirm this close relationship, the head of the goose is cut from the rest of the body, decorated, and kept for several years by the hunter.[12] In the case of the moose and the bear, the hunter makes an offering of tobacco to thank the spirits of the animal before the gutting at the place of the kill and the butchering once the animal is brought back at the camp (see Tanner 1979). This hunting and forest knowledge requires skills learned through experience on nocimic and transferred in the social and cosmological intimacy of the hunting group and the family.

Harvests are shared among the various members of the hunting group and the extended family of the ndoho uchimaau of the territory where the hunt took place. If the responsibility for their distribution lies with the ndoho uchimaau, he may delegate it to the person who killed the animals. The most prized parts—such as the organs of the moose, for example miskun (liver) and umaau (omasum), or ṇiishtaamikaat (front legs of the moose) from which pakasuun (bone marrow) is extracted—are reserved for the elders. The rest is shared among the members of the hunting group, who in turn will share it with their extended family at a makushaan held at the main camp. The makushaan is a ritual feast of commensality[13] that brings together members of one or more extended families (and occasionally guests) to share iyiniw mitchuum (iyiniw food), i.e., food from the land consisting mainly of meat and organs of small and large game, bannock (unleavened bread), donuts, and mixed salads made of vegetables (potatoes, peppers, or broccoli) and grains (rice and pasta). During the makushaan, it is common for a propitiatory offering to be made to deceased ancestors, most often to the previous ndoho uchimaau or other family members known by the elders. A plate, identical to those of the elders, is prepared and set aside before throwing the food into the fire to acknowledge the ancestors for their contribution to hunting, fishing, or trapping, and to give thanks for their transfer of hunting and land knowledge and for all the other practices for which family members are indebted to them.[14] Another first-time ritual performed at the main camps, typically during meuskumin and goose break, is e wiiwiitahaausuunaanuuhch ("walking out ceremony"). This ritual marks the first time a child leaves a dwelling and enters the forest world, establishing their role in the Iyiyiw world and acknowledging its relevance.[15]

If hunting breaks can be considered periods of family revitalization (Bousquet 2006, 46), it is mainly because the experience of the Iyiyiw world on nocimic, including camps, is most in tune with the maintenance of coexistence between human and other-than-human persons who are part of this world. This reality is most often expressed by the Iyiniwch of Waswanipi as a "(re)connection to the land," which means that they (re) connect with all these persons. The intimacy of these relationships is, however, constrained by the institutionalization of the hunting breaks. In the next section, I present two major effects: the reduction of the local diversity of Iyiniw knowledge and practices, and their regional standardization through the consecration of the goose hunt as the unifying hunt of all Iyiyiwch.

The names "goose break" and "moose break" refer to the two main hunts of the meuskumin and wastebekun seasons. However, during these seasons a multitude of other hunting and fishing activities take place (Saganash 2000). During meuskumin, nisk (goose) is not the only waterfowl hunted. Several types of iynisip (duck)[16] are also hunted. This season is also the beginning of the hunts for piyew (partridge) and kâkûs (black bear), much sought after at this time for chisheyaakupimii (bear fat). As for wastebekun, it is defined as a season of trapping, the first hunts and the last fisheries. Mûs^{w} (moose) is the most prized animal, but kâkûs[17] and amisk (beaver) are similarly favoured, especially for their meat. Small game is hunted as well.[18] Fishing is also very popular during these two seasons; it is not uncommon for some Iyiniw hunters to set fishing nets and to pull them up before leaving for the hunt or upon their return. Many kinds of fish are caught regularly throughout these hunting seasons.[19] As such, the names "goose break" and "moose break" are reductive. According to my interlocutors, the selection of these names was made within the institutions of Iyiyiw governance to the detriment of their original names, namely "fall break" and "spring break," referencing seasons that are Western concepts but are nonetheless more inclusive of the many different activities that take place during meuskumin and wastebekun.

None of the people to whom I spoke could tell me why this name change had taken place. All of them deplore it and worry about the effects of institutionalizing hunting as breaks on the valorization of local knowledge and practices. However, there is no doubt in their minds that this choice signifies a desire to homogenize local hunting and forest particularities to promote an even greater adaptation of hunting and life in the forest to the sedentary, professional, and scholastic lives of Iyiniwch families by limiting the constraints of the former on the latter. The institutionalization of hunting in the form of breaks—even more so with the imposition of a break dedicated to goose hunting, takes a more reductive turn for the Waswanipi Iyiniwch than for interior and southern communities.[20]

Doubts and questions of the Waswanipi Iyiniwch relate to the historical importance of goose hunting. Although they hunted geese prior to the mid-1970s, they did not attach the importance to the hunt that they do today, unlike the Iyiyiwch of the coastal and northern communities for whom the goose hunt has been culturally important for much longer. Recent developments in goose hunting confirm this change. The increase in importance of goose hunting among the Iyiniwch is primarily due to the disturbance of goose migration patterns caused by environmental changes attributed to the construction of the first large hydroelectric dams in the 1970s (Roué 2009, 29). This increase may also be the result of a significant redirection of other hunting activities that have now been discontinued. For example, one might consider the impact of the closure of the last trading posts for which the Iyiyiwch had long hunted fur-bearing animals such as amisk (beaver), wâpistân (marten), and pişiw (lynx). According to the Waswanipi Iyiniwch, this evolution is evidenced by the differences from the Iyiyiwch of the coastal communities who have an alternative territorial and social organization for this hunt. For example, the latter have developed land transformations to secure their goose hunting practice, including the construction of tuuhiikaan, ditches and corridors cut through the forest (Sayles and Mulrennan 2010). Within their own community territory, they further distinguish between coastal and interior hunting grounds, recognizing the former as the preferred environments for goose hunting (Scott 1986, 167). Finally, on both sides of James Bay, goose hunting is not limited to a single season as it is inland or further south; while it is certainly practised in spring and in greater abundance during the northern migration of geese, geese are also hunted during their southern migration in the fall (Berkes et al. 1995, 85, 88).

In the opinion of several Waswanipi Iyiniwch, the creation of the goose break has made goose hunting more popular than it was before, even to the point of becoming, in recent years, more important than moose hunting, which had been the most practised hunt since the moose found a natural habitat in the region in the 1930s (Feit 1978). In other words, the institutionalization of goose hunting at the national level through the creation of the goose hunting vacation tends to promote the standardization of practices and knowledge among the Iyiyiwch to the detriment of their local particularities. The intimacy that the Iyiniwch have with each other and with the other-than-human persons during these hunting breaks is undoubtedly affected. Other effects of institutionalization on the territorial intimacy of the Iyiniwch are manifested in land excursions.

PADDLING AND WALKING ON IYINIW ASTCHEE

Compared to nocimic, iyiniw astchee is a wider territory, less specifically dedicated to familial hunting activities, and where community land-based activities take place. Thus, iyiniw astchee is a territory defined by inter-family relationships of mutual aid and solidarity currently sanctioned by the community. In that sense, the community intimacy at work on iyiniw astchee is close to historical "band territoriality" (Scott 2018). To foster the experience, the Waswanipi Youth Council—with the support of the Band Council's Culture Department and other local branches of regional iyiniw institutions—has been organizing land excursions on traditional routes and itineraries across various family territories since the 2000s, namely "winter journeys" and "canoe brigades." The winter journey in which I participated consisted of a snowshoe walk of several days between Waswanipi and a main hunting camp on a family's territory where the participants stayed for one to two weeks during sheegoon (the first ice break-up, from March to April). The canoe brigade consisted of a two-week canoe trip during neebin (summer, July to August) on rivers and lakes on which families used to travel between their hunting grounds and the chiiwetau, the place of the former summer gathering site and of the old HBC trading post.

Paddling and walking on iyiniw astchee are important acts for the Iyiniwch, as they are for other Indigenous nations (Aporta 2004; Legat 2008, 2012). Joseph Neeposh, an elder from Waswanipi, explained to me the value of these land excursions while talking about the winter journey: "Cree people would always walk on the land and they would always move around from location to location every season. They want to pick up what our elders took from the land ... It is true, what they are doing" (Joseph Neeposh, personal communication, 2015). An Iyiniwch from Waswanipi whom I did not know came to sit beside me while we were waiting for the departure of the winter journey and told me the importance of this kind of activity: "What you learn on the land, you do not forget it. Afterwards, you know."

What do the participants learn from travelling on the land, paddling and walking on ancient travelling routes and itineraries? What do they retain from the knowledge that their ancestors drew from the land? I propose an answer to these questions in the following section by presenting the relationship that the Iyiyiwch have with iyiniw astchee during these land excursions, knowing that the organizers and the participants—as well as their families, the elders, and the political leaders of the community—have two objectives. The first objective is to maintain the relationship with the Iyiniw territory by following the traditional paths and waterways linked to nomadism as well as to hunting, trapping, fishing, and the fur trade. This approach facilitates the achievement of the second objective, which is to update the relevance of local knowledge according to the issues prioritized during land excursions, such as the transmission of local knowledge to the younger generations and, more broadly, the maintenance of experiencing the iyiyiw world. Intimate relationships with iyiniw astchee, however, cannot preclude the effects of the institutionalization of these excursions, particularly their bureaucratic framework and its mismatch with the social and the cosmological ways of acquiring Iyiniw knowledge.[21]

The winter journey and the canoe brigade each involved twelve to twenty "young" Iyiniwch (boys and girls), a category which, according to the criteria of the Youth Council of Waswanipi, includes Iyiniwch between the ages of thirteen and thirty-five years. This Iyiniw conception of youth places the participants in land excursions in accordance with differences between Iyiniw families in terms of access to the land and local knowledge, rather than according to a generational definition drawn from Western conceptions (Jérôme 2010; Jérôme and Gagné 2009; Poirier 2009). In fact, the programs prioritize youth participants from families whose access to the land is not guaranteed—because their family territory is either too far away from Waswanipi or too damaged by forestry cutting, or because there are no active hunters in the family—as well as youth from families who do not claim access, over youth who have access to the land because their families have a hunting territory or are regularly invited to another family's hunting territory. The latter families can more easily ensure that their children live on the land and acquire knowledge during long and regular stays at different times in their lives without needing institutional support. However, such youth are not excluded from these land excursions. Participants are taken care of by guides, usually one for each activity, who are recognized as mentors in navigating rivers and lakes and walking on snowshoes on winter paths. Depending on their availability, guides are not the same from one year to the next. In Waswanipi there are about ten such guides. One or two apprentice guides participate in the activities to be trained by the guide and to support him in his tasks. During these land excursions, the participants' experience of the Iyiniw world is multiple, depending on their routes, activities, obligations, responsibilities, and encounters.

For the winter journey in which I participated in March 2015, we covered a fifty-kilometre round trip in snowshoes over four days, between Waswanipi and the La Trêve Lake hunting camp where we stayed for a week. This loop includes sections of paths historically followed by the Iyiniwch to reach their winter hunting camps, paths used more recently, and others used exclusively for these winter journeys.

The canoe brigade in which I participated in July 2015 started from a hunting camp located inland at kilometre sixty of the Billy-Diamond Highway. The brigade of eight canoes for sixteen participants followed the historic route that many Iyiniw families used to nomadically travel between their family hunting grounds and Chiiwetau ("going back"). The latter is commonly named the "Old Post" in reference to the place where the Iyiniwch used to gather for a few weeks in the summer and where the Hudson's Bay Company trading post was built in the early nineteenth century.[22] Over a dozen days, we navigated multiple rivers, rapids, and lakes, staying at several hunting camps, historic gathering sites, and fallback sites in the event of problems.

Several activities dedicated to the transmission of local knowledge relating to fishing and trapping took place during the winter journey, once participants were settled in the hunting camp. During the canoe brigade, fishing was the only recurrent harvesting activity. Our daily life was filled with various tasks relating more generally to life on the land, whether at a main hunting camp or paddling and walking. These daily tasks mainly consisted of taking care of our clothes (sewing them or drying them over the wood stove or lying on our tents), snowshoes, toboggans, canoes, paddles (checking their condition and repairing them if necessary), and our gear. We also had to take care of ourselves: cooking, going to bed early to get enough rest, and keeping the hunting camps and staging areas clean. Nomadizing required a constant repetition of all these tasks in addition to settling quickly when we arrived and moving fast when it was time to leave, usually at the crack of dawn.

During these land excursions on iyiniw astchee, the Iyiniw world opens itself to the participants. However, one must know it a little to experience it fully and to understand the stakes, which was the case for my companions. An event on the second day of the canoe brigade made me aware of the relational dimension that the youth with whom I was paddling have with the land. After getting up at dawn to sail on Cheashquacheston Lake (Gull Lake in English), in an effort to avoid the southwest wind that usually picks up in the morning, we approached the beach where we would set up camp for the next night. We had it in our sights. The wind had not yet risen. It was still early. The water was calm. Everything was peaceful. We paddled quietly. We were six canoes behind the guide who had gone ahead with another canoe to lead us between the numerous islands in this part of the lake. We were following a more direct trajectory toward our destination than we would have if the wind had been blowing, causing the waves to be formed and hollow, and forcing us to follow the shores. Wanting to see the beach in the distance, I pointed to the horizon in multiple directions while questioning my companions about its exact location: "Is the beach that way? Or over there?" Seeing me gesticulate, my companions began to paddle faster all at once. Surprised, I started to follow the movement of my partner. After a few minutes of incomprehension, I remembered the warning of several Iyiniwch with whom I had been fishing on lakes: "Don't point to the islands on a lake, a munjoosh (monster) lives below. You would disrespect them. The wind would rise, big waves would form, and you would be in danger."[23] This was the reason for the sudden rush of my companions. I had disrespected a munjoosh! The consequences were not long in coming. After paddling a few minutes at high speed, the wind began to blow more and more strongly. The waves were forming and getting bigger and bigger. Each one threatened to tip our canoes over. We were in danger. When we arrived safely at the beach, shaken by the effort and the risk, the youth berated me in a memorable way. They all held me responsible for the danger to which we had suddenly been exposed due my lack of respect for the munjoosh.

Quite affected by their reaction and the seriousness of the situation I had caused, I learned my lesson from the Iyiniw world. I saw the depth of this type of relationship, in this case with munjoosh. I realized how much this reality of the Iyiniw world is an integral part of the youth's lives, even though most of them are participating in the canoe brigade because they do not have much knowledge of the land. I realized how much their relationship with the land is built primarily through action rather than representation. Among the Iyiyiwch, and Indigenous Peoples more broadly, acting or doing is based on personal experience—the principle of acquisition and transfer of local knowledge—which is a collective act as it involves human and other-than-human persons. Places are thus recognized as a source of relationships between many types of persons and between the different narratives of human beings who thrive there (Aporta 2004; Legat 2008). Paddling and walking on the land are vehicles of knowledge transmission and acquisition between humans and other-than-humans.

Some Iyiniw elders, whether former organizers or not, praise the merits of creating this kind of land activity, whereas other elders question them. Community valorization of iyiniw astchee through nomadism is further affirmed by participation in these land excursions at different times and places by the ndoho uchimaau of the territories crossed, and by the families of the participants, the elders, and the political leaders of the community. Visits of ndoho uchimaau on their territories and of participants' families along the route are very frequent. Elders of the community and political leaders, joined by the ndoho uchimaau of the territories crossed and by some of the participants' relatives (parents, grandparents, uncles, aunts, cousins, and nephews), make it a point of honour to welcome them as soon as they approach and arrive, and to participate in the makushaan at the end of the activity. The community intimacy that unfolds in this way contributes to valuing the participants, more specifically the lessons learned from these interpersonal experiences and the community dimensions of their actions. Land excursions thus present opportunities for the actualization of intimate relations to iyiniw astchee as a community territory.

Issues other than the diminishing transfer and acquisition of local knowledge can be identified as priorities to be addressed during these land excursions. Touching on political, therapeutic, or cultural concerns, these issues contribute to reinforcing historical inter-band links when they are organized in collaboration with other Iyiniw communities or other neighbouring First Nations. This was the case for the winter trips organized with Nemaska in 2016 and with the Anicinabe First Nation of Lac Simon and the Atikamekw First Nation of Opitciwan[24] several times during the 2000s. Land excursions can also contribute to strengthening current intercommunity ties when they are organized in a spirit of rapprochement with neighbouring Jamesian municipalities, as was the case with the 2015 canoe brigade "The Youth Canoe Exchange Expedition." According to the Iyiniw organizers, the objective was to bring together Jamesian youth and Iyiniw youth to create a mutual respectful relationship and share the Iyiniw culture with the youth of Jamesian municipalities[25] in the context of a territorial dispute between Waswanipi and Lebel-sur-Quévillon (located a hundred kilometres south of Waswanipi along Highway 113) over access to a beach on Lac Quévillon on whose shores the town is located.[26]

Some Iyiniw elders, however, are critical. Criticism of the Iyiniwch's land excursions focuses on the organizers' limited local knowledge and the limited knowledge that participants ultimately acquired. Complaints relate to the fact that in the collective setup, the ratio between a guide assisted by apprentice guides and a dozen young participants is too large to acquire and transmit local knowledge. The participants may have sufficient knowledge to have land experiences, as their reaction to my disrespect of munjoosh suggests. Little time on the land is required, and above all, knowledge reactivates once one is on the land. Experiences are available to everyone because knowledge is not possessed by humans. It is at the participants' disposal. Still, it is necessary to know how to deal with it. For that, sustained learning and a more continuous presence on the land are needed. To be sure, land excursions provide an opportunity to be on the land, but their collective framework between the guide, his apprentices, and the participants is too large in number to properly learn how to act on the land. A more propitious setup would foster a more intimate relationship. The close relation between the guide and his apprentice(s) reflects this. The apprentices gain great recognition of their competences after these excursions, significantly greater than that of the participants. The relation between the guide and the participants is not well adapted to the whole social and cosmological context of acquisition and transfer of ways of doing in the Iyiyiw world. The short tenures of the guides of these field trips, because of their regular replacement, exacerbate this situation. Above all, the fact that the relationship between a guide and the participants never continues after these excursions makes this relationship even less intimate.

These land excursions are thus distinct from the hunting breaks and their own intimate relations with and within nocimic, the extended families and the hunting groups. Despite this major difference in terms of intimacy, organized land excursions constitute crucial initiatives for the Iyiniwch of Waswanipi and for all of the Iyiyiwch. For the same reason the hunting breaks were implemented in the 1970s, the excursions fulfill the objectives of maintaining the occupation of iyiniw astchee (at the community level) and, by extension, of iyiyiw istchee (at the nation level) and the Iyiyiw way of life, with all the transformations that might arise along the way. The winter journeys and canoe brigades are further examples of the creativity of the Iyiyiwch to offer ways to "sustain relationships, obligations, and responsibilities toward the myriad of beings" of the Iyiyiw world, further examples of "strategies and practices of endurance as (r)existence" (see Blaser, Poirier, and Anthias in the introduction to this volume).

CONCLUSION

The relationships of the Iyiyiwch to nocimic and iyiniw astchee are defined by the personal and collective experience of the relationships between human and other-than-human persons through hunting, paddling, and walking, the former nourishing the latter. The family and community intimacies that emerge in coexistence with one another are transformed by the institutionalization of their practice during hunting breaks and land excursions, as well as by their priorities to pursue the occupation of the land and to support the transfer and acquisition of local knowledge. The Iyiyiwch have hunting breaks and land excursions because, like other First Nations, they control the institutions that created them (Bousquet 2006). They can therefore adapt them to their priorities and to their local or regional particularities with a "narrow margin of negotiation" in coexistence with the modalities of the sedentary, professional, and school lives of the families (Roué 2006, 21) and in acceptance of the homogenization and particularization, as well as the exclusion and inclusion of Iyiyiw knowledge, practices, and relationships produced by their institutionalization. Reflecting the complexity of continuing to live on and off the land, these entanglements show how the network of relationships are constantly reshaped to nurture intimate bonds between the beings engaged in the Iyiyiw world. *Nocimic*, *iyiniw astchee*, *nhodo istchee*, and *iyiyiw istchee* are, in that sense, different collective shapes of the "territories of life" proposed in this book (see the introduction to this volume).

The family scope of nocimic and the community scope of iyiyiw astchee can be measured by the oral mobilization of the concept of iyiyiw iituun during hunting breaks and land excursions, particularly the makushaan that punctuate both on several occasions. The mobilization of iyiyiw iituun is recurrent in the framework of the land excursions. It strongly reaffirms the objective to support the transmission and the acquisition of local knowledge by including those which are to be valued in priority and by excluding those which are secondary for that purpose. The concept of iyiyiw iituun thus contains an important public value among the Iyiniwch who share the concern for the transmission of local knowledge, whether in their respective daily lives or as administrative or political leaders responsible for dealing with this concern. Iyiyiw iituun does not have this public value in family land activities such as hunting breaks. On these occasions, no one needs to reaffirm what iyiyiw iituun is or what is done at the makushaan, although they are just as common when the hunting, fishing, or trapping has been fruitful. These processes of exclusion and inclusion are reflected in the policy definition of iyiyiw iituun as equivalent to the concept of heritage as proposed by the CNG (2008) since land excursions are part of it, while hunting breaks are not.

Hunting breaks, land excursions, and the political definition of iyiyiw iituun are ultimately adaptative endurance strategies that the Iyiyiwch employ in accordance with their ethic of "being well" (miyuu pitamtisiiwin) for which the relationship to the ancestral land needs to be sustained. Certainly, these strategies have "everything to do with living on the land and, more broadly, with 'being Cree' [sic]" and allow for the connection of "physiological well-being to social and political well-being" (Adelson 2000, 60). What brings hunting breaks, land excursions, and the political definition fundamentally closer to miyuu pitamtisiiwin are the simultaneity of the actions of doing (iituun) and being (pimaatisiiwin) in relation to the persons of the Iyiyiw world (Wattez 2020, 112–116), maintaining the Iyiyiw territorialities of intimacy. Iituun and pimaatisiiwin define each other and describe a synchronous relationship between doing and being in the Iyiyiw world that is found in Colin Scott's proposed understanding of pimaatisiiwin as the "continuous birth of the world" (2006, 61). The source of emergence, potentialities, and contingency in the Iyiyiw world might be the simultaneity of the actions of doing and being. This simultaneity is found in the relationship between cognitive action (the act of thinking) and phenomenological action (the act of experiencing) (Wattez 2020). Iituun and pimaatisiiwin cannot be apprehended or understood without each other. To do so would be to have a truncated and incomplete conception of the Iyiyiw world. In that sense, hunting breaks and land excursions are displays of miyuu pitamtisiwn, as these activities contribute to the perpetuation of the actions of doing and being according to land relation with the persons of the Iyiyiw world, here on nocimic and iyiniw astchee, maintaining while also transforming the territorial intimacies attached to them.

With ongoing challenges such as extractive projects or climate change, and considering their impact on the Iyiyiwch and their ancestral land, one wonders how the Iyiyiwch can continue to sustain family and community territorial intimacies, how these relationships will be transformed, and how their coexistence will be able to provide the Iyiyiwch with responses that enable them to adapt locally in communities or in the political and institutional areas of negotiation with the federal and provincial states.

NOTES

1. I use the endonym Iyiniw/Iyiyiw in iiyiyuu ayimuun rather than the exonym Cree in French. In iiyiyuu ayimuun, Iyiniw refers to the southern and inland dialect, while Iyiyiw refers to the northern and coastal dialect. I use Iyiniw (with the suffix -ch, the mark of the plural) when talking about the people of Waswanipi, the southernmost Iyiyiw community where I conducted several ethnographic surveys (for a PhD and an MA in social and cultural anthropology, and for an MA in social geography). I use Iyiyiw-ch when referring to the iyiyiw world (knowledge and practices) and the people of the ten communities: Waswanipi, Mistissini, Ouje-Bougoumou, Nemaska, Washaw Sibi, Whapmagoostui, Chisasibi, Wemindji, Eastmain, and Waskaganish.
2. My doctoral project in anthropology, from which this chapter is taken, is the third research project for which I conducted fieldwork with the Iyiniwch of Waswanipi after master's degree projects in anthropology in 2009 and in geography in 2008. During this last fieldwork between 2014 and 2016, I was invited to share the daily life in the "bush" of three families (during several hunting breaks, a long stay, many weekends, and several holidays) and to take part in one canoe brigade and one winter journey (for more details, see Wattez 2021).

3. For other examples of similar initiatives, see chapters in this volume by Gutierrez-Callisaya, Moritz and Qwalqwalten, and Thomassin et al.
4. Nhodo istchee is also translated as "hunting ground" or "trapline," which are the terms most used by the Iyiyiwch, as opposed to "family hunting territory," which is the accepted scientific and academic terminology. For more details on these terms and the debate on "family hunting territory," see Chaplier and Scott, 2018.
5. When I mention the CNG before 2017, it should be remembered that formerly it was the Grand Council of the Crees (Eeyou Istchee)—Cree Regional Government (CCG/EI-ARC). The CCG/EI-ARC became the CNG during a reform in 2017 (for more information, see Wattez 2024). For the sake of clarity, I refer only to the CNG in this chapter.
6. The Iyiyiwch created two other iyiyiw governance institutions in the wake of the signing of the JBNQA: the Cree School Board (CSB) and the Cree Health Board (CHB).
7. The Iyiniwch recognize six seasons: wastebekun, "the first falls" (September to October); dakotin, "the first falls and frosts" (November to December); booboon, "winter" (January to February); sheegoon, "the early spring and ice breakup" (March to April); meuskumin, "the spring thaw" (May to June); and neebin, "summer" (July to August) (Saganash 2000).
8. The settling of the Waswanipi Iyiniwch has been gradual since the beginning of the 1960s and the closing of the Hudson's Bay Company (HBC) trading post at the site of their summer gathering in 1965. Between this period and the creation of Waswanipi in 1976, their settling was rather a long-term scattering of the families on the outskirts of regional towns, or even on main highways due to occupation or the search for paid employment (Wattez 2020, 172).
9. Among the Iyiniwch, ndoho uchimaau is interchangeable with "tallyman" in English, derived from the responsibility of the nhodo uchimaau during the fur trade to manage the stocks of furs, which required counting them and tallying up prices before forwarding the furs to traders at the trading posts.
10. In order to exercise his authority as adequately as possible and, more specifically, to maintain certain parts of the territory essential for hunting, fishing, and trapping, the ndoho uchimaau may have to negotiate with non-Indigenous people, as in Waswanipi, for example with representatives of the forestry and mining companies, as well as hunters, fishermen, and vacationers. These people are numerous given the public status of the 850 kilometres of forestry roads that penetrate the territory and whose occupation most often takes place without the acknowledgement of the Iyiniwch (Feit 2005, 2004, 2017; Saganash 2000; Scott 2017).
11. The settlement encouraged the development of all-male hunting groups, whereas life in the forest required women to be "equal partners" with men (Ohmagari and Berkes 1997, 200). Women were not part of the hunting groups, but they did hunt in the vicinity of the hunting camp and participated in the preparation of the game after the men have brought it back to the camp. Recently however, in certain iyiniw families of Waswanipi, women can be part of these hunting groups. They can even be named as ndoho uchimaau. This situation can create tensions between and within hunting groups and families.
12. See Preston (1978) for more precision on the first goose killed ritual and on other types of relationships.
13. See Tanner's description (2014, 241–249) for a detailed analysis.
14. It should be noted that makushaan is not restricted to the forest universe since it also takes place in the community. In Waswanipi, the members of one or several nuclear and extended families gather, sometimes joined by other members of the community or guests depending on the celebrated occasion (births, birthdays, deaths, graduations, weddings, or community events).
15. For more precision on the walking out ceremony among the Iyiyiwch, see Tanner (2014), and among the Atikamekw Nehirowisiwok, see Jérôme (2008).
16. These are the American Black Duck, Mallard, and Gadwall (Brousseau 2010, 26).

17. The respect the Iyiniwch have for the black bear is manifested today by some families and hunters in their abstinence from hunting and consuming it. By contrast, this respect is expressed by others in their hunting and consumption of the black bear.
18. Piyew (partridge) and iynisip (duck) are hunted in this season, but less than in meuskumin. Wâpus^{w} (snowshoe hare) are trapped in this season, but less than during dakotin and booboon.
19. These are primarily miyumek^{w} (whitefish), cinusew (pike), namew (sturgeon), and ukâss (walleye).
20. They are Mistissini, Oujé-Bougoumou, Nemaska, and Washaw Sibi. The coastal and northern communities are Whapmagoostui, Chisasibi, Wemindji, Eastmain, and Waskaganish.
21. Nadasdy (2003) provides a classical study of this kind of inadequacy between state bureaucratic frameworks to foster the transmission of local knowledge and Indigenous ways of acquiring it among the Kluane First Nation in southern Yukon in Canada.
22. This trading post was operated by the Hudson's Bay Company (HBC) since 1819 after being established by the North-West Company (NWC) in 1800 (Marshall et al. 1987, 2, 65). It was the second year-round trading post in the Waswanipi Iyiniw territory. The first one was opened by the NWC in 1775 on Cheashquacheston Lake (Gull Lake).
23. Rather than pointing with a finger, the Iyiniwch will instead point to the horizon with their chin and lips.
24. The Atikamekw First Nation of Opitciwan organize their own land excursions (see Éthier 2017, 208–213).
25. The Jamesian municipalities are the towns (4), localities (3), and villages (2) created and inhabited by Quebecers since the early 1950s in the context of the industrial exploration of James Bay in Northern Quebec. In 2007, the acknowledgement of a common status as a territorial collectivity dedicated the name of Jamesia (instead of James Bay) and separated them from the Iyiyiwch communities of Iyiyiw Istchee.
26. Due to a lack of Jamesian participants and funding, this project did not take place. The expedition was, thus, focused only on the transmission and acquisition of local knowledge among the Iyiniw youth.

REFERENCES

Adelson, Naomi. 2000. *"Being Alive Well": Health and the Politics of Cree Well-Being.* University of Toronto Press.

Aporta, Claudio. 2004. "Routes, Trails and Tracks: Trail Breaking among the Inuit of Igloolik." *Études/Inuit/Studies* 28 (2): 9.

Berkes, F., A. Hughes, P.J. George, R.J. Preston, B.D. Cummins, and J. Turner. 1995. "The Persistence of Indigenous Land Use: Fish and Wildlife Harvest Areas in the Hudson and James Bay Lowland, Ontario." *Arctic* 48 (1): 81–93.

Bousquet, Marie-Pierre. 2006. "Une histoire réparée pour qui? Ce que les Algonquins du Québec commémorent de leur passé." In *Du vrai au juste: la mémoire, l'histoire et l'oubli*, edited by Michèle Baussant. Presses de l'Université Laval.

Bousquet, Marie-Pierre, and Karl S. Hele. 2019. "Introduction: Une histoire non pour détruire, mais pour éclairer les événements." In *La blessure qui dormait à points fermés. L'héritage des pensionnats autochtones au Québec*, edited by Marie-Pierre Bousquet and Karl S. Hele. Recherches amérindiennes au Québec.

Brousseau, Kevin. 2010. *Cree Forest Lexicon: Final Report.* CRDI (Cree Research and Development Institute).

Chaplier, Mélanie, and Colin Scott. 2018. "Introduction: Des castors à la terre: Construire sur les débats passés pour défaire l'enchevêtrement contemporain des territoires de chasse familiaux des Algonquiens." *Anthropologica* 60 (1): 45–60.

CHTISB (Cree Hunters and Trappers Income Security Board). 2018. Annual Report 2017–2018. Quebec.

CNG (Cree Nation Government). 2008. "Un regard neuf sur le patrimoine culturel. Mémoire soumis dans le cadre de la consultation sur le Livre vert du ministère de la Culture, des Communications et de la Condition féminine." Bibliothèque de l'Assemblée Nationale du Québec. https://www.bibliotheque.assnat.qc.ca/DepotNumerique_v2/AffichageFichier.aspx?idf=60252

Dussart, Françoise, and Sylvie Poirier, eds. 2017. *Entangled Territorialities: Negotiating Indigenous Lands in Australia and Canada.* University of Toronto Press.

Éthier, Benoit. 2017. "Orocowewin notcimik itatcihowin: Ontologie politique et contemporanéité des responsabilités et des droits territoriaux chez les Atikamekw Nehirowisiwok (Haute-Mauricie, Québec) dans le contexte des négociations territoriales globales." PhD diss., Laval University.

Feit, Harvey. 1978. "Waswanipi Realities and Adaptations: Resource Management and Cognitive Structure." PhD diss., McGill University.

Feit, Harvey. 1995. "Hunting and the Quest for Power: The James Bay Cree and Whitemen in the 20th century." In *Native Peoples: The Canadian Experience*, edited by Bruce R. Morrison and Roderick C. Wilson. McClelland & Stewart.

Feit, Harvey. 2000. "Les animaux comme partenaires de chasse: Réciprocité chez les Cris de la baie James." *Terrain* 34 (March): 123–142.

Feit, Harvey. 2004. "James Bay Crees' Life Projects and Politics: Histories of Place, Animal Partners and Enduring Relationships." In *In the Way of Development: Indigenous Peoples, Life Projects, and Globalization*, edited by Mario Blaser, Harvey Feit, and Glenn McRae. Zed Books.

Feit, Harvey. 2005. "Re-cognizing Co-management as Co-governance: Visions and Histories of Conservation at James Bay." *Anthropologica* 47 (2): 267–288.

Feit, Harvey. 2017. "Dialogues on Surviving: Eeyou Hunters' Ways of Engagement with Land, Governments and Youth." In *Entangled Territorialities: Negotiating Indigenous Lands in Australia and Canada*, edited by Francoise Dussart and Sylvie Poirier. University of Toronto Press.

Hallowell, Alfred Irving. 1992. *The Ojibwa of Berens River, Manitoba: Ethnography into History*, edited by Jennifer S.H. Brown. Harcourt Brace Jovanovich College Publishers.

Jérôme, Laurent. 2010. "Jeunesse, musique et rituels chez les Atikamekw (Haute-Mauricie, Québec): Ethnographie d'un processus d'affirmations identitaire et culturelle en milieu autochtone." PhD diss., Laval University.

Jérôme, Laurent, and Natacha Gagné, eds. 2009. *Jeunesses autochtones: affirmation, innovation et résistance dans les mondes contemporains*. Presses universitaires de Rennes.

Legat, Allice. 2008. "Walking Stories; Leaving Footprints." In *Ways of Walking: Ethnography and Practice on Foot*, edited by Jo Lee Vergunst and Tim Ingold. Routledge.

Legat, Allice. 2012. *Walking the Land, Feeding the Fire: Knowledge and Stewardship Among the Tlicho Dene*. University of Arizona Press.

Marshall, Susan, CRA (Cree Regional Authority), and CFNW (Cree First Nation of Waswanipi). 1987. *Light on the Water: A Pictorial History of the People of Waswanipi*. Waswanipi Band.

Morantz, Toby. 2002. *The White Man's Gonna Getcha: The Colonial Challenge to the Crees in Quebec*. McGill-Queen's Press.

Nadasdy, Paul. 2003. *Hunters and Bureaucrats: Power, Knowledge, and Aboriginal-State Relations in the Southwest Yukon*. UBC Press.

Ohmagari, Kayo, and Fikret Berkes. 1997. "Transmission of Indigenous Knowledge and Bush Skills Among the Western James Bay Cree Women of Subarctic Canada." *Human Ecology* 25 (2): 197–222.

Poirier, Sylvie. 2009. "Les dynamiques relationnelles des jeunes autochtones." In *Jeunesses autochtones. Affirmation, innovation et résistance dans les mondes contemporains*, edited by Laurent Jérôme and Natacha Gagné. Presses de l'Université Laval, Presses universitaires de Rennes.

Preston, Richard J. 1978. "La relation sacrée entre les Cris et les oies." *Recherches Amérindiennes au Québec* 8 (2): 147–152.

Roué, Marie. 2006. "Guérir de l'école par le retour à la terre: Les aînés Cris au secours de la génération perdue." *Revue internationale des sciences sociales* 187 (1): 19–28.

Roué, Marie. 2009. "Une oie qui traverse les frontières." *Ethnologie française* 39 (1): 23–34.

Saganash, Allan Jr. 2000. *Trapline/Forestry Project.* The Cree Model Forest of Waswanipi.

Sayles, J. S., and M. E. Mulrennan. 2010. "Securing a Future: Cree Hunters' Resistance and Flexibility to Environmental Changes, Wemindji, James Bay." *Ecology and Society* 15 (4): 22. http://www.ecologyandsociety.org/vol15/iss4/art22/.

Scott, Colin. 1986. "Hunting Territories, Hunting Bosses and Communal Production among Coastal James Bay Cree." *Anthropologica* 28 (1/2): 163.

Scott, Colin. 1989. "Knowledge Construction among the Cree Hunters: Metaphors and Literal Understanding." *Journal de la Société des Américanistes* 75 (1): 193–208.

Scott, Colin. 1997. "Property, Practice and Indigenous Rights among Quebec Cree Hunters." In *Hunters and Gatherers. Volume 2: Property, Power and Ideology*, edited by Tim Ingold, David Riches, and James Woodburn. Berg Publishers.

Scott, Colin. 2006. "Spirit and Practical Knowledge in the Person of the Bear among Wemindji Cree Hunters." *Ethnos* 71 (1): 51–66.

Scott, Colin. 2017. "The Endurance of Relational Ontology: Eeyouch and Sport Hunters." In *Entangled Territorialities: Negotiating Indigenous Lands in Australia and Canada*, edited by Françoise Dussart and Sylvie Poirier. University of Toronto Press.

Scott, Colin. 2018. "Family Territories, Community Territories: Balancing Rights and Responsibilities through Time." *Anthropologica* 60 (1): 90–105.

Tanner, Adrian. 1979. *Bringing Home Animals: Religious Ideology and Mode of Production of the Mistassini Cree Hunters.* St. Martin's Press.

Tanner, Adrian. 2004. "The Cosmology of Nature, Cultural Divergence, and the Metaphysics of Community Healing." In *Figured Worlds: Ontological Obstacles in Intercultural Relations*, edited by John R. Clammer, Sylvie Poirier, and Eric Schwimmer. University of Toronto Press.

Tanner, Adrian. 2007. "The Nature of Quebec Cree Animist Practices and Beliefs." In *La nature des esprits dans les cosmologies autochtones*, edited by Frédéric Laugrand and Jarich G. Oosten. Presses Université Laval.

Tanner, Adrian. 2014. *Bringing Home Animals. Mistissini Hunters of Northern Quebec.* 2nd ed. ISER.

Viveiros de Castro, Eduardo. 2004. "Perspectival Anthropology and the Method of Controlled Equivocation." *Tipití: Journal of the Society for the Anthropology of Lowland South America* 2 (1). https://doi.org/10.70845/2572-3626.1010.

Wattez, Paul. 2020. "Iiyiyiw iituun: l'alternative patrimoniale des Iyiyiwch. Stratégie d'auto-patrimonialisation et reconfigurations épistémologiques, politiques et ontologiques." PhD diss., University of Montreal.

Wattez, Paul. 2021. "S'impliquer, entrer en relation et se laisser affecter. Trois postures collaboratives d'une ethnographie en voie de radicalisation et de décolonisation avec les Iyiniwch de Waswanipi." In *La recherche collaborative en contextes autochtones. Réalités, enjeux et perspectives actuels*, edited by Carole Delamour, Benoit Éthier, David Bernard, Jo-Anni Joncas, and Francesca Croce. Peisaj.

Wattez, Paul. 2024. *L'alternative patrimoniale des Iyiyiwch. Savoir-faire, territoire et autonomie.* Presses de l'Université du Québec—Recherches autochtones au Québec.

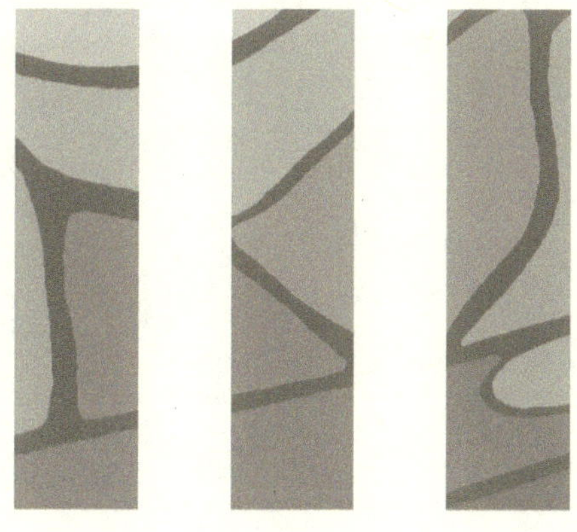

ENDURANCES

8

Annick Thomassin, Adam Nye,
Jacinda Baragud, *and* Kim Spurway

"WE DON'T WANT TO BE REFUGEES IN OUR OWN COUNTRY"

CLIMATE CHANGE, ENTANGLED TERRITORIALITIES, AND LIFE PROJECTS IN ZENADTH KES AND WALBUNJA COUNTRY, AUSTRALIA

INTRODUCTION

In the last few years, a number of scholars have highlighted the different premises delimiting Indigenous and non-Indigenous notions of sovereignty. Karine Vanthuyne and Mathieu Gauthier underline fundamental differences between Indigenous world-views and colonial settler states such as Canada, arguing that unlike settler colonial sovereignty that relies on a "legal-juridical sphere of land claims," Indigenous sovereignty "is enacted through everyday relationships with sentient territories" (2022, 296). Despite constraints imposed by the realities of being entangled in unequal relationships with settler institutions and actors, Indigenous expressions of sovereignty have endured and are still enacted in a variety of ways including legal claims, political activism, and life projects. Indigenous People also enact sovereignty through processes of everyday resurgence (Corntassel 2012; see also Éthier and Flamand, this volume), inscribed in daily actions to maintain, revive, and reimagine meaningful life projects and environmental stewardship responsibilities in relative autonomy from settler-state institutions (Morphy and Morphy 2013). In effect, Indigenous sovereignty binds together Indigenous notions of relationality—of caring for lands, waters, humans, and non-humans—on the one hand, with the concrete failures of modern settler states demonstrated through the current climate change crisis and associated extreme weather events on the other.

In this chapter, we explore how Torres Strait Islanders and Walbunja People in Australia exercise their sovereignty amid the everyday impacts of climate change. The Walbunja are one of the tribes of the Yuin Nation, Aboriginal custodians of a large section of the New South Wales (NSW) South Coast. The Torres Strait Islanders, who call their territory Zenadth Kes, are a distinct group of Indigenous Australians encompassing several heterogeneous Nations living beyond Australia's eastern tip, a stone's throw from Papua New Guinea. For both the Torres Strait Islanders and the Walbunja, the landscapes and seascapes and the non-humans are teachers and guides. Their living landscapes, modulations of the sea, tidal ebbs and flows, seasonal changes and living cycles tell them familiar stories that inform their laws and govern their daily actions on their lands and seas. Despite the radical changes wrought by ongoing colonial impositions and encroachment, Zenadth Kes's seascape and Walbunja Country[1] stories have remained comprehensible to those responsible for the stewardship of these territories. Over the last few decades, however, the seascape and Country have significantly changed their narratives. In many ways, it is as if these territories of life were now speaking a language foreign to their human relations.

As Kyle Whyte (Potawatomi Nation) stresses, humans have largely adopted a "domineering" and abusive position toward their non-human relatives, which he describes as a "massive breach of kinship" (2020, 9) and duty of "care, reciprocity and respect for consent" (7). Years of stubborn refusal by the settler society—in Australia and beyond—to rethink how as a community we relate to our territories, to each other, and to our more-than-human kin have resulted in dramatic consequences worldwide, including across Zenadth Kes and Walbunja Country. While one island's territories are progressively being engulfed by the sea, the other's Country is being destroyed by catastrophic bushfires. In both the Torres Strait Islander and Walbunja territories, community members are working hard to make sense of the new narratives conveyed by their territories and non-human kin (e.g., rising sea levels, erosion, coral bleaching, shifts in seasonal and animal migration patterns, etc.) and what they mean for their futures, interpreting them as a warning that humans must redress their abusive relationships with the lands and seas.

We adopt a "kincentric" standpoint (Salmón 2000) that emphasizes the interdependence and interconnections between humans, more-than-humans, air, soil, water, rocks, sky, and spiritual beings (Reo 2019). This approach stems from Indigenous Peoples' relational ontologies in which the non-humans are seen as part of a web of relationships and viewed as "kin," with whom humans have mutual obligations and responsibilities for care and respect. To borrow Colin Scott's words, "Relationality is ontologically primary. Relationships of (dis)respect and reciprocity (whether positive or negative) are ubiquitous and profoundly consequential in the living world, whether or not a particular cultural framing is alert to such truth" (2017, 52). As discussed by Mario Blaser, Sylvie Poirier, and Penelope Anthias in their introduction to this volume, humans are understood as being part of—and not outside—"nature," unlike in Western Judeo-Christian conceptualizations (Latour 1997, 1999). Elsewhere Poirier similarly stresses that "the land (and ancestral territories) is perceived not as a mere surface to occupy, possess and exploit, but as networks of sentient and meaningful places, the site of knowledge, experiences and transmission ... an integral dimension of one's identity" (2008, 82). These relational ontologies are the foundations of Indigenous laws, governance, and knowledge systems (Borrows 2010; Daigle 2016; Napoleon 2013). Environmental stewardship practices as well as Indigenous relational economies are framed around the moral bonds and mutual obligations linking humans and non-human relatives. This contrasts with the citizenship approach that tends to dominate the discourses around climate change action, which emphasizes personal responsibilities toward fellow citizens (within a nation or as global citizens) but maintains the human-nature divide and excludes the land, the sea, and all non-humans, denying them any form of agency and volition.

From the kincentric standpoint, the agency, stories, and teachings shared by the land, sea, weather, reefs, plants, animals, ancestors, and human relatives are central to understanding the reality of climate change. How can these stories and relationality be used to change the rhythms of what can be described as an accelerating process of colonization (Whyte 2016) driven by a relatively unquestioned "pursuit of the modernist and developmentalist notion of a good life" (Blaser, personal communication), both of which are overwhelmingly at odds with Torres Strait Islanders' and the Walbunja's enduring values, economies, and kinship responsibilities toward their territories of life? There are risks in using concepts such as climate change, as the same term is often deployed to talk about different things. It is, therefore, crucial to engage in processes of "controlled equivocation" (Blaser 2019; Viveiros de Castro 2004) to elicit the differences in perspectives that underpin understandings of climate change and climate change risks and to make visible which lifeworlds and life projects are being protected and pursued when climate change actions and solutions are proposed (see Whyte 2020). Rather than questioning the depth and breadth of scientific evidence, anthropogenic climate change is seen, from many Indigenous perspectives, as an inevitable consequence of settler states' failures of relationality with their territories and a betrayal of mutual obligations to care for and act in the best interests of our non-human kin.

This chapter explores unfolding Torres Strait Islanders' and Walbunja life projects, environmental stewardship, and sovereignty in the context of increasingly threatening climate change disruptions. It seeks to make visible the transformative continuity underpinning the resilience of their lifeworlds as well as their entanglement with the Australian settler state and global processes and examines how their stories can help rethink Indigenous and non-Indigenous interdependent futures. The chapter draws on two distinct, long-standing research relationships in which Annick Thomassin is the common denominator. In the Zenadth Kes, perspectives on Torres Strait Islanders' endurance, creative transformative continuity, and life projects emerge from Thomassin's research on the politics of fisheries and fisheries co-management in the region (beginning in 2008). This chapter presented a wonderful opportunity to collaborate with and to create a space to nurture the talent and interests of young Torres Strait Islander (Iamagal) and emerging researcher Jacinta Baragud. In Walbunja Country, the reflections we share here draw on an ongoing action-research collaboration supporting the environment stewardship resurgence along this part of the NSW South Coast. This collaboration brings together Mogo and Batemans Bay Local Aboriginal Land Councils, their ranger teams, and a small interdisciplinary team

(Indigenous knowledge, anthropology, geography, sociology, and disaster management) from the Australian National University and Western Sydney University and which includes three of the authors—Annick Thomassin (Australian National University), Adam Nye (Wabunja, Mogo Local Aboriginal Land Council), and Kim Spurway (Western Sydney University).

The thrust of the chapter involves looking at how Torres Strait Islanders and Walbunja People have gone about responding to these questions in practice and what insights can be drawn from their experiences. We briefly discuss the literature on life projects and climate change, outlining the impacts of and challenges imposed on Indigenous life projects, territories of life, and sovereignties by the Australian colonial settler state. We then describe Zenadth Kes, Walbunja Country, and their Peoples, providing a historical, environmental, and cultural context for the rest of the chapter. We describe the quotidian realities of living with the consequences of climate change. For the Torres Strait Islanders, this means rising seas, inundations, and destruction of both built and natural environments. For the Walbunja, this equates to the traumas associated with the devastation of their Country, including their non-human kin from the catastrophic bushfires of 2019–2020. We conclude with a discussion about the challenges and prospects of entangled life projects, asking whether a change is possible in the ontological relationships of the Torres Strait Islanders and Walbunja People with settler states and populations. In other words, and to echo our colleague Cristina Rojas (this volume; see also Smith et al. 2021), are the emerging alliances between Indigenous and non-Indigenous Peoples and institutions capable of engendering positive "ontological opening"?

SOVEREIGN LIFE PROJECTS AND CLIMATE CHANGE

In Australia and around the world, Indigenous Peoples, despite their negligible contributions to carbon emissions, are on the frontline of a planet-scale anthropogenic climate crisis. Indigenous communities' vulnerability to the adverse consequences of climate change is multi-faceted. Several Indigenous communities are situated in geographies among the most exposed to climate change impacts, including small islands, the Arctic, and high-altitude areas facing the most direct and immediate threats. For millennia, the communities living in these geographies have developed adaptable lifeways interdependent with the movements and needs of their land and seascapes and with more-than-human relationships. These lifeways and the capacity to maintain these relationships are now threatened by the rising sea levels and temperatures, droughts, desertification, fires, floods, cyclones, changes in marine currents, and the impacts these shifts have on plants and animals. These threats are contributing to uncertainties and increased vulnerabilities by destabilizing livelihoods, knowledge systems, and in some cases, by forcing entire communities to migrate away from their ancestral territories (Green and Ruddock 2009; Richards and Bradshaw 2017). Indigenous Peoples' vulnerability to climate change risks and impacts is also exacerbated by a series of interrelated factors including socio-economic, political and ontological marginalization, limited infrastructures, erosion of social fabric, displacement, loss of territories and resources, erosion or destruction of their knowledge, custodianship, and political systems, and experiences of intergenerational trauma.

Discourses on Indigenous vulnerability as victims of climate change are often problematic. They tend to focus on Indigenous individuals or communities as the loci of the deficits while guiding our gaze away from the ongoing processes of colonization, large-scale dispossession, and the capitalist system that structurally maintains Indigenous People's vulnerability (Haalbloom and Natcher 2012; Spurway 2018; Thomassin et al. 2018; Whyte 2016, 2017, 2020). These discourses are often used to justify the deployment of external strategies aimed at increasing Indigenous Peoples' resilience, endurance, and capacity to adapt to climate change rather than paying attention to Indigenous Peoples' perspectives, economies, environmental stewardship initiatives, and aspirations based on their intimate knowledge and deep reciprocal relationships with their territories. Indigenous Peoples' exposure to climate change risks needs to be understood in relation to the social, environmental, and spiritual injustices rooted in colonialism, industrialization, urbanization, and capitalism and which are upheld by policies, programs, laws, and economic perspectives that reproduce the asymmetrical colonial relationships that engender Indigenous vulnerabilities and hinder Indigenous initiatives and lifeways (Whyte 2016, 2020).

Anthropogenic climate change is itself a direct legacy of colonialism and Western ontologies based on human domination over the "natural world" and an endless expansion of exploitation for profit. The seismic changes Indigenous Peoples are now confronted with are similar to those they have had to adapt to since the onset of colonization in their respective territories. As Whyte puts it, Indigenous Peoples around the world are witnessing somewhat of a "colonial déjà vu" (2016). After several decades of Indigenous political struggles to have their rights recognized and of actions reaffirming their sovereignty over their ancestral territories and lives, many Indigenous communities face the prospect of being dispossessed from their territories and lifeworlds once again, forced to adapt to another cycle of colonial disruption. As Whyte suggests, their centuries-long experience of life-changing and world-threatening colonial processes could well be one of the Indigenous Peoples' strengths. On the global stage, Indigenous Peoples have been among the strongest voices of the climate justice movement and a moving force against the whole way of life imposed by the colonial project.

Since the late 1970s, there has been a progressive recognition of the value of Indigenous traditional ecological knowledge (TEK) and the positive contributions this knowledge can make to addressing environmental issues (Berkes 1993; Menzies 2006; McGregor 2014). Projects that integrate TEK with science to improve natural resource as well as disaster management practices are often driven by a non-Indigenous agenda and understandings of TEK that tend to focus on the physical and "functional" dimensions of these knowledge systems while excluding their relational, ethical, and spiritual underpinnings as well as the agency and intentionality of more-than-humans (Cruikshank 2012; Reo and Whyte 2012; Spak 2005). This process of distilling Indigenous ontological perspectives and epistemologies into knowledge of specific ecosystems or species only insofar as they are useful to dominant Western natural resource management has significantly hampered the possibility of shifting away from Western environmental management paradigms (Nadasdy 2005) and the actualization of Indigenous life projects rooted in ethics of mutual care and responsibilities for non-humans, ancestors, and future generations. In Stella Spak's words, there is a tendency to assume that "the value of TEK lies in its use by wildlife managers rather than seeing it as knowledge that might be used to re-think the unexamined cultural assumptions of how humans ought to relate to the world around them" (2005, 239).

As the global climate crisis unfolds and humanity witnesses the multiplication of "unprecedented" natural disasters and "one-in-a-century" climatic events, Indigenous Peoples' environmental management practices and TEK systems are once again being called upon in the search for solutions in climate change mitigation and adaptation (ILO 2017). In Australia, the catastrophic 2019–2020 bushfires season—which burnt over eighteen million hectares—generated discussion and interest among the broader public about the value of Aboriginal cultural burning practices (see Williamson 2022). Despite acknowledgements in public forums, such as the Royal Commission into National Natural Disaster Arrangements, that Aboriginal land and fire management practices are "not solely directed at hazard reduction" but serve wider cultural purposes (2020, 387; see also Williamson 2022), there is still very little consideration for, or understanding of, the implications of Aboriginal and Torres Strait Islanders' relational ontological perspectives on approaches to issues of climate change. Similarly, little attention is given to how Indigenous perspectives may hold radically different definitions and understandings regarding the nature of climate change, natural disasters, and risks (Altangerel and Kull 2013; Blaser 2009) as well as what actually requires protection (O'Neil et al. 2021). While the wider public tends to see climate change as a threat to human properties and infrastructures, to global and national economies, and to the quality of its carbon and resource-hungry lifestyles, for Indigenous Nations, it represents a threat to their and their non-human relatives' identities, cultures, and lifeworlds.

Despite the limits imposed by settler-colonial contexts, entanglements with colonial institutions, and—to borrow from Timothy Neale (2023)—the bureaucratic "ritual control" in which they are embedded, they can still provide entry points to enact Indigenous notions of care. Indigenous Peoples continue to enact their unceded sovereignty in their daily lives through continually evolving environmental stewardship practices and the articulations of place-based life projects, governed by their dynamic relational ontologies and perspectives of what constitutes a meaningful and respectful life. These practices enable Indigenous Peoples to honour their moral bonds and perform specific responsibilities toward their territories of life, other humans, and more-than-human beings. Indigenous stewardship duties go far beyond ensuring the sustainable use and management of natural resources, the monitoring activities that Indigenous Peoples and Indigenous ranger groups[2] are regularly contracted to conduct in scientific projects (Williamson 2022), or undertaking economic activities such as commercial fishing.

Focusing on the "everydayness," as Jeff Corntassel (Cherokee Nation, 2012) suggests, enables us to locate sovereignty within the textured complexity of the daily performance of Indigenous Peoples' relationships with and responsibilities toward their territories. This includes (but is not limited to) the enactment of their fishing, hunting, and harvesting practices and associated duties to take only what is necessary, to protect, share, and reciprocate with human and non-human relatives, and the restoration of traditional practices and ceremonies. It involves acts of resurgence such as speaking, signposting, and mapping their territories in their language (Daigle 2016). It involves the articulation of their relational economic models regarding understandings of prosperity embedded in kinship and framed around sharing and caring responsibilities, reciprocity, and respect for families, communities, and all living (and non-living) beings past, present, and future.

LIVING WITH CLIMATE CHANGE NOW ACROSS ZENADTH KES: NGAU LAGAU NUPAI BAU PUIDAN NGU (ON OUR ISLAND WE SEE THE WAVES ROLLING IN)[3]

Located in far north Queensland, Australia, in the waters between Op Daudai (Papua New Guinea) and Koey Daudai (Australia's mainland), Zenadth Kes, or Torres Strait, is an archipelago composed of over 270 islands and sand cays dispersed across a 48,000 square kilometre expanse of sea. Seventeen of these islands[4] (hosting eighteen communities) are permanently inhabited, while many more are occasionally populated and regularly visited for diverse purposes (commercial and subsistence fishing, turtle hunting, gardening, collecting eggs, ceremony, etc.).

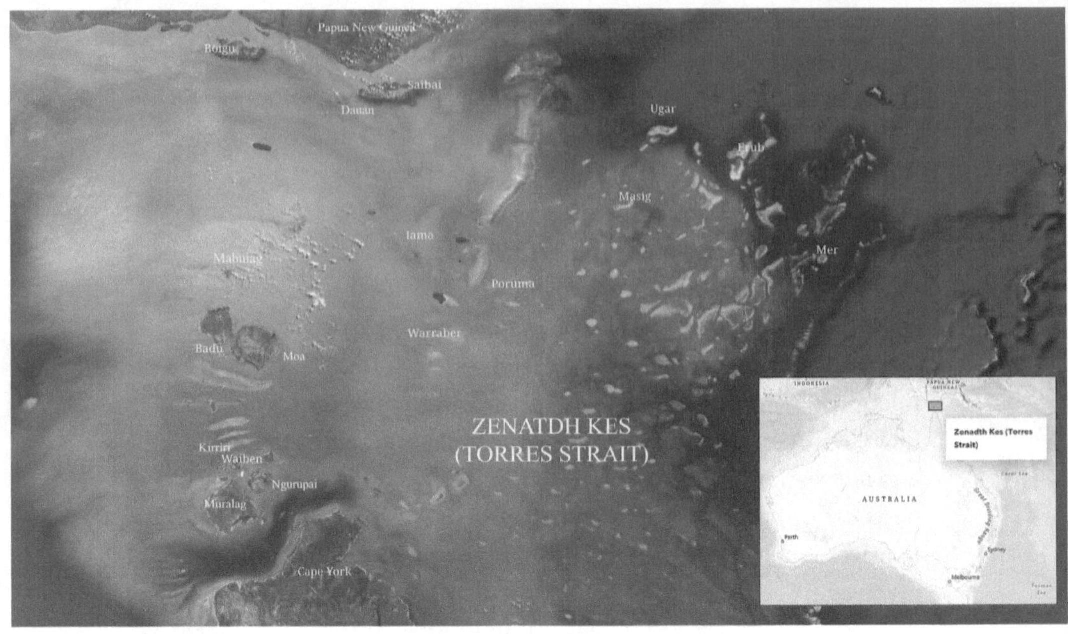

MAP 8.1 | Zenadth Kes (Torres Strait).
(Created by Annick Thomassin, 2024, with ArcGIS Storymaps.)

The Torres Strait Islanders are custodians of the region's seascape. As Melanesian Peoples, they share strong cultural and kinship ties with the Papuan Peoples of the coastal villages, islands, and Fly River estuary of Papua New Guinea's Western Province. A testament to their seafaring lifeworld and the central role they played in the extensive pre-colonial trade network connecting what is now known as Papua New Guinea and the Australian mainland, Torres Strait Islanders also share connections with Aboriginal Peoples along Cape York Peninsula's coasts.

Torres Strait Islanders' lifeways, identity, and essence are bound to their sentient seascape, created in part by the journeys and actions of ancestral beings (e.g., Waibin, Gelam, Siga, Sau, Kulka, and Malo) who constituted this marine-terrestrial-celestial environment by morphing into rock formations, nesting areas, sand cays, and hills, or by transmuting into various marine animals and constellations (Lawrie 1970; McNiven and Feldman 2003; Scott 2004; Sharp 1993). Torres Strait

Islanders also hold reciprocal moral bonds and responsibilities toward totemic animals such as koedal (crocodile), dangal (dugong), waru (sea turtle), and omer (frigate bird) (Scott 2004). Their lives are governed by the constant ebbs and flows of the ocean and the four dominant winds—naigai (north), kuki (northwest), sagerr (southeast), and zei (south)—which are the subject of stories, songs, and dances (Lawrie 1970; Lui-Chivizhe 2022).

Torres Strait Islanders have, from the outset of colonial encroachments, affirmed their sovereignty over their unceded land and sea territories. While many early encounters between Torres Strait Islanders and Europeans were marked by violence, they also engaged in trading. Contrasting with other colonial histories in Australia, it is not so much the land that was coveted by the colonists, but the vast riches found in the sea. Hence, most Torres Strait Islanders maintained their intimate engagement with their territories and seascape. From the mid-1800s, commercial fishers from around the world established pearling and bêche-de-mer stations in various parts of Zenadth Kes. Torres Strait men, women, and children joined crews of divers from the Pacific, Japan, Southeast Asia, Europe, and the Americas. While they were often coerced into doing so, many joined willingly. An extension of their seafaring and trading activities, commercial fishing has been woven into Torres Strait Islanders' relational mixed economy[5] or "hybrid economy" (see Altman 2001; Thomassin 2016) and has been a mainstay of their livelihood and culture for over 160 years. Largely controlled by porena (foreigners), the industrial fisheries that developed in the Zenadth Kes from this period led to regular collapses of commercial species stocks, exposing the fragile ecological balance of the place. As was the case with all aspects of their lives at the time, the money and wages generated by Torres Strait fishers involved in these enterprises were controlled by colonial institutions, a situation that Torres Strait Islanders have vehemently and collectively fought against since the 1920s.

From the 1910s, the relative autonomy (Morphy and Morphy 2013) gained from boat ownership enabled them to articulate their own models of economic participation and adjust their working pace and involvement in various economic segments (i.e., cash economy, subsistence fishing and gardening, trade, and gift exchange) in accordance with their lifeworld, their responsibilities to take only what they needed, as well as fishing stock and market fluctuations. As Regina Ganter writes, Torres Strait Islander boats "were co-operatively organised and reaffirmed traditional kinship structures and traditional claims to land, sea, and resources" (1994, 97).

Then and now, Torres Strait Islanders' life projects have flexibility embedded at their core, in sync with their ever-transforming seascape. On the water, commercial and customary activities interact in a synergetic way and are integral constituents of Torres Strait Islanders' dynamic, small-scale fisheries systems; understanding that these systems themselves are essential components of the communities' mixed relational economy. Torres Strait Islanders' life projects have since involved the maintenance of healthy fisheries systems and continuous political engagement to regain control over their seascape and resources based on customary marine tenure regimes, their laws and ethos of care and reciprocity toward their human and non-human kin, as well as the ambition to see these resources used in ways that benefit their community rather than mainly profiting larger, non-Islander operators based elsewhere. They have taken these political projects to various arenas, developing the Marine Strategy for the Torres Strait (Mulrennan 1993), which partly led to fishery co-management arrangements and some gains with regards to fishery licence allocation. Most notably, the landmark Akiba Decision (2013) recognized Torres Strait Islanders' non-exclusive native title rights over their sea territory. Much effort is dedicated to keeping local lifeways alive for the future generations, including developing a bilingual knowledge database, reviving and strengthening their traditional language, and rethinking their governance structure.

Torres Strait Islanders' rich and dynamic life projects are significantly entangled in their relationship with the settler-colonial institutions. The ontological asymmetries, which characterize this relationship, interact and interfere with Torres Strait Islanders' connections with and visions for their territories of life. These asymmetries are likely to become more problematic with the mounting challenges that climate change poses to the integrity of Torres Strait Islanders' environments, lifeways, economies, and the very capacity to perpetuate their cultures and customary responsibilities at home in Zenadth Kes.

As James McGoodwin et al. (2000) suggest, the rhetoric of natural resource crises can represent an obstacle for the implementation of Indigenous management practices and contribute to the reification of scientific or risk management approaches. They caution that crisis situations are "not the time to chart a new course and to bring on board inexperienced crew-members. They [the experts] might well question the wisdom of making old and new crew members 'find their sea legs' while a storm is raging" (264). Neale's work with emergency managers also echoes this perspective. To borrow his words, "the rituals of emergency management normalize and domesticate crises, both preserving and building the position and power of key elites through time" (2023, 579).

Contrasting perspectives on Torres Strait Islanders' sovereignty, their relationships with their territories, their economic well-being, and the nature of climate change risks, impacts, and mitigation and adaptation strategies will also shape Torres Strait Islanders' and Zenadth Kes futures.

AS THE SEA IS RISING

Anthropogenic climate change in Zenadth Kes is not an abstract phenomenon set to occur in a foreseeable and potentially reversible future. It is a nerve-wracking, traumatic, everyday reality that has been unfolding before Torres Strait Islanders' eyes for more than a decade. Zenadth Kes ranks among the locations considered the most vulnerable to the impacts of climate change in Australia (Hennessy et al. 2007; Steffen et al. 2014). Climate change affects the eighteen Torres Strait communities differently. The rise of the sea level is of particular concern for the six low-lying islands of Masig, Iama, Poruma, Warraber, Boigu, and Saibai. Similar to other low-lying island nations across the Pacific, Torres Strait Islander communities are increasingly impacted by increased sea levels, episodes of coral bleaching, and changes in weather patterns. This situation is expected to worsen over the next decades.

An Australian government report published in 2008 already regarded the situation as an emergency and impeding human rights crisis (ATSISJC 2008). In the late 2000s, king tides accompanied by strong winds have resulted in houses and buildings being flooded, coastal infrastructures being damaged or destroyed, and salt intrusions in wells and gardens. These floods have also reached cemeteries, damaging the resting places of ancestors and relatives.

FIGURE 8.1 | Family sheds after a king tide in 2009, Masig (Zenadth Kes). (Photo by Annick Thomassin.)

Erosion was a major preoccupation at the time. On Masig—a small coral cay covering 1.69 square kilometres and which rests at a mere three metres above sea level—walks along the beach prompt discussions about the changing seascape, about a shed built in an area now covered by water, about a road that is no longer there, and about threats to places holding recent or ancient memories, childhood dreams, and learning spaces. Invaluable heritage, sacred sites, and sites of knowledge are being eroded. Nesting areas for seabirds and turtles are disrupted.

Life rhythms and cycles are also changing. Elders on Masig recall that the winds and the sky used to tell them about the weather to come over the next three to four days, sometimes longer. The presence of certain clouds, their colour, and their shape would tell them whether it was safe to go out to sea. Such predictions are harder to make now. The weather has become less predictable. Kuki, associated with the monsoon season, has shifted from November to January or February. Christmas is now often scorching hot and dry. Particular fish and crustaceans that used to be fished at specific times of the year when they are more abundant (and succulent) have changed their habits (See Y. Mosby in O'Brien 2021).

While elected officials in the Australian parliament ponder the acceptable levels of emission reduction to avoid harms to the country's carbon-intensive economy, climate change related impacts are progressively endangering Zenadth Kes's ecosystems and entire lifeworlds. Impacts to the life of non-human relatives like the waru, dangal, and kaiar (tropical rock lobster) that are of utmost cultural, spiritual, and economic significance will have major implications for Torres Strait Islander communities' lifeways as well as their physical, mental, and spiritual well-being.

Masig's councillor, Ms. Hilda Mosby, is deeply concerned about the situation they currently find themselves in. "It is clear that we, as humans, have not upheld our responsibilities toward Mother Earth. That's what happens when you mess up with her" (ABC 2021). She worries that "building seawalls and raising houses can buy time, but in the long-term, some communities may face relocation." Like many across Zenadth Kes, leaving will only be considered as a last resort. Mosby is also worried about future generations of Torres Strait Islanders who may have to contemplate the difficult and traumatic reality of a future elsewhere. In the meantime, they are working on short- and longer-term solutions to secure the littoral, reshape their governance system, strengthen their economy, and live a good life at home for as long as possible. Many fear that they may be forced to evacuate their island on the governments' order, not on their own terms. "We don't want to be refugees in our own country ... We have our ancestors here, they are tying us to our land. We don't want to leave our loved ones behind" (Y. Mosby in O'Brien 2021).

As custodians of Zenadth Kes' seascape, Torres Strait Islanders are asserting their sovereignty and duty of care by continuously holding the Australian government accountable. In 2019, after decades of inaction to address the current and imminent problems associated with climate change and Australia's refusal to commit to reduce emissions and rethink its economy, a group of Torres Strait Islanders lodged a legal complaint with the United Nations Human Rights Committee (UNHRC) against the Australian Government for infringements on their human rights. A similar complaint was filed in the Australian

Federal Court in October 2021. Both litigations emphasize their relational perspective, the looming threat to Torres Strait Islander's place-based identity and culture, and focus on the responsibility to take care of the seascape and the non-human. While the Federal Court case is yet to be determined at the time of writing, in July 2022, the UNHRC decided in favour of the Torres Strait Islanders by determining that Australia indeed violated Islanders' human rights through climate inaction (United Nations 2023). While it may be too late to avoid out-migrations for some island communities, Torres Strait Islanders are demanding that Australia provide them with substantial support to face the increasing climate change related challenges and, most importantly, that it uphold its caring duty and responsibility for its contributions to the global issues. What they propose is for Australia and the world to commit to new life projects or, again, as Rojas (this volume) puts it, demonstrate ontological openings—dissociated from their carbon-hungry economies and utilitarian conception of nature—working collectively toward a fair transition for all, including the generations to come.

WALBUNJA COUNTRY

Some 3,600 kilometres south of Zenadth Kes, along New South Wales' South Coast, is Walbunja Country. Walbunja's ancestral territories stretch from Durras to Moruya, reaching inland to the Great Dividing Range (Donaldson 2006; NNTT 2017). The land and seascape to which the Walbunja belong are shaped by the actions of the Dreaming's ancestral beings[6]—the path they took became the regions' waterways and valleys, and the areas they chose to camp or rest became sacred sites (Donaldson 2006).

Country is dense with continuous connections, names, and stories linked to both spiritual ancestral beings and their descendants up to the present day. As Walbunja Elder Keith Nye explains, there are names, stories, and connections to every headland, bay, beach, and paddock. These stories reach into the sea, accounting for the ever-changing seascape and the kinship relationships shared with marine life. For thousands of years, Walbunja's ancestors travelled the coast at length along the Umbarra (Black Duck) Songline, which runs from

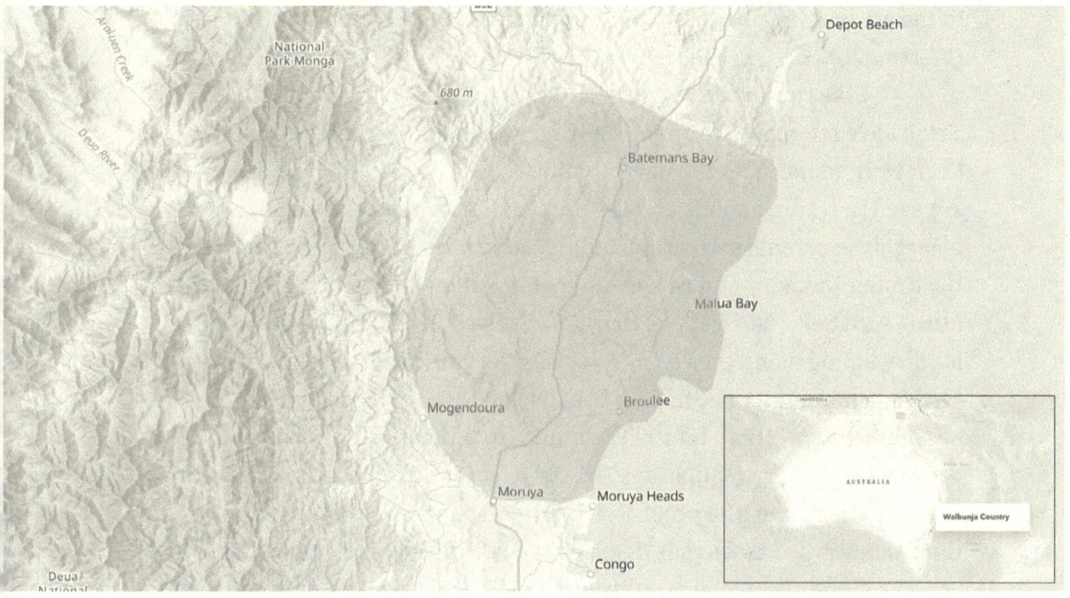

MAP 8.2 | Walbunja Country. This map shows what roughly corresponds to Walbunja territorial boundaries. These are not hard boundaries, however, testifying to the strong connections and family bonds between the local tribes and beyond. It is commonly acknowledged that the territory of the Walbunja tribe is bordered by the Clyde and Moruya rivers and by the mountain ridge to the west. Their territory also extends into the ocean. (Source: Environmental Stewardship Resurgence on Walbunja Country project, 2024, created by Annick Thomassin with ArcGIS Storymaps).

Mallacoota (State of Victoria) to the Hawkesbury River (north of Sydney) (Fuller et al. 2021). Countless middens and campsites punctuate the littoral, many of which were used until at least the 1960s, testifying to their long-term relationship with the area.

The towns of Mogo and Batemans Bay are part of a series of towns at the heart of Walbunja Country. Like so many localities, these two towns were built on the decimation (smallpox), violent confrontations, invasion, dispossession, and displacement of local Indigenous Peoples. Whalers, squatters, foresters, and gold miners came to the region to exploit its resources. From the mid-1800s, their presence led to the accelerated alienation and transformation of Walbunja territories (Watson 2014).

Like the Torres Strait Islanders, members of the Walbunja Tribe have attempted to shape their relationships with the newcomers. Creatively adapting to the new circumstances they were facing, they engaged in trading goods and services and participated in a range of emerging economic sectors, including as workers in the gold mines and the timber industry and as harvesters for settler-farmers in Mogo (White 2010). As a Saltwater People, they got involved in the commercial fisheries developing along the coast. Adapting a technique imported by early settlers, community net-fishing became a key subsistence and cultural-commercial activity for the Walbunja from the mid-1800s until the 1980s when fishery regulations started to severely impede these practices.

Over time, the progressive urbanization and privatization of their Country led to further dispossession, limiting their movements and access to important sites, traditional food, medicine, and material, and heavily impacting Walbunja community members' capacity to perform their ceremonies and customary responsibilities; further entangling their life projects with those of local and national settler economies, ontologies, and territorialities. Today, Walbunja Country is partly rural and partly urban. Their territories are facing continuous development pressure from urban expansion which has increasingly reduced the region's coastal rainforest cover and resulted in the disruption of burial grounds and other important sites. Their waters are also subjected to increased navigation and exploitation with Walbunja fishers competing with commercial and recreational fishers and the tourist industry. While their resident populations are relatively small (in 2016, Mogo and Batemans Bay had a population of 269 and 11,294 with Aboriginal populations of 36 percent and 12 percent respectively), these towns are popular touristic destinations with a significant seasonal population influx. In 2019, the Eurobodalla Shire, of which Batemans Bay is the main hub, hosted over 1.6 million visitors, most of whom congregated along the seaside over the summer holidays.

As in bigger towns and cities, the local Walbunja community has not had much of a say in the planning and expansion of these localities. Even when consultations have occurred, like during the planning of Batemans Marine Park, development and zoning have tended to disregard

Walbunja preoccupations, lifeways, and economies. Several sanctuary zones were established over Walbunja's fishing areas. Gated National Park lands and fenced private properties along the coastline and inland have restricted access to many of the fishing sites and other significant sites. The restricted access to headlands and beaches has impinged Walbunja fishers' capacity to follow schools of fish as they travel along the coast. Walbunja's beach hauling activities are further limited during peak tourist season and over weekends in the summer when the beaches are packed with visitors. These restrictions disrupt their capacity to transmit knowledge to younger generations and impact the community's health and physical, economic, emotional, and spiritual well-being as well as their sense of identity. They also prevent the Walbunja from performing their duty of care toward Country.

Contemporary Walbunja history, relationship to Country, environmental custodianship responsibilities, and economic practices have been misunderstood if not completely invisible to the general population while Walbunja arts, heritage, and pre- and early-colonial history have elicited some interest. Littoral walking tracks punctuated by interpretative panels with old photographs provide onlookers with a glimpse of Aboriginal historical connections to the region. The Eurobodalla Shire happily showcases Walbunja's past, while constraining Walbunja's contemporaneity. One of the local Elders concluded that people were more interested in their ancestors' "garbage" (i.e., middens) than in their community's life today.

Over the last decade, several initiatives have been pushed forward by the Walbunja and wider Yuin community to reassert their presence and sovereignty in Country, including the recognition of their fishing and territorial rights. In a bid to regain such rights, in 2017 the Yuin Nation (including the Walbunja) filed a comprehensive Native Title claim covering roughly 17,000 square kilometres from the Far South Coast town of Eden to the outskirts of Sydney, extending three nautical miles into their sea Country (NNTT 2017).

Walbunja's everyday sovereignty is also progressively activated through the actions of small environmental ranger teams attached to Mogo and Batemans Bay Local Aboriginal Land Councils (LALCs).[7] With the support of their respective Land Councils, the ranger teams work tenaciously with few resources to restore their environmental custodianship responsibilities and reinscribe Walbunja lifeways, place names, stories, values, and aspirations across the region's land-, sea-, and urban-scapes. Lack of ongoing secured funding means that a large part of their work consists of providing mainstream ecological services to subsidize other stewardship responsibilities. These include contracted services such as water quality testing, weed removal, and pest control.

Despite the mainstream nature of these ecological service contracts, their actions on Country remain informed by their relational ontology and the responsibilities bestowed to them through their ancestry. For example, a partnership with local oyster farmers to eradicate invasive species of oysters was conducted concurrently with a project aiming at documenting the cultural significance and biodiversity of the Walbunja coastal environment. The funds received for the revitalization of Mogo Creek enabled them to replant native bush food and medicine. The Mogo rangers undertook a mangrove rejuvenation project to enhance the health of a significant lagoon system while protecting an exposed midden from further erosion and disruption from a nearby caravan park. In the process, they deepen their relations with their territories, enabling them to identify the care that needs to be provided to specific areas.

One key custodianship responsibility the Walbunja rangers are passionate about reviving is their cultural burning duties. This project brought them to work alongside the New South Wales Rural Fire Services (RFS) to demonstrate the safety and multiple purposes underpinning this practice. From the Walbunja perspective, the use of fire is needed not only to decrease bushfire risks to communities and properties. The lands and waters of your Country tell you that burning practices regenerate the bush and return it to a healthy state, providing the best possible home for animals and a chance for threatened and endangered species to return and thrive. This is a partnership between Country, people, and non-human relatives for the well-being of all. This example demonstrates the rangers' and Walbunja community's desire to share some of their knowledge and educate the non-Indigenous population about how to relate to Country as kin.

In this context, the ranger teams have been performing their everyday sovereignty by reclaiming and reactivating relationships with their environment, rooted in their relational ontology and based on their contemporary laws, knowledge, ethics, custodianship principles, and aspirations to strengthen their decision-making power over how Country is interacted with and managed. The ongoing tensions between Walbunja's ontological perspectives and those embodied by developers, mainstream environmental managers, and disaster risks management practitioners, however, continue to pose challenges to the realization of the rangers' and Walbunja community's life projects (Spurway 2018; Thomassin et al. 2018). Nevertheless, as discussed below (see also Smith et al. 2021), there are signs of potential productive alliances and possible ontological openings emerging.

RISING FROM THE ASHES

As mentioned, the 2019–2020 bushfires in Australia destroyed an estimated 18 million hectares of land and resulted in an unprecedented loss of biodiversity and property. The territories of the Walbunja Tribe and the broader Yuin Nation were severely impacted. Large sections of the town of Mogo and parts of Batemans Bay were destroyed. This included the houses of ten Aboriginal families and the Mogo LALC's office, art gallery, and ranger shed. The LALC plays an important role for the local Aboriginal community, providing a meeting place and a wide range of services, including the environmental custodianship activities carried on by its ranger team. It was also the keeping place of cultural artefacts which were lost in the blaze.

The Walbunja community is resilient. Notwithstanding the dynamic knowledge, practices, and relations that have sustained their lifeworld on Country over millennia, they have adapted to the continuous challenges posed by ongoing colonial processes and encroachment on their territories. However, the fires have deeply scarred Country and affected the sacred bond connecting Walbunja with their land, waters, and animals, adding to their trauma. As Senior Ranger Sherrie Nye explains, "Being so connected to the land through my work and my ancestry, I'm grieving for the plants, the animals, the birds" (cited in Milton 2020). More than three years later, the scale of the devastation and its long-term impacts on the environment and cultural sites have yet to be fully grasped.

FIGURE 8.2 | Walbunja Country, January 2020. Mogo State Forest after the 2019–2020 bushfires. Nothing but ashes and burnt eucalyptus trees. (Photo by Annick Thomassin.)

For years, concerns voiced by Aboriginal communities, scientists, and fire services about increased fire risks have fallen on deaf ears. While cultural burning knowledge and practices are valued in northern Australia (Williamson 2022), Aboriginal communities in the populated southeast struggle to have a say in managing Country. Funding for ranger programs has largely been channeled away from heavily transformed urban environments. Walbunja rangers have been working for years to restore the health of Country. After years of navigating the "bureaucratic density" (Smith et al. 2021, 88) of disaster risks management with their hoops and hurdles framed by ontological Otherness, the rangers were hoping to restart their cultural burning practices over the winter of 2019, but the land was already too dry. The rest is history.

While no one event can be singled out to account for what happened, the Walbunja community and their ranger teams consider the government's inaction on climate change as negligence, a failure to listen to and perform their duty of care toward Country. The Covid-19 pandemic that hit the world a few months later exacerbated the lack of financial security of the ranger program. In Mogo, the ranger teams now only have sporadic work. The overwhelming grief triggered by the bushfires is still strongly felt and lived by members of the team.

Despite the challenges, the rangers continue to expand their capacities to care for Country properly while extending an invitation to the non-Indigenous community to open their eyes, minds, and hearts, to listen and (un)learn. This is a gracious invitation to renegotiate the terms and conditions of the settler project that currently shapes Australia's Indigenous and non-Indigenous entanglements and that constitutes a failed relationship with an abused, degraded, and neglected environment.

ENDURING YET ENTANGLED LIFE PROJECTS: SETTING THE FOUNDATION FOR NEW ONTOLOGICAL RELATIONS FOR AN AUSTRALIAN FUTURE?

The cases of Zenadth Kes and Walbunja Country provide important examples that illustrate how Indigenous Peoples must endlessly and creatively refine their life projects in the face of the seismic challenges posed to them by ongoing processes of colonization. For nearly two hundred years, Torres Strait Islanders' and Walbunja's lifeworlds and life projects have been—often severely—fragilized and destabilized by the colonial project. This colonial project is reproduced through the industrial capitalist ethos, characterized overexploitation and abuse of human and more-than-human relations—construed as resources—and maintained by policies, programs, and laws that perpetuate asymmetrical colonial relationships.

Understanding the current climate crisis as part of this colonial legacy, Indigenous Peoples' exposure to climate change risks is simultaneously engendered and amplified by these social, environmental, and spiritual injustices. For Indigenous Peoples, entanglement with the settler state's life project is not based on open, equitable arrangements between trusted partners, kin, or fellow citizens. Both examples show how deeply entangled Indigenous life projects are with actions and decisions made elsewhere—often thousands of kilometres away. Climate change is a clear manifestation of the interconnectedness of the earth's systems and entities. This is a message that Torres Strait Islanders and Walbunja Peoples are working hard to share. The hardships highlighted by Indigenous Peoples is that human systems are out of balance, and this imbalance overflows into all our relationships. The land, sea, and our non-human kin are vital to our common existence. As Torres Strait Islanders and Walbunja laws prescribe, we need to give as much as we take and take only what we need. Reciprocity is key. Both have extended an invitation to get together to shape our common futures, not simply through greener but still exploitative, profit-driven, and consumption-centred lifeways, but in ways that are respectful of our sentient world. These potentially shared life projects, however, require a significant shift in our terms of coexistence.

There is a recurrent problem in how settler institutions understand Indigenous demands that their knowledge and perspectives be acknowledged and not just tacked onto Western managerial approach to the territory. However, even these misunderstandings might provide entry points to enact Indigenous notions of care. As Spurway points out, "Indigenous [P]eoples' worldviews are increasingly recognised and valued by non-Indigenous institutions and peoples," including in the field of disaster risk management (2018, 2; see also Smith et al. 2021). While this may indicate a movement in the right direction, it remains uncertain whether this opening to Indigenous perspectives can translate into genuine efforts to understand and take seriously the relational ontologies underpinning Indigenous knowledge and practices, as decades-long engagements with TEK—often riddled with uncontrolled equivocations (see the introduction to this volume)—have demonstrated. As Whyte suggests, "While Indigenous knowledges obviously have useful information about the nature of ecological changes, it is perhaps more interesting to explore how renewing Indigenous knowledges serves the motivation of people and communities to face the challenge of climate changes" (2017, 158). Can the increasingly shared, albeit uneven, experience of climate change translate into a radical shift in non-Indigenous ways of being in the world or lead to what Poirier describes as a "path towards the political legitimacy of multiple ontologies" (2008, 77)?

Sadly, even if Australia and a majority of countries around the world would commit to decarbonize their economies within the next decade, for some low-lying Torres Strait Islander communities it may be too late to prevent large scale environmental, social, economic, and spiritual damage associated with rising sea levels. Sharing parallels with the St'át'imc's experience described by Sarah Moritz and Qwalqwalten (this volume), having to abandon their island homes would be a rupture of the sacred bonds they hold with Zenadth Kes, their ancestors, their more-than-human relatives, and an existential threat to the cultures and identities Torres Strait Islanders have developed over millennia. As Torres Strait Islanders have emphasized, if indeed they need to migrate elsewhere, they should dictate how and when, so that it reflects as closely as possible their lifeways and aspirations. These last resort life projects need to be considered carefully so that their relocation does not translate into accelerated processes of colonization.

CONCLUSION

Torres Strait Islanders and Walbunja lifeworlds are deeply entangled with wider Australian society and settler-colonial institutions. As Françoise Dussart and Sylvie Poirier argue, "whatever is entangled, in a given place and time (context), cannot easily be undone. And no matter, if changes are made to the distinctive dimension of one entity, they will impact in some fashion the other directly or indirectly" (2017, 5). Our entangled coexistence means that Indigenous life projects, territories, and enduring futures are entwined with the capacity of non-Indigenous people to recognize and support Indigenous differences, knowledges, and "territorial divergence," to value Indigenous cultures, and to enter into a renegotiation of our very terms of coexistence. It requires a radical ontological transformation—or an ontological opening—of Australia's (and other colonial nations') prevailing way of being in the world, including a shift toward embracing a relationality that emphasizes care-taking, responsibility, reciprocity, balance, and consideration for our seas, waters, lands, and each other as critical to our lifeways (see Red Nation 2020).

Torres Strait Islanders' and Walbunja's lifeworlds have been made vulnerable by more than a century of colonial encroachments, violence, dispossession, and control. Yet, they have continuously demonstrated their endurance and creative adaptability to the deep transformations and impacts that these processes continue to have on their territories of life, human and more-than-human relations, heritage, and futures. They perform this relative autonomy in the context of their everyday lives, in ways that align with their laws, values, perspectives of prosperity, and aspirations. Often misaligned with what Western institutions define as success, with its focus on profit and growth and the environment's capacity to sustain it, their articulated life projects have enabled them to sustain kinship relationships with their territories and non-human kin based on their understandings of their place in the world. Indigenous life projects, continuously refined in relation to the challenges posed to them by the colonial project, have progressively laid the foundations for the resurgence of their stewardship responsibilities and the assertion of their unceded sovereignty. As a legacy of colonization, the unfolding climate change crisis presents significant new challenges to the realization of Torres Strait Islander and Walbunja visions. For several Torres Strait Islander communities, these challenges amount to direct threats to their capacities to enact these projects at home, with ancestors, humans, and more-than-human relatives. What is a "good life" when your relations are destabilized, uprooted, or threatened with extinction?

Nevertheless, there are signs that Australians are beginning to hear the voices emerging from these territories of life, with the help of Aboriginal and Torres Strait Islander Nations. Through climate change, the planet is changing her tone, and the message is harder to ignore. Years of drought followed by dust storms and catastrophic fires, followed thereafter by floods and high-intensity cyclones, a seemingly endless succession of once-in-a-century events, is starting to hit home. At the peak of the traumatic 2019–2020 bushfire season, non-Indigenous Australians shared some of the grief for the loss of Country and way of life that Indigenous Australians have been carrying for over two hundred years. Suddenly, Indigenous knowledge, environmental management, and burning practices became more prominent—ancient solutions to a modern crisis. While Indigenous knowledge and practices are perceived as holding some solutions to the climate crisis, this shift is, for the most part, not happening purely because of more attention to and respect for Indigenous ontologies. Rather, industrial nations are beginning to understand the existential threat to themselves, although as Neale (2023) suggests, settler institutions, especially those responsible for emergency management, also demonstrate endurance and are likely to maintain their practices and "rituals" in place. Indigenous Peoples can perhaps take advantage of this shifting ontological maelstrom to push their own life projects. The question is whether the new realities that climate change carves out for most of us can provide an opportunity to (un)learn and renegotiate the terms of our coexistence, collectively re-evaluating our ways of being in the world in ways that recognize and uphold the moral bonds we share with all our relatives, including those yet to be born.

AUTHORS' NOTE

This paper was written on the lands of the Ngunnawal, Ngambri, Walbunja, and Gadigal peoples. We acknowledge and pay our respect and express our gratitude to their Elders and communities, as well as to Torres Strait Islanders' Elders and communities. We also acknowledge the remaining members of our team in Walbunja Country: Linda Carlson, Janet Hunt and the Mogo and Batemans Bay LALC ranger teams, Karen Soldatic, and Bruce Doran. We also express our gratitude to Sylvie Poirier, Mario Blaser, Carolina Tytelman, Frances Morphy, Mandy Yap, Ginibi Robinson, and Katherine Aigner for their time and valuable comments on iterations of this text. This chapter is based on research that received funds from the Social Sciences and Human Research Council of Canada (SSHRCC), the Fonds de recherche du Québec—Société et culture (FRQSC), the Australian Institute for Aboriginal and Torres Strait Islanders Studies (AIATSIS), the Federal Office for the Arts' The Indigenous Languages and Arts (ILA) program, the Australian National University First Nations Portfolio's Watervale Award, and NSW Local Land Services.

NOTES

1. "Country" is an all-encompassing Aboriginal concept referring to the sentient, intentional land and world to which Aboriginal Nations are genealogically and spiritually connected. Country and all its features were formed by the Dreaming's Creator Ancestors (Morphy and Mahood 2019; see also Myers 1991). As Adam Nye beautifully noted in a conversation, "Country is a living and spiritual connection which can in most cases only be felt and seen by those who are aware."
2. Indigenous ranger groups were established in Australia from 2007 through the federal Working on Country program (now known as Indigenous Ranger Programs). The Mogo Local Aboriginal Land Council ranger team presented in this chapter is funded independently by this program.
3. Extract of a song composed by Moses Mene (Masig Elder).
4. Part of Zenadth Kes, Hammond Island, Muralug, Ngurupai, and Waiben are the traditional territories of the Kaurareg Aboriginal Nation.
5. Relational ontology, which places the collective (which itself includes relationships with non-humans) rather than the individual at the centre of Torres Strait sociality, is a fundamental aspect defining Torres Strait Islanders' relational mixed economies (Scott 2017; Thomassin 2016).
6. For the Aboriginal Peoples, the Dreaming has created the world. As William Stanner explains, "The Dreaming is many things in one. Among them, a kind of narrative of things that once happened; a kind of charter of things that may still happen; and a kind of *logos* or principle of order transcending everything significant" (1979, 24; emphasis in original). The Dreaming is "everywhen"; it transcends time (24).
7. LALCs are a network of Land Councils constituted under the New South Wales Aboriginal Land Rights Act 1983 (ALRA). Their main mandate is to support Aboriginal land claims, the development of social and economic opportunities, and the provision of cultural and heritage services.

REFERENCES

ABC. 2021. "Climate Change Part 1: How Climate Change Is Affecting the Torres Strait." *730 Report*, April 19. Australian Broadcaster Corporation. https://www.abc.net.au/7.30/climate-change-part-1:-how-climate-change-is/13309038.

Altangerel, Khulan, and Christian A. Kull. 2013. "The Prescribed Burning Debate in Australia: Conflicts and Compatibilities." *Journal of Environmental Planning and Management* 56 (1): 103–120. https://doi.org/10.1080/09640568.2011.652831.

Altman, Jon. 2001. "Sustainable Development Options on Aboriginal Land: The Hybrid Economy in the Twenty-First Century." *CAEPR Discussion Paper 226*. Centre For Aboriginal Economic Policy Research.

ATSISJC (Aboriginal and Torres Strait Islander Social Justice Commissioner). 2008. *Native Title Report 2008*. Human Rights and Equal Opportunity Commission.

Berkes, Fikret. 1993. "Traditional Ecological Knowledge in Perspective." In *Traditional Ecological Knowledge: Concepts and Cases*, edited by Julian T. Inglis. Canadian Museum of Nature and the International Development Research Centre.

Blaser, Mario. 2009. "From Progress to Risk: Development, Participation, and Post-disciplinary Techniques of Control." *Canadian Journal of Development Studies/Revue canadienne d'études du développement* 28 (3–4): 439–454. https://doi.org/10.1080/02255189.2009.9669223.

Blaser, Mario. 2019. "On the Properly Political (Disposition for the) Anthropocene." *Anthropological Theory* 19 (1): 74–94. https://doi.org/10.1177/1463499618779745.

Borrows, John. 2010. *Canada's Indigenous Constitution*. University of Toronto Press.

Corntassel, Jeff. 2012. "Re-envisioning Resurgence: Indigenous Pathways to Decolonization and Sustainable Self-Determination." *Decolonization: Indigeneity, Education & Society* 1 (1): 86–101.

Cruikshank, Julie. 2012. "Are Glaciers 'Good to Think With'? Recognising Indigenous Environmental Knowledge." *Anthropological Forum* 22 (3): 239–250. https://doi.org/10.1080/00664677.2012.707972.

Daigle, Michelle. 2016. "Awawanenitakik: The Spatial Politics of Recognition and Relational Geographies of Indigenous Self-Determination." *The Canadian Geographer / Le Géographe canadien* 60 (2): 259–269. https://doi.org/10.1111/cag.12260.

Donaldson, Susan. 2006. *Stories about the Eurobodalla by Aboriginal People: Stage Two Eurobodalla Aboriginal Heritage Study*. Eurobodalla Shire Council / NSW Department of Environment & Heritage / Environmental & Cultural Services.

Dussart, Françoise, and Sylvie Poirier, eds. 2017. *Entangled Territorialities: Negotiating Indigenous Lands in Australia and Canada*. University of Toronto Press.

Fuller, Robert S., Graham Moore, and Jodi Edwards. 2021. "'Singing Up Country': Reawakening the Black Duck Songline, across 300km in Australia's Southeast." *The Conversation*, October 6, 2021. https://theconversation.com/singing-up-country-reawakening-the-black-duck-songline-across-300km-in-australias-southeast-167704.

Ganter, Regina J. 1994. *The Pearl-Shellers of Torres Strait: Resource Use, Development and Decline, 1860s–1960s*. Melbourne University Press.

Green, Donna, and Kirsty Ruddock. 2009. "Could Litigation Help Torres Strait Islanders Deal with Climate Impacts?" *Sustainable Development Law & Policy* 9 (2): 23–29.

Haalboom, Bethany, and David C. Natcher. 2012. "The Power and Peril of 'Vulnerability': Approaching Community Labels with Caution in Climate Change Research." *Arctic* 65 (3): 245–366. https://doi.org/10.14430/arctic4219.

Hennessy, Kevin, Blair Fitzharris, Bryson C. Bates, et al. 2007. "Australia and New Zealand. Climate Change 2007: Impacts, Adaptation and Vulnerability. Contribution of Working Group II." In *Climate Change 2007: Impacts, Adaptation and Vulnerability. Contribution of Working Group II to the Fourth Assessment Report of the Intergovernmental Panel on Climate Change*, edited by Martin L. Parry, Osvaldo F. Canziani, Jean P. Palutikof, Paul J. van der Linden and Clair E. Hanson. Cambridge University Press. https://www.ipcc.ch/site/assets/uploads/2018/03/ar4_wg2_full_report.pdf.

ILO (International Labour Office). 2017. *Indigenous Peoples and Climate Change: From Victims to Change Agents through Decent Work*. International Labour Office, Gender, Equality and Diversity Branch.

Lahn, J. 2003. "Past Visions, Present Lives: Sociality and Locality in a Torres Strait Community." PhD diss., James Cook University.

Latour, Bruno. 1997. *Nous n'avons jamais été modernes. Essai d'anthropologie symétrique*. La Découverte.

Latour, Bruno. 1999. *Politiques de la nature*. La Découverte.

Lawrie, Margaret. 1970. *Myths and Legends of Torres Strait*. University of Queensland Press.

Lui-Chivizhe, Leah. 2022. *Masked Histories: Turtle Shell Masks and Torres Strait Islander People*. Melbourne University Publishing.

McGoodwin, James R., Barbara Neis, and Lawrence Felt. 2000. "Integrating Fishery People and their Knowledge into Fisheries Science and Resource Management." In *Finding Our Sea Legs: Linking Fishery People and Their Knowledge with Science and Management*, edited by Barbara Neis and Lawrence Felt. ISER.

McGregor, Deborah. 2014. "Traditional Knowledge and Water Governance: The Ethic of Responsibility." *AlterNative: An International Journal of Indigenous Peoples* 10 (5): 493–507. https://doi.org/10.1177/117718011401000505.

McNiven, Ian, and Ricky Feldman. 2003. "Ritually Orchestrated Seascapes: Hunting Magic and Dugong Bone Mounds in Torres Strait, NE Australia." *Cambridge Archaeological Journal* 13 (2): 169–194. https://doi.org/10.1017/S0959774303000118.

Menzies, Charles R. 2006. *Traditional Ecological Knowledge and Natural Resource Management*. University of Nebraska Press.

Milton, Vanessa. 2020. "Mogo's Scattered Indigenous Families Are Still Grieving, Six Months after the Bushfires." *ABC South East NSW*, July 5. https://www.abc.net.au/news/2020-07-05/mogo-indigenous-community-six-months-after-australian-bushfires/12420464.

Morphy, Frances, and Howard Morphy. 2013. "Anthropological Theory and Government Policy in Australia's Northern Territory: The Hegemony of the 'Mainstream.'" *American Anthropologist* 115 (2): 174–187. https://doi.org/10.1111/aman.12002.

Morphy, Frances, and Kim Mahood. 2019. "Representations of Spaces and Places." In *Macquarie Atlas of Indigenous Australia*, 2nd ed., edited by Bill Arthur and Frances Morphy. Pan Mcmillan Australia.

Mulrennan, Monica E. 1993. *Towards a Marine Strategy for Torres Strait (MaSTS)*. A ustralian National University, North Australia Research Unit.

Myers, Fred. 1991. *Pintupi Country, Pintupi Self: Sentiment, Place, and Politics among Western Desert Aborigines*. University of California Press.

Nadasdy, Paul. 2005. "The Anti-Politics of TEK: The Institutionalization of Co-Management Discourse and Practice." *Anthropologica* 47 (2): 215–232. https://www.jstor.org/stable/25606237.

Napoleon, Val. 2013. "Thinking about Indigenous Legal Orders." In *Dialogues on Human Rights and Legal Pluralism*, edited by René Provost and Colleen Sheppard. Springer Netherlands.

Neale, Timothy. 2023. "Performing Control: Ritual and Divination in Australian Emergency Management." *American Ethnologist* 50 (4): 568–581. https://doi.org/10.1111/amet.13218

NNTT (National Native Title Tribunal). 2017. *Extract from the Register of Native Title Claims, Federal Court No: NSD1331/2017 / NNTT No: NC2017/003*. National Native Title Tribunal.

O'Brien, Abbie. 2021. "In a Critical Year for Climate Justice, These Torres Strait Islanders Are Leading the Fight." *SBS News*, July 4. https://www.sbs.com.au/news/article/in-a-critical-year-for-climate-justice-these-torres-strait-islanders-are-leading-the-fight/uq5xxq4it.

Poirier, Sylvie. 2008. "Reflections on Indigenous Cosmopolitics—Poetics." *Anthropologica* 50 (1): 75–85. http://www.jstor.org/stable/25605390.

The Red Nation. 2020. *The Red Deal: Indigenous Action to Save our Earth*. Common Notions and Red Media.

Reo, Nicholas J. 2019. "Inawendiwin and Relational Accountability in Anishnaabeg Studies: The Crux of the Biscuit." *Journal of Ethnobiology* 39 (1): 65–75. https://doi.org/10.2993/0278-0771-39.1.65.

Reo, Nicholas J., and Kyle P. Whyte. 2012. "Hunting and Morality as Elements of Traditional Ecological Knowledge." *Human Ecology* 40 (1): 15–27. https://doi.org/10.1007/s10745-011-9448-1.

Richards, Julie-Anne, and Simon Bradshaw. 2017. *Uprooted by Climate Change: Responding to the Growing Risk of Displacement*. Oxfam Briefing Paper November 2017. Oxfam International. https://doi.org/10.21201/2017.0964.

Royal Commission into National Natural Disaster Arrangements. 2020. "Royal Commission into National Natural Disaster Arrangements Report." Commonwealth of Australia.

Salmón, Enrique. 2000. "Kincentric Ecology: Indigenous Perceptions of the Human–Nature Relationship." *Ecological Applications* 10 (5): 1327–1332. https://doi.org/10.2307/2641288.

Scott, Colin. 2004. "'Our Feet Are on the Land, But Our Hands Are in the Sea': Knowing and Caring for Marine Territory at Erub, Torres Strait." In *Woven Histories, Dancing Lives: Torres Strait Islander Identity, Culture and History*, edited by Richard Davis. Aboriginal Studies Press.

Scott, Colin. 2017. "The Endurance of Relational Ontology: Relationships between Eeyouch and Sports Hunters." In *Entangled Territorialities: Negotiating Indigenous Lands in Australia and Canada*, edited by Françoise Dussart and Sylvie Poirier. University of Toronto Press.

Sharp, Nonie. 1993. *Stars of Tagai: The Torres Strait Islanders*. Aboriginal Studies Press.

Smith, Will, Timothy Neale, and Jessica Weir. 2021. "Persuasion without Policies: The Work of Reviving Indigenous Peoples' Fire Management in Southern Australia." *Geoforum* 120: 82–92. https://doi.org/10.1016/j.geoforum.2021.01.015.

Spak, Stella. 2005. "The Position of Indigenous Knowledge in Canadian Co-Management Organizations." *Anthropologica* 47 (2): 233–246. http://www.jstor.org/stable/25606238.

Spurway, Kim. 2018. "Critical Reflections on Indigenous Peoples' Ecological Knowledge and Disaster Risk Management in Australia: A Rapid Evidence Review." *Global Media Journal (Australian Edition)* 12 (1): 1–35.

Stanner, William E.H. 1979. *White Man Got No Dreaming: Essays 1938–1973*. ANU Press.

Steffen, Will, John Hunter, and Lesley Hugues. 2014. *Counting the Costs: Climate Change and Coastal Flooding*. Climate Council of Australia.

Thomassin, Annick. 2016. "Hybrid Economies as Life Projects? An Example from the Torres Strait." In *Engaging Indigenous Economy: Debating Diverse Approaches*, edited by William Sanders. ANU Press.

Thomassin, Annick, Timothy Neale, and Jessica K. Weir. 2018. "The Natural Hazard Sector's Engagement with Indigenous Peoples: A Critical Review of Canzus Countries." *Geographical Research* 57 (2): 164–177. https://doi.org/10.1111/1745-5871.12314.

United Nations. 2023. *Human Rights Committee under Article 5(4) of the Optional Protocol to the International Covenant on Civil and Political Rights (CCPR), Concerning Communication No. 3624/2019*.

Vanthuyne, Karine, and Mathieu Gauthier. 2022. "Mining the Land while Sustaining Iiyiyiuituwin: Exercising Indigenous Sovereignty through Collaboration in Eeyou Istchee." *Canadian Journal of Political Science/Revue canadienne de science politique* 55 (2): 279–299. https://doi.org/10.1017/S0008423922000178.

Viveiros de Castro, Eduardo. 2004. "Perspectival Anthropology and the Method of Controlled Equivocation." *Tipití: Journal of the Society for the Anthropology of Lowland South America* 2 (1): 3–20. https://doi.org/10.70845/2572-3626.1010.

Watson, Virginia. 2014. "Colonialism's Past and Present: Performing History at a Gold Rush Theme Park." *Coolabah* 13: 173–184. https://doi.org/10.1344/co201413173-184..

White, John. 2010. "Peas, Beans and Riverbanks: Seasonal Picking and Dependence in the Tuross Valley. In *Indigenous Participation in Australian Economies: Historical and Anthropological Perspectives*, edited by Ian Keen. ANU Press.

Whyte, Kyle P. 2016. "Is it Colonial DéJà Vu? Indigenous Peoples and Climate Injustice." In *Humanities for the Environment: Integrating Knowledges, Forging New Constellations of Practice*, edited by Joni Adamson, Michael Davis, and Hsinya Huang. Earthscan.

Whyte, Kyle P. 2017. "Indigenous Climate Change Studies: Indigenizing Futures, Decolonizing the Anthropocene." *English Language Notes* 55 (1–2): 153–162.

Whyte, Kyle P. 2020. "Against Crisis Epistemology." In *Routledge Handbook for Critical Indigenous Studies*, edited by Brendan Hokowhitu, Aileen Moreton-Robinson, Linda Tuhiwai-Smith, Cris Andersen, and Steve Larkin. Taylor & Francis Group.

Williamson, Bhiamie. 2022. "Cultural Burning and Public Forests: Convergences and Divergences between Aboriginal Groups and Forest Management in South-Eastern Australia." *Australian Forestry* 85 (1): 1–5. https://doi.org/10.1080/00049158.2022.2054134.

9

Sarah Moritz *and*
Qwalqwalten (Garry John)

"IT HAD THE BIGGEST SPRING SALMON RUN, IT WAS A LAND OF PLENTY FOR ALL!"

SOCIAL TRANSFORMATIONS, ST'ÁT'IMC (SALISH) KNOWLEDGE, AND TERRITORIES OF LIFE ENDURANCES IN THE BRIDGE RIVER VALLEY

"Blocking the Way of Progress"
(Re-)Visions for a "Land of Plenty"

When I was running a trapline there at Nqwáxwqten "where the eagles made nests" [in the Land of Plenty], I wanted to stay there as long as I could. Come about the end of January, I got a letter that I was supposed to leave and move anything of value to me. I gathered everything that was of value and got the money. I needed a truck to move, couldn't find anybody to do it for me. I went down to Shalalth and I went home and then all of a sudden I got another letter, that BC Electric was a private company.

And they told me that they own land now that was bought from us and they wanted us out of there and they told me that I was blocking the way of progress, that I was

evicted and if I didn't move, that they would enforce the law for me to leave. I went down to Shalalth again to look for a truck to haul our things out. I got back up there with vehicle enough to move our most valuables out and the houses and the barn were all burned down to the ground. Nothing was saved. I was homeless for about thirty years.
(Elder Qwa7yán'ak, "My eviction from my Nqwáxwqten [Marshall Creek] home," interview, July 13, 2016)

INTRODUCTION

This poignant life history event ("My eviction from my Nqwáxwqten [Marshall Creek] home") was shared by St'át'imc (Xwísten) Elder Qwa7yán'ak (Carl Alexander) during a life history interview in the summer heat of 2016. His story epitomizes some of the radical social and environmental changes in the Bridge River Valley, particularly for Interior Salish St'át'imc families who had been living, trapping, hunting, gathering, cultivating land, and fishing there until the Sama7 ("white man's") flood came to make way for their version of progress in 1948. That version of progress includes ownership claims, the social imagination of a terra nullius or "empty land," and laws at odds with St'át'imc ongoing presence and land tenure, as Qwa7yán'ak's story highlights so markedly.

The Sama7 flood story could not be more antithetical to the St'át'imc flood tradition, a creation story, in that it implies relentless dispossession, destruction, displacement, and the creation of a single materialist purpose, reality, and tradition—hydroelectric infrastructure and neoliberal prosperity—rather than land-based creation, multi-species coexistence, growth, and true origins.

Our chapter illustrates the fundamental socio-environmental changes from sQém´qem´—a "Land of Plenty" with one of the most abundant chinook salmon stocks in North America, where St'át'imc thrived—to a post-industrialist "food desert" or "plenty of water" due to industrial expansion over the past century, and examines how this plight is addressed today. Through in-depth St'át'imc Elders' focus groups (conducted in July 2013 and July/August 2014) and individual life history interviews (conducted from 2013 to 2016), our work reconstructs a variety of social and environmental continuities and changes in both memory and praxis within a holistic, inclusive, resurgent, and enduring territory of life.

Based on collaborative, community-based action and anthropological research—life history interviews, Elders' focus groups, and participation in a resource management working group—this chapter scrutinizes current efforts at documenting and mitigating impacts of collaborative water use planning. It also examines the 2011 charter, St'át'imc Hydro Settlement Agreement, which was designed to address past infringements and entails a St'át'imc knowledge–science collaborative environmental monitoring program.

Although largely displaced from this important area of their territory and the chinook fishing way of life, both through the colonial encounter and industrial development, this chapter illustrates how many St'át'imc are creatively and persistently re-enacting their knowledge of fishing, water use, and governance practices as part of their long-term goal to reclaim the Land of Plenty and finally return home. Here, returning home emerges as an incremental, relational process; St'át'imc families are advancing their collective life projects and holistic visions that become visible through the collaborative Indigenous Knowledge–Science integration process, despite having to translate and strategically employ expressions to effectively communicate with non-Indigenous, settler, and industry partners.

The following sections will critically examine our own positionalities and intellectual lineages; the entangled history of the Bridge River and hydroelectric development in the area; the processes that led to a charter hydro settlement agreement; the Indigenous Knowledge–Science relationship processes; and finally, pertinent visions for a more holistic, collaborative process and for a future that entails the continuity of the St'át'imc way of life in the area as a territory of life.

FINDING TRUTH(S): POSITIONING OURSELVES WITHIN INTELLECTUAL AND TERRITORIAL TRADITIONS

Historically and presently, a "good quality of life" in St'át'ímc terms means being deeply rooted in a life-giving and animated land, the Fraser River, its tributaries, lakes, mountains, forests, and valleys that comprise "home." It is a way of life that shall be continuously cultivated, stewarded, and maintained skillfully through keeping a respectful, reciprocal, and balanced social relationship with all beings in a diverse social community-of-life. Such balancing and balanced connections form a reliable basis for socio-ecological integrity and cultural autonomy (Moritz 2020, 2021; SGS 2016). These connections are cultivated through a complex knowledge and governance system, by maintaining land-based stories, laws, ceremonies, food, and territorial visions of autonomy and posterity. In the face of colonial, neoliberal, and large-scale industrial—especially hydroelectric, mining, and timber—impacts, St'át'ímc families are consistently challenged to creatively envision, protect, restore, and maintain such a relational good quality of life in their territory (Moritz 2012, 2020, 2021).

Our chapter illustrates the importance of different ontological orientations and "positional truths," while foregrounding St'át'imc insights, protocols, and teachings to highlight complexities of processes of communication, translation, memory, and equivocation to evoke home as a territory of life (Poirier 2013, 56). Here, animals, salmon, and other beings, such as the Bridge River, emerge as sentient, active, and communicative social agents that define knowledge of how an enduring human–animal relationality might be created and maintained. This opens up possibilities for examining fish and the river as sentient beings acting within and across diverse lifeworlds as opposed to objects, resources, species, or commodities belonging to a natural world within a prevalent Western abstraction.

We emphasize the importance of the St'át'imc relational axiom of cw7it ("shared abundance") as a set of social relationships across time and space, language codes, and human and non-human realms. We critically examine this enduring relationality in the context of collaborative water use planning and—as highlighted by St'át'imc Elders—as a key restorative vision to recover life and home. Discerningly, we adopt the term "equivocation" (Viveiros de Castro 2004) as a mode of communication between varying perspectival positions to acknowledge both the depth and limitations of our analysis of relationality in its attempt to echo a polyphony of voices and social (dis)entanglements.

Territories of life are grounded in an "ethic of connection" (Blaser, Poirier, and Anthias, this volume). They materialize and emerge through distinct forms of governance, decision-making, and actioned solidarity (see chapters by Éthier and Flamand, Gutierrez-Callisaya, and Wattez, this volume). They are entrenched and unfold through clan, family, community, and social ties with non-humans (see Thomassin et al., this volume). They are profoundly rooted in ancestral home places, vernacular, and local codes, yet their mobilization, articulation, and expression relentlessly reconcile challenges and trespasses that threaten these longstanding ties. Territories of life are resurgent, living, and anticipant, reminiscent of the good life. Their enduring quality is correlated with creative adaptability and transformative continuity and embodies a discerning cosmopolitical vision. A focus on endurances and territories of life implies a focus on laborious, collective resurgence and (r) existence (see Blaser, Poirier, and Anthias, this volume.)

Notably, many Elders emphasized that although looking at colonial, industrial, and climate change impacts is essential, a focus on positive visions, health, and teachings is just as, if not more, important for future generations. They offer an enduring vision of a territory of life that sustains positive reciprocity and shared abundance. Therefore, they asked us (specifically Sarah Moritz) to critically observe the following interrelated St'át'imc protocols for territorial, life-sustaining integrity and good relationships: nxawnánwas from St'át'imcets as "being good in every way, kind-hearted, humble, nice and gentle, meek"; xzums, "practise (genuine) respect"; gelgelús, "speaking/sharing the truth"; umná7ilh, "to share, contribute gifts (to), e.g., a potlatch"; qwámqwemt, "to have fun, amuse/enjoy oneself, be humorous"; smáwal, "life/life spirit, values inspired by giving good energy to the fire of transformation"; and nú´kw7am, "friendly, forthcoming and useful." These protocols may teach us profound lessons on shared abundance, living well, collective life projects, and respect. We hope that they fluoresce through these pages and we strive to honour them through this work, with a strong focus on gelgelús, smáwal, and umná7ilh.

A didactic equivocation that was highlighted throughout our research is the importance of considering research questions, experiences, and history from the perspective of the land, the animals, and the ancestors concerned, and transcending the personal and human way of reading and relating to the world (SLIB Land and Resources meeting, personal communication, June 2016; see also Bawaka Country et al. 2014). For example, if we want to discern the significance of the Bridge River over time, we must understand this as best as we can from the perspective of the humans, the eagles, the chinook, the rocks, the wolves, the wind, and so on (see Thomassin et al., this volume). This can be done through direct learning, dreaming, sensing, stories, ceremony, speaking the language, and connecting with the spirit of any being (anonymous Elder, personal communication, July 2016). Methodological adjustments based on a variety of perspectives are thus paramount.

To emphasize these lineages and practices of "continuity through change" (Adolph 2009), we rely on and expand on the notion of Indigenous "life projects" (cf. Blaser 2004; Feit 2004; Peterson and Myers 2016; Scott 2004). Life projects are not merely reactive or resistant to colonial, industrial, capitalist, and climate change impacts, but rather creative assertions of their own self-determined agendas while embodying local history and visions of social connectivity within a sentient "relational ecology" (Descola 2013), or "community-of-life" (Bateson 1979; Borrows 2018). These life projects and relationality shape individual and collective Salish political, social, and collaborative strategies for positioning themselves creatively vis-à-vis state and neoliberal economies as well as collaborators such as academics (Feit 2005; Li 2007; Poirier 2001). St'át'imc relational understandings of land, animals, water, and all beings provide the foundation to self-determined trajectories of resistance to universalist projects (Altman 2009).

More generally, and as a way of positioning ourselves, Moritz's research involves participatory ethnography, life history interviews, language revitalization, prolonged research stays, collaborative historiography, deep and counter-mapping, and archival research. This is based on a relational ethic of what she has come to call "research as reciprocity," a radical "action anthropology," and "research as reconciliation" (2020); some of which she has learned from the Land of Plenty and cw7it. Such research is collaborative from the time of its design to its dissemination; honours Indigenous ontology, epistemology, and protocol; and seeks to be decolonial, oriented to social and ecological justice, and to self-determination efforts (cf. Asch 2001, 2014; Smith 2010; Tax 1975). This chapter is an effort to achieve these objectives, especially by presenting a nuanced case on collaborative water use planning while foregrounding St'át'imc endurances that are formative of territories of life. Moritz argues for a relational ontological *counter-discourse* that lets us think across experience and offers an understanding of Indigenous relational ecologies as an alternative to current environmental management approaches (cf. Reddekop 2014).

Qwalqwalten's visions and mentorship (of others like Moritz) as a leader, a member of the bear clan, his long-standing experience as Tsal'alhmec title, rights, and responsibilities activist, and his ability to speak with (a) thunder, as his name implies, enable him to teach fundamental lessons toward greater autonomy, voice, power, a healthy land, and a St'át'imc-sanctioned version of truth-telling and reconciliation. In his roles and tasks that relate to creating a good life for all, he is accompanied by another thunderous speaker and activist—Pulmaqa7 (his hand drum), which helps sustain the flames of a self-determined path. His path is marked by elemental endurances that tie him to territorial home places, trails, names, and pivotal events of resistance, re-enactment, and collective record in which stories are written on the land. The authors have been joining forces for over a decade of friendship, mentorship, laughter, song, support, banter, tswan (wind-dried salmon) bartering, fishing, rides through the beautiful territory, Montreal smoked-meat sandwiches, and most of all, a profound respect for each other's lives, paths, truths, and stories. Based on such reflexive engagement with shared equivocations, methods, and friendship, we launch into the following sections, which will outline context and conflict and discuss collaborative and translation practices in more detail.

"A RIVER THAT RUNS LIKE A CREEK SOMETIMES": HYDROELECTRIC DEVELOPMENT IMPACTS ON THE LAND OF PLENTY AND THE SPRING SALMON

The Bridge River is approximately 120 kilometres long and flows southeast from the snow fields of Monmouth Mountain to connect with the Fraser River near Lillooet at their confluence. The Bridge River and its valley had already become an area of pioneer frontier-pushing, mineral claims, and fur trading when, due to its geography and volume of water, it was deemed an ideal river to be dammed for the generation of hydroelectricity. During the fur trade and early mineral explorations—including those during the "Fraser River Gold Rush" beginning in 1857—a delicate balance and abundance was maintained due to St'át'imc control, careful cultivation, and attention to mountains, water, fisheries, and traplines (Prentiss and Kujit 2012; Qwa7yán'ak, personal communication, July 2016; Qwa7yán'ak 2016; Teit 1906, 1912).

At the beginning of the twentieth century, railway, hydroelectric, and resource development caused most invasive impacts. First surveyed in 1912, the Bridge River power project had reached a preliminary stage of completion in 1934 to produce power for the locality. The Bridge River hydroelectric complex encompasses three dams and stores water for a total of four generating stations. The system uses the water of the Bridge River three times in succession to produce 492 megawatts, which amounts to 6–8 percent of British Columbia's electrical supply (see Map 9.1).

For the Land of Plenty, the consequence of this hydroelectric development included environmental degradation, flooding, the forced relocation of many St'át'imc families for the construction of several dams and generating facilities, and an almost complete depletion of the big and vital spring salmon run (Drake-Terry 1989; Elders focus group, July 2014; Evenden 2004). As another Upper St'át'imc fisher explains:

> After hydro's dams went in there were, there were many fish runs that went extinct. When the Bridge River system went in there were seventeen species of fish in Seton Lake and that was before hydro came. With the second powerhouse in 1948, I think, the salmon were trying to go into

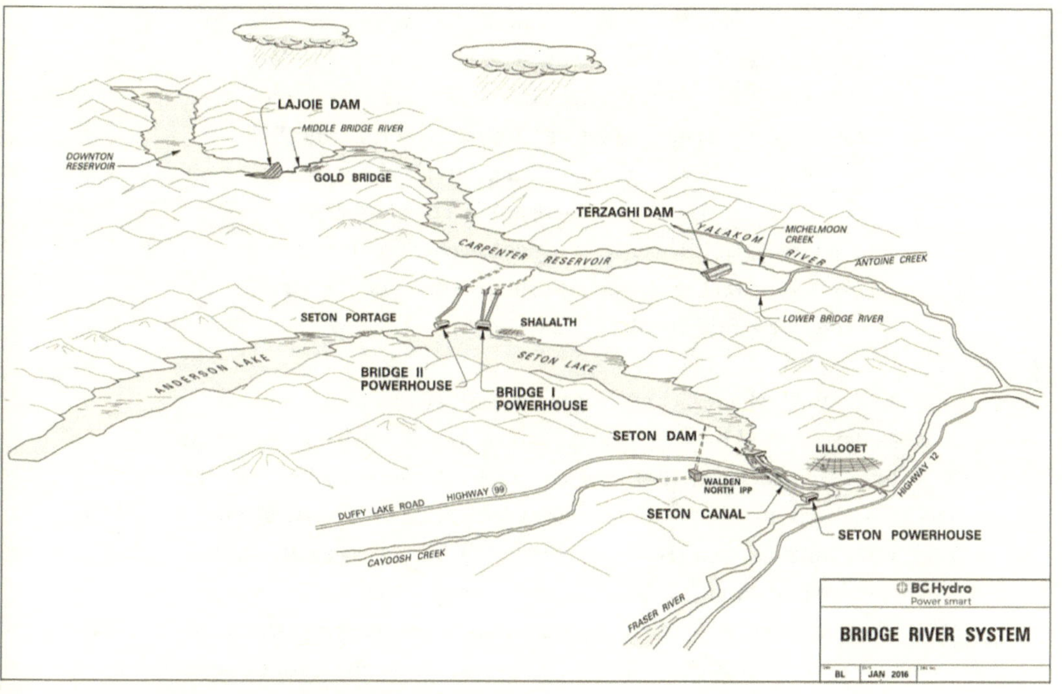

MAP 9.1 | BC Hydro's Bridge River System.

(Source: St'át'imc Government Services, 2024. Used by permission. Available from: https://statimc.ca/wp-content/uploads/2024/05/2024-Final-Annual-Operations-Update-1.pdf, page 6.)

> the powerhouse. They were confused with the fish slime on the rocks. They went the wrong way. (Personal communication, June 2014)

Xwísten's Chief Susan James summarizes the history and the impacts to the Bridge River with the following words:

> As I said, we've got ten thousand acres. Through our reserve, twenty-two kilometres. It's twenty-two kilometres long to drive through it from one end to the other. The Bridge River flows through that whole reserve. The Bridge

> River, it's a dammed river. I think the dam was built in the early sixties. I don't recall what it was like prior to the dam being built, but there is a huge dam with a huge reservoir upriver from us now. What we have is a river that runs like a creek sometimes. There's been a lot of talk about trying to rebuild the fish stocks. There are still fish in there, but they struggle. It's been a struggle to ensure that they return every year, that there's enough there to carry on the run. (Interview, SGS 2016)

In 1993, the St'át'imc Nation and BC Hydro began discussing various detrimental impacts or past grievances and infringements on St'át'imc title and rights that were caused by the existing hydroelectric facilities, dams, and transmission lines (cf. Canadian Constitution Act s.35 1982; Delgamuukw [1997]; Moritz 2012). Facing a new initiative by BC Hydro to establish a 500 kV Line through St'át'imc Territory, St'át'imc communities were obliged to react to assert their territorial authority and address (in)justice within an arising conflict of difference (Moritz 2012, 2020).

The collaborative outcomes of the conflict and the settlement negotiations include that the overall 2011 Hydro Settlement Agreement now formally commits the Province of British Columbia and St'át'imc Peoples to co-govern BC Hydro's operation and includes a trust, watershed, monitoring, and heritage plans to address impacts on St'át'imc People, in addition to financial compensation, capacity, training, and employment opportunities.

In summary, reviewing the changes to the Land of Plenty with the Elders during a focus group in July 2013, Moritz asked around the table, "If it used to be a 'Valley or Land of Plenty,' what is it now, after all these changes?" After a minute or so of reflection, she received three answers: A "food desert" (Qwa7yán'ak), "plenty of water" (Pete Alexander) and "a lost cause" (Desmond Peters Sr.). Another Elder added, "We remember. But our youth don't. Because they don't use it. They don't know the forest here, the Tlyaks, the fish, our traplines. But they should" (personal communication, July 2013). They further concluded:

> The only way to protect the land is continued use and occupation of certain areas. The young people have not seen the forest, many are not hunting or hiking and have no idea about the wilderness. What is there and what was taken. The youth are into computers and video games. We can do all this work and try and save our places that are important. But if we don't get the youth interested it is all for nothing.

A small measure of justice is BC Hydro's return of a piece of Alexander family-owned land in the Upper Bridge River area to be revitalized for community use. While this is far from previous land tenure scale, it symbolizes a hopeful beginning and references the historical call for a full "measure of justice" against colonial land theft originally demanded by the 1911 charter, Declaration of the Lillooet Tribe Chiefs, a record of endurance that has evolved through the Settlement Agreement (Qwa7yán'ak, personal communication, July 3, 2016; Qwa7yán'ak et al. 2025). Another important development in the current St'át'imc-industry relationship is the collaborative water use planning process, which we will examine critically in the following sections.

A "GIVING VALLEY": LEARNING FROM AND DOCUMENTING ST'ÁT'IMC ELDERS' KNOWLEDGE

Many Upper St'át'imc Elders remind us that this valley used to be a "giving" valley, one of provisions, reliance, trust, and a delicate balance of different forms of life (Elders focus group, July 2016, see Figure 9.1).

Qwalqwalten notes this shared abundance and interconnectedness by explaining that:

> It was called the Valley of Plenty...because it had so many berries, mushrooms, medicinal plants, and edible plants galore, a slow meandering river which was prime moose, beaver, muskrat, and deer habitat. Several species of anadromous and resident species of fish and salmon...Bears fishing. There was a balance of predators and prey that kept

FIGURE 9.1 | St'át'imc Elders focus group discussing sQémqem, the Land of Plenty (2013).

(Photograph by Sarah Moritz. Used with permission of the Elders in the photograph.)

> a delicate balance. The area had a swamp and a good forest. Prime rearing habitat for fish and amphibians...never had to hunt as far away or forage like we have to now to get stocked up. (Personal communication, May 2014)

There was an inherent dependability whereby both people and animals would always return and frequent key places in the valley, and in the case of St'át'imc, choose strategic village, settlement, and farming locations. It could be said that a regular, predictable migration of the salmon drew people to the river (Harris 2008, 61). Despite this dependability and trust, there was profound respect and knowledge not to take animal presence and shared abundance for granted. Rather, it was the key responsibility of St'át'imc to look after the land and learn and respect its way (Tiiya7, personal communication, June 2013). The Bridge River-Yalakom area was also known as a rich hunting ground. Deer, mountain goat, and mountain sheep are still hunted by members and others each fall.

The big chinook salmon run that would return regularly and abundantly was called Tlyaks'. Elders note that it was and is paramount for St'át'imc to only take as much as they need from the land and river (personal communication, July 2013). Once people have what they need for drying, smoking, canning, and freezing—that is, enough to survive and live well—it is time to stop (Qwalqwalten, personal communication, July 2014). This is a socio-ecological principle and ontological "take what you need" premise shared by many Indigenous groups (Berkes 1999; Kimmerer 2013; Kovach 2015). Many Elders agree that even if larger amounts were traded there was never full or near depletion, there was always rejuvenation and a shared concern for posterity (personal communication, July 2013). Changes to and continuities of this way of life are discussed in the following sections.

"PRECEDED BY MANY DECADES OF CONFLICT": THE 2011 HYDRO SETTLEMENT AGREEMENT AND COLLABORATIVE WATER USE PLANNING

Elder Desmond Peters Sr. also reminds us that St'át'imc who used to fish in the Bridge River Valley have resourcefully adapted to the invasive industrial impacts and reoriented themselves to mostly fish for sockeye in the Fraser River (personal communication, July 2013). Hunting is now done across the territory with people having to travel great distances to get enough to feed their families. However, there is a desire and an attempt to bring people and fish back into the area, as the Settlement Agreement now requires formal collaboration by St'át'imc and BC Hydro in Water Use Planning (WUP) through reliance on both St'át'imc (Ecological) Knowledge or Traditional Ecological Knowledge (TEK) and environmental science (SER 2013). Notably, many St'át'imc prefer the use of capitalized "St'át'imc Knowledge" for its capacity to highlight local, intimate land-based wisdom, cultural specificity, and expert knowledge status as part of more generalized pan-Indigenous TEK definitions and Western science (fieldnotes, June 2014–2016; cf. Peacock and Turner 2000). For example, St'át'imc Knowledge regarding habitat erosion, salmon health, feeding patterns, abundance of fish populations, and water quality are to guide BC Hydro's operations through collaborative monitoring and recommendation programs (SER 2013).

The 2012–2013 executive summary of the WUP summarizes this cooperation as follows:

> There are 16 Monitoring Programs that were awarded to St'át'imc Eco-Resources (SER) following the completion of the Bridge System Water Use Plan in March of 2011.Within BC, this is a unique arrangement for BC Hydro and creates efficiencies in terms of program delivery and capacity building for BC Hydro and St'át'imc ... We appreciate the support of the St'át'imc Chiefs Council which over the years worked hard to make this program a reality. The monitoring program provides an opportunity for incorporating traditional stewardship values into ongoing BC Hydro operations and will provide an informed basis for avoiding hydro impacts, mitigating them where necessary and defining future compensation activities that contribute to the overall sustainability of St'át'imc natural resources. (SER 2013, i–ii)

The collaborative process and Settlement Agreement are further contextualized and historicized in the following paragraph:

> The Bridge River Power Development Water Use Plan (WUP) monitoring program is a collaboration between BC Hydro and the St'át'imc Nation. This relationship is a recent one and was preceded by many decades of conflict due to the footprint impacts of the hydro facilities, indirect socio-economic impacts and effects on St'át'imc Traditional Territory. Following a long series of negotiations, the parties reached an historic Settlement Agreement on May 10, 2011, exactly one hundred years from the date of the "Declaration of the Lillooet Tribe." (1)

As part of that agreement, the monitoring project work attached to the WUP was directly awarded to St'át'imc Eco-Resources Ltd. (SER), a

St'át'imc resource management company. Since 2011, BC Hydro has supported St'át'imc Government Services (SGS) to build its capacity through various strategic planning initiatives, including the development of a Five-Year Fisheries Implementation Plan. This plan defines SGS fisheries objectives toward collaborative monitoring, which include:

- Maximize the benefits of fisheries and aquatic resources;
- Decision-making authority for aquatic resources and fisheries in St'át'imc Territory;
- Minimize industrial impacts;
- Restore St'át'imc watersheds to former levels of productivity;
- Employment including short-term jobs and long-term careers; and
- Capacity building

A specific collaborative monitoring program is discussed critically in the following section.

ST'ÁT'IMC-SCIENCE RELATIONALITY: THE LOWER BRIDGE RIVER SPIRITUAL AND CULTURAL VALUE MONITORING

WUP's fisheries objectives include the restoration of watersheds to former levels of productivity, minimizing industrial impacts, maximizing the benefits of fisheries, protection of fish habitat, flood control, and capacity building formally including more St'át'imc members in the implementation processes (SER 2013, 2016). Some of the Elders' knowledge on water quality and the chinook salmon run, for example, is documented and used to shape the WUP and its implementation. During our research, we focused on a specific monitoring program (LBR16: Lower Bridge River 16) that consists almost exclusively of St'át'imc Elders and leaders alongside a fisheries scientist in design, conduct, and analysis. Here, we present and critically evaluate the allegedly integrative methodology of the LBR16 and draw crucial insights for St'át'imc life projects and territorial visions.

The official program description for the LBR16 reads as follows:

> BRGMON-16 Lower Bridge River (LBR 16) Spiritual and Cultural Value Monitoring. The objective of this monitoring program is to assess the response of St'át'imc spiritual and cultural values to the flow regime on the Lower Bridge River. This monitoring program was initiated in spring of 2014 and was carried out over five years ending in 2018. (SER 2013)

This program was created collaboratively between St'át'imc representatives, Elders, and BC Hydro and SGS contracted staff but was principally directed by fisheries scientists. The first implementation phase outlines intent, purpose, conduct, and data analysis through an executive summary (SER 2016) as follows:

> The BRGMON-16 Water Use Plan (WUP) monitoring project was undertaken to measure and monitor a set of cultural and spiritual attributes of different flow discharges in the Lower Bridge River (LBR) below Terzhagi Dam. The information is needed to incorporate non-tangible inputs into a future long-term flow decision for the LBR. Between six to nine St'át'imc elders participated as evaluators to score their perceptions of cultural and spiritual values at different water flow discharges ranging between 5.1 cubic meters per second (cms) in August '14, 1.5 cms in October '14, 3 cms in March '15 and 13 cms in May '15. The Yalakom River was adopted as an adjacent (unregulated) control river and four seasonal surveys were simultaneously conducted in the LBR and the Yalakom. A total of 9 variables were evaluated at 10 sites with a scoring system that ranged between 0 (least favorable) and 4 (most favorable). The data were analyzed by means of a General Linear Model statistical approach which yielded the following results:

1. There were significant seasonal differences in BIRDSONG, water CLARITY, DIVERSITY of water movement, EDGE SMELL, MOVEMENT of the water and WADEABILITY.
2. There were significant between-river differences in BIRDSONG, EDGE SMELL, MOVEMENT of the water and WADEABILITY.
3. There were significant between-year differences in ACCESS and SMELL.
4. There were significant interactions between-season x river in BIRDSONG, water CLARITY, EDGE SMELL, SMELL, MOVEMENT and WADEABILITY.
5. There were significant interactions between river x year in water CLARITY.
6. There were significant interactions between season x year in water CLARITY.

The LBR16 (SER 2013: 47–48; see SER 2021) summary claims that its focus is different from a traditional Indigenous-science knowledge "integration" due to its focus on "the measurement of variables which were selected due to their close alignment with spiritual and cultural values" of St'át'imc collaborators. Furthermore, it emphasizes its ambitious agenda by stating that "[t]raditional approaches to the valuation of ecosystem services in river basins ... rely on 'willingness to pay' for interviews with local residents as a means for estimating resource values. The main methodological approach involves interviews with local stakeholders"[1] (SER 2016, 47–48).

While visiting one site, one fisheries scientist explained that this project is really unique and one of a kind in Canada around post-hydro water resource management due to its being in tune with the Elders' knowledge and priorities (personal communication, August 2014). At the beginning, Moritz's participation was contextualized by the project staff as that of someone who is ideally positioned and well-studied in the documentation of TEK and who could support the accuracy and diversity of knowledge documentation. The Elders and Moritz appreciated the staff's humble generosity, cordiality, and admission of the fact that the program would benefit from introducing more qualitative methods and insights.

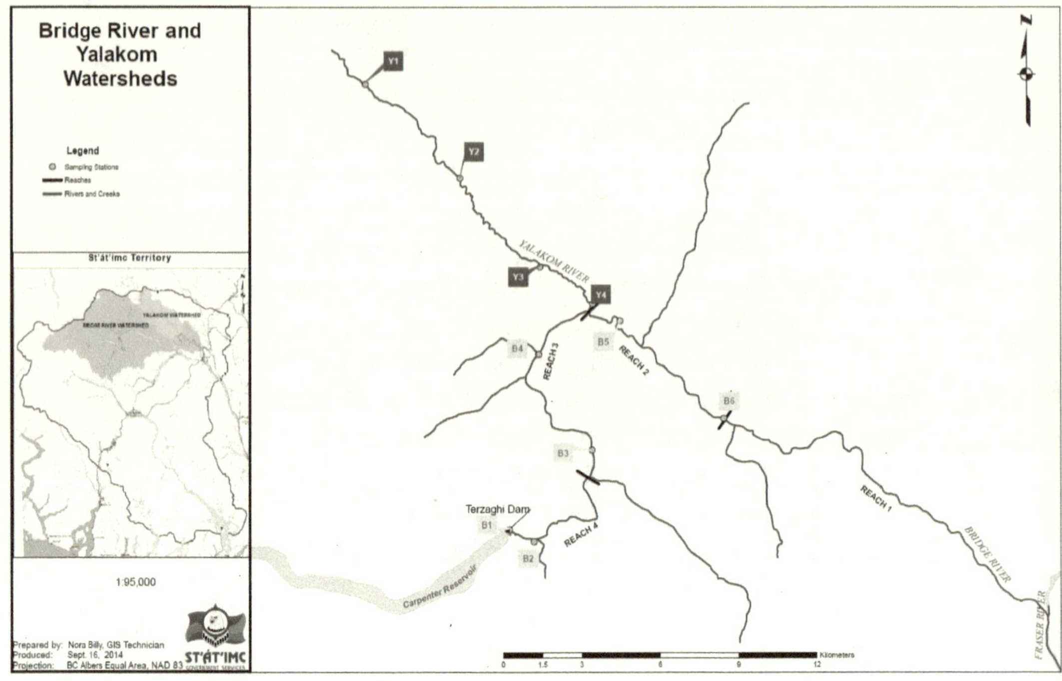

MAP 9.2 | St'át'imc Eco-Resources Spiritual and Cultural Value. Location of sampling sites in the Yalakom River and Lower Bridge River (2021).
(Source: St'át'imc Eco-Resources, 2021. Used by permission. Available from: https://www.bchydro.com/content/dam/BCHydro/customer-portal/documents/corporate/environment-sustainability/water-use-planning/lower-mainland/brgmon-16-yr5-final-report-2021-02-01.pdf, page 10.)

Moritz's role as anthropologist and guest was to observe, join site visits, and learn from Elders, particularly those who could not be interviewed at a given moment by one of the scientists or staff, many of whom are St'át'imc and thus ideally positioned to learn from and understand their own Elders. Moritz was encouraged to "add data," which would yield and support the addition of more factors, variables, and qualifiers (see Map 9.2) that could be studied, calculated, and quantified by the statistician who evaluates the data after the respective trips. These include, for example, the sound (voice of the water or birdsong) and the smell (smell of the water itself and the smell of the water's edge) (see Figure 9.2).

FIGURE 9.2 | Elder Qwa7yán'ak (Carl Alexander) at Bridge River Valley Research Site, holding horsetail.
(Photograph by Sarah Moritz. Permission by Qwa7yán'ak.)

According to the fisheries scientists and staff (see SER 2021), the statistician had suggested that more factors were needed to efficiently quantify data and that the quantification of rather qualitative, traditional, and mythological/spiritual story-type data was a complex, almost-unattainable process. Pushing for this specific methodology and focus was thus quite subversive and progressive (fieldnotes, August 2014). The statistical approach to the qualitative aspects of this project was, although partial, particularly useful for instructing BC Hydro scientists, engineers, and technicians on how to govern and amend their operations, particularly the flow regime. It enabled a middle ground as it also gave St'at'imc leaders a way to effectively communicate and negotiate with BC Hydro representatives.

While listening to and participating in conversations about the various sites during site visits, Moritz noticed that Elders, rather than focusing on the survey, wanted to remember personal historical events of significance that had happened there. They wanted to discuss names, stories, animal paths, and people's stewardship activities in both St'át'imcets and English. They wanted to point out how places along the studied sites featured in past travel, hunting, exchange, and trade routes (fieldnotes, June 2014). They wanted to show the diversity of animals, plants, roots, rocks, lichens, mushrooms, pit cooks, pit house sites, culturally modified trees (CMTs), ancestral transformer sites, and their complex interactions and relationships. They hoped to point out and document sensitive areas and related knowledge that are threatened by further industrial development and that they would like to see protected. They wanted to discuss where to build protest and "physical presence" cabins to evocatively do so. They wanted to work through and address the pain and healing related to their violent eviction and loss of livelihood, fish, traplines, and land as their home. They wanted to discuss protection and site reclamation strategies with sentences such as "if we could get back there again, we could hunt/fish/trap/gather/conduct ceremony, etc." (St'át'imc Elders, personal communication, July 2013).

They wanted to remember and represent the places visited as part of the complex social history of the Land of Plenty and as their life project given these imposed developments. They wanted to listen to the spirit of the ancestors and the diverse assemblage of all the beings that had co-created the Land of Plenty and that therefore supported just as many histories and perspectives on it. It seemed they wanted to include all those human and non-human persons, their lineages, spirits, and life histories into any current assessment of the quality of environmental protection and vision for the recreation of a good quality of life. Essentially, they wanted to discuss the meaning and contingencies of náskan úxwal´ Sqémqem´a; "I am going (back) home to the Land of Plenty" (fieldnotes, August 2014).

Letting the Elders re-establish memory, history, and relationality with the area in a way they felt appropriate taught us all in the most patient and generous way that they did not just want to focus on "a river whose spirit you will never be able to hear" because of the ongoing, silencing, and detrimental impacts on its health (Elder Qwa7yán'ak, personal communication, July 2016). Rather, all of them wished to emphasize collective endurances and visions for a more dynamic and innovative engagement with "lonely places of longstanding significance."

Therefore, the Elders' and our own understanding of the sites emerged as considerably in contrast with the scientific and statistical impetus to quantify, calculate, institutionalize, and codify what was really social, qualitative, spiritual, multi-species-related, and difficult to distil into quantifiable values and distinct categories (cf. Cruikshank 2005; McGregor 2004). What was important was not the movement or diversity of water as regulated by hydro facilities and dams but rather all that had historically yielded a diverse, nourishing, socially abundant Land of Plenty and the knowledge related to it: returning chinook stocks, deer migrating, moose using the swampy areas, mushrooms and lichens growing in abundance on jack pines for deer to find, tsawqem (Saskatoon berries, Amelanchier alnifolia) and xúsum (soapberry, Shepherdia canadensis) growing manifold on shrubs, frogs singing their songs, bears pulling chinook bones into the forest to feed the soil, and an overall reciprocal, balanced interdependence between all beings (fieldnotes, July 2014). Not (just) humans should be able to wade and smell the river but also deer, moose, bears, and mountain goats who would enable humans' wadeability by modelling examples of how to relate to and use the land (Elders, personal communication, July 2013).

In a follow-up interview Elder Qwa7yán'ak reflected on the LBR16 program's successes and impacts as follows:

> **Sarah:** We were talking about the spirit of the river. You were comparing it to a human body. I said what if somebody dies, what happens with the spirit?
>
> **Qwa7yán'ak:** We'll talk a little bit about the spirit of the river—it's gone. It's been gone ever since hydro drained the water without the fish coming through for years. Now, we are looking at others who try and get the fish back and the spirit of the river. But it's pretty hard to do because all the river isn't coming through. All the water that was coming over that smaller dam isn't going through. All that even overflow is going down through the pipes into the Seton Lake because they

have one spare pipe that takes all that excess water, sends it down into the Seton Lake. For a long time, there was nothing coming through into the Bridge River, the Lower Bridge River. The river lost its spirit. Now, hydro wants to bring it back. They're letting through three hundred cubic metres (cms) a minute. But that's not enough to bring the spring salmon through, because the spring salmon need deep water to go through. The water that is coming through has been warmed up behind the dam. It's too warm for the fish actually. It's the few that survive it go up to the pool below the dam. But that's about it. Not too many that lay their eggs. Not enough to bring the fish back. In order to bring the spring salmon back, we need a little bit more water than what comes through, even though six hundred cubic metres is coming through. It's nearly got water where there the river used to be. It's not even half up to where river used to reach. Whenever there's a danger behind the dam, maybe at the gates where they let a lot of the water through, it washes away, and the gravel where the salmon lay their eggs in. They leave nothing but rocks. That's not helping the salmon at all. We only had about four runs ever since that dam was raised. It's hard, because once the fish can't get back to where they were hatched, they just give up and die. (Personal communication, August 3, 2016)

FINDING OLD AND NEW WAYS: SCIENCE-ST'ÁT'IMC KNOWLEDGES AND FOSTERING ENDURANCES

Anthropologists may offer unique perspectives to critically examine and understand what is at stake when science and Indigenous Knowledge (IK) or Traditional Ecological Knowledge (TEK) interact and amalgamate. IK and TEK research attempts to document and employ knowledge in bureaucratic sectors of resource co-management have evoked serious criticism over the last decades (Cruikshank 2005; Irlbacher-Fox 2014;

Nadasdy 2005; Simpson 2004; Usher 2000). Frequently, these critiques have examined the social, economic, and politico-legal benefits and ramifications of Indigenous knowledge policies from an anthropological perspective. Many observers, including St'át'imc Elders and the LBR16 statistician, seem to agree that the place-based nature of St'át'imc Knowledge renders its incorporation or consideration in contexts, processes, and regimes other than its own challenging (Berkes 2009; Cruikshank 1990, 2005). Despite policy and legislative frameworks, such as the St'át'imc WUP, that attempt to include IK/TEK in environmental decision-making, it has not been an easy task. Extracting TEK from the community, knowledge holders, and Elders and inserting what is deemed relevant into management processes is reductive (McGregor 2004; Nadasdy 1999).

Julie Cruikshank, for example, is concerned that resource (co-)management scholars and practitioners increasingly seem to think that Indigenous knowledge functions as a "distinct epistemology" that can be modified and plugged into Western scientific and natural resource management regimes as necessary (2005, 269–270). In this process, she continues, everyday knowledge practices become defined, captured, recorded, codified, labelled, transcribed, de-contextualized, and "bounded as 'systems' of knowledge, [which] sets in motion processes that fracture and fragment human experience" (256). For Cruikshank, this is based on the problematic assumption or *equivocation* that different cultural views can be described in the English language and in the language of science, and that concepts considered "traditional" reflect ideas of resource managers more than those of local peoples.

LBR16 participating Elders' main critique of the way in which their knowledge and presence is valued is that a regional program must be more holistic and include more relevant history, practical knowledge, and also involve youth, whose awareness is needed to assess for contemporary and future stewardship of fisheries and water management (St'át'imc Elders focus group, July 2014). A more holistic approach would mean fewer compartmentalized "knowledge silos" (St'át'imc Eco Services officer Darwyn John, personal communication, June 13, 2013).

Based on Elders' insights, it became clear that a more holistic approach must be developed, resulting in a process and an acknowledgment based on respect for St'át'imc title, rights, and stewardship responsibilities regarding the Land of Plenty and all of St'át'imc territory. Firstly, this would require changing the current system of formal, short, prescriptive, and infrequent meetings and field site visits into an approach that is based on everyday lives, ways of remembering, and owning the land in a stewardship way. It means finding old and new ways of engaging with a changed and changing land. It also means moving from an approach of remembering and monitoring the present to an action-oriented life project approach of educating all, especially youth, and taking more direct action to reclaim, relearn, revisit, respirit, and steward the abundant ways of the Land of Plenty to become full owners again. Ideally, the focus of a (life) project that seeks to sustainably remediate or even restore the land must not be on the variables, factors, and mean value or "plenty of water" that has flooded Tlyaks' habitat and homes but on the qualitative knowing, experiencing, and bringing cw7it, shared abundance and life in its multiple forms back to the land through complex co-governance of human and non-human persons to allow it to recover and heal.

Such an approach would imply truly implementing the Water Use Plan's objective of restoring "St'át'imc watersheds to former levels of productivity" (SER 2013, 1; see SER 2021). It would also fulfill the LBR16's (SER 2016) qualifier of re-establishing a functional "interaction between people and water" beyond basic "shore access" and "wadeability" (SER 2016). In the true St'át'imc sense, it would mean "keeping the land alive" (Smith 1998); allowing St'át'imc to steward and cultivate the land to encourage the life-giving Tlyaks to return and to be invited back home (see Scott 1996, 77; Siragusa et al. 2020).

Such a call for a respectful relationship—expressed with great emphasis one hundred years ago by the signatories to the 1911 Declaration of the Lillooet Tribe—is not only necessary among the water use planning team (see Qwa7yán'ak et al. 2025). Rather, this respect should characterize all non-St'át'imc government, settler, and industry institutions in the area who would ideally request access from St'át'imc communities based on Free Prior and Informed Consent (FPIC) consultation and only move in once they have permission and collaborative support (anonymous St'át'imc Elder, personal communication, May 2013).

Nonetheless, LBR16 enabled Elders to get out onto the land and be together, reflecting on their memories, life histories, spirituality, ceremony, and culturally specific ways, and was felt to be very beneficial and important by all participants (fieldnotes, July 2014; see SER 2021). Alongside the ideal of designing the program based on everyday knowledge and stewardship practices (see Cruikshank 2005, 270), Elders appreciated the program for getting them back "onto the land" and to a considerable number of places they could not experience on a regular basis (fieldnotes, July 2014). The program was valued for its attempt to co-design and include non-tangible as well as empirical "variables," such as spirituality and cultural insights, which no other Western science-based model had genuinely attempted before. These positive attributes remained, even as the program was overall felt to be more of a "BC hydro wanting to reclaim a spirit" via hydro agreement-ordered science collaboration, a task largely incommensurable with their ongoing disruptive presence, authority, and infrastructures (Elder Qwa7yán'ak, personal communication, August 2016).

The executive and collaborative decision to focus on the more intangible terms like "spirit" and "voice" for "empirical data collection"—in both a St'át'imc and a Western scientific sense—was highly valued by Elders because they serve to empower and grant the land, water, and river the same kind of personhood and kin-based relationality that humans usually enjoy (Bird-David 2017; St'át'imc Elders, personal communication, August 2016; Hallowell 1960; Scott 1996, 2006).

A perspective that genuinely values St'át'imc Knowledge in design, conduct, and implementation opens itself up to the local stories and experiences that many St'át'imc want to embody, remember, re-enact, and use in the reclamation of the Land of Plenty. St'át'imc participating in LBR16 understand that knowing and acting upon the Land of Plenty and its transformations requires the sort of culturally specific, detailed, intimate, tacit, better-informed, lived, and long-term practical knowledge that no hydro scientist or engineer accustomed to a universalist notion of positivist expert knowledge can replicate or appropriate (see Latour 2004; Lévi-Strauss 1979; Scott 1996). However, co-existence and mutual endorsement are possible if each party acknowledges that there are both mythical/magical and abstract/empirical/rational processes, with oscillating interdependence between literal and figurative ways of knowing in both knowledge orientations (Regna Darnell, personal communication, March 2019; Scott 1996, 2013), and if neither party supports a system of power imbalance that implies subjugated knowledges (Foucault 1980; Nadasdy 1999). In this regard, Colin Scott notes: "The dominant metaphors in which Western science is embedded are 'qualitatively' different from those of relational ontologies, even though oscillation between the literal and figurative characterizes all knowledges" (personal communication, August 2019). This way we—the authors, the Elders, and the scientists—collectively experience an equivocation that "appears here as the mode of communication par excellence between different perspectival positions" (Viveiros de Castro 2004, 5); a form of intercultural equivocality and an effort to translate across perspectives and vital spaces to come to one holistic understanding that allows shared agency. Furthermore, this mode of communication points toward the endurance of territories of life as radical heterogeneity of modes of existence and non-linear notions of time and space that denote entanglements and co-presence between humans and non-humans (Blaser, Poirier, and Anthias, this volume). St'át'imc endurances of territories of life, while firmly rooted in ancestral home places and knowledge, are connected with contemporary and cumulative processes (see Dussart and Poirier 2021; Gutierrez-Callisaya, Quiroga, and Thomassin et al., this volume).

A holistic, territories of life-based St'át'imc–science collaboration manages to include all kinds of beings, salmon, and origin myths as truth; statistical variables derived from experiencing the Bridge River; St'át'imc observations of the quality of the riparian habitat; and calculated seasonal differences in individual judgements of water movement, all of which should be considered.

The LBR16 system is far from perfect, and rather opaque to the statistician trying to establish statistical significance, but it is a small measure of justice and a genuine attempt at achieving sustainable co-governance, cross-cultural translation, and understanding based on collaborative respect, positive reciprocity, and sharing in a good way for short-term and long-term goals (cf. Feit 2004, 2005; St'át'imc Elders focus group, July 2014 and 2016).

RECLAIMING THE LAND OF PLENTY?!: ST'ÁT'IMC VISIONS AND CONCLUSION

Based on the knowledge of the Land of Plenty and its transformations, during our Elders' focus group we pondered the following questions with St'át'imc Elders, leaders, and community members: What needs to be done? How can the land, its people, and the fish thrive again in cw7it, shared abundance?

One key, short-term goal was the implementation of reasonable flood control by BC Hydro, based on St'át'imc recommendations and without having to trigger the Settlement Agreement's "Dispute Resolution" mechanism or re-visit the century-old conflict (Qwalqwalten, personal communication, March 2019; SGS 2016). To quote Elder Qwa7yán'ak's:

> So whenever, in the spring especially, whenever that the water gets too heavy behind the dam, [BC Hydro] open it up full throttle, and too much water comes through. Like on a flood day. Washes all the gravel. If we kept the same amount of water coming through all the time so that they don't have to open gates all the time, that would be good. Rather than in trying to keep the water open at not only just when they are in trouble. They will be getting in trouble if they let most of the water through. Have enough water for themselves and for us. I think every day they came and were checking, the turbines and they let the water through the excess pipe, just so they could shut that one pipe down up at the intake portals, so they can stop the turbine and clean it or whatever they do. But if they allowed a little bit more water down the river then they didn't have to turn that excess pipes open. Other than that, I think the sockeye go up the dam but its spring [salmon] that they planted there and that doesn't work, because the water that is in there and it's too shallow right now. The spring salmon, they like to be in deep water, like six to seven feet down under. Now the places along as the river deepest would be about four feet. (Personal communication, July 2016)

Similarly, Qwalqwalten notes:

> Restoring the Land of Plenty and the historic spring salmon run means a more radical, exhaustive list than the status quo. It includes a fish passage over the dam, more spawning habitat, then rearing habitat, and finally a passage back over the dam when they emigrate to the ocean. Now the river is warmer. Water comes from behind the dam. The riverbed has been destroyed. The WUP vision is to restore it to a "pristine state." This may not be possible, but the fish will adapt if you give them a chance. We need that fish ladder. No more uncontrolled flooding. We need to address the water temperatures and that is both a water use planning and climate change issue. But what it really means is to get rid of the dams and facilities altogether. (Personal communication, May 2014)

Importantly, talks of decommissioning and relocating of facilities have recently begun. The process of such action is yet to be determined, but that shall partially be based on the five-point governance strategy (action, negotiation, litigation, ceremony, and communication) and LBR16 Elders' suggestions for bringing the big chinook run, Tlyaks, and other animals back (anonymous St'át'imc leader, personal communication, 2013).

In conclusion, the Water Use Plan and the LBR16 invites the kindness and generosity of the Elders who believe that speaking truthfully about the history, the good ways, and sharing their knowledge preserves knowledge and hope for all future generations (cf. Asch 2014). They participate in these processes generously, pragmatically, and with dedication while maintaining visions for restoring and rejuvenating the "food desert" into its ideal state: a Land of Plenty. This would involve bringing the animals back. As Qwalqwalten notes, it would also involve having beaver dams again, rather than hydro dams: "I can only imagine there were many beavers. Beavers provide habitat, while hydro destroys it. Beaver knows they were part of an ecosystem. Beavers lived lives ... and they died ... BC Hydro [interminably] patches cement dams and steel pipes" (personal communication, May 2019). However, this infrastructure, too, is becoming outdated. Qwa7yán'ak's adds: "Beavers didn't have to build dams in the Land of Plenty. They built along the banks of Bridge River. Beaver dams are built to accommodate their lodges, not millions of acres of land like hydro. There was no need for dams. The river was wide enough and deep enough for them" (personal communication, May 2019).

Thus, St'át'imc knowledge of the Land of Plenty and right and just relationships are profoundly entangled. St'át'imc families are asking for a recognition of these relationships as entangled forms of life and as previously existing rights to these lands and their fisheries. With this demand for recognition, they are prompting a fundamental rethinking of the bounds of "community" or "society"; as interspecies, multi-species, and kin-based relationships and communication. Fish—and the big spring salmon run—cannot conceptually or practically be separated from other beings such as the bears, beavers, or the forest; they are all necessary to ensure the integrity of the land. In the conclusive words of one St'át'imc leader: "If we have to choose a key species or practice it would have to be fish. But it should not be, there are other things in the territory and they are also important and they make each other possible" (anonymous St'át'imc leader, personal communication, 2013). St'át'imc accept the equivocation of limited cross-cultural, social, and perspectival translatability and assert that (in Western terms) they are sovereign in these lands. At the same time, however, they understand relations with non-St'át'imc and animals from the perspective that all beings are here together as equals and that they are bringing their differences to bear in creating cw7it: abundance for all.

St'át'imc model and externalize the endurances of territories of life, inclusive of all living beings, humans, and non-humans, for better relationships and sophisticated cosmopolitical visions that are resonant with this shared abundance.[2] They teach us a rooted resurgence and (r)existence based on respect, reciprocity, reverence, and responsibility. Re-establishing respectful relationships and sharing in the ethos of a real and reciprocal Land of Plenty for all is the key method for sustainability, alternative development, a social economy, and restoration as all of the St'át'imc short-term and long-term visions and practices illustrate so decisively. As such, re-establishing relationships is also one of meaningful decolonization and reconciliation across various enduring life projects that unite us. Together, they give us a roadmap of how to deal with the uncertainty and indeterminacy of failing and broken relationships. They teach the true and radical St'át'imc meaning of "home" and belonging in times of adversity.

AUTHORS' NOTE

We want to acknowledge that all our insights and engagements are chiefly shaped by the generosity, guidance, kindness, eloquence, and skill of the Úcwalmicw, the "people of the land," particularly the Elders, the ancestors, the land and all its inhabitants past, present, and future.

NOTES

1. The summary then contrasts the LBR16 program with other traditional approaches referencing St'át'imc perspectives by explaining that during "the present monitoring project monetization of spiritual and cultural values is not applicable and such considerations are not within the realm of the St'át'imc world view." To justify this empirical approach further, the summary also cites another Indigenous-science study group consisting of multiple authors who offer a balanced and critical view (cf. Berkes 1999; Simpson 2004) when they state that a "characterization of cultural benefits and impacts is least amenable to methodological solution when prevailing worldviews contain elements fundamentally at odds with efforts to quantify benefits/impacts, but that even in such cases some improvements are achievable if decision-makers are flexible regarding processes for consultation with community members and how quantification is structured" (SER 2016, 8).
2. See Moritz (2020) for a radical Boasian cosmopolitical ethos in line with our conceptualizations of endurances and territories of life in this volume.

REFERENCES

Adolph, Art (Xaxli'p Chief). 2009. *The Anthropology of Space and Place: Sxetl'*. Unpublished term paper, Thompson Rivers University.

Altman, Jon. 2009. *Beyond Closing the Gap: Valuing Diversity in Indigenous Australia.* ANU Press.

Asch, Michael. 2001. "Indigenous Self-determination and Applied Anthropology in Canada: Finding a Place to Stand." *Anthropologica* 43 (2): 201–207.

Asch, Michael. 2014. *On Being Here to Stay: Treaties and Aboriginal Rights in Canada.* University of Toronto Press.

Bateson, Gregory. 1979. *Mind and Nature: A Necessary Unity.* Bantam Books.

Bawaka Country, Sarah Wright, Sandie Suchet-Pearson, et al. 2014. "Working with and Learning from Country: Decentring Human Authority." *Cultural Geographies* 22 (2): 269–283.

Berkes, Fikret. 2009. "Indigenous Ways of Knowing and the Study of Environmental Change." *Journal of the Royal Society of New Zealand* 39 (4): 151–156.

Bird-David, Nurit. 2017. *Us, Relatives: Scaling and Plural Life in a Forager World.* University of California Press.
Blaser, Mario. 2004. "Life Projects: Indigenous Peoples' Agency and Development." In *In the Way of Development: Indigenous Peoples, Life Projects and Globalization*, edited by Mario Blaser, Harvey A. Feit, and Glenn McRae. Zed Books.
Borrows, John. 2018. "Earth-Bound: Indigenous Resurgence and Environmental Reconciliation." In *Resurgence and Reconciliation. Indigenous-Settler Relations and Earth Teachings*, edited by Michael Asch, John Borrows, and James Tully. University of Toronto Press.
Cruikshank, Julie. 1990. *Life Lived Like a Story: Life Stories of Three Yukon Native Elders.* University of Nebraska Press.
Cruikshank, Julie. 2005. *Do Glaciers Listen? Local Knowledge, Colonial Encounters, and Social Imagination.* UBC Press.
Descola, Philippe. 2013. *The Ecology of Others.* Prickly Paradigm Press.
Drake-Terry, Joanne. 1989. *The Same as Yesterday: The Lillooet Chronicle and the Theft of Their Lands and Resources.* Lillooet Tribal Council.
Dussart, Françoise, and Sylvie Poirier, eds. 2021. *Contemporary Indigenous Cosmologies and Pragmatics.* University of Alberta Press.
Evenden, Matthew D. 2004. *Fish Versus Power: An Environmental History of the Fraser River.* Cambridge University Press.
Feit, Harvey A. 2004. "James Bay Crees' Life Projects and Politics: Histories of Place, Animal Partners and Enduring Relationships." In *In the Way of Development: Indigenous Peoples, Life Projects and Globalization*, edited by Mario Blaser, Harvey A. Feit, and Glenn McRae. Zed Books.
Feit, Harvey A. 2005. "Re-cognizing Co-management as Co-governance: Visions and Histories of Conservation at James Bay." *Anthropologica* 47 (2): 267–288.
Foucault, Michael. 1980. *Power/Knowledge: Selected Interviews and Other Writings.* Pantheon Press.
Hallowell, A. Irving. 1960. "Ojibwa Ontology, Behavior and World View." In *Culture in History: Essays in Honour of Paul Radin*, edited by Stanley Diamond. Columbia University Press.
Harris, Douglas C. 2008. *Landing Native Fisheries: Indian Reserves and Fishing Rights in British Columbia, 1849–1925.* UBC Press.
Irlbacher-Fox, Stephanie. 2009. *Finding Dahshaa: Self-government, Social Suffering, and Aboriginal Policy in Canada.* UBC Press.
Kimmerer, Robin. 2013. *Braiding Sweetgrass: Indigenous Wisdom, Scientific Knowledge, and the Teachings of Plants.* Milkweed Editions.
Kovach, Margaret. 2010. *Indigenous Methodologies: Characteristics, Conversations, and Contexts.* University of Toronto Press.
Latour, Bruno. 2004. *Politics of Nature.* Harvard University Press.
Lévi-Strauss, Claude. 1979. *Myth and Meaning.* Schocken.
Li, Tania M. 2007. *The Will to Improve: Governmentality, Development, and the Practice of Politics.* Duke University Press.
McGregor, Deborah. 2004. "Coming Full Circle: Indigenous Knowledge, Environment, and Our Future." *American Indian Quarterly* 28 (3/4): 385–410.
Moritz, Sarah C. 2012. "Tsuwalhkálh Ti Tmícwa (The Land Is Ours): St'át'imc Self-Determination in the Face of Large-Scale Hydro-electric Development." Master's thesis, University of Victoria. https://dspace.library.uvic.ca/bitstream/handle/1828/4215/Moritz_Sarah_MA_2012.pdf?sequence=3&isAllowed=y
Moritz, Sarah C. 2020. "'Fishing for the Good Life': The (Boasian) Anthropology of Interior Salish St'át'imc Fisheries and Water Governance in the Fraser River Valley of British Columbia." PhD diss., McGill University. https://escholarship.mcgill.ca/concern/theses/v405sg53q

Moritz, Sarah. 2021. “Cúz̓lhkan Sqwéqwel̓ (I’m Going to Tell a Story): Revitalizing Stories to Strengthen Fish, Water and the Upper St’át’imc Salish Language.” In *Indigenous Languages and the Promise of Archives*, edited by Adrianna Link, Abby Shelton, and Patrick Spero. The University of Nebraska Press and the American Philosophical Society.

Nadasdy, Paul. 1999. “The Politics of TEK: Power and the ‘Integration’ of Knowledge.” *Arctic Anthropology* 36 (1/2): 1–18.

Nadasdy, Paul. 2005. “The Anti-politics of TEK: The Institutionalization of Co-management Discourse and Practice.” *Anthropologica* 47 (2): 215–232.

Peacock, Sandra. L., and Nancy J. Turner. 2000. “‘Just Like a Garden’: Traditional Resource Management and Biodiversity Conservation on the Interior Plateau of British Columbia.” In *Biodiversity and Native America*, edited by Paul E. Minnis and Wayne J. Elisens. University of Oklahoma Press.

Peterson, Nicolas, and Fred Myers. 2016. *Experiments in Self-determination: Histories of the Outstation Movement in Australia*. ANU Press.

Poirier, Sylvie. 2001. “Territories, Identity, and Modernity among the Atikamekw (Haut St-Maurice, Québec).” In *Aboriginal Autonomy and Development in Northern Quebec and Labrador*, edited by Colin Scott. UBC Press.

Poirier, Sylvie. 2013. “The Dynamic Reproduction of Hunter-Gatherers Ontologies and Values.” In *A Companion to the Anthropology of Religion*, edited by Janice Boddy and Michael Lambek. Wiley-Blackwell.

Prentiss, Anna Marie, and Ian Kujit. 2012. *People of the Middle Fraser Canyon: An Archaeological History*. UBC Press.

Qwa7yán’ak (Carl Alexander). 2016. *Sqwéqwel’ múta7 Sptakwlh: St’át’imcets Narratives*. Transcribed and edited by E. Callahan, H. Davis, J. Lyon, and L. Matthewson. Upper St’át’imc Language Culture and Education Society and University of British Columbia Occasional Papers in Linguistics.

Qwa7yán’ak (Carl Alexander), Qwalqwalten (Garry John), Rep’rep’sken (Morris Prosser) and Sarah C. Moritz. 2025. “‘Good Anthropology of the Past, for the Present’: James Teit, the Written and the Oral History of the Declaration of the Lillooet Tribe.” *History of Anthropology Review* 49. https://histanthro.org/notes/james-teit-and-the-declaration-of-the-lillooet-tribe/.

Reddekop, Jarrad. 2014. “Thinking Across Worlds: Indigenous Thought, Relational Ontology, and the Politics of Nature; Or, If Only Nietzsche Could Meet a Yachaj.” PhD diss., University of Western Ontario. https://ir.lib.uwo.ca/etd/2082

SER (St’át’imc Eco-Resources). 2013. Bridge River Project Water Use Plan (Executive Summary). Lillooet, BC. https://www.bchydro.com/toolbar/about/sustainability/environmental_responsibility/water-use-plans/lower-mainland/bridge-river.html.

SER (St’át’imc Eco-Resources). 2016. Bridge River Project Water Use Plan: Lower Bridge River Spiritual and Cultural Value Monitoring Implementation (Year 2). Lillooet, BC. https://www.bchydro.com/content/dam/BCHydro/customer-portal/documents/corporate/environment-sustainability/water-use-planning/lower-mainland/brgmon-16-yr2-2016-01-12.pdf.

SER (St’át’imc Eco-Resources). 2021. Bridge River Project Water Use Plan: Lower Bridge River Spiritual and Cultural Value Monitoring Implementation (Year 5). SER: Lillooet, BC. https://www.bchydro.com/content/dam/BCHydro/customer-portal/documents/corporate/environment-sustainability/water-use-planning/lower-mainland/brgmon-16-yr5-final-report-2021-02-01.pdf.

Scott, Colin. 1996. “Science for the West, Myth for the Rest? The Case of James Bay Cree Knowledge Construction.” In *Naked Science: Anthropological Inquiry into Boundaries, Power, and Knowledge*, edited by Laura Nader. Routledge.

Scott, Colin. 2004. "Conflicting Discourses of Property, Governance and Development in the Indigenous North." In *In the Way of Development: Indigenous Peoples, Life Projects and Globalization*, edited by Mario Blaser, Harvey A. Feit, and Glenn McRae. Zed Books.

Scott, Colin. 2006. "Spirit and Practical Knowledge in the Person of the Bear among Wemindji Cree Hunters." *Ethnos* 71 (1): 51–66.

Scott, Colin. 2013. "Ontology and Ethics in Cree Hunting: Animism, Totemism and Practical Knowledge." In *The Handbook of Contemporary Animism*, edited by Graham Harvey. Acumen.

SGS (St'át'imc Government Services). 2016. *St'át'imc: The Salmon People*. Film. https://www.youtube.com/watch?v=KMtdVqHDrwc

Simpson, Leanne B. 2004. "Anticolonial Strategies for the Recovery and Maintenance of Indigenous Knowledge." *American Indian Quarterly* 28 (3): 373–384.

Siragusa, Laura, Clinton N. Westman, and Sarah C. Moritz. 2020. "Shared Breath: Human and Nonhuman Copresence through Ritualized Words and Beyond." *Current Anthropology* 61 (4): 471–94.

SLRA (St'át'imc Land and Resource Authority). 2004. *Nxekmenlhkala lti tmicwa: St'át'imc Preliminary Draft Land Use Plan, Part 1*. Lillooet, BC. https://lillooet.bc.libraries.coop/files/2019/08/Nxekmenlhkalha-2004.pdf.

Smith, Joshua. 2010. "The Political Thought of Sol Tax: The Principles of Non-Assimilation and Self-Government in Action Anthropology." *Histories of Anthropology Annual* 6 (1): 129–170.

Smith, Trefor. 1998. *Our Stories Are Written on the Land: A Brief History of the Upper St'át'imc 1800–1940*. Upper St'át'imc Language, Culture and Education Society.

St'át'imc Code. 2006. *Nxékmens I St'át'imca* (Draft). St'át'imc Chiefs Council.

Tax, Sol. 1975. "Action Anthropology." *Current Anthropology* 16 (4): 514–517.

Teit, James A. 1906. "The Lillooet Indians." *Memoirs of the American Museum of Natural History* 4 (4): 193–300.

Teit, James A. 1912. "Traditions of the Lillooet Indians of British Columbia." *Journal of American Folklore* 25 (98): 287–371.

TRC (Truth and Reconciliation Commission of Canada). 2015. *Honouring the Truth, Reconciling for the Future: Summary of the Final Report of the Truth and Reconciliation Commission of Canada*. http://nctr.ca/assets/reports/Final%20Reports/Executive_Summary_English_Web.pdf

Usher, Peter J. 2000. "Traditional Ecological Knowledge in Environmental Assessment and Management." *Arctic* 53 (2): 183–193.

Viveiros de Castro, Eduardo. 2004. "Perspectival Anthropology and the Method of Controlled Equivocation." *Tipití: Journal of the Society for the Anthropology of Lowland South America* 2 (1): 1–20.

JURISPRUDENCE

Canadian Constitution Act, [1982], s. 35, "Aboriginal and Treaty Rights."

Delgamuukw v. British Columbia, [1997] 3 S.C.R. 1010.

10

Cristina Rojas

CONSTRUCTING DIVERGENT TERRITORIALITY

FROM SLAVERY TO THE CREATION OF BLACK COMMUNITIES IN WESTERN COLOMBIA

INTRODUCTION

Toward the end of the 1980s, Colombia was experiencing a political crisis associated with the advance of paramilitarism, guerrilla expansion, and a partisan political game that "depoliticized politics" and exacerbated violence (Sánchez 1991, 32). Broad social mobilization was demanding the formation of a Constituent Assembly to transform the existing 1886 constitution. The resultant 1991 constitution enshrined the nation's multi-ethnic and multicultural character and advanced recognition of the rights of Indigenous and Black populations, especially their territorial rights. Resguardos (reservations) were legalized and the Indigenous population's rights were expanded.[1] Transitional Article 55 (AT-55) prefigured the need for a law recognizing the right that Black communities had to collective land ownership. In 1993, Law 70 was passed recognizing this right. In addition to the recognition of Black populations as an "ethnic group," the law included the promise to develop measures for their economic and social development (Art. 47) and self-defined economic models (Art. 52) (Escobar 2014, 79).

Subsequent to the passing of Law 70, a debate arose concerning implicit equivalence that the law established between Indigenous and Black populations. As Peter Wade notes, the legislation traced this equivalence by referencing *ancestral roots* in connection to topics such as collective land use and productive practices (1996, 290–291). However, he also points out, this similarity was not established for issues related to territory, since the Black population was considered an "invader" of unoccupied public lands,[2] while the Indigenous population was recognized has having "original rights" to their territories. Neither was an equivalence established between Black and Indigenous Peoples with respect to Law 70's geographic scope: while no limits were established in the case of Indigenous People, in the case of the Black populations, their rights were limited to the Pacific region.

Although Indigenous and Black communities have shared a somewhat similar history in terms of subordination, I suggest there are important lessons to be learned from diverse trajectories in terms of their emancipatory practices, particularly in relation to their struggles for territories of life. Enslaved populations, once they achieved freedom, designated themselves as "free people," a process beginning in the eighteenth century and accompanied by self-defined territorial projects. In this chapter, I use the term "free people" to emphasize this sentiment of freedom accompanied by practices of "being with territory"—I also want to note that the concept of race did not yet exist, and only began to be acknowledged toward the end of the nineteenth century. Thus, I will use the term "free people," alternating it with "Black community," according to context. The relationship between *being free* and *territory* is captured in the concept of "de-enslavement and territorialization," proposed by Oscar Almario to indicate that liberation from slavery was accompanied by a "feeling and perception of territory as something unique and of one's own" (2002a, 46–47). I maintain that "being with territory" is an ontological, not a cultural, difference. In this sense, the territoriality of the Afro-Colombian communities bears a certain similarity to several Indigenous territorialities as discussed in this volume (see chapters by Tytelman and Wattez in this volume). As the editors point out in the introduction, these territorialities affirm an inherent co-emergence between that which modern notions of territoriality conceive as two components: the human population and the natural space. However, there is a difference between Indigenous and Afro-Colombian territoriality, which is particularly relevant to this chapter: while Indigenous territorialities precede modern territoriality (although today they are entangled with it), the territoriality of the free people has been generated from within modern territoriality as a divergent practice.

I use Isabelle Stengers's (2011) concept of "divergent practices" to explore the specificity of this concept of "being with territory," a specificity that partially emerges from the divergence with modern ways of "constructing territory." Echoing Stengers, Marisol de la Cadena explains that divergent "practices exist within an ecology as they diverge in assertion of what makes them feel, think, do. Unlike contradiction or difference, which require homogenous terms (to compare or make equivalent), divergence *constitutes* practices *in their heterogeneity* as they become together...while remaining distinct" (2019a, 478). She adds that establishing relationships between divergent worlds is a decolonizing political practice, the only guarantee of which is absence of assimilation (2015).

As in the introduction to this volume and in several other chapters, I too argue that the concept of territory is an equivocation. I challenge the assumption that—insofar as it signals colonial practices of power which justify the destruction of divergent worlds and their assimilation to a "one-world world" (Law 2015)—"territory" can be considered a universal. John Law (2015, 126–127) makes explicit the ontological character of divergence between different practices of territoriality through the example of Australian Aborigines and the doctrine of terra or res nullius that justified conquest (see also Pagden 2006, 17). While this doctrine implied a separation between the people and the land—the latter understood as external object to be worked on and, therefore, possessed—according to Law, for the Aborigines, the "idea of a reified reality out there, detached from the work and the rituals that constantly re-enact it, makes no sense. Land does not *belong* to people. Perhaps it would be better to say that *people* belong to the land." (127). What is at stake here, as Arturo Escobar clarifies, is not a question of beliefs (culture) but a question of "realities," because the attempt to make "a one-world world" renders multiple realities invisible (2017, 171–172). This confers on modernity the power to assume the right to be *the world*, and to subject all other worlds to its rules, to a secondary state, or to non-existence.

In this chapter, I explore the free people's practices of divergent territoriality that generated alternatives to modern practices of territoriality (including, in particular, slavery) in the haciendas of the Valle del Cauca and in the gold mines of the Pacific region. I argue that the trajectories these practices have followed throughout history bring to light a regime of visibilities and invisibilities, whose activation reveals the possibilities as well as limitations of the equivocation implied by the concept of territory. The idea of a regime of visibilities and invisibilities is inspired by Jacques Rancière when he suggests that domination operates through the organization of "the visible, the sayable, the thinkable and the possible" and that the politics of emancipation connects with this order in complex ways (2011, 240). Indeed, the discourses and practices that organize the visible, sayable, thinkable, and possible generate what I call ontological openings and closures, which means there are moments during which "being with territory" can flourish more or less to its liking, as well as moments when it is severely constrained.

To develop this argument, I begin by very briefly describing how modern/colonial territoriality unfolded in the region of Cauca through the system of slavery centred on the hacienda and the mine. Next, I focus on three non-continuous moments to illustrate the opening or closing of the free people's territorial practices (which are none other than practices of endurance leading to ontological self-constitution). The first moment, which coincides with the struggles for independence (1770–1825), is one of ontological opening, making it possible for enslaved workers of the haciendas and gold mines to break away from slavery and generate a divergent territoriality. The second period coincides with civilizing liberal reforms (1849–1880) and the conservative regeneration of the population (1882–1898). A paradox from this period relates to ontological closure for the free people of the haciendas and ontological opening for the free people previously enslaved in the mines of the Pacific. The third moment emerges around the time of the 1991 constitution, presenting contradictory tendencies of both ontological openness and closure. This contradiction gives rise to concessions over territorial rights not seen before, as well as situations of unprecedented "uprooting" (Vergara-Figueroa 2018, 17), leading to the violent separation of people from territory to produce "territories without people and de-territorialized people" (Almario and Jiménez 2004, 657). I conclude by pointing out that an analysis of this line of thinking indicates that no linear relationship exists between the regime of visibilities and invisibilities on the one hand, and moments of opening and closing on the other. This non-linearity raises a whole series of questions about enduring or striving for existence (see introduction) in contexts of ontological equivocations and deterritorialization. As a mestizo Colombian woman born in a small Andean town, and lifelong analyst of the country's (largely) violent politics, I think these questions are immensely relevant to the prospects of the recent political opening implied by the establishment of a "progressive" administration in Colombia.

MODERN/COLONIAL TERRITORIALITY: THE MINE-HACIENDA COMPLEX IN THE CAUCA REGION, A BRIEF DESCRIPTION

The Cauca region presents a clear example of the foundational role of slavery in modern/colonial Colombian territoriality. Indeed, since colonial times, the province of Cauca had the largest concentration of enslaved population in New Granada—what is today Colombia—brought during the sixteenth century to work in the gold mines of the Pacific region and in the haciendas of the Cauca Valley. A mine-hacienda complex (Colmenares 1975) allowed slave owners to complement mining and agricultural economies; to move enslaved people from one region to another; and to concentrate economic and political control of the complex in a few families, faithful to Catholic and Hispanic cultural heritage (Almario and Jiménez 2004, 45). Conservative elites were able to sustain this complex, albeit with fluctuations, until the mid-nineteenth century.

The Gold Mines of the Pacific Region

In Cauca, unlike in other regions of the Americas dedicated to tropical crops on large plantations, alluvial-type, disperse, mobile, and small-scale gold mining prevailed (Taussig 1977). Faced with the difficulty of finding Indigenous labour, mine owners resorted to importing enslaved workers toward the end of the sixteenth century.

Gold mining predominated until the second half of the nineteenth century, when the haciendas became the main source of accumulation (Almario and Jiménez 2004, 62). The mine owners lived comfortably in Popayán, Cauca's capital, from where they managed mines located in the humid jungles of the Pacific. For this purpose, they organized work crews of between ten and one hundred men, the administration of which was delegated to enslaved captains, counter-captains, and enslaved workers who served as intermediaries not only between owners and workers but also between colonial powers and farm and mine owners, thereby acquiring special status within the crews (Almario 2002a, 55–56; Romero 1991). Captains tended to be knowledgeable about colonial law, which they used to ensure their leadership, denounce abuses, and petition the government for protection. A common occurrence was the non-compliance of owners regarding their obligations toward the enslaved workers, including provision of clothing and food rations, which they compensated for by granting one day's work for personal benefit (Almario 2002a; Echeverri 2016; Romero 1991).

The Haciendas

Haciendas were rigid organizations located on the outskirts of Popayan. The owners generally delegated the management of workers to an administrator, who, in addition to providing them with food rations and a Christian education, constantly monitored them, ensuring they did not visit neighbouring towns, and whipping those who did not comply with orders as punishment. The condition of slavery became a "space of terror and death" (Romero 2017, 103).

ONTOLOGICAL OPENING IN HACIENDAS AND GOLD MINES: 1780–1825

Organizational aspects of the mine-hacienda system opened up spaces, resulting in conditions that allowed the enslaved population to free themselves from slavery, first de facto and then legally. As summarized by Oscar Almario and Orián Jiménez, "what unfolded in these areas was a de facto process of territorial occupation, supported by the dynamics of free, local societies, demographic recovery of these groups, and by their ability to construct their own territory, essentially ignoring official, national and regional land stipulations" (2004, 60). Indeed, the enslaved populations transformed the mines and the haciendas into political spaces "in the shadow" of visibility.[3] For example, the organization of work in crews for the mines facilitated emancipation by allowing participants to receive remuneration one day a week, the savings from which were used to purchase their freedom and that of their families (Almario 2002a; Jiménez 1998; Romero 1991). Juana Camacho narrates that enslaved women often sold their bodies in exchange for the promise of freedom (though not always fulfilled); earned the love and respect of their masters; breastfed white infants to appeal for the right to freedom for their excellent service; or procreated children with free men, Black and white, so they would inherit the status of free (2004, 174–175). The introduction of women into the crews also created kinship ties and broke with the nuclear, patrilineal, and patrilocal family, allowing mine workers to recognize themselves in a common ancestor, generally a woman (mother and grandmother) and to establish ties with other communities and territories (Almario and Jiménez 2004; Camacho Segura 2004; Romero 1991, 2017; Zuluaga Ramírez and Bermúdez 1997).

Almario also mentions the role played by the relation to nature in the construction of a divergent sense of existence:

> Black groups, by means of very diverse pathways, progressed from experiencing the realities of the mines as places or spaces where they were dominated and exploited by slavers, to experiencing and perceiving them as incipient territories of their own. From the realities of the mines and their rigid, legally established limitations, designed to facilitate territorial control according to the dictates of slavery, these groups came to recognize an ecologically complex environment of rivers, mountains and streams, in which they confronted the challenges of existence, reproduced life, constructed identities, and defined individual and collective meaning. (2002a, 71)

Marcela Echeverri analyzes the alliances that the enslaved population made with royalists during emancipation, at the time of crisis in the

Spanish monarchy, sparked by the Napoleonic invasion of Madrid and the removal of King Ferdinand VII in 1807 (2011; 2016, 648–649). Unlike the mine owners who rejected Spanish sovereignty, enslaved and Indigenous populations preferred to continue as the king's servants, sustaining a royalist rebellion for ten years, in which they defended the Pacific lowlands against incursions by independence forces (2016). The case of enslaved workers at the San Juan mine is a case in point. This rebellion began with a call from the governor to the enslaved population to defend the sovereignty of the king, creating the misunderstanding that the call implied an offer of freedom, thereby motivating the enslaved workers to announce to the mine owner that "the mine was now theirs and they were free" (quoted in Echevarri 2016, 174). From 1809 to 1819, the workers divided the mine amongst themselves, creating a subsistence economy that allowed them to pay for their and their families' freedom. Upon the owner's return to the mine, he found to his "surprise" that the (supposedly) enslaved population not only displayed "pride, arrogance, insubordination and neglect" (183), but acted as if they were free.

Enslaved hacienda workers also created new forms of spatiality to escape control by owners, altering places of domination by, for example, building their own roads in hacienda interstitial space, establishing river basin communities, and connecting with other communities through kinship ties (Romero 2017). They organized individual or collective escapes and created towns of escapees known as "palenques," the most renowned being El Castigo (Punishment) in the Patía River valley, which became a central point of royalist resistance in the defense of Popayán (Echeverri 2016, 105). Fleeing Black women took an active part in the formation of the palenques and used legal channels to obtain their freedom and that of their families. The growth of territorialities of the free people, however, led to a crisis of control by the landowners, which accelerated after the abolition of slavery and resulted in a paradox: the increase of free people's visibility came with a progressive ontological closure to its expression.

CIVILIZING REGIME: ONTOLOGICAL CLOSURE IN THE VALLE DEL CAUCA (1849–1886)

The Liberal government, elected in March 1849, promised freedom, progress, and civilization, their platform being grounded in ideals of the sovereign individual, an enlightened democracy, a civilized citizenship, and free trade (Rojas 2001). The government approved the abolition of slavery in 1851, while the 1853 constitution extended citizenship to all men over twenty-one years of age. However, and in response to the abolition of slavery, landowners established new forms of exploitation and control, such as semi-free land contracts, known as "terraje," which offered a small plot in exchange for family obligations to work on the farm (Almario and Jiménez 2004, 85; Garrido 2018, 95; Romero 2017, 178). This logic of domination was accompanied by repressive measures, including non-payment of improvements, expulsion of those considered pernicious, dispossession, and the destruction of dwellings (Romero 2017, 186).

Given the impetus provided to export agriculture and the crisis in mining, hacienda owners sought to increase the size of their territories, privatizing and enclosing ejidos, or communal lands. The privatization of unoccupied public lands, baldíos, comprising approximately 75 percent of the territory (LeGrand 2016), was promoted by the nation-state. According to Catherine LeGrand, in order to benefit from the program, "land entrepreneurs," politicians, lawyers, merchants, landowners, mine owners, and bankers requested access to public lands, seeking out lands already occupied by small settlers, the majority of whom had no property titles. With the assistance of lawyers, public lands occupied by settlers were privatized, leaving them no other option but to work for the new owners (71–72).[4] Thus the abolition of slavery "freed arms, without land for those arms" and "expropriated masters, but not large landowners (latifundistas)" (Aprile-Gniset 2004, 279).

In addition to employing new forms of exploitation and control, liberal reforms engendered an ontological closure, defining what was "thinkable and...possible" (Rancière 2011, 240) according to a universalized modern European civilization. As James E. Sanders notes, in the case of liberalism, the goal was to turn Black communities into "rational" people, so they would participate in politics wisely, meaning they would not "interpret their rights in too radical a manner," and so they would see their future in "the nation and the Liberal Party" (2004, 146). In other words, so that they would not deviate from liberal ideals.

This ontological closure was explicit for Indigenous Peoples, given their communal relationship with territory. As far as the liberal elites were concerned, Indigenous Peoples would never be "free citizens and active members of the democratic Republic" (Sanders 2007, 31; see also 2004a). This closure begs the question: Why were free people not excluded as well, given the concept of territoriality they had already displayed? I suggest that it was because the idea of free people with territory was "unthinkable" for Colombian liberal intellectuals. Just as Michel-Rolph Trouillot points out in the case of Haiti's revolution, which was led by enslaved people,[5] it was not as though empirical evidence of this divergent territoriality was lacking, but there existed a particular ontology that organized their world and its inhabitants that made this territoriality invisible for the liberal intellectual (1995, 73). This invisibility is further reflected in the words of Agustín Codazzi, Italian geographer and director of the Chorographic Commission,[6] for whom it was unthinkable that once having gained freedom, the manumitted would engage in other forms of life outside the dictates of European civilization:

> Suddenly finding themselves free; transiting from a state of slavery to being their own masters, with no preparation, lacking habits of freedom, without customs of virtue, and with no desire for comforts they do not know or imagine, they have gone from being servants of men to being servants of vices. Their hands are free but their hearts and souls are enslaved: they have confused independence with arrogance; the freedom to choose to work with the freedom not to work; equal rights with equal misery; and the dignity of free men with the insolence of despots. (Quoted in Almario 2015, 250–251)

In short, without civilization, the people are not free. Hence, and as the liberal intellectual José María Samper proposed, only with "education in freedom and democracy," will "the mulatto castes become one of the safest and most fruitful elements of New World civilization" (1861,

47–48). Sanders adds that, for liberals of the time, Black people were "potential citizens, but also *brute citizens who required their lead, and ignorant citizens who required education and discipline*" (2004a, 141; my emphasis). As part of their formation in citizenship, the liberal elites integrated the free people into the Democratic Societies and the National Guard,[7] to the point that, in the Valle del Cauca, the Liberal Party was identified "with [B]lackness" (Sanders 2009, 193). This support allowed liberalism to win elections, govern the province, and win civil wars.[8]

Despite the assumed impossibility (and invisibility) of other territorialities, or perhaps thanks to it, free people continued managing their territories, building towns with their own resources, settling on the banks of rivers, defining their own work schedules, congregating in groups, and avoiding being "atomized as the landowners had tried to do with the small plot owners (terrazgueros)" (Romero 2017, 182; see also Almario and Jiménez 2004, 88). Furthermore, they joined with other free people from nearby towns, escaping the landlord's authority and assigning to themselves a "certain autonomy"; they participated in markets, developed their own culture, bought land—sometimes in groups—and created economic alternatives, including tobacco cultivation and liquor production (Romero, 2017). Almario calls this coexistence "flexible landholding (terrajería)," as it facilitated the conciliation of landowners' interests with the free people-led processes of occupation and progressive social diversification within the spaces of the hacienda (2013, 46). With the abolition of slavery, some landowners suffered crises and sold their properties, which were then occupied by new groups of the free people who called themselves "comuneros."[9] In general, abandoned hacienda spaces were occupied by free people, "creating a balance between dominant and dominated" (47–48).

The reordering of social relations that came along with the end of slavery generated a multiplicity of conflicts. Large territorial entrepreneurs (real estate speculators) and landowners promoted the enclosure of the ejidos or communal lands used by communities for their survival, to which the free people responded by destroying fences and physically attacking their enemies. This, in turn, triggered reprisals in a constant cycle of conflicts that culminated with the Conservatives taking power and the establishment of a new constitution in 1886.

The free people also participated in strikes and boycotts, presented petitions and claims, and marched in public demonstrations demanding the right to land, the cessation of rent for land, and settlement on and cultivation of any land in Cauca, as long as "a second party is not severely harmed" (Sanders 2009). The "mulatto" leader, David Peña,[10] introduced a bill instituting a five-year rent moratorium and allowing anyone without land to claim three hectares on any land not fenced or cultivated by another person. Sanders explains that the greatest concern of the commission that studied the bill was the danger of "accustoming a part, perhaps the most numerous part, of society to use someone else's property without the obligation" of remuneration (2004a, 160). He furthermore affirms that for the Black population the lack of land affected their status as "citizens of a free people" (2009, 202).

I want to tweak Sanders's approach, which reduces the problem to "land distribution." As I have previously mentioned, what was at stake were different manners of making the world, as can be inferred from the elites' reasons for opposing the demands of the free people. They believed these demands to be a threat to the viability of the haciendas, given that the free people questioned private property and threatened economic progress by refusing to work for them. Elites rejected the "perverse" meaning that free people gave to freedom as a status in which elites were not needed, and all the while free people promoted the idea of withdrawing "into the bountiful and abundant lands of the tropical forests to live in relative independence" (Sanders 2004a, 147).[11] In short, freedom with territoriality posed a conflict between worlds. This perception of an ontological closure, which did not allow the free people to "be with territory," was equated to a return to slavery as claimed by the Democratic Society of Cali in 1877, formed mostly by Black people:

> Land cannot be occupied to such an extent that the other members of the community are deprived of the means of subsistence or are obligated to be the slaves of those feudal lords who do not admit onto their supposed properties any but those individuals who implicitly sell their personal independence, that is to say, their conscience and liberty, in order to be the peons and tributaries of an individual and

to cease to be citizens of a free people. (Quoted in Sanders 2004a, 159)

This conflict over divergent practices of territoriality divided the liberal elites, with one faction allying itself with conservatives demanding order and authority. In 1878, Rafael Núñez, president of Congress, warned, "We are confronting a unique dilemma: either we produce a profound administrative regeneration or face catastrophe." Once elected president, Núñez proposed a new constitution in which "the enervating particularism would be replaced by vigorous generality...Foundational codes, which define the Law, must be national." He added that "republics must be authoritative, or assume the risk of promoting permanent disorder and annihilating themselves, rather than progressing" (Quoted in Rojas 2009a, 249). During debates concerning who would be considered a citizen, Samper, now a Conservative Party militant, proposed excluding Black populations because they had no notion of what the law entails, and Indigenous populations because they were "incapable of civilization." The 1886 constitution enshrined property rights, declaring that "the Territory, including its public goods, belongs exclusively to the Nation" (Art. 4). It consolidated politics as an exclusive endeavour belonging to property-owning men, assigning them the vote to elect the nation's representatives (Art. 173). The constitution also reinstated a colonial order based on morality, religion, and the Catholic and patriarchal family, as it was dictated in "the name of God the source of all authority." It confronted the problem of divergence by declaring Colombia "a single, unified Republic and Catholicism as the nation's religion." It restricted popular classes' political participation, especially that of the free people, by prohibiting "popular political councils of a permanent nature" (Art 47). Article 121 gave the President exceptional powers to limit the rights of citizens when, in his opinion, public order might be disturbed. In short, these exceptional powers meant that the suppression of political and civil rights became an instrument for repressing the dissidence and disobedience of workers, trade unionists, and social movements, including Indigenous and free people (Uribe de Hincapié 2001, 206).

ONTOLOGICAL OPENING OF THE FREE PEOPLE OF THE PACIFIC: 1849–1991

Unlike what happened in the Valle del Cauca, where liberalism "envisioned" the possibility of assimilating the free people into civilization, without their practice of territoriality, in the Pacific, civilization was unthinkable for the Black population. Interestingly, however, the idea of progress was "thinkable" for territory if driven by the redemptive force of the white race. What is disconcerting about this situation is that, despite the ontological closure of the liberal civilizing proposal, practices of territoriality by the free people prospered continuously in this region from the second half of the nineteenth century until well into the twentieth. I suggest this was possible because, by not being "seen" as assimilable to progress, the free people enacted various forms of territoriality in the "shadow" of the thinkable. Moreover, their refusal to disappear was an example of endurance, insisting on continuing in spaces left abandoned or declared impossible by liberal projects of civilization (see the introduction to this volume).

To analyze the designation of what was "possible and thinkable" in the Pacific region during the Liberal period, I use, as a reference, the narratives of the Chorographic Commission established by the Liberal government in 1850 to study prospects for progress and the region's incorporation into the nation. Under the direction of Codazzi, the commission brought together a group of scientists who visited the Pacific in 1853. The commission divided the perceptible into two components: territory and populations. However, unlike the perception in the Valle del Cauca of Black people without territory, in the Pacific the territory was perceived as a territory without people, an empty land. For example, the census prepared by Codazzi estimated the population of Choco to be 43,649 inhabitants, not including "dispersed" Indigenous People and other "independents," and declared over 75 percent of the area to be composed of "unoccupied public lands" (Almario 2015, 55–56). The commission envisioned the territory as a possible source of progress, including the construction of an interoceanic canal that would connect the Atlantic and Pacific. Paradoxically, the commission concluded the area to be "extremely rich in gold and cultivable land," with one caveat: the Pacific was "a tomb for the white race, a hospital for the creole, and a healthy place for the African: a unique contrast *born of the different constitutions of the races in question*" (Quoted in Restrepo 2007, 32; my emphasis).

As Nancy Appelbaum notes, Codazzi believed it was possible that the Black population could one day colonize the jungle and extend its empire to the Pacific, changing the nature of the climate, modifying the impact of the swamy wetlands, and drying and destroying the forests (2016, 90). But he did not foresee the Black population effectively achieving this transformation due to what he characterized as their lack of "love for work" (90). As a result, the commission recommended a program forcing these populations to work, including the revival of vagrancy laws. I would like to propose that, in the attribution of "natural" traits to different races, at stake was the commission's perception that the Black communities lacked the capacity to transform nature into progress, a perception that emerged from translating the territorial practices of those communities into the system of values of modernity. This perception is similar to that of colonial theorists who denied property rights to hunter-gatherers because they did not transform nature (Povinelli 1995). Elizabeth Povinelli points out that according to Locke, they possess only the "acorns...pickt up under an oak or the apples... gathered from the trees"; they do not own the land on which they roam because they add nothing to it (506). The land remains empty or unoccupied (baldía) in the eyes of the Chorographic Commission because the Black community did not "work" the land; and because they exercised no "intentional activity," they could not be distinguished from animals. This is what Codazzi seems to suggest when he speaks of the "indolence" of the African race:

> Previously, they engaged in mining activities; but during the day, *neglecting to make good use of their newly acquired freedom*, they have, for the most part, abandoned such labour to live in absolute independence on the banks of the rivers, sewing a bit of plantain, corn and sugarcane, the harvest of which, together with the abundant fish in the rivers ... guarantee them a crude, but safe supply of food. (Quoted in Restrepo 2007, 30; my emphasis)

This quote suggests that when they were enslaved, Black people appeared more human due to the work they engaged in; in conditions of freedom, they resemble animals, only concerned with feeding themselves.

However, the people continued to practice ideals of territoriality "in the shadow," thanks, perhaps, to their being invisible to the elites' eyes. Some studies[12] confirm this is the case. Jacques Aprile-Gniset documents that from 1852, the free people initiated a period of agrarian colonization that continued until the twentieth century, which he describes as "prodigious territorial expansion achieved through maximum dispersion of the population and the establishment of numerous agrarian habitats" (quoted in Escobar 2010, 61). Almario argues that, despite having been denied diversity, the free people continued to develop their territorialities in which "circuits of reciprocity and redistribution of existing resources flourished; and, where, at the same time, symbolic appropriation resulted (myths, stories, legends, oral tradition)" (2001, 30). William Villa describes agrarian colonization as a "journey in freedom," in which the free

> populate an area with imaginary beings inherited from their ancestors. Likewise, events and stories of distant rivers and estuaries begin to nourish their collective memory and they learn the secrets of the forest from contact with [I]ndigenous [P]eople. During the long journey through the immense network of rivers, they understand this is territory for rebirth through music and dance, the rites of the deceased, and the network of relatives scattered along river banks; for bestowing on themselves their own form of government and searching to make history once again. (1997, 336)

According to Ulrich Oslender, after the emancipation law, the free people moved along the rivers creating "linear villages," linking identity with the "aquatic," and creating territoriality centred on the river basin, which he denominates "the logic of the river" (2001, 90). Eduardo Restrepo (1996) associates transformations in working hours, autonomy, and activities involving extractive practices, transport, and the gathering of production with the rhythm of the tide, similar to that of woodcutters and women clam diggers. Claudia Leal (2008, 2018; Leal and Van Ausdal 2013) documents that the continuation of an extractive economy, based on independent mining or diversifying into tagua and rubber, did not harm the forest and facilitated self-management of time and autonomy. For Almario, the extractive model not only maintained the landscape but also allowed successful adaptation to diverse ecosystems of forests, rivers, and mangrove by free Black people (2002b, 658).

INCLUSION OF TERRITORIES AND ETHNIC POPULATIONS WITHIN THE NATION: THE 1991 CONSTITUTION

Contrary to the ontological closure resulting from the 1886 constitution, events surrounding the 1991 constitution produced an ontological opening for Black and Indigenous populations. This opening was due, in part, to the crisis caused by the inoperability of the political system, including the constant use of the State of Siege (LeGrand 201, 19); the presence of narco-paramilitarism and its alliances with politicians and the state; and the Revolutionary Armed Forces of Colombia's (FARC) abandonment of relative institutional political presence for endorsement of a war strategy (Peñaranda 2015, 96–97). These and other factors promoted the demand for a Constituent Assembly, which, elected by popular vote, resulted in notable diversity, including three Indigenous Peoples' representatives. Although there was no representation from Black populations, they backed their demands with massive campaigns and were supported by Indigenous representatives and other constituents who identified with their cause. The 1991 constitution was a pioneer in the region, recognizing a place for Indigenous and Afro-Colombian populations within the nation, declaring it to be multi-ethnic and multicultural in nature, and assigning protection of their rights to the state. It was equally generous in acknowledging territorial rights, especially for the Indigenous population, guaranteeing recognition of their reservations (resguardos) as collective, non-alienable property (Article 329) and legalizing twenty-eight million hectares, approximately 30 percent of the national territory (Jackson 2003, 138). Transitory Article 55 of the constitution recognized the Black population's right to collective property, later followed by Law 70 of 1993, which designated the Black populations as an ethnic group and which created mechanisms for collective property titling. However, the constitution ignored the Black population's concept of "being with territory," because the idea was that Black people diverged from other groups through their culture, and their territory was designated as unoccupied public land. Indeed, Article 1 states that "[B]lack communities which have been making use of unoccupied public lands in rural shoreline areas of Pacific Basin rivers" will be recognized; Article 2, numeral 5, defines Black communities as possessing "*a culture of their own*, a shared history, and *their own traditions and customs*" (my emphasis) without referring to their concept of territoriality.

However, in debates relating to Law 70, territoriality once again becomes central as it is conceptualized as part of being Black (Escobar and Pedrosa 1996). For instance, the Second National Assembly of Black Communities in 1993 defines territory as a space of life, affirming that "we cannot be if we do not have space to live according to what we think and what we desire as a form of life" (Grueso et al. 1997, 52–53). The words of Mama Cuama, an activist for the defense of territory, could not be more eloquent regarding the notion of "being with territory" felt in the communities: "For us, territory is everything—life, food, work, sustenance; it is where we have grown up; where we find our family, the hillocks, the animals, the river; where we are happy. Without territory we have nothing, to be without territory is like being slaves again" (quoted in Lozano 2016, 24).

The constitution facilitated an ontological opening propelled by Black community mobilization, described by Hernán Cortes, one of the authors of AT55,[13] as the "largest mobilizations in the recent history of Colombia's [B]lack people" (quoted in Restrepo 2002, 39). The AT55 facilitated the capacity of these organizations to articulate their political demands and to strengthen their decision-making authority, as related to territory and resources (Ruiz-Serna 2018). In addition, communities used it as a mechanism for territorial defense at a time of dispossession and it supported the vindication of "Black culture" in certain urban communities (Restrepo 2002, 48–49; 2013). Almario describes the construction of self-defined territories, subsequent to Law 70, as an "agrarian, ethnic and social reform," accomplished without resorting to violence in one of the most violent decades in Colombia (2004, 664). These communities achieved collective titling of five million hectares, and according to their calculations, if the five million hectares of Indigenous reservations and national parks are added to theirs, ethnic groups control approximately ten million hectares throughout the Colombian Pacific (665).

Unfortunately, the ontological opening on the Pacific was brief. As Carlos Rosero, leader of the Black Communities' Process (PCN), stated, shortly after the government announced its intention to build an interoceanic canal as an alternative to the Panama Canal in 1996 (the same project considered by the Chorographic Commission a century and a half earlier), a gigantic joint offensive carried out by the army and paramilitaries in Riosucio, Chocó, resulted in the displacement of approximately twenty thousand people, one of the largest forced displacements in the country (2002, 549). He adds that something similar happened in Indigenous territories in Northern Cauca. These displacements occurred "immediately after the communities received collective titles to their territories." Almario recounts the situation of the Yurumangüí River Communal Council, which in 2000 received a collective land title for fifty-four thousand hectares and was almost immediately raided by hundreds of paramilitaries who threatened the community with massacres in the Naya and the Yurumangüí basins if their inhabitants did not leave the region (2002b, 672–674). Clearly, Black territoriality poses a danger to extractive projects and global capitalism, a fact reflected by the high number of displaced people, atrocities, and threats. However, "the people and their organizations devised a way to return and maintain contact with their territory." The destruction of Black communities implied maximum separation of people and territory, producing "deterritorialized people and territories without people" (657).

I suggest that this history of war and genocide shares—and differs from—divisions created by nineteenth-century liberalism. On the one hand, territory ceases to be perceived as that which is inaccessible, where only "rain, misery and [B]lackness" exist (Wade 1997, 143). Once a "zone of refuge" and Black colonization in the nineteenth century, the area was transformed into an "insecure space" where warlords engaged in disputes for territorial control, employing genocide, ethnocide, and all modalities of violence (Almario 2002b, 660). The territories of life inhabited by the Black population are perceived in the twenty-first century as an obstacle to be destroyed.

FINAL REFLECTIONS

The complex and violent trajectories of the Black communities' "being with territory" did not terminate with the new 1991 constitution. As noted above, the partial ontological opening the constitution provided was followed by a barrage of violence, the objective of which was to empty "ancestral territories of existing communities and demolish on-going processes of autonomous construction of territory" (Almario 2002b, 662–663). This attempt to "empty out" reached its maximum expression during the government of Alvaro Uribe (2002–2010), couched within the doctrine of "democratic security." Narco-paramilitarism sought to "cleanse the territories of politics," using terrorist strategies, including massacres, torture, and the rape of women.[14] The FARC guerrillas also said goodbye to politics and, in concentrating on a military strategy, were responsible for at least 20 percent of the massacres and more than twenty thousand kidnappings. However, even in the harshest years of the conflict, Indigenous and Black populations endured to showcase life-affirming proposals in defense of territory, including the September 2004 mobilization in which sixty-five thousand Indigenous People and peasants marched for five days, as well as the 2009 "minga of social and community resistance," proposing an agenda of community-based peace building.

During the presidency of Juan Manuel Santos (2010–2018), a peace negotiation process between the government and the FARC was initiated. During the four years of negotiations, (2012–2016), Black and Indigenous populations demanded they be allowed to participate, claiming that "neither the State nor the FARC represent us." In 2013, various Black community organizations came together and developed a proposal for "territorial peace," recognizing that what is at stake are not only "differing territorial interests, but distinct, almost irreconcilable, conceptions of territory itself," adding that "what the State considers unexploited territory, for us is 'cared for' territory. Territory is existential space, the place where one Is and Exists as a human being and as a people" (CONPA 2016, 57). In 2016, the Ethnic Commission for Peace and Defense of Territorial Rights, composed of Indigenous Peoples' organizations and Black communities, successfully negotiated the inclusion of the Ethnic Chapter within the Peace Accords. In effect, this renewed the ontological opening of the 1991 constitution, which had recognized ethnic communities' right to self-determination, autonomy and self-government, and ancestral territorial practices.[15] The Peace Accords, however, suffered a setback with the election of President Iván Duque (2018–2022). Not only was there a delay in the implementation of the agreement, but also a resumption of forced displacement of ethnic populations and increased homicides of human rights defenders. In conjunction with rising poverty and inequality, massive social mobilizations resulted during 2020 and 2021, which, among other things, defied what the government considered possible and reasonable.

On the one hand, proclamations by the Regional Indigenous Council of Cauca opened the possibility of "being with territory," including proposals for their own territorial planning models opposed to life-threatening alternatives (González Posso 2022, 74). On the other hand, the free people's proposals of territoriality, initiated in the eighteenth century, took on new life in the political movement identified by the slogan, "I am because we are," led by the Afro-Colombian activist, Francia Márquez Mina. This proposal "makes visible the interdependence between everything that exists, since it teaches us to see ourselves and to construct our identities, collectively. This means recognizing that I am, insofar as you are, that our humanity is intertwined with nature, that we are part of her, not her owners" (BBC 2022). Furthermore, politics is returned to those who did not figure within a single civilizing project—"the nobodies"—uniting emancipation proposals from Indigenous Peoples, Afro-Colombians, youth, peasants, and women.

In 2021, the Historic Pact[16]—a coalition of left-wing parties and social movements, including Indigenous and Afro-descendant organizations—elected Gustavo Petro as president and Márquez Mina as vice-president of Colombia. As Escobar points out, the unifying concept of the government program (2022–2026) "Colombia, World Power of Life" is to create conditions for humans to relearn how to coexist with non-humans and with the earth in a mutually enriching way (2022). This pact, by generating an ontological opening, once again provides evidence and makes visible the presence and plausibility of divergent territorialities. This is auspicious. However, it is also worth reflecting on the non-linear relationship between a regime of visibilities and invisibilities and the ontological opening or closing of divergent territorialities. By this

I mean that the visibility of "being with territory," in relation to modern territoriality, does not automatically translate into ontological openness, and the same happens with ontological invisibility and closure. Indeed, and as we have seen in this chapter, sometimes a divergent territoriality can endure precisely because it is not visible and, to the contrary, visibility can lead to ontological closure, as happened with the 1886 constitution. This is because by becoming visible as a divergent territoriality, the "being with territory" manifests itself as a potential challenge to modern territoriality. Of course, on occasions, becoming visible can lead to some ontological opening, as happened to a certain extent with the 1991 constitution, and as is happening now with the electoral victory of the Historic Pact. Beyond the specifics of the case, the point is that non-linearity between regimes of visibility and ontological openness raises questions about an implicit presumption, quite common in analysis, which focuses on the equivocation inherent in the concept of territory. I refer to the assumption that making divergence visible is always a good thing. The case of "being with territory" among Black communities shows us that perhaps, in some circumstances, it is preferable that the equivocation continue in the shadows so that territories of life can endure and flourish.

NOTES

1. Resguardo is the legally recognized collective ownership of an area by Indigenous Peoples, similar, to some extent, to reserves or reservations in North America, but emanating from the territorial/administrative organization of the Spanish colonial period.
2. Article 55 refers to "[B]lack communities" that have been occupying baldíos or public lands; it limits the area to "rural riversides of Pacific Basin rivers" and specifies the scope as "their traditional production practices" (Republic of Colombia 1991).
3. To undertake political activity in "the shadow" refers to a negotiation strategy, making practices considered acceptable visible, and leaving the unacceptable in the shadows (de la Cadena 2010, 359).
4. According to LeGrand, between 1827 and 1931 bondholders and large businessmen benefited from the acquisition of 2,657,000 hectares (1983, 73).
5. De-enslavement in Colombia was not accomplished through a revolution, as in Haiti. The vast majority of enslaved people bought their own freedom. At the time that the Liberal government passed the 1851 Emancipation Law, 98 percent of those enslaved was already free (McGraw 2011).
6. I will refer to this commission in the next section.
7. The Democratic Societies were created by Bogotá artisans in 1846 to defend tariffs on their products. Within government, the Liberal Party endorsed them (Sowell 1992). The National Guard was a tool for political education and support for armed struggle. To be

accepted into the Democratic Society, it was a requirement to be part of the National Guard (Sanders 2009).

8. With the support of the free people, the Liberals ruled without interruption from 1861 to 1878, and won the wars of 1851, 1860–1863, and 1876–1877.
9. Later, Almario clarifies that the comuneros were Black peasants who had systematically grabbed land from landowners, a denomination maintained even until the first decades of the twentieth century (2013).
10. He presided over the Democratic Society of Cali and was appointed as a representative to the Cauca legislature.
11. I analyze this fear of an alternative world in the next section.
12. I have already cited some of these. I draw attention to the pioneering work of Robert West (1957). For an excellent literature review, see Almario García and Jiménez (2004).
13. AT55 or Transitory Article 55 issued in the 1991 constitution required the adoption of a law recognizing the collective property rights of Black communities. This recognition was established in Law 70, Law of Black Communities, in 1993.
14. See Rojas 2009.
15. See Rojas 2023.
16. The coalition includes Colombia Humana, Unión Patriótica-Partido Comunista, Polo Democrático Alternativo, Movimiento Alternativo Indígena y Social, Partido del Trabajo de Colombia, Unidad Democrática, and Todos Somos Colombia.

REFERENCES

Almario, Oscar. 2001. "Tras las Huellas de los renacientes: por el laberinto de la etnicidad e identidad de los grupos negros o 'afrocolombianos' del Pacífico sur." In *Acción colectiva, estado y etnicidad en el Pacífico colombiano*, edited by Mauricio Pardo. Instituto Colombiano de Antropología e Historia.

Almario, Oscar. 2002a. "Desesclavización y territorialización: el trayecto inicial de la diferenciación étnica negra en el Pacífico sur colombiano, 1749–1810." In *Afrodescendientes en las Américas: trayectorias sociales e identitarias a 150 años de la abolición de la esclavitud en Colombia*, edited by Claudia Mosquera, Mauricio Pardo, and O. Hoffmann. Universidad Nacional de Colombia, Instituto Colombiano de Antropología e Historia, Institut de Recherche pour le Developpment, Instituto Latinoamericano de Servicios Legales Alternativos.

Almario, Oscar G. 2002b. "Dinámica y consecuencias del conflicto armado colombiano en el Pacífico: limpieza étnica y desterritorialización de afrocolombianos e indígenas y 'multiculturalismo' de Estado e indolencia nacional." In *Dimensiones territoriales de la guerra y la paz*, edited by Red de Estudios de Espacio Y Territorio. Universidad Nacional de Colombia.

Almario, Oscar. 2013. *La configuración moderna del Valle del Cauca, 1850–1940: espacio, poblamiento, poder y cultura*. Universidad del Cauca.

Almario, Oscar. 2015. "El Chocó en el Siglo XIX: encrucijada histórica, social, territorial y conceptual: hacia un Nuevo Siglo XIX del noroccidente colombiano." In *Hacia un nuevo siglo XIX del noroccidente colombiano. Balance bibliográfico de Antioquia, Caldas y Chocó*, edited by Oscar García Almario, Luis Javier Mesa Ortiz, and Lina Marcela Gómez González. Tomo III. Universidad Nacional de Colombia.

Almario, Oscar, and Orián Meneses Jiménez. 2004. "Aproximaciones al análisis histórico del negro en Colombia." In *Panorámica afrocolombiana. Estudios sociales en el Pacífico*, edited by Mauricio Rojas Pardo, Claudia Mosquera, and María Clemencia Ramírez. Instituto Colombiano de Antropología e Historia ICANH y Universidad Nacional de Colombia.

Appelbaum, Nancy. 1999. "Whitening the Region: Caucano Mediation and 'Antioqueño Colonization' in Nineteenth-Century Colombia." *Hispanic American Historical Review* 79 (4): 631–667.

Appelbaum, Nancy. 2016. *Mapping the Country of Regions: The Chorographic Commission of Nineteenth Century Colombia*. University of North Carolina Press.

Aprile-Gniset, Jacques. 2004. "Apuntes sobre el proceso de poblamiento del Pacífico." In *Panorámica Afrocolombiana. Estudios Sociales en el Pacífico*, edited by Mauricio Pardo, Claudia Mosquera, and María Clemencia Ramírez. Instituto Colombiano de Antropología e Historia, Universidad Nacional.

BBC. 2022. "Francia Márquez: n que consiste la filosofía Ubuntu que inspira la política de la nueva vicepresidenta de Colombia." *BBC News Mundo*, 8–22. https://www.bbc.com/mundo/noticias-america-latina-62416615.

Camacho Segura, Juana. 2004. "Silencios elocuentes, voces emergentes: reseña bibliográfica de los estudios sobre la mujer afrocolombiana." In *Panorámica afrocolombiana. Estudios sociales en el Pacífico*, edited by Mauricio Pardo Rojas, Claudia Mosquera, and María Clemencia Ramírez. Instituto Colombiano de Antropología e Historia ICANH y Universidad Nacional de Colombia.

Colmenares, Germán. 1975. *Cali: terratenientes, mineros y comerciantes. Siglo XVIII*. Universidad del Valle.

CONPA (Consejo Nacional de Paz Afrocolombiano). 2016. "Agenda de Paz Afrocolombiana." *Afrodes Colombia*. http://www.afrodescolombia.org/wp-content/uploads/2017/07/Agenda_de_paz_CONPA.Final-ilovepdf-compressed.pdf.

de la Cadena, Marisol. 2008. "Política indígena: un análisis más allá de 'la política.'" *Red de Antropologías del Mundo* (4): 139–171. http://www.ram-wan.net/html/journal-4.htm.

de la Cadena, Marisol. 2010. "Indigenous Cosmopolitics in the Andes: Conceptual Reflections beyond 'Politics.'" *Cultural Anthropology* 25 (2): 334–370.

de la Cadena. 2015. *Earth Beings: Ecologies of Practices Across Andean Worlds*. Duke University Press.

de la Cadena, Marisol. 2019a. "An Invitation to Live Together: Making the 'Complex We.'" *Environmental Humanities* 11 (2): 477–484.

de la Cadena, Marisol. 2019b. "Uncommoning Nature: Stories from the Anthropo-Not-Seen." In *Anthropos and the Material*, edited by Penny Harvey, Christian Krohn-Hansen, and Knut G. Nustad. Duke University Press.

Echeverri, Marcela. 2011. "Popular Royalists, Empire, and Politics in Southwestern New Granada, 1809–1819." *Hispanic American Historical Review* 91 (2): 237–268.

Echeverri, Marcela. 2016. *Indian and Slave Royalists in the Age of Revolution: Reform, Revolution and Royalism in the Northern Andes, 1780–1825*. Cambridge University Press.

Escobar. Arturo. 2010. *Territorios de diferencia: lugar, movimientos, vida, redes*. Envión Editores.

Escobar. Arturo. 2014. *Sentipensar con la tierra: nuevas lecturas sobre sesarrollo, territorio y diferencia*. Ediciones Unaula.

Escobar, Arturo. 2017. *Autonomía y diseño: la realización de lo comunal*. Tinta Limón.

Escobar. Arturo. 2022. "El programa de gobierno del Pacto Histórico y los desafíos planetarios." *El Espectador*, Agosto 6. https://www.elespectador.com/opinion/columnistas/arturo-escobar/el-programa-de-gobierno-del-pacto-historico-y-los-desafios-planetarios/.

Escobar, Arturo, and Alvaro Pedrosa. 1996. "Introduccion: modernidad y sesarrollo en el Pacífico colombiano." *In Pacífico desarrollo o diversidad?* edited by Arturo Escobar and Alvaro Pedrosa. CEREC ECOFONDO.

González Posso, Camilo. 2022. *Algo grande va a ocurrir en este pueblo. En abril se puso en marcha la generación del cambio*. Instituto de Estudios para el Desarrollo y la Paz.

Grueso, Libia, Carlos Rosero, and Arturo Escobar. 1997. "El proceso organizativo de comunidades negras en Colombia". *Ecología Política* (14): 47–64.
Jackson, Jean E. 2003. "La crisis en Colombia: consecuencias para los pueblos indígenas." In *El conflicto colombiano y su impacto en los países andinos*, edited by Álvaro Camacho Guizado. Universidad de los Andes.
Jiménez, Orián M. 1998. "La Conquista del Estómago: viandas, vituallas y ración negra siglos XVII y XVIII." In *Geografía humana de Colombia, tomo VI: los afrocolombianos*, edited by Luz Adriana Maya. Instituto Colombiano de Antropología e Historia.
Law, John. 2011. "What's Wrong with a One-World World?" *Distinktion: Scandinavian Journal of Social Theory* 16 (1): 126–139
Leal, Claudia. 2008. "Disputas por tagua y minas: recursos naturales y propiedad territorial en el Pacífico colombiano, 1870–1930." *Revista Colombiana de Antropología* 44 (2): 409–438.
Leal, Claudia. 2018. *Landscapes of Freedom: Building a Post-Emancipation Society in the Rainforests of Western Colombia*. The University of Arizona Press.
Leal, Claudia, and Shawn Van Ausdal. 2013. "Landscapes of Freedom and Inequality: Environmental Histories of the Pacific and Caribbean Coasts of Colombia." *DesiguALdades*, Working Paper 58. Berlin: desiguALdades.net International Research Network on Interdependent Inequalities in Latin America. https://www.desigualdades.net/Working_Papers/Search-Working-Papers/working-paper-58-_landscapes-of-freedom-and-inequality_/index.html
LeGrand, Catherine. 1986. "Los antecedentes agrarios de la violencia: el conflicto social en la frontera colombiana, 1850–1930." In *Pasado y presente de la violencia en Colombia*, edited by Gonzalo Sánchez and Ricardo Peñaranda. Fondo Editorial CEREC.
LeGrand, Catherine. 1992. "Agrarian Antecedents of Violence." In *Violence in Colombia: The Contemporary Crisis in Historical Perspective*, edited by Charles Berquist, Ricardo Penaranda, and Gonzalo Sanchez. Scholarly Resources Books.
LeGrand, Catherine. 2013. "Legal Narrâtives of Citizenship, the Social Question, and Public Order in Colombia 1915–1930 and After." *Citizenship Studies* 17 (5): 530–550.
LeGrand, Catherine. 2016. *Colonización y protesta campesina en Colombia (1850–1950)*. Universidad de los Andes, Universidad Nacional de Colombia.
LeGrand, Catherine, and Margarita González. 1983. "Campesinos y asalariados en la zona bananera de Santa Marta (1900–1935)." *Anuario Colombiano de Historia Social y de la Cultura* 11: 235–250.
Lozano, Betty Ruth. 2016. "Feminismo Negro–Afrocolombiano: ancestral, insurgente y cimarrón: un feminismo en-lugar." *Revista Intersticios de la política y la cultura* 5 (9): 23–48. https://revistas.unc.edu.ar/index.php/intersticios/article/view/14612.
McGraw, Jason. 2011. "Spectacles of Freedom: Public Manumissions, Political Rhetoric, and Citizen Mobilisation in Mid-Nineteenth-Century Colombia." *Slavery & Abolition* 32 (2): 269–288.
Oslender, Ulrich. 2001. "La lógica del rio: estructuras espaciales del proceso organizativo de los movimientos sociales de comunidades negras en el pacífico colombiano." In *Acción colectiva, estado y etnicidad en el Pacífico colombiano*, edited by Mauricio Pardo. Instituto Colombiano de Antropología e Historia.
Pagden, Ariel. 2006. "Las bases ideológicas de la disputa sobre el dominium y los derechos naturales de los indios americanos." *Revista internacional de pensamiento político* 1: 13–43.
Peñaranda, Daniel Ricardo. 2015. *Conflictos armados y reconstrucción identitaria en los Andes colombianos. El movimiento armado Quintín Lame*. Centro Nacional de Memoria Histórica.
Povinelli, Elizabeth. 1995. "Do Rocks Listen? The Cultural Politics of Apprehending Australian Aboriginal Labour." *American Anthropologist* 97 (3): 505–518.

Povinelli, Elizabeth. 2001. "Radical Worlds: The Politics of Incommensurability and Inconceivability." *Annual Review of Anthropology* 30: 319–334.

Rancière, Jacques. 2011. "Against an Ebbing Tide: An Interview with Jacques Rancière." In *Reading Rancière*, edited by Paul Bowman and Richard Stamp. Continuum.

República de Colombia. 1991. *Constitución política de Colombia.*

Restrepo, Eduardo. 1996. "Los tuqueros negros del Pacífico sur colombiano." In *Renacientes del Guandal: "grupos negros" de los ríos Satinga y Sanquianga*, edited by J.I. del Valle and Eduardo Restrepo. Biopacífico-Universidad Nacional de Colombia.

Restrepo, Eduardo. 2002. "Politicas de la alteridad: etnizacion de 'comunidad negra' en el Pacífico sur colombiano." *Journal of Latin American Anthropology* 7 (2): 34–59.

Restrepo, Eduardo. 2007. "'Negros indolentes' en las plumas de los corógrafos: raza y progreso en el occidente de la Nueva Granada de mediados del Siglo XIX." *Nómadas* April: 28–43.

Restrepo, Eduardo. 2013. *Etnización de la negridad: la invención de las 'comunidades negras' como grupo étnico en Colombia.* Editorial Universidad del Cauca.

Rojas, Cristina. 2009a. "Prácticas ciudadanas en el Gran Siglo XIX." In *Identidad, cultura y política: perspectivas conceptuales, miradas empíricas*, edited by Gabriela Castellanos Llanos and Delfín I. Grueso Vanegas. Programa Editorial Universidad del Valle.

Rojas, Cristina. 2009b. "Securing the State and Developing Social Insecurities: The Securitization of Citizenship in Contemporary Colombia." *Third World Quarterly* 30 (1): 227–245.

Rojas, Cristina. 2023. "El capítulo étnico en el acuerdo de paz de Colombia: una perspectiva desde las mujeres y organizaciones indígenas y afrocolombianas." Centro Global para el Pluralismo y Biblioteca Abierta del Proceso de Paz. https://bapp.com.co/en/the-ethnic-chapter-in-the-colombian-peace-agreement/.

Romero, Mario Diego. 1991. "Procesos de poblamiento y organización social en la costa Pacífica colombiana." *Anuario colombiano de historia social y de la cultura* 18–19: 9–31. https://revistas.unal.edu.co/index.php/achsc/article/view/35488.

Romero, Mario Diego. 2017. *Territorialidad y familia en tres sociedades negras del sur del Valle del Río Cauca.* Universidad del Valle.

Rosero, Carlos. 2002. "Los afrodescendientes y el conflicto armado en Colombia: La Resistencia en lo propio como alternativa." In *Afrodescendientes en las Américas: Trayectorias sociales e identitarias*, edited by Claudia Mosquera, Mauricio Pardo, and Odile Hoffmann. Universidad Nacional de Colombia, Instituto Colombiano de Antropología e Historia, Institut de Recherche pour le Devéloppment.

Ruiz Serna, Daniel. 2018. "When Forests Run Amok: War and Its Afterlives in Indigenous and Afro-Colombian Territories." PhD diss., McGill University.

Samper, José M. 1853. *Apuntamientos para la historia política i social de la Nueva Granada desde 1810 i especialmente de la administración del 7 de marzo.* Imprenta del Neo-Granadino.

Samper, José María. 1861. *Ensayo sobre las revoluciones políticas y la condición social de las Repúblicas colombianas (hispano-americanas).* Banco de la República Biblioteca Virtual y Editorial Centro. https://babel.banrepcultural.org/digital/collection/p17054coll10/id/2401/.

Sánchez, Gonzalo. 1991. *Guerra y política en la sociedad colombiana.* El Áncora Editores.

Sanders, James E. 2004a. *Contentious Republicans: Popular Politics, Race and Class in Nineteenth-Century Colombia.* Duke University Press.

Sanders, James E. 2004b. "'Citizens of a Free People': Popular Liberalism and Race in Nineteenth Century Southwestern Colombia." *Hispanic American Historical Review* 84 (2): 277–313.

Sanders, James. 2007. "Pertenecer a la gran familia granadina. Lucha partidista y construccion de la identidad indígena y política en el Cauca, 1849–1890." *Revista de estudios sociales* 26: 28–45.

Sanders, James E. 2009. "'Ciudadanos de un pueblo libre': liberalismo popular y raza en el suroccidente de Colombia en el Siglo XIX." *Historia crítica* 38: 172–203.
Stengers, Isabelle. 2011. "Comparison as a Matter of Concern." *Common Knowledge* 17 (1): 48–63.
Taussig, Michael. 1977. "The Evolution of Rural Wage Labour in the Cauca Valley of Colombia 1700–1970." In *Land and Labour in Latin America*, edited by Kenneth Duncan and Ian Rutledge. Cambridge University Press.
Trouillot, Michel-Rolph. 1995. *Silencing the Past: Power and the Production of History.* Beacon Press.
Uribe de Hincapié, Maria Teresa. 2001. *Nación, ciudadano y soberano.* Corporación Región.
Vergara-Figueroa, Aurora. 2018. *Afrodescendant Resistance to Deracination in Colombia. Massacre at Bellavista-Bojayá-Chocó.* Palgrave Macmillan.
Villa, William. 1997. "Movimiento social de comunidades negras en el Pacífico colombiano. La construcción de una noción de territorio y región." In *Geografía humana de Colombia. Los Afrocolombianos*, edited by Luz Adriana Maya. Instituto Colombiano de Cultura Hispánica.
Wade, Peter. 1996. "Identidad y etnicidad." In *Pacífico ¿Desarrollo o diversidad? Estado, capital y movimientos sociales en el Pacífico colombiano*, edited by Arturo Escobar and Alvaro Pedrosa. CEREC Ecofondo.
Wade, Peter. 1997. *Gente negra, nación mestiza: dinámicas de las identidades raciales en Colombia.* Siglo del Hombre Editores, Ediciones Unidandes.
West, Robert. 1957. *The Pacific Lowlands of Colombia.* Louisiana University Press.
Zuluaga Ramírez, Francisco U, and Amparo Bermúdez. 1997. *La protesta social en el suroccidente colombiano: siglo XVIII.* Instituto de Altos Estudios Jurídicos y de Relaciones Internacionales, Universidad del Valle.

CONTRIBUTORS

Penelope Anthias is Associate Professor in Human Geography at Durham University, UK. She has been conducting research on Indigenous territorial claims and hydrocarbon conflicts in the Chaco region of Bolivia since 2008. She is the author of the 2018 book *Limits to Decolonization: Indigeneity, Territory and Hydrocarbon Politics in the Bolivian Chaco* (Cornell University Press), a Spanish translation of which was published by Plural Editores in 2022. She has published numerous articles and book chapters engaging interdisciplinary debates around Indigeneity, territory, and extractivism. Penelope has recently turned to documentary film as an alternative to traditional forms of academic knowledge production. She has directed and produced two documentaries with rural communities impacted by hydrocarbon development: *Don't Touch Tariquía: The Resistance of Chiquiacá* (2022) and *Urukurenda: In Search of the Land without Evil (Ɨvɨ Maraëi)* (2025).

Jacinta Baragud is an Iamagal woman from the Kulkalgal Nation of the Torres Strait (Australia). She is a Research Officer in the College of Arts and Social Sciences at the Australian National University (ANU) and one of the key members of the project "Rekindling Japanese and Torres Strait Islander (Australia) Connections 50 Years On," funded by the Australia-Japan Foundation, the Australian Institute for Aboriginal and Torres Strait Islander Studies (AIATSIS), and the Australian Research Council Discovery Project scheme. Her research interests include Indigenous socio-economic policies, Torres Strait knowledge systems and languages, and the impacts of climate change on Indigenous communities. She is passionate about making the results of research conducted in the Torres Strait region accessible to its communities and examining the meanings and uses of historical and ongoing research information for contemporary Torres Strait societies. She lives up to her Kantok family motto: "Do your best, never give up."

Mario Blaser is Professor at Memorial University of Newfoundland (Newfoundland and Labrador, Canada). Originally from Argentina, he made the city of St. John's his home, where he lives with his two children and partner. Anthropologist by training and undisciplined by vocation, he has worked with the Yshiro nation of Paraguay since his undergraduate days and with Innu Nation of Labrador since 2009. He works in the city of St. John's with local initiatives that might strengthen what he calls "infrastructures of emplacement," his most recent obsession. He is the author of *For Emplacement: Political Ontology in Two Acts* (Duke University Press, 2025); *Storytelling Globalization from the Paraguayan Chaco and Beyond* (Duke University Press, 2010) and co-editor of *A World of Many Worlds* (Duke University Press, 2018).

Yamila Gutierrez-Callisaya is an Aymara anthropologist (Universidad Mayor de San Andres) with a master's in cultural studies and is currently a doctoral student in the Latin American cultural studies program (Universidad Andina Simon Bolivar Ecuador). She is a specialist in Indigenous issues and an activist intellectual in the political project of reconstitution of the ayllus, markas, and suyus of the Qullasuyu. She is the author of several articles, including "Mujeres aymaras y ejercicio político. Case Study in the Cantapa Marka" (2018), "The Reconstitution of the Ayllu: Politics of Decolonization" (2015), and co-author of "Niñas (des)educadas: Entre la escuela rural y los saberes del ayllu" (2011), "Pluriversidad: rostros de la interculturalidad" (2009), "Justicia comunitaria: realidades y perspectivas" (2007), and "Historia y memoria de la ch'axwa" (2005). She also works in technical assistance on gender issues, political participation, and interculturality, among other topics.

Benoit Éthier (PhD, Anthropology, Université Laval) is Professor at the School of Indigenous Studies and Director of the Participatory Mapping Laboratory at the Université du Québec en Abitibi-Témiscamingue. His research collaborations focus on Indigenous territorial issues, particularly on the question of the intergenerational transmission of territorial knowledge.

Sipi Flamand is Chief of the Atikamekw Council of Manawan and a master's student at the School of Indigenous Studies at the Université du Québec en Abitibi-Témiscamingue. His political, academic, and personal commitment is oriented toward Indigenous self-determination and the valorization of Atikamekw Nehirowisiwok philosophies and political practices.

Hernán Ruiz Fournier is a Bolivian economist with a specialty in local development and work experience as an environmentalist and an Indigenous Peoples' rights activist in the Chaco for over twenty years. He has coordinated several conservation, sustainability, and community development projects with local NGOs, particularly with the Guarani Indigenous Peoples Assembly (AGP in its Spanish acronym), and has collaborated in several research projects on natural resources, Indigenous Peoples and extractive industries. He has served as an advisor to the Constituent Assembly of Bolivia (2007) and to the Regional Assembly of the Gran Chaco of Tarija (2015–2021).

Sarah C. Moritz is a Banting Postdoctoral Fellow and socio-cultural anthropologist at Concordia University (Department of Geography, Environment and Planning) in Montréal, Canada. Her doctoral research (McGill University, Department of Anthropology) examined the social relationality and Boasian anthropology of Interior Salish St'át'imc fisheries and water governance and associated notions of a "good life" in the Fraser River Valley of today's British Columbia. She also researches and teaches Indigenous rights, human-animal relationships, stewardship practices, decolonial research methods, and the history of anthropology and science. She is the co-author of two books on environmental anthropology and Salish studies and has written numerous peer-reviewed contributions and children's books on Indigenous language, land, and legal revitalization especially regarding salmon and water. The wild salmon life cycle is her guiding metaphor that accompanies her through rivers, research, teaching, and community-based advocacy and action.

Adam Nye is a Walbunja man of the Yuin Nation, an Indigenous ranger and cultural practitioner of thirteen years from Mogo, New South Wales, Australia. Since 2015, he has been working with Annick Thomassin and Janet Hunt (Australian National University) on developing methodologies and tools (e.g., CyberTracker sequences) to enable the collection of biocultural data about Walbunja Country and supporting Mogo and Batemans Bay LALCs ranger teams' environmental stewardship initiatives. He was the lead community researcher on the Environmental Stewardship: Resurgence of the Yuin Nation, Walbunja Clan's Land and Sea Country. He is the founder of Walbunja Warrior, a business that provides environmental education, cultural services, and country experiences. His work with the tourist industry aims to bridge science and culture to create a strong connection and understanding of country for everyone.

Sylvie Poirier is Professor in the Department of Anthropology, Université Laval (Québec, Canada). She is currently editor-in-chief of *Anthropologie et sociétés*, North America's only French-language anthropology journal. She has conducted research with Indigenous People in the Australian Western Desert and with the Atikamekw, a First Nation in North-Central Quebec. In addition to numerous articles and thematic issues, she is the author of *A World of Relationships: Itineraries, Dreams and Events in the Australian Western Desert* (University of Toronto Press, 2004) and co-editor of *Figured Worlds: Ontological Obstacles in Intercultural Relations* (University of Toronto Press, 2004), *Entangled Territorialities: Negotiating Indigenous Lands in Australia and Canada*

(University of Toronto Press, 2017), and *Contemporary Indigenous Cosmologies and Pragmatics* (University of Alberta Press, 2021).

Lorna Quiroga is a PhD student in the Department of Geography and Environmental Studies at Carleton University (Ottawa, Canada). She has a BA in sociology from the University of Buenos Aires, a MA in gender studies from Memorial University of Newfoundland and Labrador, and over fifteen years of learning with Indigenous and peasant movements and activists in Paraguay. Through working for a Paraguayan human rights NGO supporting Indigenous land struggles, she had the privilege of living/sharing/learning with Enlhet-Enenlhet, Paï Tavyterä, and Yshir territories of life. Her PhD research explores ontologies of territory in collaboration with a group of Yshir artisan women of the Yshir Nation (located in the Chaco-Pantanal region).

Qwalqwalten (Garry John) is a Tsal'alh St'át'imc (Interior Salish) leader and title and rights activist. He has had many important roles in his life: he has served as elected chief for his community for over eighteen years, as St'át'imc Chiefs Council chair, as Aboriginal member to the Council of Canadians Board of Directors, as political lead to St'át'imc Government Services (SGS), and has been particularly instrumental in advising on water rights. Internally and internationally, he has fought in solidarity for Indigenous rights and title to ancestral waters. Qwalqwalten is often accompanied by another thunderous speaker and activist, Pulmaqa7 (his drum), which helps him connect to people and be heard.

Cristina Rojas is Distinguished Research Professor in the Department of Political Science at Carleton University (Ottawa, Canada). Her academic research focuses on the intersection between global and ethnic politics, peace, and citizenship rights. Presently she is leading the research project "Territory Making as World Making: Territorial Practices of Indigenous and Afro Descendent Communities in Bolivia, Colombia, and Paraguay," which is funded by the Social Sciences and Humanities Research Council. She is the author of *Civilization and Violence: Regimes of Representation in Nineteenth Century Colombia* (University of Minnesota Press, 2001) and the co-editor of *Narratives and Imaginings of Citizenship in Latin*

America (Routledge, 2014) and *Elusive Peace: International, National and Local Dimensions of Conflict in Colombia* (Palgrave Macmillan, 2005).

Scott E. Simon (PhD, Anthropology, McGill University) is Professor in the School of Sociological and Anthropological Studies, University of Ottawa, and is co-chair of the University of Ottawa Research Chair in Taiwan Studies. Since 2004, he has specialized in the study of Indigeneity and Indigenous resurgence, based on years of field research in Truku and Seediq communities. Focusing on how Indigenous Peoples affirm their own ontologies and sovereignty within ongoing colonial situations, he wrote *Sadyaq Balae: L'autochtone formosane dans tous ses états* (Presses de l'Université Laval, 2012) and *Truly Human: Indigeneity and Indigenous Resurgence on Formosa* (University of Toronto Press, 2023). His work on human–animal relations has been published in *Anthropologica*, *American Anthropologist*, *Human Organization*, and *Anthropologie et sociétés*. He has also done field research in Japan, on Ponso no tao (Orchid Island), and in Guåhan (Guam). He is the principal investigator of the SSHRC-funded project "Austronesian Worlds: Human-Animal Entanglements in the Pacific Anthropocene."

Kim Spurway (PhD, Development Studies and Political Sociology, University of New South Wales) is Senior Research Associate with the Institute for Culture and Society at Western Sydney University. Her research interests include critical approaches to humanitarian emergencies, natural disasters, climate change, Indigenous cultural approaches to natural disasters, and gender/sexuality diversity. Her current projects focus on community-based disaster resilience learning in New South Wales as well as Indigenous gender/sexuality diverse people's intersectionality and aspirations regarding socio-cultural well-being in Australia.

Annick Thomassin (PhD, McGill University) is a Canadian anthropologist and research fellow at the Australian National University. Her research intersects preoccupations of political ecology and political ontology with a particular focus on Indigenous Peoples' involvement in natural resource co-management, fisheries, perspectives on climate change, and Indigenous-state relations. She is the principal investigator of the project "Environmental Stewardship Resurgence in Walbanga Country," funded by the Australian Institute for Aboriginal and Torres Strait Islanders Studies (AIATSIS), working alongside Adam Nye. She was awarded a Wenner-Gren Foundation's Hunt Fellowship for the production of her book on the politics of fisheries co-management in the Torres Strait. She is a chief investigator (with Julie Lahn, Samantha Faulkner, and Jacinta Baragud) of the project "Rekindling Japanese and Torres Strait Islander (Australia) Connections 50 Years On," supported by the Australia-Japan Foundation, the AIATSIS, and the Australian Research Council. She is a member of the Centre for Indigenous Conservation and Development Alternatives (CICADA).

Carolina Tytelman is Adjunct Professor at the Department of Anthropology and a post-doctoral fellow at the School of Arctic and Subarctic Studies, Memorial University of Newfoundland and Labrador. Her research focuses on the interactions between people and their environments, including their construction and perception of place and their relationships with other-than-human beings, and how these issues are expressed and negotiated by different groups in the current colonial context of Canada.

Paul Wattez is an anthropologist and a post-doctoral fellow at the University of Ottawa (Ontario) and Memorial University (Newfoundland and Labrador), studying the conceptualization of "well-being" (miyiyuu pimatisiwin) among the Iyiyiwch (Cree of Quebec). His work is contextualized by a series of forestry projects occurring on the ancestral land of the Iyiyiwch of Waswanipi, and focuses on environmental realities and ontologies of conservation, extending his earlier focus on contemporary Iyiyiwch strategies and practices of cultural protection and knowledge transmission. Since 2020, he is also the Quebec Indigenous relations lead for the engineering consulting firm WSP Canada. His mandate is to support Indigenous Nations and entrepreneurs in the growth of an Indigenous economy in Quebec and to participate in social and environmental studies. He has authored several articles and co-edited a special issue of *Les cahiers du Ciéra* entitled *Points de vue et expériences autochtones sur le 375e anniversaire de la fondation de Montréal.*

INDEX

Page numbers in *italics* refer to figures and images.

www.ingramcontent.com/pod-product-compliance
Lightning Source LLC
LaVergne TN
LVHW040757070826
844660LV00025B/1169
9781772128253